FED UP

FED UP

An Insider's Take on Why the
Federal Reserve Is Bad for America

Danielle DiMartino Booth

PORTFOLIO / PENGUIN

Portfolio Penguin
An imprint of Penguin Random House LLC
375 Hudson Street
New York, New York 10014

Most Portfolio books are available at a discount when purchased in quantity for sales promotions or corporate use. Special editions, which include personalized covers, excerpts, and corporate imprints, can be created when purchased in large quantities. For more information, please call (212) 572-2232 or e-mail specialmarkets@penguinrandomhouse.com. Your local bookstore can also assist with discounted bulk purchases using the Penguin Random House corporate Business-to-Business program. For assistance in locating a participating retailer, e-mail B2B@penguinrandomhouse.com.

ISBN: 9780735211650 (hardcover)

ISBN: 9780735211667 (e-book)

Printed in the United States of America
1   3   5   7   9   10   8   6   4   2

Book design by Daniel Lagin

DEDICATION

I dedicate this book to every hardworking American who wakes up in the morning asking themselves what went wrong.

CONTENTS

FED UP

CHAPTER 1

"Groupstink"

Never in the field of monetary policy was so much gained by so few at the expense of so many.

—Michael Hartnett, Bank of America Merrill Lynch
chief investment strategist, November 1, 2015

Early morning, December 16, 2008, with a drizzle of freezing rain falling, few would even glance at the line of inconspicuous Mercury Marquis sedans pulling up to Washington, DC's Fairmont Hotel. Emerging from the luxurious four-star establishment, their Foggy Bottom home eight times a year, are eleven little-known bureaucrats with their contingent of requisite subordinates.

There is no fanfare to mark the coming momentous decision they are to take on as they comfortably settle in for the ten-minute caravan to the neoclassical white marble edifice known as the Marriner S. Eccles Federal Reserve Board Building, located at Twentieth Street and Constitution Avenue NW.

Another half dozen of their peers had already left their homes in nearby Georgetown or some other Washington suburb and they too are making their way to the same address for the all-important 9 A.M. meeting.

Only one of these bureaucrats—the chairman, a mild-mannered former professor—might have been recognized in an American airport. The rest—unelected, immune to political pressure, mostly academics, and save one, inexperienced in the intricacies of running a major corporation, or even a small business—were virtually invisible outside the narrow world they inhabited despite the enormous power they wielded.

As these seventeen people arrived, they stowed their coats and umbrellas, grabbed a cup of coffee or tea, and mingled, the low hum of their conversation perhaps more subdued than on similar occasions. The day before, the first of the two-day affair, had been extraordinary in both the dire picture it painted of the American economy and the realization that they would have to take bold and unprecedented action.

That next sleety morning, they met again, determined to take action to prop up a faltering Wall Street, hopelessly mired in the greatest financial crisis since the Great Depression. Even as they convened, the wreckage of the previous three months still burned around them. Credit markets had seized up and fears for the fate of the economy were mounting.

With a few exceptions, virtually all of those at the meeting were PhD economists who had earned doctorates at MIT, Yale, Harvard, Princeton, and other top American universities. They met under the auspices of the Federal Open Market Committee (FOMC), the decision-making body of the Federal Reserve System. They believed a lifetime of study in economic theory and monetary policy had given them unique insight to steer policy for the most powerful central bank in the world, the lender of last resort for failing Wall Street banks, and the U.S. government's last line of defense against utter financial chaos.

Created in 1913 after the Panic of 1907, the Federal Reserve was founded to keep the public's faith in the buying power of the U.S. dollar. After failing miserably in the 1930s, the Fed aimed to be more responsive. This led the institution to find discipline in the rising macroeconomic models championed by top monetary theorists. During the ensuing "Quiet Period" in American banking, deposit insurance prevented panics, the Fed controlled interest rates and manipulated the money supply, and though occasional disruptions flared, like the failure of Continental Illinois National Bank and Trust Company in 1984, no systemic risk erupted for seventy years. The Fed had tamed the volatile U.S. economy.

Until September 2008, when all hell broke loose in a worldwide panic that completely blindsided and, embarrassed the Federal Reserve. The Fed had used billions of dollars in taxpayer funds to bail out Wall Street fat cats. Everyone blamed the Fed.

Just before 9 A.M., the door to the chairman's office opened. Federal Reserve Chairman Ben Bernanke took his place in an armchair at the center of a massive oval table. The members of the FOMC found their designated places around the table; aides sat in chairs or couches against the wall. With staff, the room contained fifty or sixty people, far more than normal for this momentous occasion.

In front of each FOMC member was a microphone to record their words for posterity. To a casual observer, the content of their conversation would be obscured by economic jargon.

This day, their essential task was to vote on whether to take the "fed funds" rate—the interest rate at which banks lent money to each other in the overnight market—to the zero bound. The history-making low rate would ripple throughout the economy, affecting the price to borrow for businesses and consumers alike.

Bernanke was calm but insistent. His lifetime of study of the Great Depression indicated this was the only way. His sheer depth of knowledge about the Fed's mishandling of that tragic period was undoubtedly intimidating.

By the end of the meeting, the vote was unanimous. The FOMC officially adopted a zero-interest-rate policy in the hopes that companies teetering on the brink of insolvency would keep the lights on, keep employees on their payrolls, and keep consumers spending. It would even pay banks interest on deposits.

Free cash. We'll even pay you to take it!

As they gathered their belongings, everyone shook hands, all very collegial despite the sometimes vigorous discussion. They journeyed back to their nice homes in the toniest neighborhoods of America's richest cities: New York, Boston, Philadelphia, Chicago, Dallas, San Francisco, Washington, DC.

They returned to their lofty perches, some at the Eccles Building, others to the executive floors of Federal Reserve District Bank buildings, safely cushioned from the decision they had just made. Most of them were wealthy or had hefty defined benefit pensions. Their investments were socked away in blind trusts. They would feel no pain in their ivory towers.

It took a few months, but the Fed's mouth-to-mouth resuscitation brought gasping investment banks and hedge funds and giant corporations back to life. Wall Street rejoiced.

But the Fed's academic models never addressed one basic question: What happens to everyone else?

In the decade following that fateful day, everyday Americans began to suffer the aftereffects of the Fed's decision. By 2016, the interest rate still sat at the zero bound and the Fed's balance sheet had ballooned to $4.5 trillion, thanks to the Fed's "quantitative easing" (QE), the label given its continuing purchases of Treasuries and mortgage-backed securities.

To what end? All around are signs of an economy frozen in motion thanks to the Fed's bizarre manipulations of monetary policy, all intended to keep the economy afloat.

The direct damage inflicted on our citizenry begins with our youngest minds and scales up to every living generation in our country's midst.

The journey could begin anywhere, but let's start in Erie, Pennsylvania, an area of the country that was struggling even before 2008. The Fed's high interest rates in the 1980s killed its steel and auto industries. The zero bound has dealt the region another devastarting blow. Now, in an Erie elementary school students are given stapled copies of "Everyday Mathematics" instead of an actual textbook. After a snowstorm, twenty-one buckets were deployed to catch leaks because there was no money to repair the roof. In the last five years, the Erie school district has laid off one fifth of its employees and closed three schools to cut costs. School officials are being forced to divert budgets earmarked for kids and facilities to cover the shortfall in its teacher pension fund, starved for yield in a zero-interest-rate environment where bonds return only 1 to 2 percent.

This is not limited to Erie. By mid-2016, long-term returns for U.S. public pensions have dropped to the lowest levels ever recorded—a $1.25 trillion funding gap—forcing pension fund managers from New York to California to resort to ever-riskier investments to meet their legal obligations—and to cut services to make up the shortfall.

Ruining Americans' pension systems? The professor and the FOMC had not anticipated that particular side effect.

And then there are the millennials, the 77 million young people born between 1980 and 1995. As private equity surged into real estate, purchasing homes to be used as rentals in search of higher yields, house prices have soared and the market share of first-time home buyers has dropped to its lowest level in almost thirty years. Nearly half of males and 36 percent of females age eighteen to thirty-four live with their parents, the highest level since the 1940s.

Delaying household formation and all the consumer spending that goes with that? Not on the FOMC's radar.

Even with mortgage rates at record lows, stagnant wages have made it difficult for millennials to amass down payments. Builders anxious to maximize returns now focus on constructing expensive houses, leaving fewer starter homes for sale in urban areas favored by today's young adults. It is an ominous trend for baby boomers. For many, home equity makes up the bulk of their retirement savings.

Killing the move-up housing market? Nope, the FOMC didn't foresee that either.

Chances are pretty good that most boomers didn't get the gist of the statement released by the Fed on that December day in 2008. A certificate of deposit (CD) now pays a hair above nothing. Those boomers—my mom among them—have taken a long hard look at their retirement accounts and realized with a sense of dread that a lifetime of scrimping and risk-averse investing has left their nest eggs vulnerable to serious erosion.

With interest rates on CDs near zero, the average boomer household would need $10.6 million in principal to safely earn $15,930 in interest, the annual income at the federal poverty-line level for a family of two.

Do your folks have $10 million in savings? Mine don't.

Of course, with $10 million, CDs might not be on the table, but that's the point. Several hundred thousand dollars won't do the trick without undue risk for aging boomers.

The members of the FOMC knew their decision would screw savers and the risk-averse elderly. They didn't care. They couldn't afford to. Even when well-intentioned smart people save the world, there are always a few, or in this case, millions of inevitable casualties. *C'est la vie!*

Sadly, there were no angry protests, no million-man marches on Washington that sent shock waves through our country after the FOMC issued its press release. Only the quiet, unheralded loss of some fundamental freedoms: the freedom to save for our retirements risk free, the freedom to sleep in peace knowing our pensions are safe, and the freedom for U.S. companies to invest in our nation's future.

The FOMC's vote during its final meeting of 2008 didn't come from nowhere. It was part of a long tradition of economic interference by well-meaning bureaucrats, going back to the 1930s and accelerating with Federal Reserve Chairman Alan Greenspan in the 1980s.

Greenspan championed the era of financial deregulation that drove Wall Street to levels of greed that surprised even the most hardened investment banking veterans.

His pragmatic response to every crisis on Wall Street? Lower interest rates, which Greenspan did again and again and again. Blow bubbles and pray they don't pop.

But they always do.

In the late 1990s, dot-com companies soared far beyond true valuations; reality pricked that balloon in 2001.

In response, Greenspan again aggressively lowered interest rates and blew another bubble, this time in housing, with catastrophic results that led to the worldwide meltdown in 2008.

In response, his successor, Ben Bernanke, followed suit, pushing through a massive monetary policy experiment by lowering interest rates to zero and using QE to flood America with easy money.

He based his policies on a lifetime of academic study. His theoretical models relied on the idea of the "wealth effect," first articulated by British economist John Maynard Keynes. The concept assumed that free money would induce businesses to borrow, invest, and hire more employees. They in turn would buy homes, consume, and put savings into the stock market instead of CDs, where they would earn little to no interest. As their assets rose in value, people would spend more.

The resulting wealth-effect tide would lift all boats. Hailed as a genius by other academics, Bernanke had every confidence his theories would work.

When they didn't, when the American economy continued to stagger, Bernanke doubled down. His models couldn't be wrong; something else must be holding back the economy.

Janet Yellen, who followed Bernanke as Fed chair, maintained his radical policies with gusto, determined that households and businesses would invest, buy, consume, damn it! Though many on the FOMC sought an exit plan, Yellen was even more married to the Keynesian model of economic growth than Bernanke. She continued to advocate for more QE, and has even raised the specter of negative interest rates.

But real people haven't responded the way academics anticipated in their wealth-effect models. Individuals, small businesses, and corporations alike have been flummoxed by Fed policy and made their own rational choices unforeseen by the FOMC.

Cheap money, combined with uncertainty about the regulatory and tax landscape, has encouraged corporations to buy back their shares rather than invest in their future. Companies in the S&P 500 Index—the benchmark for America's top five hundred publically listed companies—dispersed more than $600 billion to buy back their stock in 2014, and more than $500 billion in 2015.

This strategy has been employed by companies as diverse as Apple, Bank of America, and ExxonMobil, which lost its prized AAA credit rating after one hundred years, based partially on the record amount of debt it incurred to buy back shares. Since 2005, U.S. corporations have disbursed an estimated $296,000 on share buybacks for every single new employee who has been hired.

Because that's the way the world works.

"No wonder share buybacks and corporate investment into research and development have moved inversely in recent years," wrote Rana Foroohar in an op-ed in the *Financial Times* on May 15, 2016. "It is easier for chief executives with a shelf life of three years to try to please investors by jacking up short-term share prices than to invest in things that will grow a company over the long haul."

Compared to the immediate post–World War II period, some American corporations now earn about five times more revenue from purely financial activities such as trading, hedging, tax optimization, and selling financial services, as compared to their core businesses.

As a result, the labor market has atrophied. Though lots of so-called eat, drink, and get sick jobs—for waiters, bartenders, and health care workers—have been created, Fed policy effectively pulled the plug on long-term investment and compromised high-paying job growth.

By mid-2015, only 62.6 percent of adult workers were employed or actively looking for a job, the lowest in nearly four decades. The so-called shadow unemployment rate is estimated to be as high as 23 percent. Many of these people will never come back into the workforce.

Paychecks reflect the stagnation. Unless you are among the top 10 percent of earners, your income has barely grown or declined since 2006.

Ultralow interest rates encouraged what economists refer to as "malinvestment." Yes, the shale revolution created millions of high-paying jobs for workers with little college education. But when oil prices plunged, many of those high-paying jobs evaporated as quickly as they were created.

The bailed-out auto industry drove its own form of malinvestment, pushing the subprime auto loan sector into overdrive. The last time around, Greenspan encouraged people to buy more house than they could afford. The result was a tsunami of foreclosures. This time, those same budget-strapped households have been encouraged to drive more car than their wallets can bear.

Proof: a third of all cars traded in during 2015 had loans that were "underwater." The owners had taken on debt for more than the value of the vehicles. Although the market for subprime car loans is nowhere near the size of the subprime mortgage market, it hurts the same people who can ill afford such hardships.

Of course there are those who love zero interest rates.

In five thousand years of record keeping, debt has never been cheaper. Stocks, bonds, real estate, yachts, planes, blue diamonds, you name it—Fed policies have fueled skyrocketing valuations across the full spectrum of asset classes. And bankers have happily issued debt against them all.

Paradoxically, though returns on risky investments have been consistently strong, fewer average Americans are comfortable with the risk of owning the most common of the pack—stocks.

The percentage of U.S. adults invested in the stock market fell from 65 percent in 2007 to 52 percent by the spring of 2016, a twenty-year low. Inflows into U.S. stock mutual funds—a good gauge of small-investor sentiment—were negative in six of the seven years since 2009. In 2015 alone, mutual fund investors withdrew $170.8 billion—this despite a bull market. Americans retrenched and retreated, especially those nearing retirement years. Fed-blown bubbles have decimated their savings not once, but twice.

Though they might not be able to name the Fed as the party rigging the game, their instincts remind them about the old adage: Fool me once, shame on you. Fool me twice, shame on me.

As for those mom-and-pop investors who remain in the market, they have little chance of escaping Fed policy because their assets are tied up in expensive and rigid 401(k) plans that emphasize index funds.

The Fed's artificially low interest-rate level has distorted the relationship between stocks and bonds. Rather than one providing cover when the other is in distress, asset classes have increasingly moved in concert. And though portfolio advisers make it sound safe, index investing will prove disastrous when markets finally correct.

The one true growth industry? That would be all that high cotton harvested in high finance. Since 2007, world debt has grown by about $60 trillion, enriching legions of investment bankers one bond deal at a time.

The Fed's experiment has widened the inequality gap, angering millions of people who bought into the American dream and know it's being stripped away from them. The global elite get ever richer while those who work for a living see their earnings stagnate—or worse, get laid off.

The acclaimed Noam Chomsky documentary *Requiem for the American Dream* chronicles how the "concentration of wealth and power among a small elite has polarized American society and brought about the decline of the middle class."

Chomsky's intent is to crucify conservatives. But had the predominantly liberal Fed leadership not facilitated the bad behavior of the elite by encouraging them to borrow at virtually no cost, their wealth and power would never have become as concentrated as it is today.

The ostentatiousness with which the so-called one percent has flaunted its wealth has fueled the rise of anger and extremism, leading to the presidential campaigns of Bernie Sanders on the left and Donald Trump on the right.

And politicians wonder about the genesis of a deeply divided and dispirited populace.

Central bankers have invited politicians to abdicate their leadership authority to an inbred society of PhD academics who are infected to their core with groupthink, or as I prefer to think of it: "groupstink."

Annual borrowing costs for the United States since 2008 have hovered around 1.8 percent, thanks to an overly accommodating Fed, which allowed a dysfunctional Congress and the administration of former President Barack Obama to kick the responsibility down the road. Massive spending programs, however ill conceived, got funded with little opposition. Obamacare, anyone?

According to the Congressional Budget Office (CBO), since 2008 federal debt held by the public has nearly doubled and now stands at 75 percent of gross domestic product (GDP). If this lunacy doesn't end, debt will be 110 percent of GDP by 2036, exceeding the post–World War II peak of 106 percent.

And yet feckless politicians get to brag that they've cut the deficit, a distinction lost on too many of us. Yes, it has cost less to run the government and fund the safety net. But it's done nothing to staunch the run-up in our nation's crippling debt load, which has tripled in just twenty years' time.

Were there voices of dissent to be heard in that conference room on that December day in 2008? Did anyone argue for the little guy, the cautious investor? Did someone in the room speak on behalf of pension fund managers now forced to take undue risks? What about the leadership of firms and big banks whose incentives are perverted to the extent that they no longer invest in our country's future?

The short answer is yes. I worked for one of those who pushed back against the majority. He was the lone member of the FOMC who voted against the professor's theories at that fateful meeting.

He fought the good but lonely fight, and I, in my capacity as trusted adviser, waged many a battle with him. But the sad truth is we lost the people's war. In a world rendered unsafe by banks that were too big to fail, we came to understand the Fed was simply too big to fight.

I wrote this book to tell from the inside the story of how the Fed went from being lender of last resort to savior—and then destroyer—of America's economic system.

During my nine-year tenure at the Federal Reserve Eleventh District Bank of Dallas, where I served as adviser to President Richard Fisher, I witnessed the tunnel vision and arrogance of Fed academics who can't understand that their theoretical models bear little resemblance to real life.

To tell this story, I have relied on firsthand experience, interviews with dozens of high-powered market players, reams of financial data, and publicly available documents from the Federal Reserve, including FOMC transcripts and other historical materials.

People are waking up. And it's about time. Although I do not believe it is right to end the Fed, it's high time it was upended. Every American must understand this extraordinarily powerful institution and how it affects his or her everyday life and fight back.

CHAPTER 2

Who Would Buy That Crap?

FED STATEMENT WORD COUNT: 252

EFFECTIVE FED FUNDS RATE: 5.98%

10-YR TREASURY RATE: 5.16%

FED BANKS TOTAL ASSETS: $596.1B

DATE: 1/1/2001

How do we know when irrational exuberance has unduly escalated asset values, which then become subject to unexpected and prolonged contractions as they have in Japan over the past decade?

—ALAN GREENSPAN, DECEMBER 5, 1996

As I and one hundred other members of the sales force found seats in the conference room at Credit Suisse's office a few days into January 2001, we grumbled and groused among ourselves. No Wall Street veteran liked being summoned to these dog and pony shows. That could mean only one thing: we were going to be told to sell something.

My philosophy: if something was worth being sold, it would sell itself, so why were you wasting my time?

At the front stood a handful of Harvard/Wharton investment bankers in Hermès ties, savvy enough to take off their jackets and roll up their starched sleeves in the face of an irreverent and skeptical audience.

My colleagues and I had endured the road-show parade of the late 1990s Internet boom and were now witnessing its collapse. We had lost respect for guys like the self-serving analyst who told us Enron was a "table-pounding buy!" right up until a few days before the energy behemoth filed for bankruptcy.

I had joined Donaldson, Lufkin & Jenrette in 1996 after finishing my MBA in finance and international business at the University of Texas. Inside DLJ, I was branded a rebel, a fair label since grade school, when my favorite question was "Why?"

I can't say my bosses always appreciated my attitude, but clients did, at least those with investing experience who cast jaundiced eyes at aggressive young salespeople paid on commission.

For a twenty-six-year-old woman looking to make her mark, it was a fantastic time to be on Wall Street. In early December, DLJ threw a company Christmas party at the Rainbow Room atop Rockefeller Center. I remember the endless bottles of champagne, the abundance of sushi, the dazzling view of New York at night.

I had struggled to keep body and soul together while carrying a heavy academic load with one aim: to get into a top-notch graduate program. Standing at the summit of New York's financial world, my mind sent out a thought and a thank you: "Mom, I've made it."

No one at that party was worried about Fed chairman Alan Greenspan and his "irrational exuberance" comment earlier that month. Greenspan could have increased margin requirements and stopped many traders in their tracks. He didn't, believing that an unfettered free market is the best allocator of resources. A true optimist.

I had less of his faith in mankind. In a few short months, I'd learned plenty about how the investment banking world really worked.

While in training at DLJ, my class of newly minted MBAs had watched the 1987 movie *Wall Street*. The corporate raider Gordon Gecko, played by a sleek Michael Douglas, was our role model. We adopted his mantra: "Greed is good."

We believed it, having arrived on Wall Street at the height of the dot-com mania. Yahoo went public, making instant millionaires of those who held its stock. Clients begged to buy into the next big thing.

After a few years I was working with hedge funds, mutual funds, and wealthy individuals. DLJ didn't silo its sales force, so I gained exposure to many different kinds of investors. I didn't encourage my clients to ride the

NASDAQ wave and never steered them into stuff that would have torpedoed their assets. Making money was great, but a girl's gotta sleep at night.

Not everyone felt the same way. I was shocked to see analysts, paid to be independent in their assessment of a publicly traded company's prospects, lying to investors so they could make millions of dollars on individual deals that our firm was underwriting.

I also had internal clients, the investment bankers. By day, they sold toxic stuff, which they'd never sink their own money into, out of the front door. When they got their multimillion-dollar bonuses, they'd invest in triple-tax-exempt New York municipal bonds and buy stock in Berkshire Hathaway. When the music stops and everyone else blows up, guess whose investments are liquid? That's how Wall Street survives.

Even though I played by my own rules, I was successful enough to rent an apartment on Fifth Avenue and buy Jimmy Choo shoes, on sale, of course. (I worked my way through college in retail. My motto: Never pay full price.) I was a single woman in New York at the height of HBO's *Sex and the City*!

Well, it wasn't that wild for most of us. And frankly, it got lonely. Girlfriends mattered. I hung Christmas stockings for two best friends at Christmas and had the world over for an Italian feast—literally the only time I had food besides Dijon mustard in the refrigerator, much less cooked.

During my tenure on Wall Street, from 1996 to 2002, I was only vaguely aware of the Federal Reserve as the "unseen hand." Like the Wizard of Oz behind the curtain, Greenspan pulled levers and pushed knobs to control the biggest economic system ever created. Many of my colleagues saw the Fed as an impenetrable mystery, and they accepted that the Maestro knew best on our behalf.

Greenspan rarely issued a statement after FOMC meetings to explain what the Fed would do. Anything he said about monetary policy was notoriously obscure. He had adopted the maxim of Montagu Norman, governor of the Bank of England from 1920 to 1944: "Never explain. Never excuse."

The few post-meeting notices about coming changes in monetary policy that the Fed issued were short, under two hundred words, and full of Fedspeak, code words that people on Wall Street parsed like witch doctors examining sheep entrails for clues to the future. Words like "slightly" and "moderately" in Fedspeak did not mean the same thing. Every nuance mattered.

Two years after I arrived in New York, tremors shook the markets when the hedge fund Long-Term Capital Management (LTCM) shocked the Street by declaring it was on the verge of insolvency.

The brainchild of John Meriwether, former head of bond trading at Salomon Brothers, LTCM was launched in February 1994 with $1.25 billion in capital and a cadre of hotshots who built financial models that would take bond arbitrage to never-before-seen heights of profitability.

Meriwether hired PhD economists David Mullins, former vice chairman of the Federal Reserve, and Robert C. Merton and Myron Scholes, two academics who would share the 1997 Nobel Prize in Economics for creating a new method to value derivatives. (This unusual trio should have been investors' first red flag.)

By 1996, LTCM's model-driven investments had proven phenomenally successful. The partners of the firm earned reputations as arrogant, conceited, and secretive, hiding their trades by scattering them among different banks so competitors couldn't replicate their strategies.

With its enormous success in the bond market, LTCM took its models into other areas of arbitrage: equity, swaps, and global markets. But in 1997, LTCM ran into trouble when Asian markets, starting with Thailand, began to crater.

Americans fled risky investments and piled back into Treasury bonds, causing yield spreads to widen, which had not been predicted by LTCM's models.

By 1998, these unanticipated events turned the brainiacs' assumptions on their heads. That August, when Russia defaulted on its debt, LTCM's model-driven goose was cooked. As markets sank, the hedge fund lost $2 billion in the space of a month. By September, markets had destroyed 90 percent of its equity.

LTCM's partners frantically tried to raise money but no one was lending. The hedge fund wasn't the only one flailing; fifty other firms would experience devastating losses if LTCM went under. At least $1 trillion was at risk.

Greenspan moved quickly to lower interest rates. The heads of more than a dozen of the biggest banks on Wall Street were summoned to meet with William McDonough, then president of the New York Fed District Bank, to devise a bailout plan. Bear Stearns refused to pony up, but Lehman Brothers, Goldman Sachs, Merrill Lynch, Barclays, Bankers Trust, Chase Manhattan, even two French banks agreed to contribute millions to a $3.65 billion bailout package.

Eventually LTCM was stabilized and over the next year dismantled. The management was allowed to remain; so much for tough love.

The bailout didn't require taxpayer money. But McDonough's arm-twisting proved immensely important. Wall Street breathed a sigh of relief and traded jokes about how many Nobel Laureates it took to screw in a lightbulb. (None. No one had paid the electric bill so it didn't matter!)

The criticism of Greenspan was withering. The Fed's responsibility was to supervise banks, not high-flying hedge funds. Besides, why had the Fed rescued LTCM and let five other funds go under? Greenspan had been advising central banks of foreign countries to let floundering institutions fail. The hypocrisy was obvious to his critics but not to Greenspan, who made no apologies.

"Had the failure of LTCM triggered the seizing up of markets," Greenspan told a congressional hearing, "substantial damage could have been inflicted on many market participants, including some not directly involved with the firm, and could have potentially impaired the economies of many nations, including our own."

LTCM was the canary in the coal mine for derivatives, but no one recognized it at the time. The rot unearthed by the Asian crisis continued to fester.

On February 15, 1999, Greenspan and his two colleagues from Treasury, Robert Rubin and Larry Summers, appeared on the cover of *Time* magazine, dubbed "The Committee to Save the World," as the continuing meltdown in Asian markets threatened to spread to the United States.

I grabbed a copy of the magazine at a newsstand near my apartment. The story talked about the "Three Marketeers" deregulating banks, allowing more risk-taking while at the same time encouraging the creation of complex derivatives to mitigate risk. They were hailed as geniuses. I imagined my fellow Wall Streeters going to the cathedral in my neighborhood and lighting candles. Thanks be to God and Greenspan.

In August 2000, my firm, DLJ, was purchased by Credit Suisse for $11.5 billion. By January 2001, when we were all called in for that companywide meeting, the Swiss company's stodgier, more regimented culture had already collided with DLJ's entrepreneurial spirit.

The bankers began describing their new product: a $340 million collateralized debt obligation (CDO), essentially a bond composed of home mortgages sliced into various tranches that produced income streams. Each tranche had been rated by Moody's, Standard & Poor's, and Fitch Ratings, the three most important ratings agencies. The AAA rating stood at the top, then AA, and so on down the ratings ladder until the bottom, the "equity" tranche.

The highest-rated tranches paid out first, as much as 10 percent, significantly higher than the average yield on a corporate bond with the same rating; the last to pay out was equity.

Though the equity tranche produced no income stream, as home prices rose it had the biggest upside, returning as much as 20 percent. But it also promised no guarantees. Investors could lose everything if house prices went south.

I had never heard of a CDO, nor had most people on our sales force. Everyone looked puzzled. Lew Ranieri, the legendary bond trader at Salomon Brothers, was credited with their invention and popularization.

CDOs were completely unregulated. Even as they were bailing out LTCM in 1998, Greenspan, Summers, and Rubin made sure derivatives remained beyond regulators' reach, going so far as to gang up and bully a woman named Brooksley Born in front of Congress.

Born, a highly respected lawyer with twenty years of experience in practicing derivatives law, had been appointed in 1996 by President Bill Clinton to head a small agency called the Commodity Futures Trading Commission (CFTC).

Born was alarmed at the incredible growth and opaque nature of the over-the-counter derivatives market, which included CDOs, mortgage-backed securities (MBS), credit default swaps (CDS), and many other sliced-and-diced products.

In May 1998, Born's agency published in the *Federal Register* a "concept release," a paper on proposed rule changes asking dealers and participants in the derivatives market to voluntarily submit information.

The reaction was swift and furious. Greenspan, Rubin, and Summers argued that spreading risk among thousands of market participants actually stabilized the global financial system. They and Wall Street's dog pack of lobbyists began an all-out attack on Born.

She was summoned to a lunch with Greenspan that Born has to this day refused to talk about. I can only imagine the encounter was unpleasant, Greenspan pulling out the "I know best" card, then following it with the "Who the hell are you?" card. Congressional hearings were hastily called.

CDO   Collateralized debt obligation

Greenspan, Rubin, and Summers lambasted Born, impugning her reputation and integrity.

Eventually the proposed regulations were killed. Realizing she could not effect change, Born resigned on June 1, 1999.

And the derivatives market continued to grow, made up of constantly evolving creations of smart folks like the ones standing in front of us at Credit Suisse in January 2001.

"Who would buy this crap?" I thought that morning. The highest-rated tranches should be "money good." But the rest looked dicey. I was supposed to shovel this dodgy stuff onto my hard-won clients? Nobody else said anything so I raised my hand and rephrased the question. Politely.

"Can you describe to me who would buy the equity tranche?" I asked. A friend dug a warning elbow into my side.

The guys at the front mumbled something, but the answer was really "nobody." At least nobody who understood they were taking all the risk.

I never sold any Credit Suisse CDOs, but my colleagues did, with great initial success.

By 2004, everybody wanted to get their hands on CDOs, especially the equity tranches. House prices were soaring, all but eliminating the downside risk.

In addition, investors such as pension funds could not meet their fixed obligations with low-yield government and corporate bonds. Greenspan had slashed interest rates in the aftermath of the tech implosion, dramatically cutting them from 6 percent to 5.75 percent on January 3, 2001, continuing in increments until the fed funds rate sat at 1 percent.

Derivatives offered a way out of the yield desert. Pension fund managers took the bait; so did broker-dealers, who kept robust fees coming in by originating and managing CDOs.

The CDO market exploded, with certain highly rated tranches offering much fatter returns than comparable sovereign bonds or corporate securities. By 2008, the derivatives market had quintupled to $531 trillion, up from $106 trillion in 2002.

Before 2004, when the market for CDOs and MBSs was relatively small, the pool of underlying assets was well diversified, validating the expectation that they would perform well under most circumstances.

But as the roles of banks, finance companies, and broker-dealers converged, something had to give to satisfy the immense demand. Underwriting standards were slashed. Still there were not enough loans to feed the derivative machine.

Some banks, like HSBC, acquired mortgage lenders to gain direct access to loans. Thus commercial banks' exposure to the subprime market exploded because of the sheer popularity of derivatives. risk

By the time derivatives placed the whole system at rise, I had long since put that CDO dog and pony show out of mind. On leaving Credit Suisse in early 2002, I sold my book of business to the investment bank and signed a noncompete, meaning I couldn't work at a Wall Street firm for a year.

In the DLJ training program, I'd read *Liar's Poker* by Michael Lewis, about life as a bond salesman under Ranieri at Salomon Brothers. In that world, leaving Wall Street for "equities in Dallas" equaled exile and implied failure. I didn't care. I had fallen in love and was moving to Dallas to get married. In a post-9/11 world, I had become all too aware that life was short. I was happy to give it up for a handsome, funny man named John Booth.

Even before Credit Suisse took over DLJ, I had started thinking about life after Wall Street. For several years, I'd been writing a newsletter for my clients, a hard-hitting business tool that got great feedback. That had inspired me to revisit a dream I'd had in high school, so I'd enrolled in night school at Columbia University to earn my second master's degree, this one in journalism. (Did I mention that asking questions came naturally?)

So I called up Robert Decherd, the CEO of Belo Corporation, owner of the *Dallas Morning News*, who had spoken to my class at Columbia. Since I had no track record at a newspaper, I offered to work on the business desk as an unpaid intern.

In my first week, I landed on page A1 with a story about the Pension Benefit Guaranty Corporation and how airlines were strategically bankrupting themselves to slough off pension obligations—a ploy probably dreamed up by an investment banker. Reader response was immediate and irate. The *Morning News* offered me a job. Within six months I had my own column.

After seeing outrageous tactics and deceptive practices on Wall Street, I wanted to educate the public about murky financial markets. And derivatives were among the murkiest.

CHAPTER 3

Saint Greenspan

FED STATEMENT WORD COUNT: 128

EFFECTIVE FED FUNDS RATE: 1.73%

10-YR TREASURY RATE: 5.04%

FED BANKS TOTAL ASSETS: $657.67B

DATE: 1/1/2002

The notion of a bubble bursting and the whole price level [of the housing market] coming down seems to me, as far as a nationwide phenomenon, is really quite unlikely.

—ALAN GREENSPAN, FEBRUARY 27, 2003

Bunny Harmon for Richard Fisher," said a perky female voice.

Sitting at my desk in the autumn of 2005, I thought, "Who the hell in this day and age doesn't make his own phone calls?"

Then I saw the caller ID: Dallas Federal Reserve Bank.

Could it be *that* Richard Fisher? Harvard-Stanford-Oxford smart. Diplomat, expert on trade negotiations with China, former vice chairman for the strategy firm Kissinger McLarty, hedge fund manager, and now president of the Federal Reserve Bank of Dallas.

Beyond his snazzy résumé, all I knew about Fisher was that he had a great head of silver hair and a mild case of foot-in-mouth disease.

In June 2005, a few months after he'd taken over as bank president, Fisher had appeared on CNBC and suggested the Federal Reserve was "clearly in the eighth inning of a tightening cycle" after raising short-term interest rates from 1 to 3 percent over the previous year.

"We have the ninth inning coming up in June," Fisher said. "It may have to go into extra innings."

Clearly he loved baseball metaphors.

Fisher's comments that the Fed might end its rate-tightening cycle fueled a buying spree on Wall Street, a vivid example of how Fed officials can goose markets.

In October 2005, Fisher gave another market-moving speech—a warning on government deficit spending. Blamed for a 95-point drop in the stock market, he'd been labeled a monetary hawk, tough on inflation. Unlike many other Fed District Bank presidents, whose public statements were cautious and rarely controversial, Fisher was determined to speak out and the markets noticed. But why would the president of the Dallas Fed be calling a lowly newspaper columnist?

"Sure, put him through," I said.

A deep male voice came on the line.

"You do know you're in Dallas, Texas," Fisher said with no preamble.

"Excuse me?" I said.

"I've been reading your columns," Fisher said. "You should be writing for the *Wall Street Journal*. You could be a Jon Hilsenrath or Greg Ip."

Since both are widely read columnists with a deep knowledge of financial markets, I saw where this was going. Flattery. Pure unadulterated flattery. I wondered what Fisher wanted, since a lot of my reader response came from pissed-off people who wanted me fired.

In the fall of 2005, that meant advertisers like real estate agents, home builders, and mortgage lenders. Instead of profitless companies going public, a new contagion had swept the nation.

After the high-tech bubble burst in 2000, Greenspan pushed mortgage rates down to please the Clinton and Bush White Houses, as well as Congress, which wanted to extend home ownership to more people and keep the economy humming.

At the same time, Greenspan was blowing up the industry the Fed was supposed to be regulating.

Banks traditionally profited by capturing the difference between the interest rate at which they made loans and what it cost them to borrow.

With rates so low, they had to make up what they were losing on that spread with volume, or trash their lending standards to charge higher interest rates to subprime borrowers.

Relaxed mortgage lending standards sent house prices soaring around the country, especially in California, Florida, and Nevada. Households were buying a lot more home than they could afford, courtesy of subprime mortgages. The market was so hot it had started to look suspiciously like another bubble.

The classic definition of an asset bubble was coined by economist Robert Shiller, who called it an unsustainable condition in which "price increases beget further price increases."

I preferred Warren Buffett's definition: "It's like most trends—at the beginning it's driven by fundamentals; in the end, by speculation. It's just like the old adage: 'What the wise man does in the beginning, the fool does in the end.'" By all measures of the data, the fools had piled in.

I first forecasted a housing bubble in a story that ran in the *Dallas Morning News* on January 2, 2003.

"There's definitely a housing bubble," David Tice, portfolio manager of the Dallas-based Prudent Bear Fund, told me bluntly. "Greenspan's notion that there is not one is preposterous."

I kept hearing every sort of excuse as to why it wasn't happening, wouldn't happen, couldn't happen. But by August 2003, I was truly alarmed. The greatest real estate market in history, on a tear since 1991, had peaked in July 2003, with annual sales of existing homes reaching a record high of 6.12 million.

The Fed's fingerprints were all over this boom, and not just because of Greenspan's low interest rates. In 1993, in response to initiatives by the Clinton administration to make housing more affordable for minorities and the poor, the Boston Fed produced a widely circulated paper called "Closing the Gap: A Guide to Equal Opportunity Lending."

"Lack of credit history should not be seen as a negative factor" in obtaining a mortgage, the Boston Fed guide noted. As an effort to counter "unintentional" racism in lending markets, the guide sanctioned lowering traditional mortgage-lending standards.

Not enough saved for a down payment? No problem. The Boston Fed's PhDs encouraged banks to allow loans from nonprofits or government assistance agencies to go toward a borrower's down payment, though such borrowers are more likely to default on their mortgages.

The Boston Fed distributed more than ninety thousand copies of this remarkably naïve guide. The mortgage industry, anxious to extend its reach and generate fees, embraced its suggestions.

Jeff Jacoby of the *Boston Globe* had this to say about the campaign to lower mortgage standards, writing in 1995: "[Our banks] are knowingly approving risky loans to get the feds and activists off their backs. . . . When the coming wave of foreclosures rolls through the inner city, which of today's self-congratulating bankers, politicians, and regulators plans to take the credit?"

As home prices rose, the resulting boom fueled economic growth through mortgage equity withdrawal (MEW). Homeowners turned their houses into giant ATM machines, taking cash out to pay for appliances and furniture, not to mention boats, big-screen TVs, and college tuition.

That drain of equity had a scary side. The number of subprime mortgages extended to people who could not qualify for conventional mortgages due to low income or poor credit had blasted into the stratosphere. But every adjustable-rate mortgage (ARM) contained a ticking bomb.

As interest rates rose, borrowers' mortgage payments would increase and many marginal households would no longer be able to afford their payments. If their equity had risen, they could survive—for a time—with MEW. But what happened if home values fell? Foreclosure. Multiply that by millions of mortgages.

I warned Dallas readers against buying more house than they could afford. I battened down my own hatches, clipping coupons and getting my personal household completely out of debt, even making double payments to retire our mortgage.

The data were so alarming that in April 2005 I predicted in a column that if the scorching real estate markets on the East and West coasts collapsed, the American economy would be devastated.

From 2004 to 2007, Fannie Mae and Freddie Mac, the government-sponsored enterprises (GSEs), became the biggest buyers of subprime ARMs. The insolvency of the GSEs and hundreds of other mortgage lenders could wreak havoc on an unprecedented scale.

Could the country withstand not only the loss of home equity, but the evaporation of jobs the boom had created in construction, lending, and real estate?

The enigmatic Greenspan did admit that "froth" had *perhaps* entered the housing market and must be dealt with swiftly. But his reaction was snaillike. In mid-2004, Greenspan started raising the fed funds rate incrementally by 25 basis points a time. (A basis point is one-hundredth of 1 percent.) "Gradual" became Wall Street's favorite word, a signal in the FOMC statement that Greenspan would make no sudden moves.

In the summer of 2005, Ben Bernanke, then a member of the Fed Board of Governors, tried to douse concerns about the housing market.

"We've never had a decline in house prices on a nationwide basis," said Bernanke. "So, what I think is more likely is that house prices will slow, maybe stabilize, might slow consumption spending a bit. I don't think it's going to drive the economy too far from its full employment path, though."

Greenspan told Congress in July 2005 that if housing prices fell, "they likely would be accompanied by some economic stress, though the macroeconomic implications need not be substantial."

To which I wrote a column headlined: "Reality, Fed Are at Odds."

Two of the top economists at the New York Fed released a paper in October 2005 saying, "We still find little evidence to support the existence of a national home price bubble."

But anyone with eyes could see it happening.

Greenspan continued to insist that the Fed couldn't prevent an asset price balloon, only clean up the mess left behind when it popped. I strongly disagreed. Greenspan's insistence on cutting rates from 6 percent to 1 percent in the aftermath of the tech bubble had created another, even larger bubble.

I admit I harped on this theme. I had to remind one nervous editor that Saint Greenspan was a public figure. When the villagers came, I firmly expected to see the Fed chairman carrying a pitchfork and leading the charge.

But Fisher didn't mention my criticism of the Maestro. He said that I was wasting my talent writing for a local publication when I could reach a much wider audience.

"Look, thank you very much," I said. "But I'm barefoot, pregnant, and happy as a clam." My second child was due in a few months. I joked that I was in "retirement" after the punishing pace of life on Wall Street.

"I get it," Fisher said. But before he hung up, he invited me to lunch. Sure, I said, my curiosity piqued.

Fisher was a maverick inside the Federal Reserve, the most powerful and impenetrable institution in the world. What was he like? What did he really do? What did anyone at the Federal Reserve do?

On the appointed day, I took an elevator at a downtown skyscraper to the Petroleum Club, established in 1934 during the heyday of Texas wildcatting by one hundred prominent oilmen, a private domain where they could eat, wheel and deal, and smoke cigars. Women had to dine in a separate room until 1980.

I imagined the ghost of H. L. Hunt, the founder of a Texas oil and real estate dynasty, shuddering as I—wearing a stylish dress over my baby bump—followed the waiter through the formal dining room. One of his sons, Ray L. Hunt, a self-made oilman worth billions, was chairman of the Dallas Fed Board of Directors and had crusaded for Fisher's appointment as president.

"I put on my shoes for you," I quipped as I sat down at Fisher's table.

Handsome, with piercing brown eyes and silver hair, Fisher gave new meaning to the word charismatic—old-school manners; impeccably dressed in an expensive suit and French cuffs, with cufflinks shaped like dollar signs. I had wondered if Fisher wanted to shut me up, but he had no agenda.

We chatted about the collapsing housing market over salad. By the entrée, we were deep into a discussion about my ardent belief that the financial system was headed for disaster.

Fisher made this pregnant woman feel smart and interesting. I later learned about the list of CEOs and small business owners he talked to before FOMC meetings. I'm sure Fisher made them all feel the same way.

Our lunch ended on a friendly note. *Quite nice, we'll do it again sometime, good luck with the baby . . .*

One thing was for certain, writing the column was the best job I had ever had. Not only was I fulfilling my dream of educating people about perilous markets, I was also righting the wrongs of a childhood that left me scarred by the damage debt could wreak on a family.

My brilliant but irresponsible father destroyed our family with an ever-growing mountain of unpaid bills that my hardworking mother could never overcome. The irony is, he was an investment adviser. Kind of like the doctor of yesteryear who could always be found in the smoking lounge, my dad saw himself as qualified to handle other people's money though he couldn't manage his own.

From the outside of our beautiful home, in the right neighborhood of San Antonio, we looked as if we had achieved the American Dream, but from the inside, it was a never-ending discovery of more hidden debt and the inevitable conflict it ignited between my parents. As a teenager, I learned not to answer the phone for fear it would be a bill collector. I refused to have friends over in case our shameful secret got out. Eventually my childhood home went into foreclosure and was sold on the courthouse steps for one dollar more than my parents—in the process of divorce—owed on the mortgage.

In my last semester of high school, I was one of fifteen students chosen to participate in the prestigious Scholars Program at New York University to study journalism. Half of my tuition and room and board would be paid; my family had to cover the balance. The day I received that acceptance letter was the happiest of my young life.

Of course my parents had no savings. But I was devastated to learn I couldn't apply for financial aid because my father had failed to file his income taxes for the previous few years. No tax returns, no financial aid. As far as I was concerned, no future. I vowed to quit writing that day and sadly kept that promise for many years to come. My relationship with my father never recovered.

As a result, I hated debt of all kinds. My internal risk radar constantly scanned the financial landscape for danger, shaped by my personal history.

I'd arrived on Wall Street in the midst of the greatest bull market since the Roaring Twenties. And at the height of deception—or should we say "optimistic enthusiasm."

Our DLJ sales force was subjected to the magic lantern shows by CEOs of dot-com firms whose profits existed only on paper in pro forma promises. Those lasted until the NASDAQ peaked on March 10, 2000, tumbling 37 percent over the next couple of months. Poof! Thousands of companies gone and with them investors' hard-earned money.

My master's thesis at Columbia was titled "The Daily Crystal Ball," and chronicled the intersection of two significant financial market innovations: 401(k) retirement savings plans and cable business news.

Beginning in the mid-1980s, average Americans had evolved from spectators to active participants in the stock market. Their appetite for news to track their growing portfolios propelled the rise of CNBC, a business channel inspired by sports news networks, with shows like *Squawk Box* (must viewing) and colorful commentators like Maria Bartiromo.

I had long been a CNBC addict. I loved the cascade of real-time information on the economy, the investigation of arcane market trends. (Like watching a "subtitled, multilanguage foreign movie gone mad," as one professor of pop culture described it.) Bartiromo—the original "money honey"—was my imaginary BFF.

The irony: CNBC's popularity skyrocketed even as millions of Americans lost their retirement savings in the dot-com boom and bust.

I saw my newspaper column as a way to educate people about Wall Street's deceptive ways, deciphering market-speak and clueing them in to certain realities: Beware of brilliant mutual fund managers talking their books. Tread lightly in December when brokers are trying to clean mistakes off their P&Ls. And most importantly, resist the siren call of that *table-pounding buy*.

In early 2006, those CDOs popped up again, in a column I wrote about systemic risk, a concept that most economists never think about or experience outside a textbook.

Think Great Depression, or the stock market crash of 1987, when reactionary, simultaneous, automated selling pressures succeeded in overwhelming a stock market that was supposed to be impervious to shocks.

Greenspan had ended his tenure as Fed chairman at the end of January 2006. Journalists praised him as the most visionary Fed chief of all time. As for any hardship suffered under his stewardship—well, economies are complex.

I was not in the choir singing his praises. "Though I have immense respect for Mr. Greenspan, I think it is premature to draw conclusions about his legacy until his actions work their way through the global economy," I wrote on January 30, 2006. "My fear is that we have paid a high price for the relative calm that prevailed during the Greenspan years."

In hindsight, two back-to-back columns I wrote in March 2006 about escalating systemic risk make it appear that I had psychic powers. *Step this way, Madame Danielle will read your future.*

The mortgage market in the United States had reached a record $8.7 trillion, more than twice the size of the U.S. Treasury bond market, so big and so interconnected it had the power to take down the American economy.

Whenever there were large swings in the Treasury market, automated sell or buy orders were triggered in the mortgage market. The collateral backing mortgages was stretched precariously thin; one in ten households had zero to negative home equity.

One quarter of the mortgages written in the previous year had been subprime—and the rate of subprime delinquencies was pushing 12 percent.

In the next two years, a quarter of all outstanding mortgages—an estimated $2 trillion worth—would reset at higher rates. Another reality: a record percentage of commercial banks' earning assets were mortgage related. Throw the role net money hedge funds played in mortgages for good measure. And Greenspan didn't see a problem? (Is it any wonder that years later Charlie Munger, Warren Buffett's right-hand man, would call Greenspan "an amiable idiot"? Ouch.)

I visited with Paul Kasriel, chief economist at Northern Trust Company, a wealth management firm. Known as the "econotrarian" on the Street, Kasriel told me he'd been concerned for some time that banks "had too many chips on one bet"—housing.

"Smart" mortgages had exploded in popularity and variety, including no-document, no-down-payment, skip-a-payment, adjustable-rate loans that catered to those with less than sterling credit. These too were carved into tranches like a turkey at Thanksgiving. The juicy (and relatively safe) white meat of the AAAs here, the BB-rated dark meat there, and finally the ugly bits like the neck and the gizzard, the highly profitable but precarious equity tranches.

The "cowboys"—managers of high-flying hedge funds—hungry for yield and not so concerned about risk, gobbled them all up, especially the equity tranches. That's what cowboys do. But then MBSs and CDOs were adopted by traditionally risk-averse investment firms and commercial banks' investment divisions.

By 2006, sales of these derivatives had reached $503 billion, five times the volume of just three years earlier. They relied on the credit ratings agencies' stamps of approval.

Few buyers realized that the agencies had also helped create the MBS or CDO and stood to gain from its sale. The fine print said "these ratings are just opinions and investors shouldn't rely on them." People figured the disclaimers were there to make lawyers happy. After all, it was S&P, Moody's, and Fitch; they sold trust.

But by March 2006, the problems with subprime-mortgage defaults had started to reveal themselves. As people fell behind on their mortgage payments or defaulted altogether, MBSs had racked up $25 billion in losses. The value of the $340 million Credit Suisse CDO I had been asked to sell in 2001? It had dropped by $125 million.

"So what if mortgage defaults are on the rise?" Kasriel asked. "No biggie except that U.S. commercial banks have a record exposure to the mortgage market.... If the housing bubble bursts, it is safe to say banks' ability to lend will be seriously pinched for a time."

Kasriel was less concerned with the well-collateralized and highest-rated tranches. "But somebody has to own the worst of it; hedge funds hold a lot of this toxic waste."

To juice their returns, the cowboys were buying derivatives on credit or, as they say, "leveraging them up." And who was financing the leverage on the "toxic waste"? Enormous commercial banks like HSBC. What happens when these critical backstops to the financial system themselves default?

The house of cards collapses.

Hair-raising. Systemic risk was firmly in place and virtually no one was talking about it. In a full-circle moment, I flashed to January 2001, back to that conference room at Credit Suisse. Derivatives had spread like kudzu, engulfing banks and hedge funds all over the world.

Alarmed readers peppered me with e-mails. With great timing, William "Bill" Dudley, then chief economist at Goldman Sachs, issued a report on systemic risk, monetary policy, and bubbles. He either couldn't or wouldn't acknowledge that the United States was in the middle of a big fat housing bubble.

But Dudley helpfully pointed out that the Federal Reserve "argues that asset prices should be considered in setting monetary policy only to the extent that movements in asset prices are anticipated to influence output and inflation."

So even if there was a housing bubble, the Fed wouldn't act.

"It is impossible to both achieve the central bank's mandate in managing the trade-off between growth and inflation over the near term and also limit asset bubbles," he said.

But Dudley offered reassurance: banks like Goldman had such diversified assets that no one should fear systemic risk. Blah, blah, blah.

Maybe Dudley was just shilling for his employer. After all, uninvested investors don't generate fees.

Dudley's dry words aligned with the impression he'd made years earlier when I visited Goldman Sachs to meet with economist Jan Hatzius, a pioneer in research on how households had been affected by the transformation of their homes into cash machines. Hatzius was charisma cubed, Dudley not so much.

The funny thing is: his unassuming nature fit nicely in the Federal Reserve culture. After working at Goldman Sachs from 1986 until 2007, Dudley (who had profited substantially after the company went public in 1999) would be hired by the New York Fed as the manager of its System Open Market Account (SOMA), overseeing the Fed's all-important function of buying and selling government securities.

Two words popped into my mind when I heard about Dudley's appointment to manage SOMA: How convenient. How codependent.

The New York Fed's Board of Directors always read like a Who's Who of Wall Street. In 2006, the chairman was Sanford Weill, CEO of Citigroup.

Also on the board were Dick Fuld, chairman and CEO of Lehman Brothers, and Jeffrey Immelt, CEO of GE.

In January 2007, Jamie Dimon, chairman and CEO of JPMorgan Chase (JPMC) would be appointed to succeed Weill. Goldman Sachs usually had someone in the mix.

Codependent? More like in bed together. Not a problem until your lover desperately needs a loan.

Despite evidence that the housing market was unraveling, within days of Dudley's report, the Fed moved ahead with its fifteenth teeny-tiny quarter-point consecutive interest rate hike, worried because data suggested inflation was nipping at the economy's heels.

Since the Fed is explicitly charged with combating inflation, that tweak was more important than worries about the mortgage industry. No one expressed concern about ARMs, perilously susceptible to even small hikes in the interest rate. Nor did anyone at the Fed express concerns about systemic risk.

The housing market lemmings continued marching toward the cliff. Bernanke took over as Fed chairman. But his approach was not expected to deviate from the Greenspan Doctrine. As one economist quipped, "It just doesn't make sense to make any dramatic moves when you're replacing God."

CHAPTER 4

Inside the Black Box

FED STATEMENT WORD COUNT: NO MEETING

EFFECTIVE FED FUNDS RATE: 2.28%

10-YR TREASURY RATE: 4.22%

FED BANKS TOTAL ASSETS: $807.26B

DATE: 1/1/2005

> Lunch? Aw, you gotta be kidding. Lunch is for wimps.
>
> —GORDON GECKO, IN THE 1987 MOVIE *WALL STREET*

The short, slender man with dark hair and serious eyes seemed skeptical, even wary, of the columnist sitting across his desk.

I wasn't quite sure why I was in Harvey Rosenblum's office at the Dallas Fed either.

The only other time I'd ever been inside the elegant building had been a year earlier when the bank brought in Milton Friedman for the premiere of its documentary on the legendary economist.

Staring in awe at the impressive high ceiling of the grand auditorium, I listened to Friedman's full-throated defense of free-market capitalism. Loved the guy, but it was also true that unfettered, unregulated free markets can lead to disasters. Fraud, misallocation of resources, and rampant greed can take down banks, even entire economies. I'd been warning about that for years.

That was why Rosenblum, the Dallas Fed's director of research, wanted to talk to me about a job, despite his almost palpable hostility.

Rosenblum later admitted to me that he found some of my columns "rather annoying" and a few infuriated him.

But by the autumn of 2006, my predictions were coming true. Readers' e-mails conveyed tales of woe: people were losing their homes to foreclosure. ARMs and interest-only loans—taken out when real estate prices were rising every year—had reset even as values declined. Homeowners couldn't make the higher monthly payments and couldn't sell their houses for what they owed.

Now Rosenblum was reading my stories and saying, "My God, what if she's right?"

I would come to understand that Rosenblum was a unique figure inside the Fed, a lifer dedicated to changing the institution from within. But he'd gained little traction outside his own sphere of influence, for reasons that would take me almost a decade to understand.

The Fed had contacted me after learning that the *Dallas Morning News* announced an early retirement buy-out offer. My bad luck to get into the newspaper business as print gave way to the Internet. Rosenblum told me the Fed needed writers who could translate economic research into readable prose. Did I want to work for the Federal Reserve?

My initial reaction: "Not interested." My colleagues may have thought I was Ms. Chicken Little, but my column had become one of the most popular features of the business section. In four years, I had built a deep and diverse network of sources in Washington and on Wall Street. George Goncalves, treasury strategist at Nomura Securities, and Howard Silverblatt, the walking, talking spreadsheet who personified the Standard & Poor's 500 Index, always took my calls.

Rosenblum seemed intrigued that I didn't jump at the job offer. He emphasized that the Fed needed fresh voices, appealed to my sense of duty. The Fourth of July and apple pie.

Hmmmm. I told Rosenblum that if I accepted employment at the Federal Reserve, it would indeed be to serve my country, as corny as that sounded. My sense of patriotism, especially after being in midtown New York on 9/11, was strong.

Despite my numerous slings and arrows at Greenspan, I had long revered the Fed. My late father, who left the investment advisory business to teach finance and economics at the University of Texas, would have been immensely impressed to know his daughter worked for the most important, powerful institution in the world.

Maybe I could make a difference on the inside. I felt certain there was a lack of appreciation at the Fed for the risks its policies created. In hindsight, my understanding of what really went on inside the Federal Reserve was embarrassingly shallow. I knew nothing. Nada. Zip. Zero.

But I wanted to know, and I wanted to contribute. Since I had two toddlers, I had two nonnegotiable conditions: flexible hours and I worked from home on Fridays when preschools were closed. And the Fed had to make a formal offer before the *Morning News* buy-out deal expired. He had seventy-two hours.

For Rosenblum, this was like saying "Let's get married" after a first date. Being hired into the Research Department at a Federal Reserve Bank is a process. Applicants present daylong seminars for staff economists to discuss their doctoral dissertations, areas of research interest, and economic philosophy. Are they Keynesians or Ricardians?

Somehow, Rosenblum made it happen. A formal job offer arrived just before the buy-out expiration.

When I announced I was ending my column, the avalanche of e-mails from readers was humbling. Through links on various blogs, I had built an international readership (Tel Aviv, Sydney, Plano!) and many sincerely mourned the end of my feisty reports on the economy.

One e-mail from a woman I call "Linoleum Lady" was bittersweet. She had written me a nasty note a few years earlier, mad because I warned people against taking on home equity debt through subprime ARMs. Sick of the yellow linoleum in her kitchen, she wanted to take out a loan to remodel it but her husband had shown her my column. That made her angry enough to write and tell me I was an idiot.

Now Linoleum Lady wrote to say he had finally agreed; the floor was replaced, the cabinets updated, new appliances installed. But their ARM rate had reset: they couldn't make the payments and were losing their remodeled home to foreclosure.

"I hate to say it," she wrote, "but you were right. I wish I had listened to you." Maybe so, but that didn't make me feel better.

Some readers asked why I hadn't written a column gloating "I told you so" about the housing market. My answer was simple: ladies don't dance on graves.

"A huge amount of work will be required in the coming years to address the fallout of the largest financial bubble in history," I wrote. "The ramifications extend far beyond the realm of residential real estate."

On September 29, 2006, I drove up to the security kiosk at the Federal Reserve Bank of Dallas and handed my identification to the armed guard. It had been over three years since my father had died yet I felt his presence so strongly it was like he was sitting in the car beside me.

"Hi, it's my first day," I said to the guard. "I'm going to be working in the Research Department."

He studied my ID, then lowered the mechanized steel bollards that barred entry. I drove through and was soon blocked by another security gate. A light finally flashed on and the second gate rose. I drove past guards in a glassed-in room, who scrutinized me and then opened the door to the parking garage.

Inside the building, I walked down a long hallway through double sets of sliding glass doors and into a vestibule where a representative from Human Resources waited to greet me.

My possessions went one way through an X-ray machine and I went another, into what looked like a European phone booth with bulletproof glass. I was trapped for a few moments before the other side of the booth opened.

I grabbed my belongings, feeling lucky I hadn't been frisked. We walked down a glassed-in corridor that ran alongside a courtyard of meticulously manicured hedges and flowers to more elevators.

In a low-ceilinged basement bright with fluorescent lights I met more armed guards. They inked my fingerprints, took a picture, and promised I would have my official magnetized Dallas Federal Reserve Bank badge by the end of the day. At this point, I suspected it was easier to break into Fort Knox than the Dallas Fed.

My HR guide led me back to the lobby, wished me good luck, and that was the last I would see of her. Alone, I ascended to the twelfth floor, domain of the Research Department.

I stepped into eerie silence. Home to thirty-five economists, the floor was library quiet and smelled sterile, like a hospital.

A receptionist showed me to my new work space. My heart sank. Not only small and claustrophobic, the little gray cubicle had no television feed and therefore no access to my CNBC lifeline.

The contrast between my first day on the job at the Fed and my first day on Wall Street in 1996 couldn't have been more dramatic.

As a newly minted MBA in the training program, I had walked onto the trading floor at DLJ to be slapped in the face by cacophony. Phones ringing, people yelling, multiple TVs tuned to financial news.

And the aroma. It smelled, literally, like red meat. For lunch, traders ordered steak from Smith & Wollensky and ate at their desks. Leaving your chair for a meal during the trading day meant you weren't serious about your job.

The Dallas Fed: no noise, no smell, no bustle. And everybody left their desks for lunch.

The Fed at first seemed like utopia, a cocoon of calm occupied by highly educated people cosseted by creature comforts in keeping with their lofty goal: safeguarding America's economy.

Occupying a starkly modern limestone building on the northern edge of downtown, the bank was the most beautiful place I had ever worked. A soaring lobby of marble, glass, and steel faced toward the striking skyline of the city. An extensive collection of art—paintings, pen-and-ink drawings, lithographs, collages, and sculpture by well-known regional artists—was featured throughout the fourteen-story building.

In all about 1,100 people worked at the Dallas Fed, including economists, bank auditors, accountants and guards, lots of guards.

The entire first floor of the bank—six acres of office space—was dedicated to its financial operations. From the well-appointed gym to the subsidized cafeteria and executive dining room, the bank catered to its employees' every need. (And yes, Fed employees can do all their banking there at a credit union.)

Some of my colleagues arrived early in the morning to work out, shower, and eat breakfast. Four hours later they headed to the executive dining room for competitive discourse on the latest iteration of their models over long lunches.

The common cafeteria suited me just fine. The food was darn good and so cheap some people even bought dinner to take home to the spouse and kids. Some habits are hard to break. I usually ate a bowl of soup (50 cents, crackers included) at my desk, my eyes glued to the *Wall Street Journal* live feed on my computer.

The Fed's permanent meal subsidy never failed to remind me it was an entity that operated outside the business cycle. It's not that Wall Street didn't have its fair share of perks; it's that perks came and went. In the aftermath of the dot-com bust, our travel was downgraded from the Four Seasons to the Marriott. Entertainment budgets were slashed. And one day, to no one's surprise, we received an e-mail informing us that the cafeteria would no longer be subsidized. Those were the days you'd be at your desk late into the night, proving you were worthy to keep your chair.

And then there was the Fed. One of the few times there was hustle and bustle: 5 P.M. on the nose. The security guards locked open the doors to allow for the cavalcade of humanity to rush the exits.

To say employees were coddled is not an exaggeration, at least compared to the outside world. Platinum benefits included Cadillac health care, plus a 401(k) with matching contributions by the Fed *and* a defined benefit pension system, an increasingly rare perk.

And workloads were lighter than any I had ever witnessed in the private sector. An employee in another division of the bank confided to me that during a year-end review, her boss criticized her for being "too productive," thus putting others in a bad light. Furious, she began looking for another job where her initiative was rewarded. She landed at a certain large retailer in Seattle.

Technological innovations that have streamlined banking worldwide have cut costs at the Fed as they have in the private sector. The dwindling need for check processing has shrunk lower-skilled Fed jobs, taking total employment from 23,000 to 17,398 by 2009.

It's a myth that the Federal Reserve is nonprofit. It earns billions of dollars per year through various financial functions; after expenses, most of the profits go straight to Treasury.

Thanks to the explosive growth of its balance sheet, the Fed has reaped escalating profits in recent years. All those bonds pay interest. In 2015, it posted record earnings of $97.7 billion.

But its expenses are borne by the taxpayer. From the General Accounting Office (GAO): "The Federal Reserve is a self-financing entity that deducts its expenses from its revenues and transfers the remaining amounts to the U.S. Treasury. Because an additional dollar of Federal Reserve cost is an additional dollar of lost federal revenue, the costs of operating the Federal Reserve System are borne by U.S. taxpayers just like the costs of any federal agency."

Its profitability doesn't keep the Fed's enemies at bay. From the day after it was created to today's late-night infomercials, the Fed has always had its fair share of thoughtful critics and witch-hunters. One of the Fed's most dogged detractors was from my hometown.

An aggressive congressional investigation in the 1990s spearheaded by Congressman Henry B. González (D-Tex.) attacked the Fed as unaccountable and spendthrift. The central bank, he reminded the House of Representatives, "was not struck from the brow of Jove, the Greek God. It is an institution that is the creature of Congress."

In response to González's persistence, the Fed streamlined its operations, ditched its fleet of fifty airplanes used to cart checks across the country, and cut redundancies in its operations. The District Banks now fight tooth and nail to preserve their functionality. Otherwise they are just fortresslike office buildings housing highly paid PhDs.

The Atlanta Fed landed the processing of the nation's electronic checks. The Cleveland Fed was awarded the job of handling paper checks. In addition to trading government securities, the New York Fed holds a half million bars of gold bullion owned by domestic entities and foreign governments in a basement vault—and supervises Wall Street, of course.

And the Dallas Fed?

From the top floor of the Dallas Fed, I could look down into the courtyard below and see a large green dollar sign fashioned from carefully pruned hedges—an amusing reminder that the bank literally sits atop a gargantuan pile of cash.

At any given time, the vault beneath the building—five stories deep and two football fields long, with two doors that each weigh twenty-two tons—contains hundreds of millions of dollars in newly printed greenbacks ready to be rolled out to area banks.

The Dallas Fed's vault holds up to 2,800 cash "buses," large steel carts with windows that can contain anywhere from $300,000 to $30 million, depending on the denomination of the bills.

Maintaining a high level of security twenty-four hours a day is the Dallas Fed's single largest line-item expense. The Federal Reserve has its own law enforcement unit, with hundreds of cameras, armored trucks, and delivery vehicles that pass through sophisticated monitoring of undercarriages for explosives.

I was certainly copacetic with safeguarding the monetary goods. My grandmother ignited my fascination with hard currency. During my summers in Connecticut, I sat with her late at night counting out pennies, nickels, dimes, and quarters from the sales at two DiMartino Sunoco stations off Exit 51 in East Haven. We fashioned the coins into rolls so she could make the bank deposit the next morning.

As a child I crammed my piggy bank with quarters and the occasional dollar bill. As an adult I think of money as an instantaneous transfer of electrons when I swipe my debit card at the grocery or gas station, or the wire transfer of pay to my bank account.

But an informal tour of the building's basement left me dumbfounded. Giant stacks of crisp $20 and $100 bills. Shiny new coins in huge bags. *Ka-ching!*

The proximity of the Bureau of Engraving and Printing in Fort Worth is the reason the Dallas Fed has the primary responsibility for distributing currency to member banks around the country. The plant produces about 70 percent of the money made in the United States. (The rest is printed and distributed by the Bureau of Engraving and Printing plant in the District of Columbia.)

The U.S. Mint produces coins in Philadelphia, Denver, and San Francisco, which are then circulated by the Dallas, Philadelphia, Denver, and San Francisco Fed District Banks.

With about $1.45 trillion worth of U.S. currency in circulation, almost half of the transactions in America are paid for in cash.

As the Dallas Fed tells visitors, the nation's estimated 107 billion cash transactions per year require money to be "durable, portable, divisible, scarce, uniform and acceptable." The U.S. dollar is regarded as the strongest, most reliable currency in the world.

Without cash, the nation's economy would grind to a halt. And not just at Walmart, McDonald's, and hair salons. Strip clubs would go under. The drug trade would implode. Red-light districts would go dark. And the Texas State Fair wouldn't be as rowdy. For the three raucous weeks of the State Fair each year, millions of dollars flood into the Dallas Fed for safekeeping at night, and the next morning millions go back out to handle sales of corn dogs, beer, and deep-fried Oreos.

I learned fun facts about money. Look in your wallet. The face of each Federal Reserve Note bears a letter, starting with the "A" of the Boston Fed (District 1), and ending with the "L" (District 12) of the San Francisco Fed. "K" is for Dallas, District 11.

Paper money is composed of 75 percent cotton and 25 percent linen. By passing through so many dirty, sweaty hands, a $1 bill lasts an average of 5.8 years in circulation. The $10 bill has the shortest life span, surviving only a little over 4.5 years before it must be replaced. Hundred-dollar bills—except for those stuffed under mattresses and locked into safes—typically last fifteen years before being pulled from use. Coins can last decades.

Why are issues of $2 bills abject failures? Probably because they are too easy to confuse with $1 bills. Two-dollar bills have never caught on with the public and remain a niche fascination for collectors and Vegas gamblers.

As used currency flows into the Dallas Fed from member banks, enormous machines scan an average of one hundred thousand bills per hour. About 36 million tattered and defaced currency notes are replaced each month with crisp new bills.

Specially trained examiners identify and pull fake bills. The Bureau of Engraving and Printing uses anticounterfeiting techniques that include a 3-D security thread, microprinting, and color-shifting ink. In one day, the Dallas Fed's inspectors might find as many as fifteen phony bills. These are given to the Secret Service to be traced to their creators if possible.

In the basement of the Dallas Fed sits a giant shredder that destroys about $20 million in unfit currency every single business day. Some of the shredded cash is used to train dogs to sniff for money used in illegal activities. Some is given to Goodwill or other such programs for workers to package shredded cash into bags as novelty items. The vast majority is dumped in landfills.

In a weird way, seeing all that currency being diced, sliced, and discarded like so much mulch brought back painful memories. Money—and the lack of it—had powerfully shaped my life. Debt was my monster in the closet. I took home a small bag of shredded cash to remind me why I was at the Fed.

My initial job was to translate the Fed's economic research into readable material for the public, as part of its mission to improve financial and economic literacy.

The people I worked with in the Research Department, three dozen PhD economists with degrees from the world's top universities, were scary book smart. At least it seemed that they were, based on their credentials and the arcane language that they spoke among themselves.

From the beginning, I could sense my new colleagues at the Dallas Fed didn't take me seriously, which I initially attributed to my Wall Street wardrobe: Brooks Brothers suit, Hermès scarf, Jimmy Choo shoes, diamond earrings. The economists wore monochrome and sensible footwear, which I quickly learned matched their personalities. *Note to self—lose the stilettos.*

Within days I realized that it wasn't my outfits they disdained. I didn't have a PhD. As far as they were concerned, I had nothing interesting or valuable to say.

This presented my type A personality an immediate challenge. I arrived at work bursting to discuss alarming economic data erupting on all fronts. Stock market volatility, the collapsing subprime mortgage industry, and the mountain of household debt was unnerving. And not a sounding board for miles.

My new colleagues shrugged, uninterested. They believed any housing crisis would be regional. After all, their boss Bernanke had said just that. Their indifference—and subtle hostility—was maddening.

As far as I could tell, none of them watched CNBC in the morning. Of course they read the financial newspapers, if they bothered to check their mailboxes. I was often unnerved to find days of the *Financial Times* stacked up in someone's box. How could anybody ignore the news in this quickly unraveling world?

The economists were satisfied parsing backward-looking data to predict future events using their mathematical models. Financial data in real time were useless to them until it had been "seasonally adjusted," codified, and extruded into charts.

Seasonal adjustments in data are used to smooth out aberrations in financial activity. For example, the consumption of gasoline might be higher in the summer months than in winter. Economists adjust the data to get a clear look at a general trend.

Makes sense, but sometimes seasonally adjusted data require long periods to be of real use. By then the world may have changed and the data are no longer valid. (At a conference, I chuckled when an economist stood at a podium deriding the rigidities of the "dismal science." Somewhat vertically challenged with a bald head, Wells Fargo's Mark Vitner remarked, "If you seasonally adjust me, I'm George Clooney.")

This created a weird disconnect every time I went to work.

Inside the Dallas Fed, there was no housing bubble. ARMs were the greatest financial innovation to ever bless the middle class. Mortgage equity withdrawal was fueling a fantastic wealth effect. Derivatives were sophisticated financial instruments that diffused risk. All of the Fed's eccentric econometric models showed the future was rosy, that baby boomers would retire with record levels of prosperity.

I believed none of those things were true.

I believed that Greenspan, above all others, had blood on his hands. Not only had Greenspan publicly encouraged home buyers to take out ARMs, he had assured them that despite home prices trending well above their hundred-year average, all was well.

Now Bernanke was in charge. Hadn't he read about people in California's Inland Empire making fifty thousand dollars a year and somehow qualifying for mortgages to buy a half dozen homes?

How could he not find trouble in the 125 percent loan-to-value toxic garbage trading hands? And that's what Wall Street traders called it.

Didn't Bernanke see that the era of deregulation, with the fall of the last remnants of the Glass-Steagall Act of 1933, had let Pandora out of her box? Did he not know that Pandora was now a wild alcoholic thanks to Greenspan lowering interest rates from 6.5 percent to 1 percent? And then raising rates at such a predictable pace it kept markets in a comatose state?

This inexplicable act had set off a speculative fervor that eclipsed that of the Roaring Twenties, thanks to investors' increasingly desperate search for yield.

My colleagues in the Research Department thought it ridiculous that

I—the new kid on the block—arrived every morning with my hair on fire. I was convinced a monetary asteroid was heading in our direction, aimed directly at the American Dream.

You could almost see them shaking their heads and thinking, *Only two master's degrees, poor girl. Probably nothing to be done...*

On paper, my coworkers at the Dallas Fed were more qualified than I was to analyze and predict the economy. Masters of the Phillips Curve, Okun's Law, and the Taylor Rule, schooled in the stringent field of macroeconomics, they studied data to discern patterns for the benefit of the Federal Reserve decision-making process.

They wore their PhDs like T-shirts. There was a distinct hierarchy: MIT, Harvard, Yale, Princeton, and the University of Chicago sat at the top, in that order. Their papers appeared in prestigious academic journals with titles like "VAR Estimation and Forecasting When Data Are Subject to Revision." And "Lifecycle-Consistent Female Labor Supply with Nonlinear Taxes: Evidence from Unobserved Effects Panel Data Models with Censoring, Selection and Endogeneity."

Each morning I greeted Carlos, a Fed lifer born in Argentina, whose dissertation was fittingly titled "Inflation Processes in Latin America." Nearly always in his trademark sweater with leather patches on the elbows, he seemed to wander the office floor with coffee mug in hand.

In a corner office reigned senior economist John V. Duca, Yale undergrad, Princeton PhD, latest greatest paper called "Mutual Funds and the Evolving Long-Run Effects of Stock Wealth on U.S. Consumption." Fascinating guy. Top-ranked economist, based on the number of times other economists cited his papers in their papers.

Few had even the slightest interest in financial markets. Nor in talking to me. Because of my lack of academic accomplishments, I didn't qualify to breathe their air. It was a shock to be treated with such obvious condescension.

In those first few months, while trying to figure out which planet my colleagues had come from, I contemplated the purpose of the Federal Reserve. It all came down to trust.

Created after a massive stock market collapse and subsequent bank failures that decimated depositors' savings, the Federal Reserve exists so that the American public can maintain faith in its monetary system.

This vital responsibility is carried out by an organization with an arcane, complex, and peculiar decision-making apparatus that is virtually opaque to outsiders.

The Fed mother ship on Constitution Avenue in Washington, DC, is linked to twelve District Bank satellites located in Boston, New York, Philadelphia, Cleveland, Richmond, Atlanta, Chicago, St. Louis, Minneapolis, Kansas City, Dallas, and San Francisco, occupying real estate valued at $2.3 billion.

Though the Fed's "factory" functions—bank supervision, management of currency, paper-check processing, and electronic payments—command 83 percent of the central bank's resources, it's the sexy 17 percent related to monetary policy that attracts the attention of the press and financial markets.

Setting monetary policy is the job of the Federal Open Market Committee (FOMC), composed of the seven members of the Board of Governors in Washington and the presidents of the twelve District Banks. At full complement, the FOMC consists of nineteen people, though it's not unusual for governors' seats to go unfilled.

By law, the FOMC is required to meet at least four times a year, but it usually meets eight times a year—about every six weeks—under the leadership of the chairman.

Governors vote at every meeting. Save for the New York Fed, which has a permanent vote, the presidents of District Banks vote on a rolling basis, giving each a voice on the committee one year out of every three—except for Chicago and Cleveland, who vote every other year.

As a reminder, among other things, the FOMC sets the fed funds interest rate, the rate at which commercial banks lend reserve balances to each other on an uncollateralized basis in the overnight market.

Think of the precrisis monetary system as a giant seesaw. Some banks had extra reserves, some a shortage. When the Fed bought and sold Treasury bonds, money flowed up and down as banks met their liquidity and credit needs.

The Federal Reserve has always advertised itself as being above politics, impervious to outside influence. This is, of course, nonsense.

The chairman is appointed to a four-year term by the president of the United States and must be confirmed by the Senate. Members of the Board of Governors are appointed to staggered fourteen-year terms by the president and are also approved by the Senate. It is common for governors to be appointed to an unfilled term if someone resigns before the end of their tenure. But the governors cannot be removed for their policy views—not by the chairman, or the president, or Congress. They have complete and total immunity.

Their pay is somewhat parsimonious, compared to the responsibility. In 2015, Fed governors earned annual salaries of $179,700. The chairman earned $199,700. (The head of the European Central Bank, Mario Draghi, earns more than twice as much as the head of the Fed, receiving $518,264 in 2013.)

Presidents choose the chairman and governors their advisers tell them will do their bidding. If the opposing party controls the Senate, it blocks appointments deemed too partisan. For most of President Barack Obama's time in office, the Board of Governors operated with two vacant seats because the Republican-dominated Senate refused to confirm certain nominees.

In theory, FOMC members pledge to put partisan politics aside when they begin their terms. Few do, though most strive to maintain objective demeanors. There are exceptions who flaunt their leanings. One member of the Board of Governors, Daniel Tarullo, still sported an Obama sticker on the bumper of his car in the Fed parking garage long after his appointment, and Governor Lael Brainard was revealed as a donor to Hillary Clinton's presidential campaign.

Overt strong-arming of permanent voting members of the FOMC rarely happens, but everyone knows who butters their bread and where they might land when they leave. The notion of some superior objectivity inside the institution is naïve at best.

The politicking is hardly contained inside the Beltway. The Fed was gerrymandered from its inception.

When the Fed was created more than a hundred years ago, politics dictated where the twelve banks ended up. Some were placed in obvious turn-of-the-century economic powerhouses like New York, Chicago, Cleveland, and St. Louis.

But in smaller cities, politics reigned. The Kansas City bank should have been on the other side of the river in Kansas, not in Missouri. Republicans controlled Kansas at the time and Democrats were in charge of the White House; as a result, Missouri is the only state to boast two Fed District Banks.

The Texas bank should have been in San Antonio, then the state's biggest city. While a strong banking industry, central location, and railroad access made Dallas an acceptable choice, heavy lobbying by George Bannerman Dealey, publisher of the *Dallas Morning News*, sealed the deal.

The San Francisco Fed covers Alaska, Arizona, California, Idaho, Hawaii, Oregon, Utah, and Washington, a massive geographical area that according to yesteryear's cartographers was a mere economic footnote that could be represented with just one Fed. (Alaska and Hawaii were added to the Fed system after they became states in 1959.)

Each of the dozen District Banks has a board of directors that nominates a president/CEO to serve a five-year term. The presidents' pay outstrips that of Fed governors and the chairman; in 2009, the average salary of the twelve District Bank presidents was $340,323.

Their appointments must be approved by the Board of Governors. Though rarely disclosed in the press, some District Bank boards have had their nominations quietly scuttled.

When a District Bank president has overstayed his or her welcome, he or she will not be fired but will perhaps receive an employment offer from a university or corporation too enticing to be refused. Wink, wink. A different kind of politics.

One former insider has described the Federal Reserve System as a giant pyramid made of Jell-O. You know, the wiggly lime or cherry gelatin dessert.

The pyramid's objective is analyzing economic data, building consensus, and pushing the information up the pyramid for decision makers at the top.

Whack the Jell-O pyramid in the middle, kick it again and again, run into it full speed like an NFL tackle—no matter how hard you punch, it shudders and wiggles and absorbs the hit, and then returns to its original shape.

That Jell-O pyramid starts on the bottom with operations at the Fed District Banks, which are hybrids—part private, part government.

In addition to operations—processing payments and distributing currency—they supervise and regulate depository institutions under their jurisdiction. "Sup & Reg" is vital but gets little respect from those above.

Halfway up the pyramid are the Research Departments of each District Bank.

Next level up is the Washington mother ship's legion of economists, who have the ear of the Fed Chair. Consider them to be the Grand Pooh-Bahs of PhDs. (Their e-mail addresses end in .gov, while District Bank employees' e-mails end in .org.)

The District Bank presidents occupy one stratum of the FOMC, with the Board of Governors one layer above.

The FOMC's vice chair, always the president of the New York Fed, is second-in-command. At the peak of the pyramid reigns the Fed chairman.

By law—according to the 1977 amendment of the Federal Reserve Act—the FOMC has two mandates: maintain "price stability" and maximize employment. In other words, safeguard what a greenback can buy while employing as much of the population as possible. Its tools are short-term interest rates and the money supply.

When I joined the Fed, the mystique was mesmerizing. No other institution in the world had such power, such prestige.

However, once inside, I confronted an uncomfortable question: Why were so many of its highly-educated and well-paid economists oblivious as the worst financial crisis since the Great Depression was about to break over their heads?

Why had Greenspan been so resolutely blind to the housing bubble his low-interest-rate policies had created?

Why didn't Bernanke sound an alarm instead of repeatedly opining that the housing crisis was "likely to be contained"?

Why was Janet Yellen, then president of the Federal Reserve Bank of San Francisco, astonishingly clueless as the housing market in her region imploded? And later, why couldn't Yellen—an economist known for her brilliant forecasting skills—foresee the consequences of the Fed's disastrous zero-interest-rate policies after she succeeded Bernanke as Fed chairman?

Over the next nine years, as I scaled the outer walls of the Federal Reserve pyramid, always an outsider looking in, I grew more and more alarmed.

The Fed leaders we entrusted with our financial fate had in fact precipitated the crisis. After restoring the basic plumbing of the financial system, that same institution then dealt it another series of deadly blows. Instead of fortifying the American economy, they have repeatedly made it more vulnerable.

Grasping the modus operandi of the Federal Reserve requires first anchoring in your mind two words: hubris and myopia.

We know better than you. Only our models can decipher and predict the economy.

The Fed's battalion of economists—from the top down—believe that their training in the world's top universities and their unique schooling in analysis gives them wisdom and insight, when in fact their training often blinds them to reality.

I witnessed this elitism and tunnel vision hard at work in the halls of the Dallas Fed's Research Department on a daily basis.

Virtually no one I met at the bank had ever worked on Wall Street, managed a business, or handled their own investments. They were discouraged from actively investing in the financial markets because the institution's access to confidential data could be used for fraudulent purposes. They rarely talked to people outside their spheres.

And their standard of success? Getting published in peer-reviewed journals by cranking out academic studies that impressed people just like them. If their work proved wrong, well, no harm, no foul. Nobody was ever fired.

But most economists are long on theory and short on practical results.

Economist John Kenneth Galbraith in 1978 famously predicted that General Motors so dominated the auto business that other companies would be foolish to try to compete. At the time, the unionized GM held 46 percent of the market. But other auto companies eroded its dominance over the next three decades. In 2008, GM was rescued with a government bailout. By 2014, the auto giant commanded just 17 percent of the market.

Consensus among economists is endemic, and sometimes hilarious.

A letter published in the *Times* of London on March 30, 1981, signed by 364 prominent economists, predicted that Margaret Thatcher's stringent fiscal policies would be disastrous. The UK's spectacular economic turnaround proved they were dead wrong.

Their absurd collective blunder prompted Geoffrey Howe, chancellor of the exchequer, to observe that an economist was like a "man who knows 364 ways of making love, but doesn't know any women."

A 1991 report by the American Economics Association looked at the training economists were receiving at universities. It concluded that the programs "may be turning out a generation with too many idiot savants, skilled in technique but innocent of real economic issues."

At one top university, grad students couldn't "figure out why barbers' wages have risen over time," but they could solve "a two-sector general equilibrium model with disembodied technical progress in one sector."

"Central banking thrives on a pervasive impression that [it] is an esoteric art," wrote Karl Brunner, an economics professor and Fed critic, in 1981. "Access to this art and its proper execution is confined to the initiated elite. The esoteric nature of the art is moreover revealed by an inherent impossibility to articulate its insights in explicit and intelligible words and sentences."

Even Greenspan dinged his chosen profession. "A surprising problem is that a number of economists are not able to distinguish between the economic models we construct and the real world," he said in 1984 when he was a private consultant.

By the 1990s, many Wall Street and corporate entities concluded that PhD economists were a drain on overhead.

In 1996, my first year on Wall Street, the *New York Times* wrote a story pointing out that IBM, which had employed more than two dozen in-house economists in the 1970s and '80s, had canned them all. Many other major corporations like General Electric had done the same, preferring to use commercial services. Why? Because high-paid economists' predictions were unreliable.

"Research economists have shown little interest in improving forecasting techniques or testing the models," Ray Fair, professor at Yale University, told the *Times*. It was cheaper for companies to outsource the crystal ball gazing and focus on hedging risk by relying on financial derivatives.

While corporate America shed its academic economists, the Fed bulked up, adding to its ranks and increasing its dependency on their methods and models.

In 1970, the Federal Reserve had about twenty-five thousand employees. By 2005, the number of employees had dropped to seventeen thousand as the Fed streamlined its operations. But the percentage of professional economists had grown exponentially; the system now has about a thousand PhD economists. According to the San Francisco Fed, the Federal Reserve is the single largest employer of PhD economists in the nation, and presumably the world.

For decades, the Fed also has provided contract work and "visiting appointments" to hundreds of academic economists who specialize in monetary and financial subjects. They dare not bite the hand that feeds. If you don't believe me, take economist Milton Friedman's word for it: "The Fed's relatively enhanced standing among the public has been aided by the fact the Fed has always paid a great deal of attention to soothing the people in the media and buying up most of its likely critics."

At the Board of Governors, the huge staff of PhD economists is managed by the three "barons," as the directors of Research and Statistics, International Finance, and Monetary Affairs are known. At one point, all three were graduates of MIT. Insiders began calling them and their staff the "MIT Mafia."

By 2006, when Bernanke (ditto, PhD from MIT) was named chairman, PhD economists had so overtaken the central bank that former Fed vice chairman Alan Blinder said that having a doctorate in economics was probably a prerequisite for the top spot.

"Otherwise," said Blinder, a Princeton economics professor, "the Fed's staff will run technical rings around you."

It wasn't always so.

Fed chairman William McChesney Martin, a former stockbroker and president of the New York Stock Exchange, is credited with shaping the modern economist-dominated Fed. Under his tenure, from 1951 to 1970, the Fed's central focus shifted from bank regulation to managing the economy by manipulating monetary policy.

But during Martin's reign, there were few economists outside academia. The turning point came in the 1960s, when American universities hosted a PhD explosion. Currently, of the estimated 50,000 PhDs granted each year by U.S. universities, about 1,100 are in economics. A sizable portion of these newly minted "doctors" go to work at the Fed.

The first Fed chairman to have a PhD was the eminent Columbia University professor Dr. Arthur F. Burns (1970–78), who has been widely criticized as one of the worst to hold the office in the institution's history. Fed chairman Paul Volcker had a master's degree in economics but no doctorate. He's widely regarded as one of the best Fed chairmen in history because he vanquished double-digit inflation (created by Burns) during the 1980s. Go figure.

As for the Maestro, Greenspan dropped out of the doctoral program at Columbia University in 1951, failing to complete his dissertation. After chairing the Council of Economic Advisers in the Nixon and Ford administrations, he obtained a PhD from New York University in 1977.

But his paper went missing for years, removed from NYU's Bobst Library at Greenspan's request. The missing document gave rise to the suspicion that his doctorate was honorary, composed of recycled articles cut and pasted together.

When one of two known copies was finally unearthed by *Barron's* in 2008, it was revealed to be previously published work totaling about 180 pages. A legitimate thesis perhaps, but not groundbreaking.

The big surprise: in his dissertation Greenspan addressed housing bubbles. "There is no perpetual motion machine which generates an ever-rising path for the prices of homes," he wrote. It's too bad he didn't believe his own words.

Over the last two decades, as top universities have churned out students trained in analyzing the economy through complex, highly technical mathematical models, their forecasting abilities haven't improved a bit.

A study at the Cleveland Fed in 2007 showed that, over the previous twenty-three years, "economists have had trouble producing forecasts that were superior to naïve predictions . . . none of the economists in our sample was able to demonstrate consistent superiority in forecasting accuracy."

When researchers at the Federal Reserve and Treasury tried to reproduce the results of sixty-seven papers from thirteen prestigious journals, they found that in half the cases—even after contacting the authors for more information—the results were not replicable, making their conclusions as reliable as a coin toss.

Many times the issue cited was poor data. However, in nine cases, even when researchers had access to the right data and computer code, the results could not be replicated.

One researcher involved with the study said that a survey of economists revealed that more than a third admitted to "searching for control variables until you get the desired results."

I call this "fudging the data."

Despite their profession's obvious shortcomings, academic economists have literally overrun the Fed from top to bottom. Governor Blinder was only the fourth or fifth PhD plucked from academia in the Fed's eighty-year history when he was appointed in 1994.

"Janet Yellen followed quickly, and the floodgates opened," Blinder said. "Now it's normal, even expected."

By 2006, four of the five Fed governors and seven District Bank presidents had PhDs in economics, very different from the past, when they traditionally came from the ranks of banking, those on the receiving end of Fed policy.

The overwhelming dominance of academics goes a long way toward explaining why the financial crisis of 2008 blindsided the Fed.

Called before Congress during the ongoing implosion of Wall Street in October 2008, Greenspan, his upper lip visibly quivering, admitted that he was shocked to discover a defect in his free-market model of the economic system. He didn't acknowledge, however, that there was nothing free market about the Fed and its fixing of interest rates.

At the opposite end of the intellectual spectrum sat Nobel Prize–winner Shiller. The Yale economist expressed no shock; he had predicted the crisis of 2008 and also nailed its cause with one simple word: "groupthink," the tendency to agree with others' viewpoints. Groupstink.

At the top of the pyramid now sits Janet Yellen. Under her leadership, the Fed has struggled to extricate itself and the American economy from years of policy blunders that have positioned our economy on the precipice of another financial crisis that could dwarf that of 2008.

It's worth asking: Why did Greenspan, Bernanke, and Yellen—for all of their prestige—so completely misread the American economy and fail to comprehend how extraordinarily interconnected the global financial system was until it blew up in their faces?

Hard to believe, but it all comes down to hubris and myopia. *We know best. Our models say this will work.* And not a thing has changed.

CHAPTER 5

The First Tremors

FED STATEMENT WORD COUNT: 216

EFFECTIVE FED FUNDS RATE: 4.29%

10-YR TREASURY RATE: 4.42%

FED BANKS TOTAL ASSETS: $828.90B

DATE: 1/1/2006

With respect to their safety, derivatives, for the most part, are traded among very sophisticated financial institutions and individuals who have considerable incentive to understand them and use them properly.

—Ben Bernanke, November 15, 2005

The most accurate term for the view from inside the Dallas Fed when I arrived in the autumn of 2006 was "complacent." No sense of alarm.

Timothy Geithner experienced the same thing upon his confirmation as president of the New York Fed in late 2003.

The massive fortress at 33 Liberty Street in downtown Manhattan encompasses an entire city block. Fourteen stories high, with five stories underground, it was designed to resemble an Italian Renaissance palace. Powerful, impregnable.

If the Marriner S. Eccles Federal Reserve Board Building on Constitution

Avenue in Washington is the Fed's brain, the imposing stone behemoth on Liberty Street is the Fed's beating heart.

When Geithner set foot in the door, neither the brain nor the heart of the Fed sensed any danger.

Fed economists had "growing confidence that derivatives and other financial innovations designed to hedge and distribute risk—along with better monetary policy to respond to downturns and better technology to smooth out inventory cycles—had made devastating crises a thing of the past," Geithner said in his memoir, *Stress Test*.

A protégé of Rubin and Summers, Geithner had no experience on Wall Street or in banking. He had a lot to learn about the New York Fed, which occupies a unique place in the Fed's ecosystem.

The New York Fed is first among equals, like a firstborn son. Its relationship to Wall Street explains why the president of the New York Fed always has a vote and holds a permanent position as the vice chairman of the FOMC.

Like the other District Banks, the New York Fed has a Research Department, populated by its own army of PhDs. It also has Sup & Reg, responsible for the oversight of the most dominant and rapacious banks on the planet.

But the New York Fed has two functions not replicated anywhere else, the SOMA, a team that buys and sells U.S. securities in the "Operations Room," and the Markets Desk.

Manned by dozens of analysts, the Markets Desk gathers intelligence on financial markets from Wall Street and other financial centers and distributes it—like a heart pumping blood—to the Board of Governors and the eleven other District Bank presidents.

After spending most of his career in government service, Geithner—though an intelligent man—was woefully unprepared for the vital and complex role of leading the New York Fed. It was just another posting after a life in government service. That Geithner was even appointed illustrates the Fed's political nature.

Born in 1961, Timothy Geithner had grown up all over the world. His father worked for the U.S. Agency for International Development (USAID) in Zimbabwe and Zambia. Hired by the Ford Foundation, he moved the family to India, then Thailand. The elder Geithner's moves from one global hot spot to another with USAID and the Ford Foundation prompted some to speculate that he really worked for the CIA!

Geithner graduated from high school at the International School in Bangkok. He attended Dartmouth, earning a degree in government and Asian studies. Geithner took only one economics class, which he found "especially dreary." He followed that with a master's degree in international economics and East Asian studies from Johns Hopkins University.

He joined the U.S. Treasury Department in 1988 after three years as an Asia specialist at the consulting firm Kissinger Associates (which later became Kissinger McLarty), his only stint in the private sector.

From 1998 to 2001, Geithner served as undersecretary of International Affairs under both Rubin and Summers, participating in negotiations involving various crises including the bailout of LTCM, the Mexican peso crisis, and the Asian meltdown.

In October 2003, after rotating through positions at the Council on Foreign Relations and the International Monetary Fund (IMF), Geithner was named president of the New York Fed.

Geithner's appointment was met by snarky rumblings on the Street referring to him as a lackey for Summers and Rubin, the dynamic duo who championed deregulation of the financial system.

His mentors were perceived to have maneuvered "their guy" into the second most powerful position at the Federal Reserve. Oh, by the way, the New York Fed was the primary regulator for Citigroup, where Rubin sat on the board of directors.

Geithner's new job had previously been held by people with robust egos like Benjamin Strong (the first president of the New York Fed), Gerry Corrigan (at the helm during the crash of 1987), and Paul Volcker (from 1975 to August 1979, when he became chairman). Wrist twisters and ear biters to a man.

Though compulsively profane, flinging obscenities at the drop of a hat, Geithner was gracious and professional with colleagues. Rubin described Geithner as "elbow-less," with a calm and easy manner.

Geithner later admitted that his previous jobs "mostly exposed me to talented senior bankers and selection bias probably gave me an impression that the U.S. financial sector was more capable and ethical than it really was." An understatement if there ever was one.

A lawyer at the New York Fed, who at times played basketball with Geithner on the Fed's fourteenth-floor court, described his boss as a fantastic player with a notable lack of nerve when it came to making the big shot.

"At the moment of truth, his gaze often became curiously unsteady, his hands seemingly shaky," wrote Andrew Huszar, who worked at the New York Fed nine years. He sensed Geithner was too cautious, a man "who seemed to float above the action."

Employed in Sup & Reg, which reported directly to the bank president, Huzsar portrayed a work environment "in complete disarray."

At a critical moment in Wall Street history, when the biggest banks were frenetically spitting out toxic securities, the six-hundred-person Sup & Reg division suffered from high turnover and vicious internal politics.

"The only thing it seemed to excel at was demoralizing the bright, idealistic minds it was recruiting from the nation's finest graduate schools," Huszar said. One quarter of the department left each year. Regulators obsessively focused on possible systemic risk from hedge funds, not banks.

The New York Fed was always looking in the rearview mirror and not at the road ahead. The ghost of LTCM haunted the halls of 33 Liberty and Wall Street knew it. Hedge funds' higher-paid PhDs were and always will be one step ahead of the Fed, outmaneuvering their regulators.

And the one in charge at this critical juncture was a newbie who preferred long lunches at the Four Seasons to getting dirt under his fingernails.

In the senior regulatory strategy sessions Huszar attended, Geithner "simply peppered the room with questions, rather than providing any concrete direction." Instead of trying to fix Sup & Reg from within, Geithner began filling other key positions with people he trusted from Goldman Sachs, JPMC, and American Express.

Geithner would later portray himself as one who did not share the confidence in derivatives that he found at the New York Fed, citing the first speech he gave as president in 2004.

"I tried to push back against complacency," Geithner wrote, "telling a room full of bankers that the wonders of the new financial world would not necessarily prevent catastrophic failures of major institutions, and should not inspire delusions of safety on Wall Street. . . . I suggested that financial innovation was driving risk and leverage into corners of the financial system with weaker supervision, and that our tools for monitoring systemic risk weren't keeping up."

Hmmm. Geithner's memory doesn't match the actual text of his speech, which painted a picture of the system's financial stability and, yep, complacency.

Though Geithner mentioned that financial innovation presented "significant challenges," he expressed no warnings, sounded no alarms. Bankers had heard this speech a hundred times over rubber chicken. In fact, beyond reiterating that banks must have "a sufficient cushion against adversity," Geithner's speech was the opposite of a warning.

He sounded like Greenspan, Rubin, and Summers all rolled up into one. He'd been involved in the public shaming of Brooksley Born. Can't bring up the risks of derivatives now.

Geithner later admitted that he didn't anticipate the mortgage crisis or understand the systemic risk it would trigger. His research staff, using the most sophisticated models and complex analysis in the world, sounded no alarms. Nor did his Markets Desk.

At the Dallas Fed, Rosenblum had started to question whether the consensus-building tradition was distorting the Fed's ability to analyze the increasingly interconnected global economy and protect the integrity of the banking system. Fisher had taught him a lot about the way market participants really operated, far out on the ledge of risk. Though he treasured the Fed's DNA, especially its collegiality, Rosenblum was the opposite of complacent.

Years later, I learned Rosenblum knew the easiest way to get me into the bank was to claim he needed another economics writer. He realized I had a nose for the rot that lurked in financial markets that he and Fed insiders lacked. What were they missing and why?

Rosenblum often pointed out that people's behavior never read the economists' models.

"These people gang up academically on naysayers," he told me. "If it's not in their models, they shut it out." Any challenge from outside was rejected.

Despite his efforts, Rosenblum had been unable to change the culture from the inside. "Willful blindness" and "monetary myopia" had become his private terms for the Fed's tunnel vision.

After learning that economists at the Dallas Fed didn't have my connections to various producers of data, I cast a wide net. I brought in Morgan Stanley's weekly "Global Market Analyst," which focuses on global inflation. To track housing data, I helped the bank obtain RealtyTrac's full historic series of the consultancy's monthly, quarterly, and annual statistics on state and national foreclosures. And I secured Case-Shiller housing data back to 1890 for use by the macroeconomics group, plus mortgage and banking research from Fitch Ratings Credit Research, Standard & Poor's, and Credit Derivatives Research.

At Rosenblum's direction, I went to New York in October 2006 to attend the annual Bank Credit Analyst conference. I intended to shore up my Wall Street sources, find new ones, and obtain data sources, the more proprietary the better, stuff like the pricing of CDO tranches, patterns of home equity withdrawal, internal credit-card data that dug so deep you knew whether Americans were buying diapers at Target or trinkets at Tiffany's. Economists at the Dallas Fed rarely sought out such data sets on their own.

Usually an upbeat affair, the BCA conference in 2006 proved disturbing. Harvard professor Niall Ferguson asked a strange question: Why hadn't the recent assassination of a Russian central banker, a Thai coup d'état, and a North Korean nuclear bomb test triggered a stock market rout?

The room, full of chattering investors from twenty-seven countries, went instantly silent, a sign Ferguson had hit a nerve.

Risk and volatility measures of financial markets hovered at record low levels even as Iraq descended into civil war and most oil-producing countries were in conflict zones.

Ferguson drew a striking parallel to a 1914 news story about the American stock market rallying a month after the assassination of Archduke Franz Ferdinand. We all knew what happened after that. The Great War.

What to make of the disconnect between the front page and the financial markets? High liquidity, AAA credit ratings, and the slicing and dicing of risk had deluded everyone into thinking we lived in a safe world.

The rest of my trip was devoted to interviewing top economists at investment banks, hedge funds, and ratings agencies, who I found dramatically more forthcoming now that I was inside the Fed.

They conveyed private thoughts, knowing that whatever they said would remain confidential and proud that their insights would be used by Fed policymakers.

I found some of their revelations reckless, even by Wall Street standards. CDOs and their variations (CDO squared, CDO cubed) had become so complex even the investment banks' highly paid PhDs didn't understand them.

"Almost everyone mentioned that they felt CDOs to be the potential source of systemic risk," I reported to Rosenblum, "mainly because the reach of the market cannot be accurately measured nor is the 'other side of the trade' a guarantee. The Fed could endear itself to Wall Street by at least threatening to facilitate transparency in this murkiest of markets."

This was shocking to me. When Wall Street begs to be regulated, beware. People in New York kept using the term "uncharted territory" when discussing CDOs. It made me think of an ancient map with the inscription on the edge, "Here be monsters."

Most on the Street felt the risk to the economy from hedge funds collapsing was slight as long as they "blew up" one at a time. Treasury had just conducted a sensitivity analysis to assess what single event could throw the markets into a tailspin. The answer: a failed trade on the proprietary book or the "prop desk" at Goldman Sachs. The prop desks of the biggest banks— and Goldman was the biggest—traded on their own behalf.

The consensus reaction: Goldman collapsing? Nah. Never happen.

During my years at the Fed, I relied on my Wall Street sources to divulge their unspoken fears and share proprietary data. My contacts often revealed concerns they would never tell a journalist, or even their colleagues, as if my Fed hat conferred a confessor role. I became priest and psychiatrist.

Their fascination with the Fed was deeply unsettling. Did they know people on the FOMC were mere mortals? That most were PhDs who had never made a payroll, much less worked on Wall Street?

And yet they hung on to every utterance by Bernanke as they had with Greenspan. They paced their hallways anxious for the newswires to report each FOMC statement, released immediately after the meetings. Three weeks later, when the more in-depth "minutes" became available, people scoured them for clues that could signal expectations about future rate hikes or cuts so they could position their books accordingly.

My Street sources taught me the fine art of diplomacy. Traders and analysts pressed me for inside information, constantly looking for an edge. They knew any indiscretion was grounds for my dismissal. That didn't stop them from trying.

CHAPTER 6

Front-running the Fed

FED STATEMENT WORD COUNT: 173

EFFECTIVE FED FUNDS RATE: 5.25%

10-YR TREASURY RATE: 4.76%

FED BANKS TOTAL ASSETS: $865.73B

DATE: 1/1/2007

First, if the bubble were to collapse on its own, would the effect on the economy be exceedingly large? Second, is it unlikely that the Fed could mitigate the consequences? Third, is monetary policy the best tool to use to deflate a house-price bubble?

My answers to these questions in the shortest possible form are, 'no,' 'no,' and 'no.'"

—JANET YELLEN, SEPTEMBER 27, 2005

When Harvey Rosenblum walked into the San Francisco Federal Reserve Bank in early 2005, he anticipated being welcomed with open arms by his friend Janet Yellen.

The Dallas Fed had commissioned a documentary to commemorate the ninetieth birthday of Milton Friedman. The film would celebrate the twenty-fifth anniversary of the release of *Free to Choose*, a groundbreaking ten-part PBS TV series and a companion book, written by Friedman and his wife, Rose, also titled *Free to Choose*.

Since the Nobel Prize–winning Friedman lived in San Francisco,

Rosenblum flew out with the filmmaker to interview the economist at the Fed Bank where Yellen had recently been named president.

But when Rosenblum was ushered into her office, Yellen lit into him, very out of keeping with her usual mild demeanor. She told Rosenblum she had never invited Friedman to the San Francisco Fed because he had always been such a strong critic of the system.

"She called Friedman an enemy of the Fed," Rosenblum said. "That was offensive to me. She was talking about one of my gods."

A Keynesian on steroids, Yellen was an avid believer in government stimulus to keep the economy humming. Friedman's attitude that government should "get the hell out of the way" was anathema to her.

Stunned, Rosenblum applied his motto: WWGD.

What Would Greenspan Do?

Greenspan would have said, "Let the best ideas win."

Rosenblum believed Yellen's rigid approach was not in keeping with the Fed's ethos. Her attitude toward Friedman was a slap in the face not just to Rosenblum, but to the Fed's culture as he knew it, his life's work.

Rosenblum had joined the Chicago Fed in August 1970, when the Fed was under the disastrous leadership of Burns, who had written a definitive book on business cycles. Pressured by President Richard Nixon, Burns would institute policies that resulted in double-digit inflation.

Rosenblum had studied under economist Robert E. Weintraub, a Milton Friedman student who often complained about the ineptitude of the Fed. "I joined to bring new ideas to the institution," Rosenblum said.

At the Chicago Fed, Rosenblum rose to associate director of Research. Papers by Fed economists went up the chain to the Research Department in Washington, where they were approved or sent back with "suggestions" for improvement. Or deep-sixed.

Volcker ran a similarly tight ship, according to Rosenblum. Speak out of school and "they'd sit you down with five [economist] thugs, and they'd beat you up mentally so you'd never do it again."

Greenspan loosened the intellectual environment. Rosenblum more frequently expressed contrarian views, figuring that if he went too far, someone at the Board of Governors would give him a call and say, "Harvey, can you back off a bit?" That happened a few times under Greenspan, but always "with a velvet hammer."

In 1983, Rosenblum organized a conference to be held in Dallas for a select handful of economists. Each District Bank and the Board of Governors sent participants.

During the lunch break, the bank's dining room was so crowded Rosenblum couldn't find a spot to eat with his peers. He saw an elegant fellow with white hair sitting at a table by himself. Rosenblum sat down and introduced himself. Surprise. The loner was Robert Boykin, president of the Dallas Fed.

A lawyer, Boykin had served in various capacities at the bank for forty years, rising through the ranks to become president.

"We had a grand conversation," Rosenblum said. The topic turned to the Dallas Fed's proposed new logo, which his employees were resisting.

"I said, 'Dammit Bob, you're the president of the bank,'" Rosenblum says. "Can't you sell your own idea?"

A few months later, Rosenblum was told by his boss: "You may be getting a call from Dallas." In 1985, when the position opened up, Boykin hired him as director of Research.

Though Rosenblum was a Yankee from Connecticut, the son of a struggling door-to-door salesman who read the *Wall Street Journal* every day, moving to the Lone Star State was his dream come true. Rosenblum had become an honorary Texan during a postcollege trip to Yellowstone, when he'd awakened to find two couples from Texas had set up their tents next to his campsite. They adopted him, teaching him their lingo. He bought a Western hat and started dreaming in a Texas drawl.

He treasured a photograph of himself taken during a party on a friend's rooftop terrace overlooking Wrigley Field. Published in a Chicago newspaper, there's the sober-minded Fed economist, wearing nothing but shorts and a cowboy hat. "Somehow I knew Dallas was where I was supposed to end up," he said.

At lunch with Boykin in 1985, Rosenblum met a fascinating man who would become a close friend: Richard Fisher. Rosenblum was struck by Fisher's sheer likability, intellectual curiosity, and his intense fascination with the inner workings of the Fed.

"From the day I met him, Fisher wanted to be a central banker," Rosenblum said. "It was his dream job."

One of Fisher's early mentors, Robert Roosa, a former senior official of the

Fed and undersecretary of the Treasury, had inspired him to think of the Fed as the ultimate public service. Another mentor, Paul Volcker, would inspire Fisher's laserlike focus on the dangers of an overreaching central bank.

Fisher and Rosenblum hit it off, their philosophies about managing the economy similar if not always identical.

When he first arrived, Rosenblum had some tough adjustments. The Dallas Research Department had been rudderless for years. Rosenblum inherited several dozen economists, mostly unseasoned in economic policy matters.

Before their hire, economists at the Fed were given the assurance they could research their particular field of interest with the goal of publishing in prestigious journals. Publishing raised the economist's profile and thus benefited the Fed. Their work for the Fed was limited to a few reports a year. Thus an economist could spend as much as half of his workday on his or her own research; some stretched that to 90 percent.

Rosenblum's philosophy didn't fit the mold. He felt that Fed economists should focus on the ten most important issues that would be on the Fed chairman's mind before he even formulated the thoughts.

But no matter how hard he tried, many Fed economists could not be steered. Few wanted to study issues of obvious importance to the public. Should gambling be legalized? How did gun control affect the economy? Should Dallas City Hall use public funds to build a football arena? Nope. They'd rather research an area that would win kudos from their peers, the more esoteric the better.

Rosenblum felt the problem had become more acute over time as the study of economics at America's top universities emphasized complex mathematical modeling. Mastering that esoteric language assured advancement in the world of PhD economists.

But could it predict serious problems in the economy? Short answer, no.

When Rosenblum arrived in the mid-1980s, the Dallas Fed's reputation probably would have been ranked eleventh out of twelve regional banks, or the "Sleepy Fed," in the view of economist Michael Cox, who spent over thirty years at the bank. (He's now a professor at Southern Methodist University.)

Under the leadership of Rosenblum, the Dallas bank improved dramatically and became known as the Free-Market Fed.

Rosenblum encouraged Cox and his new hires to think outside the box. As a champion of "creative destruction," a seemingly paradoxical concept developed by renowned economist Joseph Schumpeter, Cox published frequently and about issues the public cared about, an anomaly in the Fed system.

But the field of economics was undergoing a sea change, literally. The "saltwater" economists (East and West coasts, Harvard, Keynes, pro-government regulation and intervention) were challenging the "freshwater" economists (Midwest, University of Chicago, Friedman, free-market philosophy).

The San Francisco bank became known as the Keynesian Fed. The St. Louis Fed, which had a core of economists devoted to Friedman's ideas, became the home of the "monetarists," those with faith that the money supply determined economic conditions.

The New York Fed, of course, had long been considered the Wall Street Fed. As the Free-Market Fed, Dallas was the only Fed bank that would have let me—a non-PhD who didn't subscribe to any particular economic orthodoxy—in the door.

Whatever their canon, economists study the world through the lens of concrete measurable data, like unemployment, household wealth, housing, oil prices, inflation.

The financial system is under constant stress. Economists perceive these stresses as an equation: equilibrium, shock, adjustment, return to equilibrium. As a society, we are interested not only in how we return to equilibrium, but in the adjustment costs. Economists quantify and analyze those shocks. They have certain sets of values and assumptions and look for data sets that quantify the concepts they want to study.

But their models and data sets rarely incorporated financial markets, despite the fact that market stressors periodically threatened the economy.

Beginning in the late 1980s, technical innovations like computer program trading changed the financial world's methods of hedging risk. But precious few had been stress tested or studied by Fed economists.

In his goal to shake things up, Rosenblum approached hiring by looking for variety in schools of economic thought and "vintage," or the era candidates received their doctorate. "Vintages tend to ossify," Rosenblum said. "Every five years you have to make sure you are bringing in new ideas. Diversity does matter."

Though women have become more represented in the field of economics, blacks and other minorities have not. Rosenblum estimates the percentage of black PhD economists at around 2 percent. More than half of PhD economists trained at American universities are foreign nationals, often from Russia or China. Many cannot get clearance to work at the Fed without jumping through a lot of hoops. But whether they are from Nebraska or Nepal, if they graduate from a top American university program, they have similar training.

Rosenblum considered economics a craft—half art, half science. But in his view the study of economics was moving toward becoming a branch of engineering, with the main focus on mathematics. Not a welcome development.

Over time, economists he hired who had fresh ideas didn't change the Fed culture. They attended conferences with other Fed folks. They saw what it took to get ahead, to gain prestige, to be asked to sit on panels. Instead of changing the culture, they were co-opted, sucked into the Jell-O pyramid.

Rosenblum was working at the Dallas Fed on the momentous morning of October 19, 1987, when Greenspan, just a few months into his tenure as Fed chairman, flew from Washington to Dallas to be the keynote speaker at the American Bankers Association conference. While he was in the air, the Dow Jones Industrial Average (DJIA) fell 508 points.

When Greenspan landed in Dallas, a Fed employee handed him one of those brick cell phones. The Reagan White House was in a panic.

"Get me to my hotel," Greenspan said. The speech was canceled. The next morning, Air Force One picked up the Fed chairman and flew him back to Washington to save the world economy.

"Black Monday," when the market fell by 22.6 percent in one day, remains the single worst day for the American stock market. Over three days, the S&P 500 Index shed 28.5 percent of its value. Investors lost about $1 trillion in wealth. The debacle was widely blamed on program trading—when stocks dropped to a certain price, computers dumped them—combined with a potent brew of market hysteria.

But the day after, October 20, 1987, marked a more significant point in Wall Street history. The FOMC slashed the fed funds rate by half a percentage point to just under 7 percent.

Then the mother of all storks delivered the "Greenspan Put" with the release of this one-sentence statement: "The Federal Reserve, consistent with its responsibilities as the Nation's central bank, affirmed today its readiness to serve as a source of liquidity to support the economic and financial system."

As Pavlov was to dogs, the Fed was to market players. They would come to understand and embrace the commitment Greenspan had made by putting a floor under losses. Investors could continue piling into risk, confident the market now offered a built-in "put" option. (A put is a contract that allows the owner to profit if the price of an underlying security declines.)

Over the next few months, the FOMC repeatedly took overnight interest rates lower and lower. Sometimes, as an added bonus, the Fed would even give trading desks advance notice. How awesome was that, traders must have thought, the ability to position their books to profit before the fact, a license to front-run the Fed!

Greenspan's actions ushered in the period of prosperity later dubbed the Great Moderation, the slaying of capitalism's volatile business cycle of creation and destruction. Fewer bankruptcies, fewer disruptions in markets, steadier sailing.

Though Rosenblum became a passionate defender of the Great Moderation, something continued to vex him. With hindsight, the causes of the 1987 crash became obvious. The Fed's army of economists had missed them. What would be the next disaster they wouldn't see coming?

CHAPTER 7

The Maverick

FED STATEMENT WORD COUNT: 250
EFFECTIVE FED FUNDS RATE: 3.94%
10-YR TREASURY RATE: 3.74%
FED BANKS TOTAL ASSETS: $900.26B
DATE: 1/1/2008

It is not the responsibility of the Federal Reserve—nor would it be appropriate—to protect lenders and investors from the consequences of their financial decisions.

—BEN BERNANKE, JACKSON HOLE, AUGUST 2007

A half dozen men flung one leg up on the massive boardroom table and hiked up their pants. Ostrich, alligator, elephant, and even some lowly cowhide. Custom made, one and all. Who had the best?

I had to laugh at this cowboy boot showdown, Texas style. What was this, the Honky-tonk Fed?

Soon after I joined the bank, I was bestowed the privilege of taking notes at the monthly meeting of this very prestigious board of directors. Privilege, meaning no one else wanted the job.

As clerical as the task was, the experience provided a fascinating glimpse into the workings of the top floor, home of the boardroom and executive offices.

All twelve District Banks have a board of directors elected from their regions. Unlike members of the Board of Governors, they are not isolated from their constituents.

In the 1990s, Congress and the public began pushing for an end to the dominance inside the Fed of middle-aged white bankers. By 2006, women and minority members sat on the Dallas Fed and other Fed boards.

At all District Banks, the board of nine includes three bankers elected by commercial banks in the district (Class A), three nonbanker business leaders elected by member banks (Class B), and three chosen by the Fed's Board of Governors to represent the general public, maybe university presidents, leaders of nonprofits, or CEOs (Class C).

Everything that occurred on the floors below was geared toward informing the president and his board about current economic conditions and bank health in the Eleventh District—an area covering 360,000 square miles, population 27 million, with branches in El Paso, San Antonio, and Houston.

The Dallas Fed is a $100 billion bankers' bank, overseeing 37 state-chartered member banks and 522 bank holding companies, with assets ranging from less than $20 million to more than $50 billion. It also supervises 92 savings and loan holding companies.

Larger than life, Fisher dominated the building in a way few other Fed presidents did. He knew everyone of political consequence in Dallas and most of those in Washington. He was also one of the wealthiest District Bank presidents, worth about $21 million. (As required by Fed rules, his assets had been put into the management of a blind trust.)

Despite his patrician appearance, Fisher came from a hardscrabble background, one that makes his ascent into the rarified air of the Federal Reserve even more astonishing.

On the wall of his office, Fisher displayed a prized possession: a small, framed scrap of blue paper, the receipt for the "head tax" that his father paid in the 1940s when crossing the border from Mexico into California to see his wife.

His father was like a character out of a Dickens novel. Leslie Fisher was born in 1904 in Toowoomba, a small town in Queensland, Australia. Abandoned by his mother, at the age of six Les was picked up by police with his father and charged with begging.

Consigned to an orphanage, Les was later placed with a series of foster families, and often treated with brutality. As a teenager, he lived by his wits on the streets.

Somehow the resourceful young man made his way to South Africa, where in 1936 he married a beauty named Magnhild Andersen. Born in Jagersfontein to Norwegian parents, Magnhild was known as Babe.

The young couple eventually sailed to America. Due to a quirk in immigration laws, authorities admitted Babe but not Les.

They made their way to California in 1941. Babe rented rooms at a boardinghouse in Los Angeles; Les had to live across the border in Tijuana, Mexico, until he could get legal status. He made sport of outsmarting the bookies at the Tijuana race track and visited his wife whenever possible.

Though born in Los Angeles in 1949, their third son, Richard, was conceived while his parents were in Shanghai attempting to collect a debt. They barely escaped the mainland before Communist revolutionary Mao Tse-tung closed down the docks.

"I was delivered on March 18, 1949, in Los Angeles as an American," Fisher said. "But I was manufactured in China."

So, Australian father, South African/Norwegian mother, conceived in China, born in the United States—a fitting preamble for the glittering international career to come.

Soon after Richard's birth, the family moved to Mexico City, where his father eked out a living. Les was finally granted admission to America in 1948, after years of crisscrossing the border. Eventually, the family landed in Miami, Florida. Eleven-year-old Richard spoke fluent Spanish but had to repeat a grade to improve his English.

Florida was not the promised land. At one point, Richard rode a bus with his mother to pawn her wedding ring.

But finally the spirited kid caught a lucky break. Cuban students had inundated Florida after the Castro revolution of 1959. The school principal, who couldn't speak Spanish, corralled young Richard to help translate. Good grades followed.

When the family again moved, this time back to Southern California, his stellar academic record qualified Richard for an experimental program at a junior high that used a math curriculum developed by Yale University.

Richard aced his math classes and won a scholarship to the Admiral

Farragut Academy, a private military-style boarding school then based in New Jersey.

The nomadic childhood behind him, Fisher thrived, excelling in the classroom, playing football, working summers in a diner. By dint of hard work and personality, his trajectory shot skyward. On graduating high school, Fisher spent two years at the U.S. Naval Academy, then transferred to Harvard, where he graduated cum laude in 1971 with a bachelor's degree in economics.

During a year at Oxford University, Fisher studied Latin American history and politics. At a reception given for American students by Congressman Jim Collins, Fisher's fate collided with Texas.

He had spied Collins's pretty daughter Nancy in his classes. They married and moved to California, where Fisher earned an MBA from Stanford.

Upon graduating, Fisher set his sights on Wall Street. He got a job at the investment bank of Brown Brothers Harriman & Company, where he specialized in fixed-income securities and foreign exchange markets. There he learned the first rule of banking: "Know your customer."

Despite the extraordinary odds against him, Fisher had arrived at the epicenter of the financial world, with family connections to the inner workings of America's political establishment.

But it wasn't enough.

"I'll never make it here," Fisher thought, as he stood on the ferry between Ellis Island and the tip of Manhattan, holding his firstborn child in his arms. It was 1976, the two-hundredth anniversary of America's founding, and he'd taken his son to the iconic point of entry for so many hopeful immigrants.

In one generation, Fisher had achieved success far beyond his father's dreams. But in a flash, Fisher realized that if they stayed in Manhattan, he'd be just another Ivy Leaguer who toiled at investment banks built by others.

With this epiphany was born a maverick who, like many before him, pulled up stakes and moved to Texas, where a popular bumper sticker proclaims: "I wasn't born in Texas, but I got here as fast as I could."

His wife preferred Houston over her hometown, but Fisher pressed for Dallas, a brash city where the landscape was wide open. In Fisher's words, anyone could succeed in Dallas in the 1970s if they had "the brains of a squirrel."

He started his own investment company, embracing the Texas ethos of working hard, striding tall, and speaking plain. It would take Texans a few decades to figure out Fisher and embrace him as one of their own.

In the end, Fisher had to leave to come back in full glory, serving in both the Jimmy Carter and Bill Clinton administrations, for a while living in Japan. As Deputy U.S. Trade Representative with the rank of ambassador, he was involved in negotiating the terms of the North American Free Trade Agreement (NAFTA). When he returned to private enterprise, Fisher built a fortune with Fisher Capital Management and Fisher Ewing Partners.

Fisher's intense focus and energy came to play in every aspect of the bank—his erudition on display even in the lobby, where visitors were greeted with a video of him speaking in a dazzling multimedia exhibit.

His many speeches—sometimes in far-flung places like Hong Kong and Dubai—often made news. Journalists loved Fisher because he challenged Fed orthodoxy and, as an avid consumer of history and pop culture, could always be counted on for a pithy or funny quote.

In one speech, with a hat tip to the Canadian "looney," Fisher invented a currency issued by Texas called the burrito. What would happen if the Lone Star State issued burritos out of thin air and created its own central bank?

He wasn't afraid to take on sacred cows, giving a widely reported speech in November 2006 that criticized Greenspan and the Fed for relying on poor data to justify keeping the fed funds rate low for too long and thus fueling the housing bubble.

"Poor data led to a policy action that amplified speculative activity in housing and other markets," Fisher said. "Today . . . the housing market is undergoing a substantial correction and inflicting real costs to millions of homeowners across the country. It is complicating the [Fed's] task of achieving . . . sustainable noninflationary growth." Greg Ip of the *Wall Street Journal* called it "an apparent and rare in-house critique."

And he had a self-deprecating side. Describing his failed effort to win election to the U.S. Senate in 1994, when he ran as a Democrat against the popular Republican Kay Bailey Hutchison, Fisher said, "Veni, Vidi, Defici: I came, I saw, I lost."

Big personalities like Fisher's and boisterous exchanges typified meetings of the Dallas Fed Board of Directors, wildly different from the mummified floors below.

Once a month, Dallas Fed employees donned their Sunday best for the invasion of bigwigs like board chairman Jim Hackett, CEO of Anadarko Petroleum, one of the world's largest publicly traded oil and gas exploration and production companies. (Ray Hunt was the previous chairman. You get the feeling that oil and energy might be important at this particular Fed bank?)

Most board members were strong, brash men who strutted into the building wearing suits and cowboy boots, people like Herb Kelleher, CEO of Southwest Airlines, a cheery force of nature and an inveterate lip kisser. During my year of note-taking, I learned to dodge or pucker up.

Kelleher's philosophy of life was simple: "Wild Turkey whiskey and Philip Morris cigarettes are essential to the maintenance of human life." The Dallas Fed designated a bathroom for his smoke break because in the 15 minutes allotted, Kelleher couldn't get out of the building, smoke and get back through security in time.

In the prearranged "boot smackdown," Fisher, Hackett, Kelleher, and a handful of other men threw their legs up on the massive table to compare their custom-made footwear. Joe Kim King, CEO of the Brady National Bank, probably won on sheer authenticity. King's tumbleweed-inspired observations on life, drawn from his day job as a goat farmer, kept everyone in stitches.

Why was King on the board? His bank—actually a $280 million organization called Texas Country Bancshares with six locations—is a small but robust institution smack-dab in the geographical center of the state, exposed to the vagaries of agriculture, ranching, and petroleum. The town of Brady calls itself the "Heart of Texas," which makes King an excellent representative of the state's rural heritage.

In the Eleventh District, disciplined banking roots run deep. In 1932, when the Fed started providing loans to bankrupt financial institutions, the Dallas bank warned: "Credit is exactly like morphine. Either credit or morphine used habitually leads inevitably to the gutter."

Eight decades later, the board still prided itself on its conservative banking standards.

Fisher may have failed at the polls but he knew how to work a room, schmoozing and soaking up stories.

He and Hackett controlled the amount of time each member had to relate what was going on in their corner of the Eleventh District. Nobody ever came empty-handed. Their anecdotes often ended up in Fisher's speeches or statements at an FOMC meeting.

The CEO of Whataburger might talk about average fast-food ticket totals. You know the economy is struggling when people stick to the 99-cent menu items. King might opine about drought and farm foreclosures—and the personalities and antics of goats.

In the 1980s, Texas had wallowed in recession triggered by the collapse of oil prices and the savings and loan fiasco. The two coasts were booming, but Texas lost population. The oil-field industry dropped by two thirds. The Fed and state regulators had to close hundreds of banks.

At the end of a particularly rough period, a journalist asked the state's lead bank regulator how many institutions would go under the following year. He paused, then said, "156." The journalist was wowed by his prognostication. Not so impressive, the regulator said. The state had only enough auditors and other personnel to close three banks per week. Fifty-two times three equaled 156.

But the tide had turned. Fisher marched into FOMC meetings boasting about the Eleventh District's robust economy. Texas could legitimately claim to be the nation's top job engine. Major businesses pulled up stakes and relocated to Texas by the thousands.

Each of the other Fed District Banks has a similar board of directors, though I bet most of the members don't wear cowboy boots.

Why are the boards of directors at Fed District Banks relevant, since the District presidents have a vote only every three years? In fact, to listen to boastful staffers at the New York Fed and the Board of Governors—who have permanent voting status—District presidents like Fisher don't matter.

But the Dallas Fed's board members are people running banks and other companies. This extended "Fed family" understands how interest rate changes and credit availability affects their survival.

Fisher knew how to exploit his staff to show off the sheer brainpower at his beck and call. Rosenblum usually brought in an economist or two to make a presentation. It was always a treat when Rosenblum, never dry and wonky, was the main attraction.

Rosenblum had announced his retirement a few months before Fisher was appointed president. He planned to teach, consult, sit on a few boards.

But Fisher had grand plans. He pleaded with Rosenblum to stay. He wanted Rosenblum's gravitas, loyalty, and reputation at his back. Fisher needed to make withdrawals at will from Rosenblum's extensive memory bank. Most of all, Rosenblum understood the MIT Mafia.

District Bank economists got the snooty treatment from the Washington and New York Fed economists, who considered themselves the elite. The pecking order was brutal. In Rosenblum's opinion, the New York Fed had an inordinate amount of influence within the organization.

So Rosenblum agreed to stay as Fisher's right-hand man. The first few years were bumpy. Other members of the FOMC regarded Fisher as the brash new kid on the block. Not an economist and too outspoken. But Rosenblum had his back.

Though I continued to attend board meetings, my stenography days were short-lived. After one year at the Dallas Fed, I found myself behind that same podium making a presentation to Fisher and the board, Rosenblum looking on with pride.

The transformation of my role at the bank began on February 7, 2007, when HSBC Holdings announced that its bad debts for the previous year would total more than $10.5 billion—20 percent over expectations—due to problems in its portfolio of subprime mortgage derivatives.

This was the Code Red moment I'd been preparing for since that CDO presentation at Credit Suisse: systemic risk bleeding from housing to a major bank.

I leaped up from my chair and made a beeline to the corner office of John V. Duca, the only person on the floor who I had discovered might share my alarm.

Duca had worked in Washington, where he'd earned bragging rights by briefing Greenspan. (Inside the Fed it's not who you know, it's who you brief.)

In Dallas, Duca had seen the 1980s S&L debacle and the oil bust up close. He saw signs disaster could happen again, this time on a national basis, and had written several papers about the housing market.

I was thrilled to find a like mind. Duca loved my access to "real-time" data sets. Since Fed economists rely on seasonally adjusted data, their conclusions always trail well behind rapidly unfolding events. Duca wanted to compensate for some of that lag.

Like his peers, Duca had a high regard for himself. He took every opportunity to remind me I had only two master's degrees, not a doctorate, but at least one of them was from the Ivy League. And if it was any consolation, I was the best-dressed person in the bank. Gee, thanks.

My father had faced such academic pretentiousness as a university instructor; despite high ratings from students and an MBA in finance, he was forever branded as inferior by the PhDs. The Fed's brand of snobbery finally helped me understand how that grated on my father's spirit.

Looking at the data from HSBC's announcement, Duca and I agreed that a catastrophe was brewing, but it seemed like we were the only ones inside the Fed who thought so. A few weeks later, Bernanke gave a speech that brushed aside concerns about systemic risk.

"The impact on the broader economy and financial markets of the problems in the subprime market seems likely to be contained," Bernanke calmly assured Congress. "In particular, mortgages to prime borrowers and fixed-rate mortgages to all classes of borrowers continue to perform well, with low rates of delinquency."

That's the misinformation the Washington Fed economists and the Markets Desk were feeding the FOMC.

But Bernanke was only referring to "prime" borrowers. The previous year, low- or no-document loans comprised over 80 percent of near-prime, 55 percent of jumbo, and 50 percent of subprime mortgages. Reports of fraud had mounted. Defaults had escalated exponentially, housing prices were dropping, and home builders were declaring bankruptcy left and right. On April 2, 2007, New Century Financial Corporation, a leading subprime mortgage lender, filed for Chapter 11 protection.

With Rosenblum's encouragement, I began working with Duca on an Economic Letter to be published by the Dallas Fed, called "The Rise and Fall of Subprime Mortgages."

It proved a challenging but rewarding partnership. I admired how a seasoned economist like Duca could use data sets like an artist uses clay. He sculpted graphs and charts that brought complex material into sharp and understandable focus. (Published in November 2007, this remains one of the most cited Fed papers on the subprime debacle.)

The next month, Duca, Rosenblum, and I published another Economic Letter, called "From Complacency to Crisis: Financial Risk Taking in the

Early 21st Century." It was the first Fed paper to sound the alarm about the risky business of CDOs.

Duca was thrilled by the number of Internet hits the papers generated. However, though the papers would be footnoted by other economists and authors, inside the institution little had changed.

As coauthor of two Fed papers, my predictions about subprime mortgages and the potential for systemic risk had been validated. My decision to leave journalism and join the Fed was beginning to pay off, at least in my mind.

However, I wasn't quite finished with my barefoot and pregnant days.

On October 1, 2007, seven months' pregnant with twins, I was forced by my doctor to go on bed rest. When I returned to the Dallas Fed, I would find my role at the bank radically changed.

CHAPTER 8

The Inner Sanctum

FED STATEMENT WORD COUNT: 248

EFFECTIVE FED FUNDS RATE: 2.00%

10-YR TREASURY RATE: 4.10%

FED BANKS TOTAL ASSETS: $892.71B

DATE: 6/1/2008

While the decline in housing activity has been significant and will probably continue for a while longer, I think the concerns we used to hear about the possibility of a devastating collapse—one that might be big enough to cause a recession in the U.S. economy—have been largely allayed.

—JANET YELLEN, JANUARY 22, 2007

J ust minutes into the morning session of the FOMC on June 30, 2005, Chairman Greenspan handed control to Dino Kos, manager of the SOMA for the New York Fed.

Kos immediately proceeded to slap the manicured hand of the committee's newest member.

Earlier that month, Fisher had made the quote in the financial press about the FOMC being in the "eighth inning" of a rate-tightening cycle. His words had triggered a trading frenzy and required Greenspan and others to do damage control.

"Market participants briefly flirted with the notion that the tightening cycle would end as early as this meeting, after President Fisher's comments on June 1 and the weak employment report two days later," said Kos. "But subsequent remarks by the Chairman in his [congressional] testimony and by other Committee members quickly reversed sentiment."

In other words, we cleaned up your little mess. Please don't do that again. An unusual start for a new member of the FOMC.

But Fisher was an extraordinary addition to the table.

Before his first FOMC meeting, Fisher had gone to pay his respects to Alan Greenspan. He asked, "Now that I'm in the inner sanctum, what do you require?"

"Just speak the truth, Richard," Greenspan told him.

In his inaugural statement to the FOMC on May 3, 2005, Fisher had sent a message not only to the fellow members but the three powerful barons, the directors of Research and Statistics, International Finance, and Monetary Affairs. He'd been anticipating this moment for twenty-five years.

Fisher mentioned his background—"having spent the last five years as a strategic adviser to UPS, Exxon, EDS, and Wal-Mart, etc."—and the fact that he'd had dinner the previous Sunday night with a handful of CEOs of transnational corporations and the Crown Prince of Saudi Arabia.

"It was a small group that met to discuss what they thought was going on in energy prices, for what it's worth. . . . As summarized by the CEO who will remain unnamed but who runs the largest oil company in the world, the market seems to be pricing in a supply disruption some time this winter."

Got that? A: Fisher's no academic. B: He understands markets. C: He knows the Crown Prince of Saudi Arabia. Unlike the majority of those seated around the massive oval table, he'd been in the trenches as a manager of a hedge fund (Wall Street) and as a diplomat involved in negotiating the terms of NAFTA (government), and had been retained by the world's biggest players for strategic advice (private enterprise).

Fisher described "a noticeable dissonance" between the staff's economic reports and "the tenor of the discussion" around the FOMC table in the previous few months. Fisher's extensive contacts and experience were telling him something was amiss in the economy. He had real problems with the Fed's designated measure of inflation, "core" personal consumption expenditure (PCE), which ignores the prices of food and energy and thus did not reflect inflation's true level.

Greenspan, in the final few months of his term as Fed chairman, didn't blink an eye at the braggadocio of the new guy.

During his long tenure, dozens of people had come and gone from the FOMC. Greenspan couldn't hire them or fire them. He couldn't give them raises. He couldn't take away their staffs.

What he could do was find out where they stood and either move them to his point of view or get out in front of them like a drum major with a runaway marching band. At this Greenspan proved a genius. He rarely faced dissent on the FOMC.

After Fisher spoke, the woman who was his complete antithesis, tiny, colorless Janet Yellen, took the microphone.

With her white hair, limited makeup, and strong Brooklyn accent, Yellen looked and sounded like the professor who puts you to sleep in Econ 101.

Yellen offered no sports metaphors but indicated all seemed rosy in the Twelfth District. Core inflation measures were "uncomfortably and unexpectedly high," but Yellen's contacts in the business community, outside of Los Angeles and the Bay Area, remained "quite upbeat about the economy." She didn't think the FOMC should "overreact" when fundamentals for growth appeared to remain relatively sound. (A little kick in the pants to Fisher.)

Yellen did not mention the sizzling housing markets of California, Nevada, and Arizona. Like Greenspan, she had an unshakeable faith that any housing tribulations would remain regional. Sitting at the epicenter of the greatest housing bubble in U.S. history, Yellen had no appreciation for what the markets were screaming.

But the alarm outside the Fed had grown to such a pitch that Greenspan announced the special topic of the next FOMC meeting: Had a housing bubble developed? If so, what should the Fed do about it?

In June, after a marathon presentation by five Fed economists, FOMC members concluded that their data had provided great insights and even offered comfort. No nationwide housing bubble seemed in play. MBSs and CDOs were barely mentioned.

The Fed even ran simulations on how the economy was likely to respond to falling home prices with its computer model, called FRB/US. "Ferbus" was used to anticipate how the economy might respond to changes in interest rates and various outside shocks.

"Assuming that the FRB/US model does a good job of capturing the macroeconomic implications of declining house prices, such an event does not pose a particularly difficult challenge for monetary policy," said John Williams, a top analyst at the San Francisco Fed, during the debate. (He would later become the bank's president.) "The model showed the economy could weather a 20% drop in home prices with small increases in unemployment and modest cuts in interest rates."

So Ferbus thought everything was dandy. The FOMC agreed to raise the fed funds rate 25 basis points. There were no dissents.

Flash forward almost a year.

The White House Correspondents' Dinner on Saturday, April 29, 2006, was one of those Washington affairs where policymakers, politicians, and journalists rubbed shoulders—and a party Ben Bernanke would never forget.

Bernanke had taken over as chairman just four months earlier. One of his stated goals was improving communication and transparency at the Fed. (WWGD? Probably spit out his coffee.)

That week, Bernanke had testified to Congress for the first time in his new role. At the party, Bernanke chatted with anchor Maria Bartiromo.

On Monday morning, Bartiromo reported Bernanke's "surprising comments" on the air.

"Ben Bernanke told me over the weekend the media and the markets got it wrong last week in speculating the Fed is done raising interest rates," Bartiromo said.

Her story set off turmoil in the markets. Bernanke learned the hard way there is no such thing as idle chitchat by a Fed chairman. That's one reason the closemouthed Greenspan was considered notoriously boring at dinner parties and stubbornly opaque in his public statements.

At first Bernanke stonewalled, refusing to confirm Bartiromo's story. A month later he fessed up.

"Senator, that episode you refer to was a lapse of judgment on my part," Bernanke told Sen. Jim Bunning (R-Ky.) during a hearing of the Senate Banking Committee. "In the future, my communications with the public and the markets will be entirely through regular and formal channels."

The *New York Times* described Bernanke's slip as a "small one" compared to Richard Fisher's much larger "faux pas" the previous June.

"Fisher's comment was at odds with most other signals from Fed policymakers, and it turned out to be wildly wrong," the *Times* story said. "The Fed has raised rates eight times since he spoke and is widely expected to raise them a ninth time at its meeting on June 28 and 29. Fisher has complained that CNBC dropped the last part of his comment, which was that the 'game' might well go into extra innings. He has been more cautious in his public comments ever since."

Exactly how Fisher's comments were a more egregious mistake than Bernanke's was unclear, except that the chairman's off-the-cuff remarks at a party did not hint at a "new turn in policy"—and that Bernanke was far more important than Fisher, a mere District Bank president in a flyover state.

Privately, Fisher was worried there were media moles inside the Fed, based on what he was reading in the financial press.

Journalists and Fed watchers eagerly anticipate the release of the FOMC statement, always issued at 2 P.M. on the Wednesday after the meeting, reporting any action (or inaction) the FOMC has taken.

The minutes, released three weeks later, go into more detail but rarely communicate internal discussions, just the economic conditions reported by the Fed's staff. They are often massaged in response to the market's reaction in the intervening period.

If the FOMC statement and minutes don't get the hoped-for response from the markets, Fed insiders can leak information to a journalist to get a message across. Sometimes a reporter would print "what Bernanke is thinking" ahead of the FOMC meeting, as if Bernanke or an ally was testing the wind.

Gossips often fingered Jon Hilsenrath of the *Wall Street Journal* as a major culprit; some dubbed him "Fedwire." Market watchers started tracking Hilsenrath's stories. And Fed watchers started tracking the number of words in FOMC statements. The more verbiage, the more worry.

Prior to 1994, the FOMC didn't even announce the outcome of its meetings. No statement, no minutes, nothing to indicate what, if anything, had been decided.

The investigation by "Henry B." compelled the Fed to move toward more transparency.

In February 1994, Greenspan issued the first postmeeting statement after the FOMC raised the fed funds rate, the first tightening since 1989. The statement was spare: ninety-nine words in four sentences.

For the next five years, the FOMC released a statement only if a change was made. In May 1999, responding to pressure for further transparency, the Fed pivoted and decided to release a statement after each FOMC meeting, regardless of action, to specify the target level of the fed funds rate, and to provide "forward guidance" regarding the balance of risks.

But the biggest change was the decision to release lightly edited but otherwise—at least theoretically—complete transcripts of every meeting, with a delay of five years.

In some ways transparency backfired. Previously, the FOMC meetings had been unscripted exchanges. But when members of the FOMC started receiving preliminary drafts of transcripts, they discovered that they were not necessarily eloquent orators.

Everyone began reading scripted comments. Meetings were no longer arenas in which to argue and influence fellow FOMC members. All persuasion had to be exercised ahead of time. This concentrated power even more solidly in the hands of the chairman, who could visit individually with governors before meetings.

The transcripts didn't include tone of voice, body language, and conversations in the men's room (or ladies' room) during the breaks. Raised voices were neutered. Even so, the transcripts provided more insight into the FOMC decision-making process.

During Fisher's first six months on the FOMC, staffers were coming up to Rosenblum and asking, "Who is this guy?" They paid close attention for a few months, but started tuning Fisher out, sneaking looks underneath the table at their BlackBerries during his comments. (This was before people figured out BlackBerries could be used to eavesdrop on conversations and had to be left outside the room.)

Bottom line: he wasn't a PhD economist. Fisher emphasized what CEOs and other business leaders reported about the economy, rarely relying on academic studies. Fed economists regarded Yellen and Bernanke as the intellectual heavy hitters at the table.

Yellen's Research Department had a strong reputation for producing top-notch studies on labor and unemployment, one of the Fed's stated mandates. In contrast, Fisher's contributions were regarded as anecdotal and possibly too entertaining.

Rosenblum conceded that the Dallas Fed didn't have the system's strongest Research Department. Under Fisher's leadership, the Dallas Fed established the Globalization and Monetary Policy Institute in 2007, with an advisory board of top economists, including Martin Feldstein, John Taylor, Ken Rogoff, Glenn Hubbard, and Nobel Laureate Finn Kydland.

"It improved a lot when he was there," Rosenblum said, "but Fisher was rarely able to go into a meeting and say 'I had my Research Department look at this and we're going to be publishing a study on it.' He was viewed as seat of the pants. He may have been right, but nobody can outeconometric the Reserve Board staff."

Each night before an FOMC meeting, Rosenblum met Fisher for dinner to discuss the next day's strategy. Fisher rarely read from a script, though he might have notes. Fisher's comments often provided a better look at where the economy was going than other speakers, at least in hindsight. But his charm and lack of a PhD meant that many on the FOMC and board staff did not take him seriously.

During FOMC meetings, Rosenblum watched his boss closely. He might get up and give him a note during the proceedings, or confer with Fisher in the hall, offering the perspective of a macroeconomist. "But he followed his own counsel."

Over time, Rosenblum saw Fisher leave a mark on the FOMC. Other bank presidents began bringing in more real-world reports from the trenches.

"The Fed is drowning in data," Rosenblum said. "We're not drowning in 'what does that data mean?' I think Fisher tried to do that."

A few District Bank presidents got irritated because Fisher, who had a wide circle of acquaintances, felt no qualms about calling a CEO in another district to get information. Could Fisher help it if he was friends with the head of FedEx?

Or perhaps they worried what the CEOs who talked to Fisher divulged about their own District Bank presidents. Top corporate leaders in Yellen's district—even bankers on her own board of directors—thought she was a clueless academic more interested in labor issues than the dilemmas of those running businesses. They cringed at the idea of Yellen going to meet the CEO of Wells Fargo. She was even more inept when it came to bank Sup & Reg.

By January 30, 2007, Fisher had been in the job almost two years. The mood was buoyant around the FOMC table at the start of a two-day meeting that included all the major Fed players whose lives and careers would be so dramatically impacted over the next few years.

Fisher sat in his designated chair with Rosenblum in a seat against the wall near the door to the chairman's office. There he could catch Fisher's eye and also read Bernanke's body language, signaling like a first-base coach if necessary. He also could overhear snatches of dialogue as the chairman retreated to his office during breaks or after meetings.

On taking charge, Bernanke had gotten off on the wrong foot with Rosenblum.

During his first visit to a District Bank after being appointed chairman, Bernanke had watched Rosenblum make a presentation to the Dallas board.

Both Fisher and Rosenblum had problems with the way the Fed determined the core PCE inflation rate, which ignored the costs of food and fuel.

But what prices do people remember most? What they pay for gasoline at the pump and the price of a gallon of milk? Any elevation in those prices signaled to consumers that inflation was rising. By ignoring those trends, the Fed eroded its credibility.

Dallas Fed senior economist Jim Dolmas came up with a method of calculating core inflation called the "trimmed mean analysis." It looked at the price movements of 178 personal consumption items that matter to average consumers—in a data set that goes back to 1977—and stripped away both the highest and lowest monthly price changes for those goods to come up with the underlying trend.

Rosenblum and Fisher felt this method was better able to gauge the direction and speed of "approaching inflationary winds," in Rosenblum's words. Fisher invited Bernanke to the Dallas Fed to hear what they had come up with.

In the middle of Rosenblum's presentation, Bernanke interrupted him. "Why would you want to do something stupid like that?" Bernanke asked. "Why would you use one forecast when you can use twenty?"

Deeply offended that Bernanke would demean him in front of Fisher and the board, Rosenblum replied: "Simplicity has its virtues."

Bernanke's reaction revealed a lot about the new chairman.

"I don't think he was trying to put me down," Rosenblum said. "But simplicity is not how you get published. At the board, there's this attitude of 'We have a monopoly on truth.'"

At each FOMC, Bernanke, who had become the alpha intellectual during his years as a governor, sat midtable in the chair once occupied by the Maestro.

With Bernanke's ascension, the charisma of the chairman dropped precipitously. On a scale of 1 to 10, Rosenblum rated Greenspan a 3 or 9, depending on his mood and necessity. Bernanke rated a 2. Yellen barely registered at 0.7. (For comparison, Fisher would score a 9, former President Bill Clinton an off-the-chart 11.)

The dynamics of the meetings changed. "Greenspan had great listening skills when he needed to use them," Rosenblum said. "Bernanke was trying to be the un-Greenspan." Not that Bernanke wasn't listening, but over time, he fixated on his academic theories. Real-life reports by Fisher and other District Bank presidents counted for little.

Bernanke would later tell the BBC that FOMC meetings are "very scripted" and quite dull, but in January 2007, the Fed was about to embark on a roller coaster ride.

Everybody pulled out the stack of previously supplied charts and graphs on the economy created by New York and Washington economists. Then began the two "go-rounds" of the District Bank presidents. First they spoke about their regional economies, then their policy preferences.

Fisher and Yellen appeared to be living in different universes.

Fisher bragged about the Eleventh District's vigorous economy and summarized his conversations with twenty-five CEOs. He went on so long and in such detail that the next day he would apologize: "I was a bit loquacious, and apparently, for some, too anecdotally explicit, if not excessive."

Yellen, in contrast, spoke in the paper-dry tones of an economist; no input from CEOs, no district anecdotes, no pop culture references. Just the facts, ma'am. She did offer that, in her opinion, while housing was a concern, "I think the prospects for a really serious housing collapse that spreads to consumer spending have diminished substantially."

From her perch as president of the San Francisco Fed, Yellen presided over one of the most dynamic and problematic regions of the United States.

The Twelfth District looks across the Pacific Ocean to Asian markets that wreaked havoc on the U.S. economy and financial system in the late

1990s. Two financial centers, San Francisco and Los Angeles, call the district home. The Fed must supervise and regulate banks and monitor economic instabilities in areas as diverse as Las Vegas, Seattle, and Phoenix.

Quite a challenge. Virtually all of Yellen's career had been spent in academia or government. She had no experience with Sup & Reg, unfortunate given the complexity and criminality taking place inside many institutions in her district.

The biography of the most prominent female economist in the world bore some surface similarities to Fisher's. Yellen's grandparents had been Yiddish-speaking Polish immigrants who arrived in New York and settled on the Lower East Side around the turn of the twentieth century. Her parents were born in 1906 and 1907, their lives profoundly affected by the Great Depression.

American medical schools had quotas limiting Jewish students, so her father, Julius Yellen, had been forced to leave the United States to become a doctor. He was just beginning his practice in Brooklyn when he tripped down a flight of stairs and fractured his skull. The injury permanently damaged his eyesight. His wife, Anna, gave up her job teaching elementary school to chauffeur her husband on his rounds.

Born in 1946 when her father was forty, Yellen graduated valedictorian of Fort Hamilton High School. The accident her father suffered gave Janet empathy for those who struggled their way up the economic ladder, one disaster away from unemployment and penury.

She intended to study philosophy at Brown University, but instead switched to economics, graduating in 1967.

"What I really liked about economics was that it provided a rigorous, analytical way of thinking about issues that have great impact on people's lives," Yellen told Nicholas Lemann of the *New Yorker*. "Economics is a subject that really relates to core aspects of human well-being and there's a methodology for thinking about those things. This was a very appealing combination to me."

In her senior year, Yellen heard legendary Yale economist James Tobin talk about the "life-cycle model of consumption." He had served on John F. Kennedy's Council of Economic Advisers, had been an academic adviser to the Federal Reserve, and sang the praises of working for government.

"Tobin was a person who really impressed me, because he had a passion for social justice and for public policy," Yellen said. She applied to Yale's graduate school to study with him.

Of the two dozen economists who earned their PhDs from Yale in 1971, Yellen was the only woman. She embraced Tobin's dual passions and aspired to get involved in public policymaking at the highest levels.

Yellen taught at Harvard until 1976 but did not receive tenure. In a charming twist of fate, she met her husband at the Fed in Washington, where as young economists both did brief stints before moving to England. They taught at the London School of Economics from 1978 to 1980, when they were hired by the University of California, Berkeley, a bastion of neo-Keynesian economics. (Bill Dudley earned his PhD at Berkeley in 1982.)

In addition to teaching, Yellen researched unemployment. She and her husband frequently coauthored papers, often dealing with ideas like "efficiency wage theory."

In 1994, Yellen received the opportunity she had long been seeking when President Bill Clinton appointed her to a full fourteen-year term on the Fed's Board of Governors. She described herself as a "non-ideological pragmatist," and expressed her confidence in the positive contribution that "a predictable, well-executed monetary policy can make to economic growth."

She gave a succinct summary of her views of the Fed's purpose in 1995, when the Fed was debating proposed legislation that would make price stability the central bank's sole mandate at the expense of unemployment.

"Who would be prepared to believe that the FOMC is single-mindedly going to pursue an inflation target regardless of real economic performance, if not even the Bundesbank is prepared to go that far?" she said, citing the German central bank's efforts to minimize economic downturns. "So, that means that the targets are going to be perceived as a hoax. . . . They are not going to be any more believable than I would be if I told my child that I was going to cut off his hand if he put it in the candy drawer."

Three years later, Yellen's profile jumped higher when Clinton named her head of his Council of Economic Advisers.

After President George Bush took office in 2001, Yellen went back to Berkeley but didn't have to wait long to return to the FOMC. In 2004, she was named president of the San Francisco Fed. Though Yellen voted only every third year, she was still in the game, her sights set on a higher prize.

Though Yellen had developed a reputation as a whiz in economic forecasting, she remained oblivious as the housing market in her region imploded on multiple fronts—even more amazing considering the mental firepower at her own breakfast table.

Her husband is George A. Akerlof, corecipient of the 2001 Nobel Prize for Economics. (Actually, it's the Sveriges Riksbank Prize in Economic Sciences in Memory of Alfred Nobel.) Both are quiet, modest academics, their economic and political philosophies closely aligned.

"Not only did our personalities mesh perfectly," Akerlof wrote about their marriage after he won the Nobel Prize, "but we have also always been in all but perfect agreement about macroeconomics." Insiders at the Fed joked that the two lovebirds took economics textbooks on vacation as beach reading. Their son is also an economist.

Together they have been successful not only professionally but financially. A public disclosure statement in 2012 showed Yellen and Akerlof had assets valued between $4.8 million and $13.2 million, held in a living trust created in 1992. (The forms require only ranges.) Their investments included stock in Pfizer and OfficeMax, and a stamp collection valued between $15,000 and $50,000. In addition to her income of about $200,000 a year as chairman, their income from several defined benefit pensions totaled $22,000 per month.

Though both are strident Keynesians, Yellen rarely says anything dramatic in her public speeches, unlike her husband.

In January 2007, departing president Akerlof spoke at the annual meeting of the American Economic Association (AEA), which represents most American academic economists. He went for the jugular, taking on the sacred cow of the economics profession, Milton Friedman.

Friedman had thrown down the gauntlet for the free-market system in 1968, when he was president of the AEA. He argued in a speech to the same body that the economy works best for most people when government intervention is limited. He posited that there was a "natural rate" of unemployment; going below that point risked spiraling wages and inflation.

Friedman's philosophies profoundly influenced economists like Volcker and Greenspan. The Great Moderation could be seen as validation that Friedman was right.

However, stock bubbles and rising inequality suggested all was not well. Akerlof argued that Friedman's approach was based on false assumptions about human behavior. Friedman's "misleading" theories had led to "misguided" policies.

Akerlof called for a return to "sensible economics." Identify a problem. Ask what government can do. Adopt appropriate interventions. In other words, we're the government and we're here to help.

The problem: the government in the form of the Fed was helping too much. Its insistence on the existence of the wealth effect fueled the formation of bubbles.

If only Akerlof could have channeled the ghost of Austrian economist Ludwig von Mises, he would have realized "sensibility" was much more obvious to the naked eye.

The financial markets had been subjected to overreaching intervention in one form or another since Greenspan assumed leadership of the Fed. Less intrusive Fed policy would have allowed for the price discovery so essential to market functionality and the prevention of the boom-and-bust cycles that so worried von Mises in his day.

In 2003, Akerlof had given an interview to the German magazine *Der Spiegel* that made clear his own extreme views. Akerlof blasted the George W. Bush administration as the worst in two hundred years.

"It has engaged in extraordinarily irresponsible policies not only foreign and economic but also in social and environmental policy," Akerlof said. He considered the Bush tax cuts and subsequent run-up of government deficits to $455 billion in fiscal 2003 outrageous because they benefited only the rich.

"In the long term, a deficit of this magnitude is not manageable," Akerlof said. "This is not normal government policy. Now is the time for people to engage in civil disobedience."

Akerlof didn't chain himself to the massive double doors of the Eccles Building. At any rate, the magazine story was in German and got zero play in the United States. Nor did her husband's views hamper Yellen's career.

As president of the San Francisco Fed, Yellen picked up in her peripheral vision that there were some concerns about housing.

"I'm sorry that light bulbs didn't go off in my head a couple of years before they really did," she told the *New Yorker* years later. "I was hearing stuff that was scary. And I wouldn't have seen it in the data."

So the San Francisco Fed's data were clearly lacking.

The potential of housing to ignite systemic risk never crossed Yellen's mind. "I absolutely did not see it as something that could take the financial system down."

Yellen would have been well served by actually talking to people in the trenches—the out-of-control mortgage brokers, the house flippers, the Realtors, and home builders who unwittingly would contribute to the coming disaster. Heck, all she had to do was read the newspapers.

In May 2006, Ameriquest, an Orange County–based subprime lender, announced it would cut 3,800 jobs and close all 229 of its retail branches. That same month, Merit Financial, based in Washington State, filed for bankruptcy, firing all but 80 of its 410 employees. In early January 2007, Ownit Mortgage Solutions, another Southern California subprime lender, filed for Chapter 11 bankruptcy protection.

And yet in a speech in Reno on January 22, 2007, Yellen brushed off concerns about a housing bubble, spectacularly obvious in Nevada.

"While the decline in housing activity has been significant and will probably continue for a while longer," Yellen said, "I think the concerns we used to hear about the possibility of a devastating collapse—one that might be big enough to cause a recession in the U.S. economy—have been largely allayed."

A month later, she continued on her Pollyanna path while speaking in Sacramento. "Outside of housing and domestic autos, the rest of the economy has been doing quite well," Yellen said. "The risk of an outright downturn has receded along with the early signs of stabilization of housing markets. In summary, I believe that a soft landing is the most likely outcome over the next year or two."

Though Yellen perceived no significant threat, Fisher sounded an early alarm on the FOMC despite public comments that the financial system and economy were strong enough to weather the storm.

"On the housing front, I have been bearish—more bearish than anybody at this table," Fisher said in May 2007. "I am more concerned than I was before. We can go through the numbers, but I think it is best expressed by the CEO of one of the five big builders, who said that in March he was arguing internally with his board that the headlines were worse than reality and now reality is worse than the headlines."

At the June 2007 FOMC meeting, after news that two Bear Stearns hedge funds were in trouble due to toxic MBSs, Geithner dismissed concerns by saying "direct exposure of the counterparties to Bear Stearns is very, very small compared with other things."

Fisher begged to differ. "I was once a hedge fund manager—I know all the tricks that are played there, including, by the way, the valuation of underlying securities—in a day when the business was less sophisticated than it is now," Fisher said. "I don't feel I understand this issue ... I don't think the issue is contained. I do think there is enormous risk."

Fisher's fears were realized.

The Bear Stearns High-Grade Structured Credit Strategies Enhanced Leverage Fund held $638 million of investor capital and gross long positions of $11.15 billion in the first quarter. (Even the name of the subprime mortage fund screamed risk.) The second fund had $925 million of investor capital and gross long positions of $9.682 billion. Bear injected money to prevent a fire sale, but the two funds filed for bankruptcy on July 31.

By the August 2007 FOMC meeting, Yellen had no choice but to echo Fisher's alarm. She called the housing sector a "600-pound gorilla in the room" and remarked that the "risk for further significant deterioration in the housing market, with house prices falling and mortgage delinquencies rising further, causes me appreciable angst."

But Bernanke remained sanguine. "I think the odds are that the market will stabilize," he said. "Most credits are pretty strong except for parts of the mortgage market."

Few inside the Fed staff had connected the dots between toxic MBSs and CDOs, and the instruments banks employed to lend to one another in the overnight and commercial paper markets.

In fact, Dudley (of the Berkeley mafia) told the FOMC on August 7: "We've done quite a bit of work trying to identify some of the funding operations surrounding Bear Stearns, Countrywide, and some of the commercial paper programs." Corporations issue commercial paper or debt to finance short-term liabilities. "There is some strain, but so far it looks as though nothing is really imminent in those areas. Now could that change quickly? Absolutely."

And with lightning speed, it changed.

In early August 2007, I was in Connecticut visiting my family, my last travel opportunity before pregnancy would keep me tethered to home.

Standing in my aunt's kitchen on Sunday morning, watching *CNBC In-*

ternational, I learned the "yen carry trade" had started to unravel. Currency traders who borrowed Japanese currency at a low interest rate, converted it to U.S. dollars, then bought higher-yielding bonds had been caught with their pants down when exchange rates suddenly shifted.

About $1 trillion had been invested in the yen carry trade by mid-2007. Most currency traders who indulged in this tactic were highly leveraged and chased returns by investing in subprime mortgage derivatives. I called Rosenblum.

"It's started, Harvey," I said calmly. "The yen carry trade is unwinding." The appetite for risky assets was beginning to change as the yen rallied.

Rosenblum listened, asked lots of questions, and hung up more informed but unsure what to do. He never reacted as if I were a hysterical pregnant woman, but I wouldn't have blamed him.

At the September 2007 FOMC meeting, Bernanke pushed through a larger than expected rate cut—50 basis points to 4.75 percent. The Fed, Fisher argued, was giving in to a "siren call" to "indulge rather than discipline risky financial behavior."

But the chairman and his allies on the FOMC "had lost patience with this argument," Bernanke wrote in his memoir. "As the central bank, we have a responsibility to help markets function normally and to promote economic activity broadly speaking."

Throughout the FOMC transcripts for 2007, two words never appear: "AIG" and "Lehman."

Malignant stars were aligning for a once-in-a-century global economic meltdown. Though precious few inside the Fed saw the crisis coming, it is patently false to suggest insiders hadn't been fairly warned.

CHAPTER 9

"Luddite!"

FED STATEMENT WORD COUNT: 378

EFFECTIVE FED FUNDS RATE: 0.21%

10-YR TREASURY RATE: 3.72%

FED BANKS TOTAL ASSETS: $2,025.57B

DATE: 6/1/2009

Not only have individual financial institutions become less vulnerable to shocks from underlying risk factors, but also the financial system as a whole has become more resilient.

—ALAN GREENSPAN, 2003

Every August, the Kansas City Fed hosts a small but prestigious conference of central bankers and distinguished economists from around the world at Jackson Hole, Wyoming.

The Kansas City Fed first started doing an annual conference in 1978. But the conference got little attention outside the insular world of Fed economists.

So the bank rethought its approach. They knew Chairman Volcker loved to fly-fish. To attach his prestige to the conference, they looked around their district—which includes Oklahoma, Colorado, Kansas, Nebraska, Wyoming, northern New Mexico, and western Missouri—for the perfect fishing spot.

Jackson Hole, a breathtaking valley with a view of the Grand Teton Mountains, was the only place in the district that had waters cold enough for trout fishing in August.

The first Jackson Hole Economic Policy Symposium took place in 1982. Volcker showed up. The beauty of the landscape, the opportunity for urban economists to hike, fish, and ride horses—acting like rugged outdoorsmen while exchanging views with fellow monetary policymakers—soon made the annual conference a hot ticket for those lucky enough to get an invitation.

Rosenblum never missed a chance to attend. There he built relationships that spanned continents and made connections with others inside the Fed but outside the formal FOMC meetings. He went white-water rafting with people like Dudley, definitely a bonding experience. Donald Kohn usually led a grueling mountain hike dubbed the Kohn Death March.

But Jackson Hole was also the place to hear significant theories propounded by top monetary theorists.

In 2005, economist Raghuram G. Rajan was anointed to give an important paper at a critical juncture.

It was Greenspan's last year as chairman. The most powerful and well-known figures in monetary policymaking would be in attendance, making the occasion a celebration of his long reign as America's central banker.

Rajan was invited to laud Greenspan's leadership and congratulate him for making the world's financial system safer, recognition of his own rising star.

The son of an Indian civil servant, Rajan had grown up in Indonesia, Sri Lanka, and Belgium. He joined the University of Chicago's business school in 1991. In 2003, he received the first Fischer Black Prize, awarded to the person under forty who has contributed most to the theory and practice of finance. Later that year, Rajan was named chief economist for the IMF, the youngest person and first non-Westerner to hold that job. It was a great honor to be asked to praise Greenspan for making the world's financial system more stable.

On August 26, one presenter after another praised Greenspan for his approach to monetary policy, which a Fed summary described as "discretionary, flexible, and based on a deep understanding of economic data and business conditions." Guided by eleven key principles, a "hallmark of the Greenspan era was reliance on what he himself has characterized as a 'risk management' approach to monetary policy. Under this approach, policy-makers guard against low-probability outcomes that might have outsized adverse effects on the economy."

Well, I wouldn't have put it that way. Guarding against "low-probability outcomes" surely would exclude blowing a magnificent housing bubble.

The next day, Rajan stepped up to the lectern and delivered a very different paper from the one the Kansas City Fed organizers anticipated: "Has Financial Development Made the World Riskier?" His answer was an unequivocal yes.

Rajan argued that technological innovation, deregulation, and institutional transformations had eroded the traditional banking virtues of stewardship and prudence. Investment banking on Greenspan's watch had been profoundly transformed for the worse.

Rajan used compensation for investment bankers and other finance executives to illustrate his point.

Salaries, bonuses, and other perks run into millions of dollars a year for many investment bankers, a hot-button topic both on and off Wall Street. According to a study covering the years 2003 to 2007, the CEOs of Wall Street's biggest banks earned an average of $30 million annually, more than double the $12 million in compensation for nonbank Fortune 50 CEOs.

Once remunerated by a fixed salary, financial managers in deregulated banks vied with each other and institutions like mutual funds to attract investors' cash.

Because their pay was increasingly tied to short-term returns, managers tried to maximize their compensation by betting on complex derivatives with potentially huge payoffs. Though a price decline of the securities could be disastrous, the probability of such an event—the "tail risk"—was low.

Since financial managers' pay is set relative to their peers, everyone follows the same path. A herd instinct takes over. But if something went wrong, the results could be ruinous. The more crowded the trade, the greater the chance an unexpected turn in prices would cascade from institution to institution and potentially throughout the entire system.

Rajan pointed to credit default swaps—a type of insurance—as examples of financial innovations that posed enormous danger. Some of the financial institutions making bets using CDSs also held some of the same underlying securities on their books. If these failed, the risk would be magnified, putting the banking system itself in peril.

"The interbank market could freeze up, and one could well have a full-blown financial crisis," Rajan concluded. Banks would no longer trust each other. The result could be a catastrophic meltdown.

Rajan's paper was received as a slap in the face to Greenspan, the Fed, and the economic theories championed by top American economists like Summers, who was in the audience.

It's a good thing starchy academics would never resort to violence. But their disdain for Rajan was palpable.

"I felt like an early Christian who had wandered into a convention of half-starved lions," Rajan later wrote.

Summers, then president of Harvard University, lambasted Rajan, saying he found the paper's "basic, slightly Luddite premise" to be "largely misguided."

Campaigning to become Greenspan's successor, Summers perhaps saw Rajan's paper as an attack on him. Summers had championed privatization and deregulation of financial institutions. He had shepherded the passage of the Commodity Futures Modernization Act, which banned regulation of derivatives.

And high-paid Wall Street CEOs hired him for advice. (Public disclosure forms showed that from 2001 until 2008, Summers earned $20 million in consultancy fees from the financial industry.) No wonder Summers thought Rajan was a Luddite.

The Fed's house view was expressed by Governor Donald Kohn, also in line to succeed Greenspan.

Kohn's words dripped with condescension.

"As a consequence of greater diversification of risks and of sources of funds," Kohn said, "problems in the financial sector are less likely to intensify shocks hitting the economy and financial markets [thus] I do not share Raghu's nostalgia for the systemic-risk implications of bank-dominated finance."

Kohn argued that policies to stem risk-taking would "result in less accurate asset pricing, reduce public welfare on balance, and definitely be at odds with the tradition of policy excellence of the person [Greenspan] whose era we are examining at this conference."

The shocking folly of his argument is easy to see in hindsight. But Kohn—steeped in the Fed's narrow worldview and economic models— could not conceive of a situation in which he was wrong.

CHAPTER 10

Helpless

FED STATEMENT WORD COUNT: 547

EFFECTIVE FED FUNDS RATE: 0.11%

10-YR TREASURY RATE: 3.73%

FED BANKS TOTAL ASSETS: $2,246.89B

DATE: 1/1/2010

It's a boy! It's a girl!

—DR. JAMES RICHARDS, OB/GYN, DECEMBER 7, 2007

The blaring alarm startled all three of us: me; my husband, John; and the neonatal pediatrician. A nurse rushed into the small room, shoved us all aside, put her hands into the openings of the crib, and gave Baby John a good shake. His lips had already turned a light shade of blue. His heart had stopped, which all but stopped mine.

Our four-day-old son had been admitted to the step-down nursery just prior to our discharge from the hospital. It was a precautionary measure, since the younger of our twins could not hold his body heat.

The doctor sat two trembling parents down and explained that the Lord does indeed move in mysterious ways. Had we taken Baby John home, we almost certainly would have lost him to sudden infant death syndrome. Now that he was on a heart monitor, he would be in safe hands until he passed the test of time: five days without triggering the alarm. Each time he set off the alarm, the clock reset itself back to the first-day mark.

Two buildings over, across fields of ice, my daughter, Carolyn, slept in the neonatal intensive care unit. I had yet to lay eyes on her. At exactly 6 P.M. on December 7, 2007, she had emerged blue due to oxygen depletion, followed forty seconds later by little John.

A historic ice storm had paralyzed Dallas and made transport between the nurseries all but impossible for me. The emergency C-section had taken place in the blink of an eye when doctors determined the weight of water on my heart showed I could no longer withstand the strain of the pregnancy. The blood vessels from my knees down had burst and I was stuck in a wheelchair while I healed. So John sat vigil by our baby daughter's side until the ice melted.

I had never felt so helpless or terrified in my life. Incapable of sleep, I asked John to bring my Fed laptop up to the hospital. For ten days, I slept with one eye open waiting for that alarm to go off, able to calm my mind while he slept by pulling out my laptop and monitoring the markets.

Work had been my salvation when I was stuck on bed rest during October and November 2007. My mom arrived to help since I couldn't pick up anything larger than a gallon of milk.

I kept the TV tuned to CNBC, though the sound was usually muted. And my laptop was right beside me, at risk of being crushed when toddlers William and Henry came barreling across the bed in fits of happy giggles.

So much was taking place in world financial markets while I sat tight, safeguarding the growth of my double cargo until my December due date.

The rolling disaster rippled around the world.

Insomnia kept me up late. Instead of *I Love Lucy* reruns, I watched the BBC as thousands of Brits queued to withdraw one billion pounds from Northern Rock, the biggest UK bank run in over a century.

Markets sniff out the weakest links in the system. The cost of protecting the debt of big U.S. investment banks became the train wreck I couldn't stop watching.

I began following bank credit default swaps. These insurance securities could be used to bet for or against the survival of any financial entity—for example, the sovereign debt of Iceland or the corporate bonds of General Motors. Propped up on a mountain of pillows, I tracked bank CDSs in a spreadsheet.

My Economic Letter on subprime mortgages, published on November 1, was the first article the reading public would see with my name on it since I had vanished into the invisibility of the Fed.

I felt proud, though very isolated, as tumultuous events unfolded. But, as my CDS spreadsheets evolved into a daily digest of sorts, I gained two private readers.

One morning before dawn, I added a bit of analysis to my daily spreadsheet, stuck on an obvious title, "Daily Briefing," addressed it to Richard Fisher, copied Harvey Rosenblum, and hit send.

Within five minutes, I received a reply from Fisher, with whom I'd had little interaction to date at the bank: "Great stuff! Thanks. Keep it coming." There I was, big as a whale but electrified because the president of the bank had responded within minutes.

Up until that moment, Fisher had been the charismatic Renaissance man on the fourteenth floor. Now I knew he was an early riser, and for the first time I realized he was literally my neighbor. His house in Highland Park was only a few blocks away from ours. He went from mythical big boss in the heavens to a living, breathing mortal with one e-mail response.

As the markets melted that November, the daily briefing for Fisher gave my bedridden self a sense of purpose and kept my mind off my precarious physical state.

Even so, by the first week of December, I was about to crawl out of my skin. On December 6, President Bush appeared on TV outlining a plan to help more than a million homeowners facing foreclosure. It would have been more helpful had they not bought more home than they could afford in the first place, but I was beyond caring.

The next afternoon, when John ferried me to the doctor's office, I struggled to make the short walk from the hospital parking lot to the lobby elevator—lungs wheezing, heart racing, despite my agonizingly slow steps.

"Hop on the scales, honey!" chirped the nurse. Every OB appointment starts the same happy way, by weighing in. Not bad, she said, noting that I had gained two pounds on my chart. However, the nurse, in her brisk and skinny efficiency, was wrong. The scale actually revealed that I had gained twelve pounds since my last visit.

Vanity almost stopped me from pointing out to my OB that his nurse had made a mistake. But confess I did. He instantly reached for a blood pressure cuff, which told him all he needed to know. My heart was giving way, threatening the two babies' lives.

Within minutes I was in an operating room, any vestige of control swept aside.

As luck would have it, excellent doctors and nurses brought us through the fear and anxiety. Two weeks later, we returned home triumphant with two healthy babies. On a chilly Christmas morning, John and I gave thanks to be celebrating with our four children. We laugh to this day when Baby John, whom we now call Bruiser, gets chilled so easily. His cold nature saved his life.

The holidays that year raced before my eyes at record speed. Before I knew it, I was back at work, though my old routine was never to stage a comeback.

One morning in late February 2008, my BlackBerry buzzed. I'd gotten to the YMCA at 5:30 A.M. and was only halfway through my elliptical routine. But I stopped, grabbed a towel, and reached for the phone. The screen gave no number, just said "Restricted."

It was Fisher, the only person in my world with a private cell phone number.

"Danielle, can you get me the latest S&P 500 top-line growth forecast as of yesterday's close?" Fisher asked. The stock market had gone full manic-depressive. Fisher was headed to an FOMC meeting in a few hours and wanted the most up-to-date figures in hand. Thankfully, it was an hour later on the East Coast. I e-mailed Howard Silverblatt at S&P and had a spreadsheet in Fisher's hands inside a half hour.

On my first day back at the Dallas Fed in mid-February 2008, I had settled back into my cubicle and connected my laptop to its docking station. My first action: bookmarking the Mortgage Lender Implode-O-Meter.

A Web site started in late 2006 by a twenty-seven-year-old computer geek, the Implode-O-Meter tracked the collapse of independent mortgage lenders.

The troubled Countrywide, the most recognized name in mortgage lending, had avoided disaster when it was acquired in a fire sale by Bank of America for $4 billion in early January 2008.

I checked the Implode-O-Meter several times a day, horrified at the grim toll the subprime disaster was taking on the rank and file.

Throughout my maternity leave, I had maintained my sanity by communicating the market's upheavals in my daily briefings to Fisher. He wanted the day's events honed and condensed to one page, no more. Though we rarely talked, Fisher often zapped back a response or a question.

That first day back at work, I had been issued an encrypted BlackBerry. I was instructed to keep it charged and accessible at all times so that President Fisher could get in touch with me around the clock. My security clearance was promptly upgraded.

I'm sure my colleagues were puzzled, though they would never admit it. I'd left the building as a nobody and returned as someone having direct communication with the bank president. Status at the Fed was determined by access to policymakers and tended to be limited to officers. (I rebuffed the handful of times management offered to put my name in for an officer position.)

The focus of my work at the Fed shifted to Fisher's daily briefings. This was his year on the voting rotation, the markets were in turmoil, and Fisher wanted me and my research on call.

Transcripts from FOMC meetings in 2008 reveal that the Fed misjudged the depth and severity of the evolving crisis at almost every turn.

The soft-spoken, dignified Bernanke had been in the job two years. He began 2008 with a deep sense of unease.

Born in 1953, Bernanke grew up in Dillon, South Carolina. His parents had been one of the first Jewish families in the small Southern town.

His academic credentials were second to none in his own insular world. Though a scholar of the Great Depression, Bernanke had zero experience on Wall Street or in finance. When vetted for the job as Fed chairman by the White House, he said so little that one interviewer worried he lacked "assertiveness." But Bernanke knew the destructive nature of systemic risk and how it could spread like wildfire once ignited.

In 2002, Bernanke, while on the Board of Governors, had paid tribute to Milton Friedman at a conference at the University of Chicago. Acknowledging Friedman's work on the Depression and his criticism that the Fed's tight monetary policy had deepened its deprivations for millions of Americans, Bernanke told Friedman, "We did it. We're very sorry. But we promise not to do it again."

After years of downplaying the housing crisis, Bernanke had finally awakened to the imminent danger. The markets were in turmoil, with the S&P 500 Index down over 16 percent by the third week of January.

On Monday, January 21, Martin Luther King Day, Bernanke went into his office believing dramatic action by the Fed was needed before the next FOMC meeting, scheduled for January 30. Though it was a holiday, an emergency videoconference of the FOMC was called for 6 P.M. that evening. The word went out to all members of the FOMC to get to a secured videoconference line and dial in.

In a special room at the Fed, the faces of far-flung members of the FOMC appeared on individual video monitors. It was like a game of the TV show *Hollywood Squares,* the monetary policy version.

"Obviously it's not our job to target stock values or to protect stock investors," Bernanke said. "But I think that this is a symptom of both sharply mounting concerns about the economy and increasing problems in credit markets. On the economy, the data and the information that we can glean from financial markets reflect a growing belief that the United States is in for a deep and protracted recession."

Bernanke wanted to cut the fed funds rate to indicate the Fed was "on top of the situation."

He got pushback from several Fed District presidents, including Fisher. (He was on the call but not eligible to vote until the official FOMC meeting in January. Bernanke admitted in his memoir that he wanted to cut rates at the teleconference before Fisher and Charles Plosser, president of the Philadelphia Fed, would have the vote in order to minimize dissents. His plan all along was a two-step cut.)

"What do we get for this?" Fisher asked. "What expectations do we build in for future decision making?" He pointed out that the economic data provided by Fed staffers were mixed and their projections often proved wrong.

"This action will not be viewed in the marketplace as anything other than a direct response to the stock market," said William Poole, president of the St. Louis Fed. He argued the FOMC should wait until the next meeting and voted against the move.

But Bernanke pressed the FOMC, which approved his proposal for a drastic interest rate cut despite Poole's dissent.

The next morning, the Fed shocked the markets, slashing the fed funds rate by 75 basis points—the largest single cut since the 1980s—from 4.25 to 3.5 percent.

The unexpected rate cut and breaking news that Jérôme Kerviel, a rogue junior trader at the French investment house Société Générale, had racked up trading losses of $7 billion, foreshadowed the bumpy ride.

Kerviel's bizarre maneuvers involved huge market trades placed on various stock exchanges and was probably behind the sudden drop in foreign equity markets. Still, the random and unpredictable nature of the markets had Bernanke frazzled. Throughout 2008, he gave the impression that, more often than not, he was flying by the seat of his pants.

Unlike Bernanke, Fisher was a seasoned veteran of "manic markets," a phrase he used with great frequency. I never saw him rattled by the ups and downs of the DJIA.

In the five regular FOMC meetings from January through August 2008, as Bernanke continued to push interest rates lower, Fisher dissented from the majority FOMC vote every time. (Twice Plosser joined him.) This pattern of dissents was highly unusual. Fisher repeatedly stressed that the Fed should not be seen as reacting to market fluctuations.

As Fisher's prominence as a dissenting Fed banker grew, I descended into the weeds, combing for market intelligence. He once introduced me as his "eyes and ears" on the financial markets. I preferred to think of myself as a French pig sniffing out risk truffles.

As providence would have it, I came along as Fisher saw an opportunity to make his mark at the Federal Reserve. We both regarded the institution as too opaque, too chairman driven, too insular, and too beholden to Wall Street.

My work for Fisher put me on a collision course with the Markets Desk. The Desk chief was now Bill Dudley, rapidly moving up the Fed hierarchy.

Seeds of doubt about the reliability of the Desk's analysis had been planted in Fisher's mind during his three years on the FOMC and had grown into a deep suspicion.

What this one-woman "markets desk" produced for Fisher was invaluable to his independence: real-time information on the markets not generated by the New York Fed, with its revolving door to banks like Goldman Sachs.

Many on the Street entertained various conspiracy theories about the Desk. It was long rumored that analysts there leaked information to bond traders, allowing them to front-run the FOMC's next move.

I didn't know if the stories were true, but the reports coming off the Desk always smelled like "sell-side" research to me. Rosier, less willing to highlight escalating risks, as if they too benefited from rising markets.

Strange. The Desk and I had many contacts in common. I would be at a meeting with one of my sources on Wall Street and hear, "Oh yeah, so-and-so was just here from the New York Fed." The funny thing is, I would come away with vastly different impressions than my counterparts on the Desk.

Maybe it comes down to location. Whatever the reason, New York Fed analysts are steeped in the same worldview as those at Goldman and Morgan Stanley.

Fisher refused to blindly accept the Desk's analysis as gospel. Time and again, Fisher warned me not to get cozy with my counterparts in New York. Keep my views clean. Stay objective. Observe the data for myself. Report back.

In the spring of 2008, the nation's financial woes had briefly receded from the front pages. But the signs were growing more ominous each week. Systemic risk hadn't disappeared, it had just submerged, like a fire in a vein of coal.

The previous year's problems had raised concerns at the highest levels. On March 13, Treasury Secretary Henry "Hank" Paulson released recommendations from the President's Working Group on Financial Markets (PWG).

Composed of the heads of Treasury (Paulson), the Federal Reserve (Bernanke), the New York Fed (Geithner), the Securities and Exchange Commission, and the Commodity Futures Trading Commission, the PWG was established in 1988 after the stock market crash by President Ronald Reagan to "enhance the integrity, efficiency, orderliness, and competitiveness of our nation's financial markets while maintaining investor confidence."

The shadowy nature of the PWG sparked conspiracy theories about secret cabals manipulating markets. In 1997, a *Washington Post* reporter interviewed various members of the group and nicknamed the PWG the "plunge protection team."

Now, two years after home prices peaked, the "plunge protection team" turned its attention to the bubble's fallout.

The PWG recommended six broad changes by market players: stronger transparency and disclosure; stronger risk awareness on the part of regulators and all market participants; more diligent risk management by all participants; stronger capital management; stronger regulatory policies; and stronger market infrastructure.

Could the PWG have shown up any later for the party? Its recommendations reinforced the image of cluelessness, especially of the Fed.

In early March, the price of CDSs for Wall Street banks skyrocketed, with the priciest policy attached to Bear Stearns, weakened by the hedge fund collapses of 2007.

"The Bear" had always been the scrappiest, least highbrow of all the "bulge bracket" firms on Wall Street. ("Bulge bracket" is slang for investment banks whose names are listed most prominently on the "tombstone" or front of a stock-offering prospectus.)

Founded in 1923, Bear was one of the first brokerages on Wall Street to go public, in 1985. Though not a large firm, it had tentacles in every financial business imaginable—and one of the Street's highest exposures to subprime mortgages.

Since 1993, Bear had been headed by James E. "Jimmy" Cayne, a one-time scrap-iron dealer and professional bridge player who joined the firm in 1969 after his girlfriend demanded he get a real job.

He'd been hired by Alan "Ace" Greenberg, a swashbuckling adventurer who shared his passion for high-stakes bridge. After Cayne boasted that he was a better bridge player than Greenberg and always would be, Greenberg hired him for seventy thousand dollars a year.

Cayne proved a natural bond salesman, quickly rising inside the firm. The world-class card player rubbed elbows with America's highest-profile bridge enthusiasts, including Malcolm Forbes, Warren Buffett, and Laurence Tisch (chief of CBS), who would become his first big client.

Besides his obsession with bridge, Cayne was known for his high-flying lifestyle and his blunt manner. He once told a mother who ran a small investment firm that her eleven-year-son had a "rotten handshake" and was "going nowhere in life." He was less polite to his underlings.

Under the leadership of Greenberg and Cayne, Bear loaded up on derivatives. Its business model relied on ever-appreciating asset values. When markets rise, brokers underwrite more fee-generating deals. Higher values require less collateral, freeing up money for other investments.

Bear was even known for its savvy risk managers. Nicknamed "ferrets," these valuable employees sniffed out hidden hazards in trades.

By 2006, Bear's stock was flying high at $170 per share. Cayne earned $34 million in pay that year and became the first Wall Street CEO to own a stake in his company worth more than $1 billion.

With a winner-take-all philosophy, Cayne and his ferrets were true believers in Wall Street Darwinism.

I had great affection for folks in the trenches at Bear Stearns; they'd proved to be valuable allies when I was at DLJ.

In those days, I traded a lot of junk bonds. Eventually I realized dealers on my own desk were jacking up prices to build in extra profits for themselves. After I became friendly with people on the bond desk at Bear, I'd quietly call one of my buddies and ask, "How bad is my own desk ripping my head off?"

They'd get me realistic pricing. I'd take that back to my traders to finagle a better deal for my client. The DLJ bond desk didn't need to pad its sizable commission at my clients' expense. That brand of greed was one of my pet peeves about Wall Street.

Dudley would later call the Bear Stearns debacle in March 2008 an old-fashioned bank run, just like that depicted in the 1946 movie *It's a Wonderful Life*, played out in real time on CNBC.

But it had really started in 2007, during the ten-day crisis as its hedge funds crumbled. Cayne, age seventy-three, had come under attack for being AWOL, playing a bridge tournament in Nashville instead of tending to agitated investors.

Cayne exhibited a bizarre indifference during this tumultuous period. He often neglected to keep a cell phone or e-mail device with him. On Thursday afternoon, he'd helicopter from Manhattan to his vacation home in Deal, New Jersey, to play golf over three-day weekends at the ritzy Hollywood Golf Club. Though he paid for the flights himself (at $1,700 a pop), his behavior reinforced the image of an out-of-touch Wall Street titan unresponsive to his customers' woes.

Top-level execs at Bear insisted they never had a problem reaching him. But the investing community got the impression Cayne was off in la-la land, especially after the *Wall Street Journal* reported that, in addition to his ubiquitous Cuban cigars, he had been seen smoking marijuana during bridge tournaments. (He denied smoking pot.) As Bear's hedge funds imploded, Cayne's reputation took a hit. He had been forced out of his job as CEO by year's end.

Meanwhile short sellers were on the prowl, with Bear squarely in their crosshairs. As its stock price dropped, many suspected that unscrupulous traders had launched a so-called "bear raid" on "the Bear."

Consider short sellers to be Wall Street's checks and balances. They place bets that pay off only if the stock of a company goes down. Bear Stearns and other investment banks worked with short sellers all the time and also engaged in this tactic on their own behalf.

While some people call aggressive short sellers vultures, they serve a vital purpose as cleansing agents of the financial ecosystem.

Wall Street and corporate America have always had companies at which fraud is being perpetrated. That's why Enron, Tyco, and WorldCom deserved to go down.

Though initially creative and entrepreneurial, Enron resorted to deceiving regulators and its own shareholders. Short sellers legitimately bet against its stock, taking out a dirty operator to the betterment of the industry.

Sometimes short sellers prey upon companies that are vulnerable due to poor management, risk intoxication, or plain bad luck. That described Bear Stearns to a tee. By mid-March, it was apparent that short-selling wolves were determined to cull Bear from the herd.

Beginning on March 10, rumors and the memory of the previous year's hedge funds debacle prompted skittish investors to pull $17 billion from Bear in two days. The price of its stock fell 60 percent as word got out.

Early on March 12, the company issued a press release denying that Bear was in trouble. Later that morning, a few minutes after 9 A.M., CNBC reporter David Faber interviewed Bear CEO Alan Schwartz on camera. He asked him about reports that Goldman Sachs wouldn't "accept the counterparty risk of Bear Stearns." Schwartz denied it, but the bombshell allegation by Faber escalated the run.

On March 13, Schwartz called the SEC and the Fed. Bear was out of money and needed an emergency line of credit. By the end of the day, Fed officials descended on Bear's Madison Avenue headquarters to scrutinize its books.

On March 14, Schwartz admitted to Bloomberg that in the previous twenty-four hours, the firm's liquidity had "significantly deteriorated" as panicky investors tried to cash out.

Watching Bear's collapse and the quickly spreading contagion was nerve wracking, even from my spot in front of the break room TV at the Dallas Fed, the only other TV I'd seen in the building outside of Fisher's office. Lenders' trust in each other's balance sheets eroded and it wasn't contained to Bear Stearns. Overnight liquidity evaporated and counterparty risk exploded.

The word "counterparty" refers to legal entities on opposite sides of a transaction. (The word became widely used after the Basel I Accord in 1988.) For every buyer there must be a seller; for example, if a hedge fund must sell assets to raise money, but the agreed counterparty to a transaction refuses to buy, the hedge fund risks being stuck with a worthless asset.

On March 14, I ran up to Fisher's office with my own concerns. JPMC had the largest counterparty exposure to the struggling brokerage.

"If Bear Stearns goes, it's going to blow a huge hole in JPMorgan's balance sheet," I said. Because of JPMC's immense size and importance, that was like saying the American economy was aboard the *Titanic* as it steamed toward the mother of all icebergs.

Fisher and Rosenblum were on the "daily call" between members of the FOMC and the Markets Desk. The Desk was rattled, fearing the brokerage might not be able to play its role in the overnight repurchase or "repo" market because its cash reserves had dropped so precipitously.

Bear Stearns was a major player in the repo market, the liquidity engine that banks and brokers use to lend cash to each other overnight.

This mechanism fills various needs, most often to keep operating funds on hand or to keep cash or liquid securities required as reserves. It's a market built on trust. The loans are often "rolled over" from one day to the next. Relationships and transactions in the repo markets are highly intertwined.

But the problem was much bigger than one limping brokerage. Bear's troubles had ensnared the much larger and more important JPMC, the largest derivatives trader on Wall Street. If JPMC collapsed, the ripple effect would seize up the global derivatives market.

The *Financial Times* reported that Fed officials feared this "would cause the broker to default on its related contracts, sparking a daisy chain of defaults across the banking sector."

Bear Stearns had revealed the disease infecting the financial system and was simply too interconnected to be allowed to fail. Over one harrowing March weekend, Bernanke, Geithner, and Paulson joined forces, the new "Committee to Save the World."

Bernanke, the nonassertive academic, bore the responsibility of the global economy on his shoulders. Compared to Greenspan, Bernanke had a deeper understanding of the way the Fed had exacerbated banking troubles during the Great Depression. He'd studied it all his professional life.

Geithner, the elbow-less civil servant, kept such a low profile that in March 2008 one reporter called him the New York Fed's "quiet skipper" with an "aversion to the spotlight." Despite his inexperience on Wall Street, he knew what the government could and couldn't (or wouldn't) do.

And Paulson, a human skyscraper with a Wall Street pedigree second to none, had relationships and rivalries with top CEOs that went back decades.

At six foot seven, Paulson was an imposing figure used to getting his way. In the *New Yorker*, writer James B. Stewart described Paulson as "tall, excitable, garrulous, and supremely self-confident," a man who once told a colleague "I didn't get the charm gene."

A practicing Christian Scientist who grew up in an affluent area of Chicago, Paulson graduated from Dartmouth and Harvard Business School. He spent the next thirty years at Goldman Sachs, making his way up the ladder to COO.

Unlike Geithner, Paulson threw muscular elbows. He had seized control of the firm in 1998 from Jon Corzine and served as Goldman's CEO until 2006, when President George W. Bush appointed him treasury secretary.

When he took the job, Paulson's annual paycheck went from $38 million to $183,500. But he would have no trouble paying the bills. His estimated equity stake in Goldman stock totaled $700 million.

Government ethics laws required Paulson to divest himself of his Goldman holdings. But the move to government service saved him as much as $50 million thanks to a clause in tax law passed in 1989, a substantial perk of public office.

Section 1043 of the Internal Revenue Code provides that individuals in the Executive Branch forced to sell stock to comply with federal conflict-of-interest rules can defer paying capital gains tax, provided that the proceeds are then reinvested in government securities, diversified index funds, or similar investments. The rule is intended to "minimize the burden of public service."

Thus Paulson would avoid a huge tax bill on the capital gains of his Goldman stock, which had more than doubled in value since the firm went public in May 1999. A pretty big incentive to spend a few years in Washington.

Paulson went so far as to specify that he would have no interaction with Goldman executives for his entire term as treasury secretary, saying, "I believe that these steps will ensure that I avoid even the appearance of a conflict of interest in the performance of my duties as Secretary of the Treasury."

So Bernanke understood the history, Geithner had the government insider knowledge, and Paulson knew the egos and anxieties of Wall Street CEOs.

When it became clear that a miracle was needed to deal with Bear Stearns, this eclectic trio, led by the aggressive Paulson, went to work on Jamie Dimon, the charismatic, pugnacious, and wily CEO of JPMC.

Dimon had fought his way up the Wall Street ladder not once but twice.

I had been on Wall Street for two years when one of the most memorable high-level power struggles broke out at Citigroup between CEO Sandy Weill and Dimon, his second-in-command.

Over fifteen years, the two had built Citigroup into a financial empire like no other. Despite their long relationship, the ambitious Dimon was fired in November 1998 by Weill for nipping too closely at his heels. Weill would later say firing Dimon was one of the biggest mistakes of his career.

Dimon clawed his way back into the executive suite and by the end of 2006, he had become president, CEO, and chairman of JPMC, one of the most prestigious and powerful jobs in the financial world. To top it off, in January 2007 Dimon began serving a three-year term on the New York Fed's Board of Directors.

Bear Stearns's death rattles could have been a nightmare for Dimon. But his response became a triumph.

The scene is now part of Wall Street legend: When his cell phone rang on the evening of March 13, Dimon was annoyed. Sitting in his favorite Greek restaurant in midtown Manhattan, he was celebrating his fifty-second birthday with his wife, his parents, and one of his three daughters.

Though he didn't recognize the number and didn't want to be disturbed, Dimon answered the call. It was Gary Parr, a Lazard executive working on the Bear rescue.

Bear Stearns was in dire straits. "We have a real issue here and we need to be talking to you and your team," Parr said. "They're in desperate shape. They need a lot of money." Could JPMC make Bear Stearns an emergency loan before the opening of business the next morning? They had twelve hours.

Walking out of the restaurant so he would not be overheard, Dimon asked if Bear was in touch with Paulson or Bernanke. Yes, Parr said, Bear had been dealing with the duo from the Fed and Treasury all day.

Dimon started calling his deputies to find out more about the situation at Bear, like a general rallying his underlings to arms. What was in it for JPMC? What was the downside risk?

At first Dimon was reluctant, telling Geithner that buying Bear Stearns would weaken his own bank. But in the end, the trio presented Dimon with a huge opportunity. Take over Bear Stearns. We'll make you an offer you can't refuse.

Bear's collapse had flipped a switch that changed the rules of the game. The Federal Reserve's mandate—Section 13(3)—provides that on a formal invocation, the Board of Governors, by the affirmative vote of not fewer than five members, can take an action that is "unusual and exigent" and is required "for the purpose of providing liquidity to the financial system." (Note that this does not require an FOMC vote.) The rule opens the door for the Fed to be the true "lender of last resort."

At Bernanke's bidding, the Board of Governors held an emergency telephone conference on Friday, March 14, at 5 A.M. and voted to authorize the New York Fed to loan up to $30 billion to JPMC to bail out Bear Stearns.

The transaction was carried out by the New York Fed's SOMA through a newly created entity called Maiden Lane LLC. (The New York Fed is bordered by a street with that name.)

The New York Fed loaned Maiden Lane about $28 billion to purchase approximately $30 billion in toxic assets from Bear Stearns. JPMC lent Maiden Lane about $1.15 billion for a ten-year term, accruing interest at the primary credit rate plus 450 basis points.

Though Dimon first agreed to pay only two dollars per share for Bear's stock, that price triggered howls from shareholders and threats of lawsuits.

JPMC ended up acquiring Bear Stearns for about ten dollars per share, or $270 million, signing the merger agreement on Sunday, March 16. The fire sale included Bear's brand-new midtown Manhattan headquarters, valued at $1 billion.

The gallows humor on Wall Street held that karma had to wait a long time, but Bear Stearns got its just deserts. During the 1998 bailout of LTCM by sixteen financial institutions, one investment banker refused to write a check: Jimmy Cayne.

A decade after that Fed-orchestrated bailout, *Fortune* magazine would dub Cayne "the Nero of the credit crisis," playing bridge, puffing cigars, and smoking pot while his company burned down around him.

Dimon came out smelling like a rose. He had proven his mettle as a "big swinging dick" by insisting that the Fed sweeten the pot by providing JPMC with downside protection to cover the risk of the unknown.

The rescue's fallout for the Fed was swift and unflattering. Congress and the press blasted Bernanke, Geithner, and Paulson for inflaming "moral hazard."

The term "moral hazard" refers to the problem created when one party (an investment bank) engages in risky behavior, knowing that it will be rescued by a second party (the Federal Reserve or the taxpayers), which will incur the cost.

Paulson fully grasped what was at stake. During the negotiations over Bear's salvage, he insisted that the rescue had to hurt. He pushed for the deal to be done at two dollars per share. The bailout had to be humiliating.

Unfortunately, Bear's bailout sent the opposite message to Wall Street: once again, the Fed has our back.

But what was the alternative? Dimon had the full-blown threat of international financial instability on his side in negotiations with Bear and the Fed.

It made me angry to see TV news reports of Bear's former employees leaving the building lugging their belongings, looking like a bomb had gone off. Bear's fourteen thousand employees faced the loss not only of their jobs, but the value of stock held in the company, their retirement, their kids' college tuition.

And I was livid at Greenspan. Bear Stearns had gotten greedy, but the underlying conditions that allowed it to grow so spectacularly and fall so hard wouldn't have existed if Greenspan had the spine to stand up to Wall Street beginning in 1987.

"Gambling has been fed by knowledge that, if disaster struck, someone else—borrowers, investors, taxpayers—would end up bearing at least some of the losses," wrote the *Economist*. At every stop on the securitization gravy train, investment banks generated big fees for themselves. They had no incentive to tap the brakes.

Bear's top executives and even its ferrets allowed themselves to be deluded that the risk to themselves and their firm was minimal because they'd purchased default insurance. But that policy didn't cover an old-fashioned bank run.

Most at the Fed believed that Bear's demise had broken the daisy chain. The fall of another bank was unlikely.

Fed governor Kevin Warsh, a seasoned veteran of Morgan Stanley, was an exception. Only thirty-five when appointed in 2006 by President Bush, Warsh had a law degree from Harvard, not a PhD in economics. The youngest governor in Fed history, Warsh was also the wealthiest member of the FOMC, thanks to his wife, Jane, an heir to the Estée Lauder fortune. In 2006, their combined wealth was estimated at $65.8 to $116.5 million.

Many on the FOMC assumed that Warsh, who bears a resemblance to the actor Tom Cruise, was too good-looking, too rich, and too young to make a serious contribution. But Warsh turned out to be one of Bernanke's most valuable allies during the crisis, his savvy liaison to Wall Street.

At the March 18, 2008, FOMC meeting, just two days after Bear's rescue, Warsh shared his concerns that many other financial institutions were undercapitalized. Geithner disagreed.

"It is very hard to make the judgment now that the financial system as a whole or the banking system as a whole is undercapitalized," Geithner said. "But based on everything we know today, if you look at very pessimistic estimates of the scale of losses across the financial system, on average relative to capital, they do not justify that concern."

Taxpayers, who couldn't appreciate how high the stakes were—to say nothing of the complicated plumbing of the financial system—understood only one thing: the Fed had bailed out some Wall Street fat cats. They demanded answers.

Within a few weeks Congress paraded all the major participants in the

Bear Stearns drama in front of hearings. Geithner insisted that the Fed had to act or risk "a greater probability of widespread insolvencies, severe and protracted damage to the financial system and, ultimately, to the economy as a whole."

Bear's CEO Schwartz maintained that the wool had been pulled over his eyes by the New York Fed in the days before the firm went under. On Friday, March 14, Schwartz believed that the Fed would provide an emergency funding arrangement that gave him up to twenty-eight days to find a buyer.

But late that same night, Paulson told him that he misunderstood the terms of the deal. Schwartz had only until Sunday night, when Asian markets opened. The deal with JPMC was his only option.

In return for the $30 billion taxpayer loan to JPMC, the Fed acquired investment-grade securities and MBSs. A dedicated manager would be appointed to handle the disposition of the assets over a ten-year period, with JPMC agreeing to absorb the first $1 billion of any potential losses.

It was a fantastic deal—for Jamie Dimon. The Fed had left Bear no negotiating power. "Buying a house," Dimon told Congress, "is not the same as buying a house on fire."

Bernanke and Paulson came under swift and scathing criticism from lawmakers. Senator Jim Bunning called for both to resign. Economist Nouriel Roubini called their actions "socialism for the rich, the well connected, and Wall Street."

The Fed's reputation took it on the chin. "Our system has many strengths," Geithner testified. "But to be direct about it, I think we've suffered a very damaging blow to confidence in the credibility of our financial system." Though Geithner was talking about the economy at large, the Bear rescue also marked the beginning of the unraveling of the Fed's mystique.

The SEC opened an investigation into possible illegal manipulation of Bear's stock by certain well-known short sellers. But the stock manipulation investigation went nowhere. Shorts who operate in the shadows know how to cover their tracks.

The mystery was finally solved in March 2016, when records of the Financial Crisis Inquiry Commission (FCIC) were released, indicating that Faber's source was, as long suspected, Kyle Bass, a Dallas-based hedge fund operator and notorious short seller.

It's worth explaining because the situation would be repeated by many other firms as they desperately scrambled to save themselves in the months to come.

Thomas Marano, head of mortgages at Bear, told government investigators that he had contacted Bass to ask about his reluctance to trade with Bear.

Bass had asked other Wall Street firms to "novate," or take his place, in trades of CDSs with Bear. In other words, Bass wanted someone to take on his counterparty risk.

"There were several investors who tried to novate, but Kyle Bass was memorable because I reached out to him to find out his concerns," Marano said. "I heard on CNBC that he had told them that he had tried to novate with Goldman, and they said that they would maybe take it, but he wasn't sure."

Faber did not use Bass's name on the air. But Marano seemed to believe he did.

Goldman had been inundated with so many requests for novations "facing" Bear Stearns that it stopped taking such requests to comply with its own risk management rules.

Late on Tuesday, March 11, when Bass's firm, Hayman Capital Management, tried to close out a $5 billion subprime derivative position, Goldman Sachs refused to take the novation.

"Our trading desk would prefer to stay facing Hayman," a Goldman Sachs employee wrote in an e-mail to Bass early the next morning. "We do not want to face Bear."

But a few minutes later, Goldman sent an e-mail—time-stamped 9:04 A.M.—to say it would accept the trade. That occurred at almost the same time Faber dropped his nuclear bomb on Schwartz.

"The news hit the Street that Goldman had refused a routine transaction with one of the other big five investment banks," the government report later said. "The message: don't rely on Bear Stearns."

Rumor, panic, and fear killed the victim—aided by a huge dollop of hubris.

The best description of what happened to Bear was offered by a chastened Cayne in testimony to the FCIC.

Bear had about $12.5 billion in loans on its books with either deficient or no documentation—more than the company's total value. "That was the business," Cayne said. "What was, really, industry practice. In retrospect, in hindsight, I would say leverage was too high."

Testifying to Congress, Bernanke sounded like the captain of a sailboat who had encountered an unexpected hurricane and was desperately trying to prevent his boat from capsizing.

The Fed was "fighting against the wind," Bernanke said. In a presidential election year, he faced intense political pressure as unemployment and foreclosures mounted.

"With financial conditions fragile, the sudden failure of Bear Stearns likely would have led to a chaotic unwinding of positions in those markets and could have severely shaken confidence," Bernanke said. "The damage caused by a default by Bear Stearns could have been severe and extremely difficult to contain."

Bernanke predicted that the economy would probably slow still further, maybe even slip into recession, but "much necessary economic and financial adjustment has already taken place, and *monetary and fiscal policies are in train that should support a return to growth in the second half of this year and next year*" (emphasis mine).

In addition to cutting interest rates at its March FOMC meeting, the Fed had taken other actions that were "at least offsetting significantly the headwinds coming from these financial factors."

Bernanke was "reasonably confident" that the Fed would recover its money and stressed the unusual nature of the situation, the broadest use of the Fed's credit authority since the Depression. Bernanke portrayed the Fed's actions as a one-time event, concluding, "It has never happened before and I hope it never happens again."

CHAPTER 11

Slapped in the Face
by the Invisible Hand

FED STATEMENT WORD COUNT: 434

EFFECTIVE FED FUNDS RATE: 0.17%

10-YR TREASURY RATE: 3.39%

FED BANKS TOTAL ASSETS: $2,443.52B

DATE: 1/1/2011

You want to put out the fire first and then worry about the fire code.

—BEN BERNANKE, DECEMBER 1, 2008

Among the economists at the Dallas Fed, Bernanke's optimism pre-vailed. The Bear Stearns rescue was the punctuation mark that ended the paragraph. Bernanke would trim the sails to right the founder-ing ship.

I disagreed. The demise of the Bear was a flashing red light that shouted "DANGER." My colleagues rolled their eyes.

Rosenblum treated me with a new respect. The chain of events was playing out as I had predicted. He and I began collaborating on a paper on moral hazard. It would make Rosenblum no fans at the Board of Governors.

The bailout both relieved and alarmed the financial press.

The *Economist* wrote that the Fed was "taking the unprecedented (and, some say, disturbing) step of financing up to $30 billion of Bear's weakest assets. This could cost the central bank several billion dollars if those assets fall in value."

The fear of the unknown prompted the Fed, for the first time ever, to extend lending at its discount window to all bond dealers.

Under previous rules, only institutions offering depository insurance or under strict regulatory oversight were allowed to use the discount window, paying a penalty fee for the privilege. Now any distressed investment bank, broker, or commercial bank was allowed to come, hat in hand, to use the window.

The *Economist* expressed skepticism at this development, saying that fear persisted because the "new Fed window is untested and the very act of drawing on it could rattle markets." No bank wanted to be perceived as the next sick buffalo.

Inside the Fed, the academics naïvely assumed that just because the window was opened it would be used. The people who had been in the market, such as Fisher and myself, knew the stigma associated with the discount window. Borrowers might as well invite speculators into the boardroom to short their stock.

Fisher told the FOMC that if the Fed could coax some "big boys" to access the discount window, "it could be a life-changing event in removing the stigma."

To encourage lending, the Fed at its March 2008 FOMC meeting dropped interest rates again, to 2.25 percent. Fisher dissented, as he would again in April when the FOMC again lowered rates.

Fisher wanted to raise rates instead of lower them. This got under Bernanke's skin. Bernanke "vented" in an e-mail to Kohn the day after the 10 to 1 vote with the subject line "WWGD?": "I find myself conciliating holders of the unreasonable opinion that we should be tightening even as the economy and financial system are in a precarious position and inflation/commodity pressures appear to be easing."

Like Rosenblum, Bernanke had internalized Greenspan's approach to monetary policymaking. The Fed's tradition of consensus was so powerful "in that context a 'no' vote represents a strong statement of disagreement," Bernanke wrote in his memoir. "Too many dissents, I worried, could undermine our credibility."

But tradition be damned, Fisher refused to be a yes man. He always feared the consequences of "pushing on a string"—a phrase with a venerable history at the Fed.

In 1935, Federal Reserve Chairman Marriner Eccles testified during hearings on the Banking Act that little could be done with monetary policy to stimulate growth.

"You mean you cannot push on a string?" Congressman Alan Goldsborough said.

"That is a very good way to put it, one cannot push on a string," Eccles said. "We are in the depths of a depression and . . . beyond creating an easy money situation through reduction of discount rates . . . there is very little, if anything, that the [federal] reserve organization can do toward bringing about recovery."

Fisher feared the same thing was happening. In the middle of what would become known as his year of dissent, he sat down for an interview with the *Wall Street Journal*.

"It's really a question of, are we getting the bang for the buck?" Fisher asked. "And clearly we're not. The system was sputtering and I began to feel that at 3.5%. After that, that's when I dissented," referring to his January 2008 dissent, when the FOMC lowered the fed funds rate to 3 percent.

The problem wasn't interest rates. Banks didn't begin making loans because they first had to shore up their capital bases to cover potential losses from their own toxic waste.

"The U.S. economy was suffering from a breakdown of the nervous system and they wanted to use conventional macroeconomic tools," said Rosenblum years later. "None of these people had ever been through a financial crisis. Their response was the height of tunnel vision, shortsightedness and myopia."

The Fed's medicine was incapable of treating the disease in the system, but they insisted on using it. By doing so, they began to cripple the very banks they desperately needed to convalesce.

In an attempt to keep things flowing, the Fed expanded the type of assets it would accept as collateral from distressed banks, reduced penalty rates to virtually nothing, and speeded up auctions of quality bonds, so banks could put those on their balance sheets and off-load the junk onto the Fed. But there was still no stampede to the discount window.

Buyers of securities had disappeared; the great derivatives locomotive had slammed on the brakes, causing the train cars behind to slam into one another, derail, and slide off the mountain.

In mid-April 2008, the IMF warned that potential losses from the credit crunch foreshadowed by Bear's fall could surpass $1 trillion. As if on cue, Swiss bank UBS reported an $11.5 billion loss and announced that it would cut 5,500 jobs by the middle of 2009.

The bond issuers were the next to get hit. On May 13, MBIA, the world's largest bond insurer, reported $2.4 billion in losses due to write-downs of CDSs. By early June, Moody's announced it would probably downgrade MBIA and the second-largest player, Ambac. S&P followed two days later with a similar announcement.

If only the monoline bond insurers had stuck to their original business of insuring municipal bonds. But the potential for fee generation by selling insurance for CDOs was too tempting.

One after another, financial institutions announced deep losses. The $5.4 billion loss announced by American International Group (AIG), a massive underwater depth charge waiting to explode, was lost in the parade.

The next systemic risk flare-up came from the West Coast. On July 11, 2008, IndyMac Federal Bank, a subprime lender based in Los Angeles and valued at $30 billion, was placed in receivership by the Office of Thrift Supervision (OTS).

Inexplicably, the OTS downgraded IndyMac without informing Yellen, whose bank had been in the process of offering IndyMac loans. What did the OTS know that Yellen didn't?

That week, Congressman Barney Frank (D-Mass.) characterized as "solid" the future prospects of Fannie Mae and Freddie Mac, the two mammoth GSEs that guaranteed three out of every four mortgages in America. And made huge contributions to his political campaigns.

Frank had blocked all attempts by the Bush administration to rein in excesses at Fannie and Freddie. "The more people exaggerate a threat of safety and soundness [at Fannie and Freddie]," Frank said, "the more people conjure up the possibility of serious financial losses to the Treasury, which I do not see. I think we see entities that are fundamentally sound financially."

But the GSEs were on a greasy slide to ruin. The companies had combined outstanding liabilities of $5.4 trillion. By early September, the Fed would be forced to take control of both Fannie and Freddie.

Though Wall Street banks had raised vast sums of capital to buffer themselves against losses, it became apparent by the summer of 2008 that the Fed's hope of containing systemic risk had failed. The *Financial Times* published a table showing worldwide bank write-offs had swelled to $450 billion since January 2007.

As the second quarter ended, investment firms announced more record losses. Merrill Lynch reported write-downs of $4.9 billion on its mortgage-related assets, followed by Citigroup with a loss of $5.2 billion and $7 billion in write-downs, and Wachovia with a loss of $8.9 billion.

The magnitude of the damages got Main Street's attention. On July 31, 2008, panicked depositors withdrew $10 billion from Washington Mutual (WAMU).

In what can only be described as desperation, big banks began selling toxic assets at discounted rates to private equity firms. Though many banks were swept into this fire sale, Merrill Lynch became the poster child, announcing on July 29 that it had sold $36 billion in CDOs for $6.7 billion, or 22 cents on the dollar. Just twelve days earlier, those same CDOs had been valued at $11.1 billion. Had the CDOs suddenly dropped 40 percent of their value?

Or did no one know what they were worth in this lightning-fast market?

Around this time, the New York Fed received a job application from a soft-spoken Hungarian immigrant named Zoltan Pozsar. He attached a paper he had written for Moody's Analytics, "The Rise and Fall of the Shadow Banking System," along with a rudimentary map.

Like me, Pozsar was a finance major and non-PhD. His work vividly reveals how an outsider sometimes sees things more clearly than those inside a system.

Now pay attention, because shadow banking is what caused the financial crisis of 2008. Though the subprime housing market was the virus, shadow banking transmitted the virus and nearly killed the patient. The Fed's army of a thousand "doctors of economics" had no understanding of its enormity and significance. It took a Hungarian with a green card, a fierce curiosity, and a vigorous work ethic to see what was hiding in plain sight.

Born in 1978, Pozsar came to the United States when he was twenty-four, after receiving a graduate degree in finance from a university in South Korea. Definitely not the Ivy League.

He had been working for six years as senior economist and right-hand man for Mark Zandi, chief economist for Moody's Analytics. Somewhat bored with his day job, at night and on the weekends Pozsar began working on a side project that he found fascinating: the structure and growth of the shadow banking system.

The term "shadow banking" had first been coined at the Fed's 2007 Jackson Hole symposium by Paul McCulley, then chief economist of Pacific Investment Management Company (Pimco). Son of a Baptist preacher, McCulley has a knack for colorful metaphors.

During a panel discussion on housing and monetary policy, McCulley used the phrase to describe "the whole alphabet soup of levered up non-bank investment conduits, vehicles, and structures." He described what had occurred in the summer of 2007 as Bear Stearns's hedge funds cratered, the result of a "mighty gulf between the Fed's liquidity cup and the shadow banking system's parched liquidity lips."

Humorous. But the not-so-funny thing is that entities created by Wall Street's largest investment firms made up the backbone of the shadow banking system.

And nobody wanted to talk about it. Shadow banking implied something sinister, mysterious, evil.

In late May, Pozsar sent his paper to the New York Fed. He heard nothing for a month.

Out of the blue he got a message from Bill Dudley: No one on his Markets Desk understood shadow banking. Did he want a job? Pozsar joined the Desk as a senior trader/analyst on August 25, 2008, and was assigned to cover the corporate debt market for the FOMC and Treasury. Though he got a better job offer from a top hedge fund, Pozsar turned it down, saying, "No, I'm going to do this public service at the Fed." My kind of guy.

Pozsar's initial paper outlined the "constellation of forces that drove the emergence of the network of highly-leveraged off-balance-sheet vehicles—the shadow banking system—that is at the heart of the credit crisis."

Off-balance sheet (OBS) is an accounting maneuver used by companies to reduce their debt levels for reporting purposes. Enron perfected the use of OBS partnerships to hide its true liabilities from regulators and shareholders. Many at the Fed believed the OBS demon had been forever exorcized with Enron's fall. But the demon had grown and metastasized, spreading little cancers throughout the financial system.

The resurrection of OBS vehicles had been made possible because banking had been reshaped by deregulation, innovation, and competition. Then the Fed lowered interest rates, creating "an abundance of credit for borrowers and a scarcity of yield for investors." (Thank you, Alan Greenspan!)

Pozsar pinpointed the 1988 Basel I Accord as the main catalyst for the growth and advances of "credit risk transfer instruments" like CDOs, MBSs, asset-backed securities (ABS), asset-backed commercial paper (ABCP), commercial mortgage-backed securities (CMBS), and so on.

Issued after the banking crises of the late 1980s, the new Basel rules required that banks meet a minimum capital requirement and hold even more against riskier assets. For investment bankers seeking to maximize profits, and thus their own compensation, the changes created the need to hide liabilities in the shadows.

As deregulation dissolved barriers to entry in the banking industry, the number of new financial entities exploded, fueled by the demand to finance derivatives backed by an astonishing array of collateral such as taxi medallion loans, intellectual property cash flows, aircraft leases, even pop stars' music royalties.

Financial firms began to employ entities called structured investment vehicles (SIV) and conduits to hold these assets OBS.

Nobody talked about them.

"Indeed, before the subprime financial crisis, few market participants knew that SIVs even existed," Pozsar told me. "There was no institutionalized effort to understand the shadow banking system until I got to the Fed."

Conduits typically held the raw material like whole loans or mortgages and could be especially dangerous.

Think of the game "hot potato." The potato has to be thrown to the next person as soon as possible or you get burned.

The minute a bank or mortgage firm originated a loan, the clock started ticking. In the early years of the housing boom, banks were exposed to mortgage risks for only as long as it took to assemble the pieces of the MBS and off-load it. Buy it. Build it. Sell it. Game over.

But as the derivatives business grew, banks began to accumulate warehouses of mortgage loans in conduits. As the percentage of subprime mortgages increased, that magnified the risk.

SIVs held the structured debts, the sliced and diced hot potatoes, some more combustible than others. To maximize returns, banks often retained most of the "super-senior" investments they created in SIVs. The super-senior tranches were perceived to be so risk free that banks regarded them as "money good."

This "safety," Pozsar said, allowed banks "to reduce the capital associated with the super-senior investments and supercharge their returns on book equity."

This was classic regulatory arbitrage. Bank managers were not unaware of the risks they courted. Wall Street has simply never kowtowed to regulations that pull the plug on profitable businesses. They always find their way around them.

SIVs typically borrowed fifteen dollars for every one dollar in assets. But conduits were 100 percent debt financed, Pozsar said, "essentially being levered to infinity."

At their peak in 2008, the IMF estimated assets held by banks in SIVs at $400 billion and in conduits at $1.4 trillion. The sheer success of the OBS entities created ever more risk.

When high demand meets low supply, what happens? The creation of substitutes, often good-looking but not quite the same, like Marilyn Monroe impersonators. CDO managers and underwriters began using credit default swaps to mimic the returns on MBSs, wrapping them in insurance from monoline bond insurers like AIG.

So-called synthetic CDOs magnified the level of leverage and credit risk in the system, indeed, in Pozsar's words, "exponentially so."

At the epicenter of Pozsar's rudimentary map was the repo system, in which commercial banks and large corporations make overnight loans to each other. (More about repo later.)

Repo connected to the "risk originators" such as finance companies, bank holding companies, commercial banks, and broker-dealers. Those connected to "risks originated for sale": CDOs, MBSs, ABSs, and so on. These in turn branched to SIVs and conduits.

This massive web of debt was issued in capital markets completely outside regulators' purview.

Between the lines Pozsar drew little "explosions" to signal where breakdowns could occur. Near the center of the map was a black box labeled "CREDIT DEFAULT SWAPS," atop which was a dark cloud with a lightning bolt shooting out. Talk about speaking volumes.

Others had awakened to the danger. Just as Pozsar was getting his fingerprints inked for his badge at the New York Fed, a paper delivered at the August 2008 Jackson Hole conference by another outsider described other market mechanisms that rendered the shadow banking system even more dangerous.

Called "The Panic of 2007," the paper by Yale professor Gary Gorton ignited a debate inside the Fed about the shadow banking system that rages still.

After hearing Gorton's ideas, Professor Randall Wright at the University of Wisconsin, a brilliant monetary theorist, commented, "I have no idea what Gary said just now, but I know it's really, really important, so I'm going to sit down and study this until I get it."

If only there had been more thinkers like Wright and Gorton (and Pozsar!) inside the Fed.

Gorton was in a unique position to observe the events of August 2007, when multiple hedge funds crashed.

His research career focused on banking, financial crises, and banking panics. But he also had practical experience. Starting in 1996, Gorton worked as a consultant at AIG Financial Products (AIGFP), a tiny London-based division of the insurance giant. (Remember that name.) He advised the company on structured credit, credit derivatives, and commodity futures. So he had theory and practice to give him insight.

Gorton pointed out that the collapse of numerous hedge funds in the summer of 2007 had been triggered by "wholesale" panics, not "retail" panics like the bank runs of the 1880s, 1907, and the 1930s. Those bank runs ended when the Federal Deposit Insurance Corporation was created in 1934, insuring bank accounts up to one hundred thousand dollars.

During the American banking world's so-called Quiet Period—from 1934 to 2007—some banks failed and thrifts went under, but those did not contaminate the broader banking system.

However, the financial system had undergone deep and treacherous structural changes, negating the fundamental assumptions held by economists about the way the economy worked.

"Economists view the world as being the outcome of the 'invisible hand,' that is, a world where private decisions are unknowingly guided by prices to allocate resources efficiently," Gorton said.

He'd described the first thing I had ever learned from my father about laissez-faire—the philosophy cherished by all Fed economists—as first described in Adam Smith's *The Wealth of Nations*.

"The credit crisis raises the question of how it is that we could get slapped in the face by the invisible hand," Gorton said. (Gorton's quotes are taken from an updated paper that developed his ideas more fully.) "What happened? Many private decisions were made, over a long time, which created the shadow banking system."

In fact, the Fed was a very visible hand, manipulating many private decisions predominantly due to the search for yield.

My own efforts to understand the shadow banking system, with its extraordinary structures and complex terminology, would present the greatest intellectual challenge of my career.

But here goes.

First, realize the trading of derivatives is nothing like trading stocks. When a public company is born, its stock is sold for the first time in an initial public offering. Shares are then bought and sold in the secondary market, also known as the stock market. All trades are transparent and settled in kind, three days after the trade is executed, by delivering the stock. This is Securities 101.

Now, put derivatives at the opposite end of the transparency spectrum in every way.

Performing due diligence on these complex instruments was nearly impossible, even for sophisticated players. Out of this ignorance grew an over-reliance on credit ratings from agencies like Moody's.

The basic task performed by the credit rating agencies was to strip derivatives of their individuality. Whether it was David Bowie pioneering securities derived from the perpetual value his music had created or a 30-year conventional mortgage, once a credit rating had been assigned, investors were agnostic. Bowie's AAA-rated royalties and the AAA mortgage on the house next door were interchangeable, or as Gorton said, "informationally insensitive."

But there was no "stock market" for derivatives.

"Instead," Gorton said, "the secondary market is organized around dealer banks and depends on intermediation via the repurchase market."

Ah, the repurchase or "repo" market, largely concealed from retail investors. Gorton could offer no official statistics about the size of the overall repo market, but unofficial guesses estimated it at $10 trillion.

At its most basic, the repo market is a form of overnight borrowing. From Investopedia: "A dealer or other holder of government securities (usually T-bills) sells the securities to a lender and agrees to repurchase them at an agreed future date at an agreed price."

Repo is used by corporations and other large institutional investors to provide safety and liquidity. The most commonly used form is a "tri-party repo agreement," in which a third party—a custodian bank or clearing organization called the "collateral agent"—serves as an intermediary between the counterparties, or two sides, of a deal.

In a typical tri-party repo, the collateral agent acts on behalf of both buyer and seller, receiving and delivering the securities and cash. The collateral agent protects investors.

The agent prices the securities, which may be discounted—given a "haircut"—to reflect market conditions. A haircut of 5 percent means that a "bank" can borrow ninety-five dollars for each hundred dollars in pledged collateral.

In 2007, when the value of the pledged collateral for Bear Stearns's MBSs began to collapse, panic set in. Other investment banks and hedge funds incited "runs" on their shadow bank counterparts at other financial institutions by refusing to renew repo agreements or by punitively increasing the haircuts.

But the most dangerous piece of the repo puzzle, Gorton said, was that the underlying collateral had been "rehypothecated"—or used as collateral in another transaction with another party.

Let's break it down. In an example of hypothecation, Barney provides a twenty-thousand-dollar loan to Aunt Mabel to buy a car. She makes payments; the car is his collateral. But Barney needs money to remodel his kitchen. So he asks Sidney for a loan, using his revenue stream from Aunt Mabel's car payments as collateral. Now Aunt Mabel's car loan has been hypothecated.

If Sidney takes out a loan against Barney's payments to him, Aunt Mabel's original loan would now be "rehypothecated."

Thus the collateral was backing more than its actual value. A classic house of cards.

As to the extent of rehypothecation in the shadow banking system, Gorton explained that there was literally no data. Zilch.

So the Fed had no official figures on the size of the repo market. Nothing official on repo haircuts. Nothing on rehypothecation.

Shocking. The Fed had allowed this system to flourish under its nose and had no clue as to its size, structure, or danger.

The price of repo haircuts (or cost of collateral) had been essentially zero until August 2007, when it started to rise. A year later, the price shot up, forcing the shadow banking system either to "shrink, borrow or get an equity injection" to make up for the loss, Gorton said. Some firms were forced to sell assets. This caused prices to go down, creating a vicious cycle.

No private agent or clearinghouse had the wherewithal to buy the assets. And the Fed didn't have deployable tools to stem the panic, especially astonishing because the New York Fed was a major participant in the repo market by making collateralized loans to so-called primary dealers.

Designated by the Fed, twenty or so primary dealers must meet certain liquidity requirements, promise to purchase the majority of Treasuries at auction, and redistribute them to clients, creating a secondary market. In exchange for being among the chosen ones, dealers agreed to provide market intelligence to the Fed. Among the primary dealers in 2008 were Lehman Brothers, Merrill Lynch, and Citigroup.

The Fed conducted repos with primary dealers via auctions to implement monetary policy, temporarily adding or draining reserve balances to the banking system as needed. The typical loan term was overnight, sometimes up to fourteen days, and though rare, even up to sixty-five days.

At the initiative of the SOMA, dealers bid on borrowing money against various types of collateral; in reverse repos, dealers offered interest rates at which they would lend money to the Fed. The Fed's collateral was usually Treasury bills.

The Fed typically used a clearing bank to manage the collateral. It accepted only three types of general collateral (GC): marketable U.S. Treasury securities; certain U.S. agency obligations, and certain agency "pass-throughs" (like Fannie Mae or Freddie Mac MBSs).

The "GC" designation means that the collateral is "fungible," or mutually interchangeable, the same way a $20 bill can buy you lunch or a pair of flip-flops.

The importance of fungibility cannot be overstated. The repo market rests on the understanding that the collateral exchanged has an indisputable value.

Primary dealers used Fed repos every day to acquire funds or put funds to use for short periods. Completely benign, because there was a strict "no rehypothecation" rule at the Fed.

Outside the Fed, rehypothecation was allowed with permission of the client who, in compensation for the additional risk, received a discount.

Throw a wrench into the repo system and the world's financial system comes to a shuddering halt.

Shadow banking, combined with the Fed's utter lack of understanding about the true shape of the financial system, set the stage for the catastrophic meltdown of September 2008.

CHAPTER 12

Heads Must Roll

FED STATEMENT WORD COUNT: 454
EFFECTIVE FED FUNDS RATE: 0.09%
10-YR TREASURY RATE: 3.00%
FED BANKS TOTAL ASSETS: $2,865.25B
DATE: 6/1/2011

Some critics have argued that [the Fed's] approach to policy is too undisciplined—judgmental, seemingly discretionary, and difficult to explain. The Federal Reserve should, some conclude, attempt to be more formal in its operations by tying its actions solely to the prescriptions of a formal policy rule. That any approach along these lines would lead to an improvement in economic performance, however, is highly doubtful.

—ALAN GREENSPAN, AUGUST 2003

After Bear's fall, short sellers resumed their hunt. On March 20, 2008, Maria Bartiromo of CNBC called Erin Callan, Lehman Brothers's young and inexperienced CFO, and asked point-blank: "Is Lehman next?"

"Categorically no," replied Callan with characteristic confidence.

At age forty-two, Callan had been appointed CFO in September 2007, plucked from obscurity by CEO Dick Fuld and COO Joe Gregory. Young, glamorous, and articulate, Callan handled herself well with the media.

A few days after her interview with Bartiromo, Callan received a stand-ing ovation from the Lehman trading floor. During the first-quarter earnings call, she had announced Lehman had posted a profit of $489 mil-lion, marking its fifty-fifth consecutive profitable quarter. Amazing since Citigroup and Merrill Lynch had posted sizable losses. Lehman's stock price jumped 46 percent.

A few weeks later, after presiding over Lehman's annual meeting, Fuld brushed off concerns about systemic risk.

"The worst of the impact on the financial services industry is behind us," he said. Wall Street gossips wondered: Did Lehman have better risk managers—or somebody cooking their books?

Investors soon found out. On June 9, Lehman reported its second-quarter earnings: a loss of $2.8 billion. The stock price tanked.

Several days later, a half dozen Lehman senior executives met with Fuld. The perception that Lehman was circling the drain had to be stopped.

"The board has to deliver a head to the Street," one of the execs told Fuld. Preferably two.

Forced into a corner, Fuld lopped off the called-for heads, firing Callan and demoting Gregory. Suddenly, the financial world realized Lehman's troubles went deep.

Founded in 1850 as a cotton trading business in Montgomery, Ala-bama, Lehman had long enjoyed a reputation for prudence and sound man-agement. As it evolved, Lehman survived financial catastrophes like the Panic of 1907, the Great Depression, and two world wars.

But it wouldn't survive the hubris of one of the most successful CEOs in Wall Street history.

Before joining DLJ in 1996, I had interviewed at Lehman, which was aggressively hiring because Fuld, named CEO in 1994, wanted to hit the top of the bulge bracket rankings. Goldman Sachs and Morgan Stanley had long been considered the crème de la crème of investment banks. Fuld was determined Lehman would rise to the same stature.

Wall Street's lean, mean, fighting machine, Fuld earned the nickname "Gorilla" because of his broad, sloping forehead, his intense stare, his ten-dency to grunt instead of speak in complete sentences, and what one col-league described as his "animalistic presence." Fuld embraced his inner ape by installing a life-size gorilla in his office.

Like his mentor Lew Glucksman, Fuld carried a chip on his shoulder the size of a two-by-four and believed doing business meant going to war.

"Every day is a battle," he'd say. "You've got to kill the enemy." At the height of the crisis, Fuld handed out plastic swords to symbolize their fight against nefarious forces trying to take Lehman down. He lashed out at rumor-mongering short sellers, insisting that by managing risk, "I will hurt the shorts and that is my goal."

From an upper-middle-class family, Fuld had joined Lehman fresh out of college. Lehman was a merchant bank when Fuld arrived, growing young companies by helping them find capital and develop business strategies. Fuld would later describe working with "gentlemen who knew what it meant when they said, 'I am your banker.'"

Fuld started in commercial paper and worked his way up. Under Glucksman's stormy leadership, the company eventually foundered and merged with American Express. After that relationship soured, American Express spun Lehman off into a stand-alone company.

When Lehman went public in 1994, Fuld steered Lehman from a fixed-income house—the bond market—into the financial innovations taking hold on Wall Street.

Fuld prided himself on building a team culture inside Lehman. Many of his hires had grown up poor. Few had Ivy League degrees. He paid bonuses largely in stock, which they couldn't sell for five years. That built loyalty and a sense of ownership—and fueled infighting and turf wars.

People either loved Lehman or they left, often the victims of Fuld's fiery temper, unceasing demands, and high self-regard. Whatever his methods, Lehman's earnings grew and its stock started to rise.

Professor Mark Stein of the University of Leicester in the UK later wrote a business management study titled "When Does Narcissistic Leadership Become Problematic? Dick Fuld at Lehman Brothers."

Narcissists are often drawn to positions of power and prestige; their self-absorption and obsessive traits can be positive (constructive) or negative (reactive) for a company. Wall Street attracts narcissists like ants to honey.

Stein concluded that Fuld's "slightly militaristic and brutal way" instilled the company with a "sense of purpose and direction."

Fuld knew the only way to reach the level of the big banks was to supercharge revenues. For that he needed leverage. By 2008, Lehman had borrowed thirty-two dollars for every dollar in its coffers. The ratio at Goldman Sachs and Merrill Lynch? More like twenty-five dollars to a dollar.

Under Fuld's leadership the storied firm thrived, becoming a dominant force in subprime mortgages. But the most significant engine of its success was commercial real estate.

From 2003 through 2007, the firm reported almost $16 billion in profits. Success brought Fuld immense wealth. He owned five homes, from a $25 million apartment on Park Avenue to a $19 million compound in Sun Valley, Idaho. His compensation for the years 2000 to 2007 was estimated at $550 million. By one friend's assessment, the price tag for Fuld's lavish lifestyle hovered around $5 million a year.

But then Lehman's fortunes began to stagger. To see why, one had to look no further than McAllister Ranch, an ambitious development in California's Inland Empire.

On May 29, 2007, even as the California housing market buckled, Lehman Brothers partnered with Tishman Speyer to acquire Archstone-Smith, one of America's largest owners of multifamily properties, for $22.2 billion, the biggest deal Lehman had ever done.

McAllister Ranch was one of Archstone's largest assets. The 2,000-acre development near Bakersfield, encircling a Greg Norman–designed golf course, would feature six thousand homes marketed for $190,000 to $450,000. Two hours from Los Angeles, the boating, fishing, beach club, and other recreational features promised to lure buyers seeking more house for less money.

When colleagues warned that real estate had peaked, Fuld reacted by firing his enemies and plowed ahead with the deal. By May 2008, only a year after Lehman's investment, McAllister Ranch lay desolate, the clubhouse half finished, the golf course only weeds. The disastrous project came to symbolize Fuld's arrogance and self-deception.

As his outrageous bets caught up with the firm, the stock slump continued. To save Lehman, Fuld went to war, determined to report a profitable third quarter. He slashed Lehman's residential mortgage portfolio by 31 percent and that of commercial mortgages by 19 percent. But nothing worked. Fuld attempted to broker deals to sell shares of the company to South Korean or Chinese banks. Those last-ditch efforts would fail.

Years later Fuld would emerge from self-imposed exile to describe what happened to Lehman as a "perfect storm," a confluence of the build-up of a bull market mentality, the government's insistence that everyone could own a home, abnormally low interest rates, and easy credit.

As Fuld described it, the sheer amount of money sloshing around the global financial system was staggering.

Private equity firms had $300 billion under management in 2000; by 2008, that had more than doubled to $800 billion.

In 2000, about four thousand hedge funds managed $500 billion; by 2008, there were ten thousand hedge funds controlling $1.8 trillion. Investors thirsty for yield flooded into these riskier classes of assets.

That insatiable demand drove up equity values, balance sheets, and the need for financing. This heady brew was stirred into an overheated vat with little regulation or market supervision.

Then the Fed took away its famous punch bowl, raising interest rates and choking off the party. The crisis became a "self-fulfilling economic loop."

Fuld's bottom line: The Fed did it, not me.

Well, he wasn't entirely wrong. But Fuld refused to look in the mirror. There he would have seen the arrogant "Master of the Universe" so reckless with other people's money that he ignored reality.

As Lehman's stock tanked, Fuld began peppering Paulson with phone calls, trying to find an exit route.

The treasury secretary wasn't helpful. Bail out the Gorilla? Paulson recognized he was dealing with moral hazard in spades.

It again seemed as if Dimon would come to the rescue. On September 9, at the Fed's urging, JPMC agreed to loan Lehman operating funds; without the deal, Lehman would have had to close its doors the next day. But Lehman had to come up with $5 billion in extra collateral. It couldn't.

"As long as I am alive this firm will never be sold," Fuld had told the *Wall Street Journal* in late 2007. "And if it is sold after I die, I will reach back from the grave and prevent it." Now, one foot in the grave, he frantically began seeking buyers.

On September 10, Lehman reported a loss of $3.9 billion and $7.8 billion in credit-linked write-downs. Though the firm wasn't saddled with massive CDO debt like Merrill Lynch, Lehman had $40 billion in highly illiquid real estate.

Lehman announced it was putting up assets for sale and spinning the commercial real estate division into a separate company, but Fuld could not find an investment bank willing to pay his price.

On the morning of September 12, Bernanke had his weekly breakfast with Paulson. News reports had quoted anonymous Treasury sources indicating Paulson would refuse government assistance to Lehman.

Paulson admitted he had authorized the leaks. He had lassoed two potential buyers: Bank of America and the UK-based Barclays. But they sought the Fed's help.

That morning, Bernanke and Paulson hashed out a plan to get other banks to form a consortium like that employed to bail out LTCM.

On Friday night, September 12, a remarkable meeting occurred in a conference room at the New York Fed. Among those invited were Dimon; John Thain, CEO of Merrill Lynch; Vikram Pandit of Citigroup; Brady Dougan of Credit Suisse Group; John Mack of Morgan Stanley; and Lloyd Blankfein, CEO of Goldman Sachs. Representatives of several European banks with offices in New York were included. (Potential suitors BoA and Barclays were not invited.)

Geithner and Paulson worked on the CEOs. A Lehman failure could torpedo them all.

Paulson's adamant stance—"no public money"—became a source of friction between him and Geithner. "I began to worry that he actually meant it," Geithner later wrote.

The group had forty-eight hours—until the opening of business on Monday—to avert catastrophe. Meetings continued all weekend, with CEOs broken into teams to tackle various issues. They came close to getting an agreement that they would guarantee up to $70 billion of Lehman's troubled assets that any suitor would be loath to accept.

Bank of America CEO Ken Lewis had agreed to contemplate a takeover of Lehman. But Geithner grew concerned after learning BofA hadn't sent in a due diligence team.

Lewis was battling the Fed over details involving his takeover of Countrywide. Bernanke had promised to handle the Countrywide issue, but Lewis refused to consider Lehman until he had assurances from the Fed in writing.

"If you don't believe the word of the chairman of the Fed," Geithner told him, "we have a larger problem." Maybe Lewis was remembering Bear Stearns's Alan Schwartz, who believed the New York Fed had given him twenty-eight days to find funding—but he didn't get it in writing.

Thain had resisted a plan to sell his own company earlier in the week. But sitting in the Fed's hotbox over the weekend forced Thain to face reality. He must save Mother Merrill.

Thain approached BoA, which coveted Merrill's "thundering herd" of sixteen thousand retail brokers. A deal would be announced on Monday, September 15, saving Merrill Lynch from the chopping block.

That left Barclays as Lehman's last hope. At 10 A.M. Sunday morning, September 14, it seemed as if a deal with the British bank would go through. But it derailed. According to Paulson, "They did not want the problems of the U.S. banking system infecting the British banking system."

Later that morning, when the banks' head honchos again met at the Fed, Geithner and Paulson told them the Barclays deal was kaput. Lehman would not be saved. As Paulson put it, "The British screwed us."

At Treasury, the idea had taken hold that though Lehman's collapse would be horrible, investors had had time to get out, since its problems had been known for months.

"Everybody in some part of their brain thought it was a good thing for Lehman Brothers to go under," a Treasury official told the *New Yorker*. "Was this ten percent of the brain? I don't know. . . . But the thought was there somewhere."

If so, they were extraordinarily shortsighted.

As events unfolded, Pozsar was getting up every morning for the 4 A.M. shift as markets in Europe opened, then participating in calls with Treasury, the Fed, and the White House. Though new to the Desk, he was the only one who really understood the shadow banking system. (Pozsar would be seconded to the Research Department to help create credit backstops for ailing banks.)

Word of Lehman's imminent demise leaked out. Lehman employees rushed to the company's headquarters to get their belongings, fearing the building would be sealed off and its contents seized the next morning.

Lehman filed for bankruptcy on Monday, September 15, the largest such court action in U.S. history, valued at $639 billion.

News that Lehman would not be rescued sent Fuld into shock. He later insisted the firm could have survived, claiming Lehman had equity capital of $28 billion, a Tier 1 capital ratio of 11 percent, and unencumbered collateral of $127 billion.

Besides, the Fed had saved Bear Stearns. Why not Lehman Brothers?

Bernanke, Geithner, and Paulson didn't have long to pat themselves on the back for preventing moral hazard. Within hours of Lehman's bankruptcy filing, AIG went into cardiac arrest.

The largest insurance company in the world, with assets estimated at $1 trillion, AIG had four main lines of business: general insurance, life insurance and annuities, asset management, and financial services, with 116,000 employees and offices in 130 countries.

The sudden turmoil stemmed from AIG Financial Products (AIGFP), the 377-person division based in London, where Yale professor Gary Gorton had worked.

AIGFP had written about $500 billion worth of insurance on every conceivable type of derivative.

Started in 1987 by Joseph J. Cassano, a former Drexel Burnham Lambert executive, AIGFP first waded into the derivatives market with interest rate swaps, "plain vanilla" products.

But ten years later, as derivatives evolved, Cassano's division was approached by JPMC with the idea to write insurance on CDOs and similar securities. Because the securities had AAA ratings, Cassano assumed they would rarely pay any claims. AIG's high credit rating meant it didn't have to post collateral on the insurance it issued.

Cassano had found the goose that laid diamond-encrusted platinum eggs. The unit's revenues in 1999 were $737 million; six years later they topped $3.26 billion. Fat profit margins meant high levels of compensation for Cassano.

At a conference in 2007, Cassano boasted that his company worked with a "global swath" of the world's premier "banks and investment banks, pension funds, endowments, foundations, insurance companies, hedge funds, money managers, high-net-worth individuals, municipalities and sovereigns and supranationals."

Most of AIG's industry peers who had followed them into such markets hedged their exposure by buying their own insurance. AIGFP did not, seeing little to no risk in its financial models.

"It is hard for us, without being flippant, to even see a scenario within any kind of realm of reason that would see us losing one dollar in any of these transactions," Cassano had said.

But by early 2008, it was clear that the cocky Cassano's imagination had been woefully inadequate, even delusional. As earnings collapsed, Cassano was forced into retirement in March.

AIGFP had issued more policies on derivatives than it had cash to cover. The "black swan" event of Lehman's collapse triggered the largest margin call of all time. AIG faced paying billions of dollars to banks all around the world.

The failure of parent company AIG could have triggered a global banking cataclysm. No wonder Paulson couldn't sleep and was throwing up during this period, as he later said in his memoir.

I can only imagine his anxiety. I was pacing in my kitchen night after night, watching *CNBC International* for any clues of what was to come.

On the evening of September 13, a Saturday, AIG CEO Robert B. Willumstad called the New York Fed and pleaded for help. AIG was preparing to post a fourth-quarter loss of $62 billion, the largest in U.S. corporate history. The firm needed $40 billion to stay alive.

Geithner told him, sorry, no can do. "There will be no public support" for AIG, he said. The financial industry had to find a solution.

On September 15, all three credit agencies downgraded AIG's rating, forcing the insurance giant to post $14.5 billion in collateral. Though AIG had far more than that in assets—close to $1 trillion—it couldn't raise the cash quickly enough to stave off disaster.

The next day, the Fed injected $70 billion into credit markets to unfreeze overnight lending, but with little effect. European bankers were calling Bernanke, demanding that he do whatever it took to prevent an AIG bankruptcy.

Paulson, Geithner, and Bernanke worried that saving AIG so soon after refusing to help Lehman would appear erratic and unfair. They had to prepare the Bush administration for the fallout.

At 6 P.M. Paulson and Bernanke briefed members of the House and Senate leadership. They had little choice, Bernanke explained. AIG was one of the ten most popular stocks in Americans' 401(k) accounts. The Fed would have to loan AIG $85 billion.

"Do you have eighty-five billion?" asked Rep. Barney Frank.

"I have eight hundred billion," Bernanke replied, a reminder that the Fed could "print" money.

On September 17, the Fed invoked the "unusual and exigent" clause and agreed to bail out AIG for $85 billion through a fund called Maiden Lane II, giving taxpayers a 79.9 percent stake in the company. (It was my thirty-eighth birthday. I felt I had aged a decade over the last twelve months.)

Eventually the bailout would total $184.6 billion, with the Fed taking a 92 percent government stake.

Paulson informed Willumstad that he had to go. Another head rolled down Wall Street, coming to rest alongside that of Dick Fuld.

Bernanke and crew didn't have even a moment to catch their breath when Lehman's collapse ricocheted and blindsided them again.

CHAPTER 13

Breaking the Buck

FED STATEMENT WORD COUNT: 420

EFFECTIVE FED FUNDS RATE: 0.08%

10-YR TREASURY RATE: 1.97%

FED BANKS TOTAL ASSETS: $2,919.55B

DATE: 1/1/2012

Will capitalist economies operate at full employment in the absence of routine intervention? Certainly not. Do policymakers have the knowledge and ability to improve macroeconomic outcomes rather than make matters worse? Yes.

—JANET YELLEN, APRIL 1999

When Bruce R. Bent Sr. and his wife landed in Rome on September 15, they were looking forward to a lovely holiday to celebrate their fiftieth wedding anniversary. The chairman of the Reserve Management Company, Bent had been one of the originators of the country's first money market mutual fund (MMF) in 1970.

Not long after he arrived in Italy, Bent got a frantic call from his son, Bruce Bent II, the firm's vice chairman. In the wake of Lehman's collapse, panicked investors had triggered a run on the fund. By the time the senior Bent was able to get back to New York, the net asset value (NAV) of his company's Reserve Primary Fund, a behemoth valued at $62 billion, had "broken the buck."

Describing this development as unthinkable is an understatement.

An MMF invests in low-risk securities like commercial paper, government securities, and certificates of deposit. To investors, MMFs were cash equivalents: low yield but zero risk.

Normally the NAV of MMFs is kept at one dollar. On September 17, the Reserve Primary Fund was forced to lower its share value to 97 cents because of exposure to Lehman's commercial paper. No other MMF had broken the buck since 1994, in the aftermath of the bankruptcy of Orange County, California.

The news was "really, really bad," said Don Phillips, one of the founders of Morningstar. "You talk about Lehman and Merrill having been stellar institutions, but 'breaking the buck' is sacred territory."

And scores of other MMFs, a $3.6 trillion industry, had lethal exposure to Lehman commercial paper.

Lehman and AIG had played with fire and their shareholders got burned. But what about Aunt Mabel, who slept well at night knowing her savings were safely invested in an MMF, as risk free as a Treasury bill?

The Reserve Primary Fund's board of directors directed their fury at the Fed and Paulson. "Paulson and Bernanke totally fucked this up," the chief investment officer said in a board meeting. "I don't think they thought this God-damned thing through, to figure out what the ripple effects would be."

Lehman's demise triggered a tsunami that swept the globe in waves.

"Lehman Brothers begat the Reserve collapse, which begat the money-market run, so the money-market funds wouldn't buy commercial paper," a Treasury official told the *New Yorker*. "The commercial-paper market was on the brink of destruction. At this point, the banking system stops functioning. You're pulling four trillion [dollars] out of the private sector [money-market funds] and giving it to the government in the form of T-bills. That was commercial paper funding GE, Citigroup, FedEx, all the commercial-paper issues. This was systemic risk. Suddenly, you have a global bank holiday."

At this juncture, I was producing not one but two briefings a day for Fisher. He asked me to do a special in-depth report on the commercial paper market.

On the night of Wednesday, September 17, Bernanke met with his top aides, while Paulson and Geithner and their crews listened on speakerphone from Washington and New York.

"We cannot do this alone anymore," Bernanke said. "We have to go to Congress and get some authority."

They argued and agonized. Paulson fretted that their admission of the emergency circumstances would further destabilize markets.

Finally, someone in New York pushed the mute button, pleading with Geithner to explain that if they didn't go to Congress immediately, "there will be shantytowns and soup lines across the country."

With that, Bernanke found his voice and cut Paulson off. "Hank! Listen to me," he said. "We are done."

The Great Depression scholar Bernanke unleashed a lecture on the hot-shot Wall Street CEO. Bernanke went on for fifteen minutes in what one call participant described as "an encyclopedic tour de force." They had reached the limits of the Fed's authority. Paulson stood down.

The next morning, Thursday, September 18, Paulson and Bernanke met with President Bush, who made a short statement from the Oval Office to soothe investors' anxieties and prevent further runs. Treasury announced it would provide up to $50 billion in funding to insure MMFs, just like the FDIC insured bank accounts. That calmed some nerves, but the bank runs continued.

Paulson beseeched a small group of congressional leaders that evening to pass legislation that would let the government buy up to $700 billion in toxic assets from the impacted banks.

"We are in danger of a broad systemic collapse, and action needs to be taken urgently to head it off," Paulson said. "We need the authority to spend several hundred billion." The price tag was rapidly rising.

Bernanke added a historical perspective. "The kind of financial collapse that we're now on the brink of is always followed by a deep, long recession," he said. "If we aren't able to head this off, the next generation of economists will be writing not about the thirties but about this."

He predicted that they could see "a twenty-per-cent decline in the stock market, unemployment at nine to ten percent, the failure of GM [General Motors], certainly, and other large corporate failures. It would be very bad."

With the blessing of President Bush, on Friday before markets opened, Paulson issued a statement outlining his proposed "troubled-asset relief program" (TARP) to remove "illiquid assets that are weighing down our financial institutions and threatening our economy."

Wall Street breathed a sigh of relief. The stock market rallied. The calm didn't last.

Short sellers had turned their attention away from Lehman to the walking wounded like Morgan Stanley, even Goldman Sachs. They drove down stock prices and kept the fear alive. At the urging of the Fed and Treasury, the SEC board on September 19 voted unanimously to impose a temporary ban on the short selling of 799 stocks. Those who legitimately used short positions to hedge risk were outraged. This wasn't China, after all.

On September 21, Goldman Sachs and Morgan Stanley converted to bank holding companies to gain access to government rescue funds.

In the meantime, the run on Washington Mutual continued. In the week ending September 23, depositors withdrew $17 billion. WAMU was sold the next day to JPMC for $1.9 billion. (Which brings up the question: What would the world financial system have done without Jamie Dimon?)

The bloody, bloody Monday of the financial crisis occurred on September 29, when the U.S. House of Representatives voted down the proposed $700 billion bank bailout bill.

In a vicious backlash, the DJIA crashed, falling 778 points, while the S&P 500 fell by 8.8 percent. But the biggest bloodletting was reserved for the stocks of financial firms, which lost 65 percent of their value in one day.

A chastened Congress and White House approved TARP on October 3, the plan they had voted down days before.

Central banks worldwide scrambled to contain the carnage. One after another, governments injected money into their banking systems and financial markets to stem the tide of systemic risk.

Throughout the fall of 2008, even I was amazed that things had gotten this bad. I installed more televisions in my home so I could move from room to room without missing a single minute of market action. Every day seemed to bring a "holy crap" moment.

My Wall Street contacts were going without sleep, wondering if they would lose their jobs, their retirement holdings. Everybody wanted to know why the Fed's responses kept changing. The Fed had one set of rules for Bear, another for Lehman, yet another for AIG. And then there was Goldman Sachs.

A story in the *New York Times* revealed that Blankfein, CEO of Goldman, had huddled in a private meeting with Geithner at the New York Fed on the morning of September 15, and confided, "the rivets are coming off the submarine."

As crowned ruler of Wall Street, Goldman was also AIG's largest trading partner and a major customer of AIGFP. Goldman acted as a tri-party repo agent for trades between AIG and other clients. The insurer's collapse would blow a $20 billion hole in Goldman's gut.

Paulson had been ethically bound to sever communication with Goldman. Though Paulson had not attended the meeting with Blankfein on September 15, the treasury secretary could no longer avoid dealing with his former firm if he hoped to stem the crisis.

So Paulson requested and obtained conflict-of-interest waivers from the White House and Treasury on September 17, the day Goldman's exposure to AIG was revealed to Fed officials.

But phone records later obtained by the *New York Times* revealed Paulson held frequent conversations with Blankfein and other Goldman personnel long before he sought the waiver.

As early as August 2007, when the markets for asset-backed commercial paper stuttered to a halt, Paulson called Blankfein a dozen times. Over that period, the treasury secretary spoke with Fuld six times, with Jamie Dimon four times, and only twice with Thain of Merrill Lynch.

In fact, Paulson spoke with Blankfein twenty-six times before seeking a waiver.

"We don't know what they talked about," said Samuel L. Hayes, a professor emeritus at Harvard Business School. "Obviously there was an enormous amount at stake for Goldman in whether or not the AIG contracts would be made whole. So I think the burden is now on Mr. Paulson to demonstrate that there was no exchange of information one way or the other that influenced the ultimate decision of the government to essentially provide a blank check for AIG's contracts."

Paulson's spokesperson would later say that the ethics regulations didn't prevent him from speaking to members of his former firm to keep up with "market developments" and that Fed officials handled the primary role in negotiating and crafting the AIG bailout, not the treasury secretary.

But two "senior government officials" who demanded anonymity told the *New York Times* that Paulson was "closely involved in decisions to rescue AIG."

"It's clear he [Paulson] had a conflict of interest," Rep. Cliff Stearns (R-Fla.) later told the *New York Times*. "He was covering himself with this waiver because he knew he had a conflict of interest with his telephone calls and with his actions. Even though he had no money in Goldman, he had a vested interest in Goldman's success, in terms of his own reputation and historical perspective."

The public was making no distinction between Paulson at Treasury and Bernanke at the Fed. The Fed's long-standing problems with communicating the reason for its actions were on vivid display during this weeklong debacle and the months that followed, exacerbated by the Fed's insistence that one of two reports it made to Congress on AIG remain confidential instead of being released to the public.

The Fed's on-again, off-again attitude toward bailouts had gotten an airing in front of Congress on September 24. Bernanke had insisted he believed Lehman's failure would be "absolutely catastrophic. . . . I never wavered in my view that we should do absolutely everything possible we could to prevent a collapse."

But in the end he had failed.

"The Federal Reserve and the Treasury declined to commit public funds to support the institution," he had said. The firm's problems had been known for some time. "Thus, we judged that investors and counterparties had had time to take precautionary measures."

Bernanke modified that answer a few months later when he told Congress that regulations prohibited any action by the Fed because Lehman did not have solid assets against which a loan could be secured. Under the "unusual and exigent" clause, the Fed could lend large sums of money only to firms that had sufficient collateral.

"The only way we could have saved Lehman would have been by breaking the law," Bernanke said. "I was not prepared to go beyond my legal authorities."

But why hadn't he said so at the time? Did he and Geithner consider asking Congress for the necessary authority if such a legal constraint existed?

A few years later, in a hearing before the FCIC, Bernanke added this caveat: even if the Fed had fudged the rules, Lehman was too far gone to save. The panic had taken hold as Lehman's lenders and counterparties tried to recoup their own assets.

"The view was that failure was essentially certain in either case," Bernanke said. If the Fed had given Lehman the emergency funding it required, it would still have collapsed, leaving taxpayers holding tens of billions of dollars in assets nobody wanted.

What if the Fed had given Lehman time to work out a deal with Barclays? Maybe the panic would have ebbed. Think of the jobs saved, the calm restored. In December 2008, the *New York Times* called the failure of the Fed to save Lehman "an epic blunder."

A person involved with both negotiations later told *New York Magazine* that the Fed "could have found a way to save Lehman." Perhaps Paulson believed that the Gorilla's head needed to roll down Wall Street in all its bloody glory.

If Cayne was Nero, Fuld would become the 2008 face of Wall Street greed and decadence. At a hearing before Congress, Rep. John Mica (R-Fla.) told Fuld, "If you haven't discovered your role, you're the villain."

It's hard to feel sorry for Fuld. But the collapse of Lehman cost him as much as $1 billion; he'd kept much of his wealth in Lehman stock. And was Fuld that much different from his peers? After all, soon after being appointed CEO of Merrill Lynch in early 2008, Thain had spent $1.22 million to remodel his office. The price tag included a pair of guest chairs ($87,784), a nineteenth-century credenza ($68,179), a coffee table ($5,852), and a fancy trash can ($1,405).

Steve Rattner, chairman of Willett Advisors, had worked with Fuld in the 1980s. "Some have faulted Dick for having run an incredibly leveraged firm, for not having enough capital," Rattner later said. "But he was also unlucky, because if Lehman had been first and Bear Stearns second, they would have saved Lehman and Jimmy Cayne would have become the poster boy of the crisis."

Tom Russo, former chief legal officer at Lehman, who later went to work as chief counsel for AIG, also cut Fuld some slack.

"You can't look at Lehman in isolation," Russo said. "You have to look at it within the context of Bear, Fannie, and Freddie.... Lehman was simply in the wrong place at the wrong time, because everyone got bailed out, except Lehman."

Maybe, but Fuld was also his own worst enemy. He never accepted responsibility for ratcheting up the risk that led to Lehman's fall. "I think I missed the violence of the market and how it spread from one asset class to another," Fuld later said.

The crisis put the New York Fed on the map in a way that it had never been before. Pozsar helped create backstop facilities for every fault line in the shadow banking system. The Fed needed to inject liquidity into the right places. With lines of credit open at every conceivable central bank, the New York Fed was running the world.

Coordination of decisions by the world's central banks was tricky. Word could not leak out ahead of time. A special meeting of the FOMC by video-conference was called for the afternoon of October 7.

Because they happened to be in New York at the time, Fisher and Plosser joined Geithner at the New York Fed, with all three men on the same camera.

"I just wanted to point out that I have assembled a historic coalition in New York of hawks on both sides of me today," Geithner quipped to Bernanke, who was watching by video in Washington.

"Mr. Chairman, we enjoy visiting Third World countries," Fisher joked back.

"We just thought we would outflank him," Plosser joined in, "but we haven't succeeded."

The financial crisis had raised Geithner's profile to such heights that after the election of President Barack Obama, he was seen as the natural successor to his mentors Summers and Rubin as treasury secretary.

And Dudley, the former Goldman Sachs chief economist, was chosen to take Geithner's place as president of the New York Fed, despite the fact that Goldman was viewed as having too much sway at Treasury and the Fed.

Since the 1930s, Goldman Sachs had a history of encouraging its partners to become involved in public service. Make your money then make your mark. Public service by its alumni gave the firm undeniable clout. The revolving door between government and Goldman Sachs—or "Government Sachs," as the joke went—was never more pronounced than during the 2008 meltdown.

Goldman veteran Neel T. Kashkari became Paulson's right-hand man during the crisis. To lead AIG, Paulson selected Edward M. Liddy, a Goldman director since 2003. To oversee TARP, Paulson turned to Kashkari, who then picked another former Goldman exec to fill a top role on his staff.

But Paulson's actions raised questions about the level of the firm's power inside government, as if Treasury were a "de facto Goldman division," as the *New York Times* put it in October 2008.

Of course, Goldman expats paid a price to serve, but few became career government officials. Their experiences paid off when they cycled back to Wall Street.

Some had feet in both camps. During the financial crisis, the chairman of the New York Fed's Board of Directors was Stephen Friedman, a former Goldman chairman who still sat on the firm's board.

As a Class C Fed board director, he was chosen to represent the public. Yeah, right.

Once Goldman became a holding company, thus a bank the Fed supervised, conflict-of-interest rules prohibited Friedman, who owned 46,000 shares of Goldman stock, from sitting on the Fed board. But on October 6, Geithner asked the Board of Governors to grant Friedman a waiver.

While awaiting the decision, in December Friedman bought an additional 37,300 Goldman shares. Friedman didn't inform the New York Fed board, which didn't have a policy at the time requiring notice of new stock purchases.

The Fed waiver was approved on January 22; the next day, Friedman bought 15,300 more shares because, as he put it, they were "cheap." That brought his holdings to 98,600 shares.

The Fed's bailout of AIG allowed it to pay Goldman what it owed the investment bank: $8.1 billion. Goldman's stock rallied—as Friedman knew it would—and by late spring his purchases had earned a profit of $5 million.

A former president of the Cleveland Fed contended that Friedman should not have been granted a waiver to remain on the board. "You can't get permission to violate the law," said Jerry Jordan.

To top it off, Friedman did the trades even while leading the search for Geithner's successor—who turned out to be Dudley! Government Sachs indeed.

By the end of 2008, American households had lost 16 percent of their household wealth. Actions taken by the Fed and Treasury were universally unpopular. But inside the Fed, they were viewed as absolutely necessary to prevent massive unemployment. The banking system was like the nation's power grid. The Fed had to keep the lights on.

Before the crisis, I viewed blood on the Street simply as damage done to my former peers and their families. But the catastrophe highlighted in rude form a perverse sort of trickle-down economics. As bad as things ever get for those on Wall Street, the damage that trickles down to Main Street is always exponentially worse.

CHAPTER 14

Breaching the Zero Bound

FED STATEMENT WORD COUNT: 485
EFFECTIVE FED FUNDS RATE: 0.16%
10-YR TREASURY RATE: 1.62%
FED BANKS TOTAL ASSETS: $2,863.55B
DATE: 6/1/2012

The U.S. government has a technology, called a printing press (or today, its electronic equivalent), that allows it to produce as many U.S. dollars as it wishes at no cost.

—BEN BERNANKE, NOVEMBER 21, 2002

Bernanke gave a speech on December 1, 2008, that was meant to reassure but spooked financial markets just the same.

His news that the Fed "might" start buying U.S. Treasuries pushed yields to record lows. He intimated that the Fed "might" lower interest rates, which were sitting at 1 percent. It seemed that "Helicopter Ben"—a nickname Bernanke resented—again wanted to shovel money out of the cockpit.

The nickname referred to a famous speech made by then Fed governor Bernanke in 2002 called "Deflation: Making Sure 'It' Doesn't Happen Here." He talked about avoiding the monetary doldrums that permeated Japan and outlined the strategies the Fed could use to battle deflation, like taking interest rates to zero and "printing" money. He mentioned Milton Friedman's famous quote about dropping cash out of helicopters to induce spending—and the nickname stuck to him!

This speech cemented Bernanke's reputation as an intellectual giant inside the Fed. To investors, his convictions equated to an insurance policy against potential losses.

But the unfortunate nickname and the Fed's inability to clearly communicate its policies and intentions frustrated Fisher. Regardless of what Bernanke meant to convey, any hint the Fed would take action propped up the stock market. In the "fog of war," as Bernanke described it, controlling the message was a secondary concern.

The 2008 transcripts of FOMC meetings showcase the Fed's policy committee at its best and its worst: seventeen smart men and women wrestling with extraordinary times, too little or too much information, and a blinkered mind-set.

The transcripts do not include meetings at which smaller groups of Fed and Treasury officials worked on the bailouts of Bear Stearns, Lehman, and AIG.

Nor do they include the impromptu meetings like the one that Bernanke held at Jackson Hole in August 2007. As hedge funds tanked and credit markets trembled, Bernanke pulled a handful of top Fed officials into an empty conference room to talk about a possible Fed response. In the room: Geithner, Governors Kohn and Warsh, Dudley, and board secretary Brian Madigan.

With these core supporters, Bernanke outlined his theories on the zero bound and quantitative easing. Geithner would later call the game plan the "Bernanke Doctrine." (This meeting is absent from Bernanke's memoir, perhaps because he knew it was less than kosher.) Though no action was taken at the time, substantive policy strategies were predetermined, to be fleshed out a year later at the Jackson Hole symposium in August 2008.

No record was made of the meeting. Fisher and Rosenblum were not made aware of this secret discussion—an example of how Fed officials sometimes skirt transparency policies when it suits them. And the impromptu meeting is illustrative of how the chairman, his top allies, and staff perceive the conversation around the FOMC table.

On the day the committee meets, they listen politely. But some actions are preordained. Participants are given two or three possible policy statements, with wording that is then delicately tweaked to reflect the group's consensus.

But the possibilities are dictated by the chairman and staff, not the result of freewheeling discussion around the table. The chairman knows which statement he wants and works on the governors behind the scenes before the FOMC meeting to bring them to his point of view.

From 1936, when the FOMC first met in its current structure, through 2014, 94 percent of all votes have been cast in favor of the policy directive adopted by the committee, according to a study by the St. Louis Fed.

Dissents are not unprecedented. From 1936 to 1995, the number of dissents by governors (219) exceeded those by District Bank presidents (174).

However, from 1995 to 2014, governors toed the line, with only two dissents, compared with sixty-seven by District Bank presidents. Did the publication of transcripts, which compelled the chairman to use persuasion well before the meetings, actually reduce dissent?

After each regular FOMC meeting, at precisely 2 P.M. Eastern Standard Time, the Fed issues a press release with ten to twelve sentences explaining any changes it had made to the fed funds rate, who voted for and against the move and why, and a short statement about economic news that led to its decision. Throughout the crisis, it almost always included the promise that "the Committee will continue to monitor economic and financial developments and will act as needed to promote sustainable economic growth and price stability."

In Dallas, the statement was released at 1 P.M. I would run up the staircase to the break room television so I could watch as a reporter on CNBC read the statement and see how the markets reacted. I was usually the only person watching.

As the crisis descended, the FOMC statement release became a highly anticipated moment for financial markets—and the pistol fired at the start of a race. It lifted the curtain on the "blackout" period, allowing FOMC members to sprint to the nearest TV camera.

During the blackout—which lasts from the Tuesday a week before the meeting until the Thursday morning after the meeting—FOMC members are prohibited from discussing monetary policy with outsiders. This means not only the press, but their barbers, their financial advisers, even other Fed officials, without proper clearance. To prevent traders from gaming the system, no one must know the policy proposals on the table.

After the end of the blackout, Fed officials are allowed to give speeches or interviews to support or criticize the FOMC's actions. Fisher often made the short trip north to New York for the early show on CNBC, first out of the gate to explain his vote.

Greenspan ignored the blackout, though Fed public affairs liked to pretend he didn't, according to former Fed governor Laurence Meyer's book *A Term at the Fed*.

A top economics forecaster, Meyer had to sell his very profitable business to join the Fed, serving from 1996 through 2001. Once he arrived, Meyer was shocked to discover that many of his sophisticated models failed in practice—an honest admission that theory doesn't always hold up.

Meyer differentiated between "sanctioned and unsanctioned signaling." The sanctioned variety meant that the FOMC had reached a consensus and had encouraged the chairman to signal it to the markets. The unsanctioned signal occurred when the chairman or any member of the FOMC leaked information that didn't have prior approval of the committee.

But Greenspan had no qualms about issuing unsanctioned signals or speaking to reporters during the so-called blackout period. (Meyer was once stunned to see a prominent reporter leave Greenspan's office the Monday before an FOMC meeting.) Bernanke and his closest allies continued that tradition through surrogates, including Bill Dudley.

At the FOMC meeting on January 29–30, 2008, Dudley sounded an alarm regarding the Fed's lack of information about the shadow banking system, though he didn't call it that. He mentioned problems with monoline insurers like AIG. But the New York Fed had no direct dialogue with them.

"Unfortunately, there is not much transparency as to the counterparty exposures of the guarantors on a firm-by-firm, asset-class-by-asset class, or security-by-security basis," Dudley said.

Little did the committee realize the bomb Dudley had just dropped inside the conference room. But there was no call to arms, no explanation that in early 2008, the shadow banking system, at $20 trillion, dwarfed the $12 trillion conventional banking system. (By the way, Dudley had no idea how big it was; those figures come from a 2011 paper written by economists at the St. Louis Fed.)

Geithner admitted the New York Fed had not been in touch with the monoline insurers like AIG.

"We have had extensive conversations with the New York State Insurance Commissioner, who is the lead supervisor of many of them, but not all of them," Geithner said. "It turns out that office also has very little information, particularly on the stuff that is on the leading edge of concern, which is to whom they sold credit protection and on what."

The January 2008 meeting ended with the FOMC slashing the fed funds rate to 3 percent, with a 9 to 1 vote. (Only a week earlier, in a teleconference vote, a nerve-wracked Bernanke had pushed to cut the rate to 3.5 percent.) Officially sworn in as a voting member for the year, Fisher told the committee that he had prayed over it, but couldn't join the majority. He preferred no change in the fed funds rate.

"When the market is in the depressive phase of . . . a bipolar disorder," Fisher said, "crafting policy to satisfy it is like feeding Jabba the Hutt—doing so is fruitless, if not dangerous, because it will simply insist on more." He entered his first dissent of the year.

The meeting had a flash of dark humor. Fed governor Frederic Mishkin, speaking of staffers' efforts to report positive news, said the situation reminded him of the Monty Python film *Life of Brian*, which ends with the characters being crucified while singing "Always Look on the Bright Side of Life."

In a March 10 conference call, Richmond Fed president Jeffrey Lacker expressed concern about the Fed's creation of the Term Securities Lending Facility (TSLF), which would lend government bonds in return for toxic MBSs and other problem assets.

The Fed "could equally well rationalize buying tech stocks in late 2000," Lacker said. "This proposal crosses a bright line that we drew for ourselves in the 1970s in order to limit our involvement in housing finance."

Once that line was breached, there was no going back. As the crisis deepened, the Fed increasingly trespassed its mandated boundaries.

The tenor of the March 18 meeting—held just after the rescue of Bear Stearns—was contentious. Bernanke wanted to cut rates again. Fisher was adamant that a rate cut wouldn't help.

"The root problem is a problem of liquidity, solvency, and trust," Fisher insisted. Even Exxon was having trouble with its commercial paper funding.

"We [the Fed] are the water main, and yet the grass is turning brown," Fisher said. "The water is not getting to the grass because the piping is clogged with all the hair and residue and all of the ugly stuff that has been building up . . . that we allowed to happen over a long period of time. I don't believe that cutting the fed funds rate addresses the issue. I do believe that the measures we have undertaken recently to enhance liquidity, to improve the functioning of the system, and to address the solvency issues are of significant import."

Fisher drew a line in the sand. "I am not going to vote for further cuts," he said bluntly.

The FOMC approved cutting the fed funds rate by three quarters of a percent to 2.25 percent. Plosser and Fisher dissented, widening the crack in the unified front usually presented by the Fed.

Unintentionally, the March 2008 meeting provided a hilarious lesson in Fedspeak.

Some context: the economy was under stress after Bear's collapse. Deflation posed an impending risk, but the FOMC was instead worried about rising inflation.

Those participating in the discussion about the crafting of the FOMC statement included Bernanke, Geithner, Fed governors Randall Kroszner, Kohn, Mishkin, and Warsh, Fed District Bank presidents Charles Evans (Chicago) and Dennis Lockhart (Atlanta), and Fed secretary Madigan.

MR. KOHN: On inflation expectations, because they haven't risen very much, I agree with President Geithner. I like the fact that we tell people we are aware, but we could say "have edged higher" or something like that instead of "risen."

MR. MISHKIN: We could use my "smidgen" word, but "edged higher" is better.

MR. KOHN: Went up a smidge.

CHAIRMAN BERNANKE: All right. President Evans.

MR. EVANS: "Edged higher" is an unusual phrase.

MR. MISHKIN: "Have risen somewhat"?

MR. MADIGAN: I think an issue with "edged higher" is that it really does sound as though you have some very specific measures in mind.

CHAIRMAN BERNANKE: Brian, do you have a thought on "risen" versus "risen somewhat" versus taking it out?

MR. MADIGAN: I think if you take it out that very much raises the question of what to do with that language in red about the factors that would push inflation down. It would be tough to drop the inflation expectations thought and not have inflation expectations mentioned anywhere in the paragraph. There would just be vacant space where you had, at least in previous minutes, referred to it.

CHAIRMAN BERNANKE: Anyone else? Bill.

MR. DUDLEY: Adding just the word "slightly"—"risen slightly"—gets to your point.

MR. MISHKIN: "Slightly" or "somewhat" risen.

MR. WARSH: Brian, does "somewhat" mitigate it a little, or does that highlight it?

MR. MADIGAN: I'm not sure. I mean, in my mind it mitigates it.

VICE CHAIRMAN GEITHNER: Somewhat.

MR. KROSZNER: Is "slightly" better than "somewhat"?

MR. KOHN: "Somewhat" is bigger than "slightly."

MR. EVANS: That is 50 versus 25 [basis points] in the old days.

MR. LOCKHART: Mr. Chairman, if I understand the discussion about this, when you say "some indicators have risen somewhat," you are getting into territory that seems sort of mealy-mouthed.

CHAIRMAN BERNANKE: Right.

MR. KOHN: "Risen a little"?

MR. KROSZNER: What is wrong with "slightly"?

CHAIRMAN BERNANKE: All right.

I might have run screaming from the room.

The April 30, 2008, FOMC meeting began with Bernanke's assessment that things had calmed down after Bear's rescue. "Let me first say that I think we ought to at least modestly congratulate ourselves that we have made some progress," Bernanke said.

Yellen, not a voting member, offered her opinion that though the economy had slowed, she did not anticipate a long recession.

To Yellen, Bear Stearns was an isolated event. She expected GDP growth of 1.5 percent during the second half of the year and opined "the likelihood of a severe financial panic has diminished." Yellen added that the Bush administration had recently announced a fiscal stimulus package, and tax rebates would likely "provide a bigger bang for the buck" than similar measures in 2001.

Classic Keynesian economics. Spread the money around. Prosperity will follow. If only.

The meeting ended with Bernanke prevailing upon the FOMC to cut the fed funds rate to 2 percent. Fisher and Plosser again dissented, believing further cuts to the fed funds rate were not only ineffective, but counterproductive.

In June, the FOMC voted to keep the fed funds target rate at 2 percent. The statement sounded a note of calm. "Although downside risks to growth remain, they appear to have diminished somewhat, and the upside risks to inflation and inflation expectations have increased."

Fisher dissented, again insisting the Fed needed to raise the fed funds rate. He made the same solitary stand in August, marking five dissents in a row.

"I think it would be wise, just to shift my analogy here and think in canine terms, to take a newspaper across the snout and call for a 25 basis point increase," Fisher said. "We're always talking about tightening at some point. I think it just becomes increasingly difficult to take that first step." Little did he know.

But Fisher had become the Lone Ranger. Bernanke had a plan that required he stick to the 2007 Jackson Hole script. He was focused on the fed funds rate, not the risks from the shadow banking system. Had a task force been deployed to better understand those connections, there would have been no existential crisis following Lehman's failure. There would have been no Lehman failure. They would never have let it go.

In September, the peanut butter hit the fan, as Rosenblum liked to say. The September 2008 FOMC meeting, held a day after the death of Lehman

Brothers and the day the Fed bailed out AIG, must have felt like a funeral. Seventeen gloomy Fed officials veered off their usual prewritten statements to assess the carnage.

A frustrated Bernanke sounded pistol-whipped. He lamented that the Fed had no policies that defined the terms and circumstances under which the government would and should intervene.

"We don't have a set of criteria, we don't have fiscal backstops, and we don't have clear congressional intent," Bernanke said. "So in each event, in each instance, even though there is this sort of unavoidable ad hoc character to it, we are trying to make a judgment about the costs—from a fiscal perspective, from a moral hazard perspective, and so on—of taking action versus the real possibility in some cases that you might have very severe consequences for the financial system, and, therefore, for the economy of not taking action. Frankly, I am decidedly confused and very muddled about this."

Bernanke was not alone in his muddle. One Fed chief economist in attendance sounded a surreal note of optimism: "Our projection [is] that we're going to get a stabilization in housing in 2009."

In the go-round, Yellen expressed her belief that the economy would escape serious fallout from the financial crisis, but she had become more pessimistic. She managed to throw out some humor at the Fed's darkest hour.

"For example, East Bay plastic surgeons and dentists note that patients are deferring elective procedures," she said. Everyone laughed. "Reservations are no longer necessary at many high-end restaurants. And the Silicon Valley Country Club, with a $250,000 entrance fee and seven-to-eight-year waiting list, has seen the number of would-be new members shrink to a mere thirteen." Such are the economic signposts in California's richest neighborhoods.

Striking a more serious tone, Yellen expressed concern. "The interaction of higher unemployment with the housing and financial markets raises the potential for even worse news—namely, an intensification of the adverse feedback loop we have long worried about and are now experiencing." She was right about that.

Fisher argued for no action on the fed funds rate. "Money doesn't talk, it swears," Fisher said, quoting Bob Dylan. "When you swear, you get emotional.

If you blaspheme, you lose control. I think the main thing we must do in this policy decision today is not to lose control, to show a steady hand."

For once Bernanke agreed. The fed funds rate would be held at 2 percent. "I also agree with those who say that, when the time comes, we do need to be prompt at removing accommodation," Bernanke said, throwing the hawks a bone.

In the end, Fisher voted with the majority, aware any dissent might be misunderstood as criticism of Bernanke's extraordinary actions in the previous week.

Despite misgivings, Fisher voted again with the majority at the gloomy October 28–29, 2008, meeting. The economic news and forecasts were so dire the FOMC voted to cut the fed funds rate again, down to one percent.

Yellen, knowing she would rotate into a voting position come January 2009, began flexing her Keynesian muscles, arguing that propping up the banking system was not enough.

"We are fighting an uphill battle against falling home prices, an economy in recession, and collapsing confidence," Yellen said. "It is not clear whether these steps will reopen credit flows to households and businesses, especially those with less than sterling credit."

More government money was needed. "Given the seriousness of the situation," Yellen said, "I believe that we should put as much stimulus into the system as we can as soon as we can."

Meanwhile the New York Fed was operating 24/7, opening swap lines with foreign banks, handling issues with AIG, TARP, GM, Chrysler, Freddie and Fannie, the Primary Reserve Fund, and the sudden meltdown of Citigroup.

The last FOMC meeting of 2008 took place on December 15–16. The task: to assess the extraordinary state of the financial markets and discuss taking the fed funds rate to zero for the first time since the Great Depression.

Bernanke had nothing less than "regime change" in mind.

On the first day, the standing-room-only meeting was packed with Fed staff. The question Bernanke put on the table: Do we take the interest rate to zero immediately or gradually? At this historic meeting, Fisher challenged Bernanke repeatedly.

Geithner, nominated to take Paulson's job, did not attend. Dudley, awaiting confirmation as the president of the New York Fed, took the floor armed with charts and graphs.

"The recent sharp deterioration in the macroeconomic outlook and the forced deleveraging of the nonbank portion of the financial sector have led to sharp declines in asset values during the past few months," Dudley said. "These losses are likely to intensify the vise on financial firm balance sheets, and that is likely to further impede the Federal Reserve's efforts to ease financial conditions. As a consequence, a broadening of our suite of liquidity facilities that bypass banks and dealers may prove to be necessary."

My translation: Everybody's screwed and we're out of ammo.

Enter QE and ZIRP. Quantitative easing meant pumping money into the system by buying Treasury bonds. Zero-interest-rate policy meant taking the fed funds rate to the zero bound. In addition, the Fed would actually pay interest on some bank reserves. Bernanke had outlined this approach in the "Helicopter Ben" speech in 2002 and a 2004 paper called "Monetary Policy Alternatives at the Zero Bound." He'd had this plan in his back pocket since the impromptu Jackson Hole meeting in August 2007.

The Fed was following the Bank of Japan into territory that, so far, hadn't worked for them.

Fisher's concern had been building since the meeting in October. Alarmed, he challenged Bernanke's proposal, self-deprecation barely hiding his sarcasm.

"I am the least well-educated on this subject matter and not as erudite in my understanding," said Fisher. "What we have been doing is implicitly acknowledging that standard monetary tools are not as effective as they could be because of the financial frictions that we have encountered in the marketplace. . . . If we are going to target the monetary base, I worry about the operational consequences of doing so, since it seems to me that is an open-ended question."

James B. Bullard, president of the St. Louis Fed, Plosser, and Lacker also weighed in with doubts.

"We don't have any models to draw on," Lacker said. "In any event, even were we to focus solely on our primary objectives for growth and inflation . . . I think we would have a great deal of difficulty figuring out a quantitative relationship between the monetary base at the zero bound and our objectives."

Plosser also seemed skeptical. "Once we are in the situation in which our policy rate is effectively zero, it does become a constraint on monetary policy. . . . Eventually, however, we would need to bring policy rates back up in line with economic conditions, to avoid a permanent increase in long-run inflation expectations. That will be a tricky task to be sure."

Yellen spoke at length in support of the zero bound. "We could also consider using the FOMC minutes to provide quantitative information on our expectations." Massage the minutes. See how the market reacts.

It is doubtful the average American household comprehends how manipulative the Fed is when it comes to communication. Three weeks after the FOMC, the "minutes" are deployed as just another monetary tool.

Fisher jumped in again after Yellen's long speech.

"Mr. Chairman," Fisher said, "my colleague Harvey Rosenblum made an interesting point the other day that we're at risk of being perceived as migrating from the patron saints of Milton Friedman and John Taylor to a new patron saint—Rube Goldberg."

Interesting choice of "saints." Friedman suggested to a colleague that the country would be better off if all the Fed's data were programmed into a computer to make all the policy decisions, because when the FOMC did it, "things get messed up."

And Rube Goldberg: saint of cobbling odds and ends together to create a rickety machine that does nothing useful.

Fisher maintained that cutting the fed funds rate to zero was misguided, a "diversion of our focus and energy." He warned that the Fed should not adhere to the "old orthodoxy" of manipulating interest rates. Superlow interest rates had gotten the economy and financial markets into this mess in the first place.

"Adding to our difficulties is the fact that we simply do not know how financial intermediaries or money and capital markets will behave and function when interest rates get this low," Fisher said.

Japan had been wallowing in a zero-interest-rate environment for years. By following its lead, the Fed risked fostering zombie corporations and banks.

"I have worked and lived in Japan and we have learned from what they've done," Fisher said. "But the fact is that we have no sustained experience in the modern era in the United States with T-bill rates and the effective fed funds rate trading near zero. We do know that money market funds will become unprofitable if rates get much lower. Let me just say to those who sort of dismiss that"—meaning Yellen—"I think we might look a little foolish if we drove some of them out of business, especially after creating two special facilities to support their continued intermediation functions on the basis that they were critically needed for their roles in the commercial paper market." The Fed also would be risking the destruction of banks that depend on depositors to maintain profitability.

The afternoon session ended with Bernanke saying they would reconvene next morning; he asked the bank presidents to keep their go-round briefs short. "Just to remind you that there's a reception and dinner available for your convenience. There will be no business conducted at that dinner. Thank you. See you in the morning."

Fisher skipped the FOMC dinner. He stayed at the Chevy Chase Club; it was cheaper than the Fairmont, and also quieter. He had a rum punch with his meal, then went for a long, cold walk in the woods around the Club, going over his brief in his head, fully aware of the ramifications of the FOMC's vote the next day.

He had no doubts about what he was going to do. He rarely tossed and turned before momentous decisions. At age nineteen, he'd been aboard a boat called *The Following Sea* when it was overtaken by a terrific storm two hundred miles southeast of San Diego. The boat sank, throwing Fisher into the ocean.

"I spent the night in the water before being rescued at dawn by the Mexican Coast Guard," he told me. "I vowed while I was lost at sea that if I survived that horrific night, I would never be afraid of any challenge again."

Before bed, Fisher prayed, as he did before all FOMC meetings, just as he had since his days of taking exams at Harvard: "If I am worthy, then show me the way." He slept soundly.

The next morning started with staff projections, which were uniformly gloomy. The go-round, in which each district bank president reported regional conditions, was replete with anecdotes of the dire conditions cascading from Wall Street to Main Street.

Despite the bad news, a handful of them expressed skepticism about the zero bound. Fisher raised his main concern: would Bernanke's extraordinary "regime change" really work as anticipated? At the time, the "real" fed funds rate, which subtracts inflation from the quoted rate, was nearly minus 2 percent.

Fisher insisted that establishing a fed funds rate between zero and one quarter percent would trigger an "enormous backlash" from bankers and money market funds, arguing that it was counterproductive, and it created an unnecessary distraction. Fisher mentioned one CEO who was "quite pleased that he could borrow $40 million over the weekend for a total of $250." The back and forth came to a head, with Fisher saying he would vote against the rest of the committee.

Bernanke held firm. "Today is the end of the old regime," Bernanke said. "We have hit zero."

The tension in the room was palpable as Bernanke called for a vote. Ten people voted yes for taking the rate to zero immediately. "With some reluctance," Plosser said, "I will vote yes."

Fisher entered the only no vote. His opposition was a terrible affront to Bernanke after all he had been through in the previous four months.

The meeting broke for a quick lunch. Rosenblum pulled him aside and tried his best to convince Fisher to take one for the team. Nothing less than the Fed's spirit of consensus, its collegiality, its credibility was at stake.

Though he often heeded Rosenblum's advice, Fisher always marched to his own drummer.

Fisher excused himself to take a solitary walk. He paced a long hall of the Eccles Building, wearing a groove in the tile. He wrestled with his thoughts, the immense responsibility, the "no confidence" message a dissent would send to the public.

After the break, Bernanke made an unusual announcement, no doubt with pride: "On consideration, in order to maintain a united front with the Committee, President Fisher changed his vote to 'yes' on the resolution."

Fisher had argued for Main Street, worried about the precedent the Fed was setting. At the time, the public had no idea he had dissented. It would be five years before the transcript would be released, noting his initial vote. Even then, Fisher was attacked by the press for being shortsighted. After all, Bernanke had saved the day!

CHAPTER 15

The Walking Dead

FED STATEMENT WORD COUNT: 645

EFFECTIVE FED FUNDS RATE: 0.14%

10-YR TREASURY RATE: 1.91%

FED BANKS TOTAL ASSETS: $3,008.70B

DATE: 1/1/2013

> I will be the first to say that it is always difficult to get monetary policy just right. But the Fed's analytical prowess is top-notch, and our forecasting record is second to none.
>
> —JANET YELLEN, JUNE 30, 2009

As I walked into the Research Department's conference room at the Dallas Fed one Monday morning in early 2009, I felt a knot as big as one of my Italian grandmother's meatballs lodged in my gut. Sweaty palms, heart palpitations.

Two dozen economists sat around the huge table, their analysts and assistants in chairs against the conference room wall, maybe forty people in total. When I took a chair, the eyes of a few economists swiveled to look at me as if to say, "What is *she* doing here?"

It was my first presentation at a "pre-brief." I was thrilled. Another step closer to my mission. But I also felt like throwing up.

For nearly three years I had endured the economists' snide remarks, their snobbery, their intellectual arrogance. Now I would be an open target.

The Friday before each FOMC meeting, three economists chosen by Rosenblum formally briefed Fisher on the developments in regional, national, and international economies since the FOMC had last met. This event happens at all the District Banks, same day, same time.

The pre-brief occurs on the Monday of that week to give all the department's economists a forum to challenge their peers' data, models, and conclusions before the reports are edited, printed, and collated. The official Briefing Book is hand-delivered to the president the Thursday before the formal briefing on Friday at 10 A.M.

(This is in addition to the Beige Book, with analysis of economic conditions in each district, received by FOMC members two weeks before each meeting. FOMC members also received the Greenbook with staff forecasts, and the Bluebook with staff analysis of monetary policy alternatives, which were merged in June 2010 to become the Tealbook. Reams of material to digest, but with a significant lag in tumultuous times.)

My predictions had been profoundly validated by the events of the previous fall. Showing his belief that the Fed needed to include the financial system in its economic assessments, Rosenblum broke new ground by adding my reports, now labeled "Markets Brief," to the Dallas Briefing Book, highlighting my rising stature inside the Fed. The economists reacted like Rosenblum wanted to add a heretical book to the Bible.

I first had to undergo a more detailed background check. Upgraded from a Class III to a Class II Clearance, I was given access to "restricted controlled" documents dealing with policy input.

Rosenblum presided over these three-hour marathons. He opened by handing out bottles of his special "Rosenblum" wine (no relation) to recognize those whose papers had been published in a prestigious journal since the previous meeting.

Then it was time for the tigers to feed, ripping each other's work to shreds, challenging their charts, their seasonal adjustment methodology. Gulp.

The pre-brief order is the same as that for the formal briefing, a go-round style. Economists loved to walk through their reports one graph at a time. It was the only forum to show off their wares.

My nervousness dissipated soon after I was called on. Naked curiosity was on everyone's faces as I started with a recap of the first few months of 2009.

The year had started in chaos as the aftermath of the crisis throttled the economy. In January, the S&P 500 Index got off to the worst start in its history. The DJIA was down more than 50 percent from its peak in October 2007—similar to the decline recorded in October 2002, and the same magnitude of the early stages of the Great Depression.

Blackstone Group CEO Steve Schwarzman estimated the crisis had destroyed 45 percent of global wealth. *Pfffftttt!* Into thin air.

The Fed's bailouts had propped up the sickest patients with shots of penicillin, but the disease—the debt-driven risk that had built up in the system—could not be easily cured, even with ZIRP and QE.

A stock market rally for the ages in March had been triggered by an announcement by Citigroup that it would return to profitability for the first time since late 2007.

But, as I explained, Citigroup's recovery was smoke and mirrors. Accounting tricks. New rules allowed banks to move so-called "legacy assets" off their balance sheets; mark-to-market accounting was suspended. Nothing had changed but perceptions.

Jumbo loans, commercial real estate, and credit card debt had been written down to a small extent, but not to the level the intensity of the recession suggested was necessary.

The deluded "groupthink" was that time would heal the legacy assets on bank balance sheets. But most of these assets would never again flirt with par value. Until the necessary catharsis took place, policymakers would be unable to take the markets and financial system off monetary life support.

Yes, there was a rally in distressed debt. But a rally gone too far is vulnerable to a shot fired from anywhere within the financial system. A steadier rebound would have laid the groundwork for a more orderly unwinding of the multitude of nonfinancial firms destined to fail in the coming years.

That marked the end of my brief. Whew. I could breathe. The economists had a few questions, but my work was based on sources of information with which they were unfamiliar. I wasn't speaking their language. Even so, it never got easier.

That Friday morning, I convened with Rosenblum, Duca, and about a dozen other Fed economists to formally brief Fisher.

True to form, he had digested the three-inch-thick document and did not need a chart-by-chart explanation. Briskly he went around the table, asking for any important updates. When Fisher called on me, I added several bullet points on the latest market developments. Fisher understood market-speak and Rosenblum was a quick and willing study.

Over time, I tended to be the contrarian in the room, but that wasn't my goal. Lacking Class I clearance, I had to get up and leave during the policy discussion over the two or three proposals requiring the FOMC's vote. There was immense peacocking among those who were allowed to stay.

Though it was taboo to recognize it inside the Fed, and I didn't dare put it in my report, Greenspan's legacy as the Maestro had been thoroughly tarnished.

The general realization that Greenspan and the Fed had actually created the conditions that made the debacle possible was a real wake-up call. The *Wall Street Journal* revisited Rajan's prescient paper at Jackson Hole in 2005. If Rajan had seen the crisis coming, why hadn't Greenspan and his acolytes at the Fed?

And why had the Fed sacrificed Lehman? From the moment Lehman filed for bankruptcy, financial firms struggled to extract their money from its associated shadow banks. As the *New York Times* put it, Lehman had become the Roach Motel of Wall Street. Investors had checked in, but they couldn't check out.

Counterparties were trying to disentangle their assets—complex derivatives, futures, options, stocks and bonds—from Lehman, which was now being dismantled by bankruptcy administrators in the United States and the UK. Some funds could take write-offs and live to see another day. For others, Lehman's collapse proved a death knell.

The Fed had been forced by its own mistakes into creating an elaborate alphabet soup of backstops for the shadow banking system, which included:

- The Commercial Paper Funding Facility (CPFF), to backstop commercial paper and asset-backed commercial paper (ABCP) issuance of loan originators and loan warehouses.
- The Term Asset-Backed Securities Loan Facility (TALF), to backstop asset-backed securities (ABSs). (This is not to be confused with the Term Securities Lending Facility [TSLF], which provided twenty-eight-day liquidity to primary dealers.)
- Maiden Lane LLC, to backstop Bear Stearns's ABS warehouse.

- Maiden Lane II LLC, to backstop AIG's various mortgage-backed securities.
- Maiden Lane III LLC, to backstop AIG's toxic credit default swaps and CDOs.
- The Term Auction Facility (TAF) and the Foreign Exchange (FX), to handle swaps with foreign central banks.
- The Primary Dealer Credit Facility (PDCF), to backstop the tri-party repo system.
- And finally, the Money Market Investor Funding Facility (MMIFF).

These Fed-created facilities put a floor under the shadow banking system and finally checked the run. (These didn't include the various programs created by the FDIC, the Treasury, or Congress.)

The loans the Fed made were secret. Vermont Rep. Bernie Sanders, an avowed socialist who in 2015 launched a run for president as a Democrat, later sponsored legislation that compelled the Fed to disclose financial details of its extraordinary efforts to save Wall Street.

Released in late November 2011, the data, which covered twenty-one thousand Fed emergency loans totaling $3.3 trillion, revealed for the first time how close some of the biggest names on Wall Street came to the brink of disaster. The release gave details like the borrowers' names, amount borrowed, interest rate charged, even collateral.

The Fed's backstops rescued even Wall Street's healthiest players. Morgan Stanley accessed the PDCF 212 times for the year from March 2008 to March 2009. Goldman Sachs borrowed overnight from the Fed 84 times for a total of $600 billion.

Foreign banks also queued up for these loans after Lehman fell on September 15, 2008: Barclays Capital, Deutsche Bank, BNP Paribas, and UBS. (The European Central Bank used the Fed's swap lines 271 times.)

TAF, which allowed banks to avoid the stigma of the discount window to obtain emergency funding, was accessed by Citigroup twenty-six times, MetLife Bank nineteen times, and JPMC seven times. (TAF ended in March 2010.)

TALF provided one-month emergency loans against certain collateral to top investment banks including Goldman Sachs (fifty-two times), Morgan Stanley (thirty-four times), Citigroup (sixty-five times). Big bond companies also relied on TALF, including Pimco, which borrowed $7.1 billion.

The CPFF, created in October 2008, was used by GE, Chrysler Financial Services, AIG, and GMAC. These Fed loans also went outside the traditional banking world, to McDonald's Corporation, Verizon, and the sovereign Korea Development Bank. (Those who used the stigmatized discount window remained confidential.)

The single neediest day? December 5, 2008, when the Fed loaned a combined $1.2 trillion.

After the data release, Fisher defended the Fed's actions as the lender of last resort. "We took an enormous amount of risk with the people's money," he said. "And we didn't lose a dime, and in fact, we made money on every one of them." It was a rare moment when Fisher and Bernanke were on the same page.

After the financial crisis, at every FOMC meeting the Fed was drawn into embracing broad responsibility not only for stabilizing the financial system, but for reviving job growth, strengthening the housing market, and making sure all children got proper orthodontia.

Okay, I made that last one up. But the Fed's dual mandate of maximizing employment and minimizing inflation had been crumpled into a ball and thrown into the trash as it shifted from putting out the fire to rebuilding the burned-out house.

At the FOMC meeting in January 2009, Fisher, who no longer had a vote, warned that the Fed's ZIRP and QE could backfire.

"It strikes me that there is enormous fear in the marketplace about the potential for open-ended stimulus in fiscal policy," Fisher said, "and there is great concern that we will acquiesce by monetizing fiscal policy."

Technically it takes two to tango to monetize the debt. The Treasury first issues the debt and the Federal Reserve buys that same debt, which increases the money supply. Effectively, it gives Congress an open checkbook and allows policymakers to put off making hard choices that budgetary constraints would otherwise force. The idea always made Fisher's blood boil. And with good reason. Unconstrained politicians? Need I say more?

His fellow hawk Lacker fretted that the Fed's interventions would interfere with the creative destruction needed to clear out deadwood, uncompetitive industry players who would gain access to the bond market and, by doing so, keep the lights on. Did someone mention zombie banks in Japan?

"People make choices on their way to making adjustments," Lacker said.

"Would these leveraged borrowers like there to be a greater demand for their liabilities? Yes. This all looks as though demand is low. I will ask you a question. The buggy whip industry—is that sector broken?"

After Obama's election in November, rumors had swirled that Summers and Volcker were being considered for treasury secretary. But Obama wasn't ready for a changing of the guard. He tapped Geithner as Paulson's replacement, a vivid illustration that the New York Fed presidency can be a stepping-stone to greater power.

Geithner was sworn in as treasury secretary after clearing up a small matter of unpaid taxes, writing a check for $42,702, which included interest, for unreported income from 2001 to 2004. (Hadn't anyone noticed that small problem when he was vetted to be New York Fed president?)

Bernanke's term wouldn't be up for another year. Obama could have made his displeasure known and pressured the chairman to step aside if he felt change was needed. But Obama wanted Bernanke to stay.

On February 9, 2009, Bernanke called a special videoconference meeting of the FOMC to give everyone a heads-up about the Fed's potential role in a proposal by Geithner for banks to undergo "stress tests."

"As you'll see when I go through the plan with you, the details are fairly lacking," Bernanke told the disembodied heads on TV monitors. "That, in part, is on purpose. The political strategy is to provide an overall structure with some detail, but not a great deal of detail, with the idea that the public discussion and the congressional discussion will create some buy-in on the political side. It's like selling a car: Only when the customer is sold on the leather seats do you actually reveal the price."

You could also call this a bait and switch. Bernanke was getting the hang of this Washington thing.

Calling BoA and Citigroup the Fed's "problem children," Bernanke explained that the strategy was "to provide the framework to get the Congress involved within certain parameters, and then, only when there is some consensus on how the plan will work and what the key elements will be, to negotiate whether additional funding beyond $350 billion is necessary."

Call me cynical, but I do like to know what my used car will cost before I buy it.

There were political advantages to keeping the cost on the down low. "I will say that both I and the staff—Bill Dudley and others—are somewhat concerned, at least given the way things stand now, about the market reaction," Bernanke said. "First, the lack of details will create some uncertainty and concern. . . . Secondly, I think the markets will be disappointed in the following sense: As I will describe, this is a real truth-telling kind of plan. . . . It's not about using accounting principles to give [banks] back-door capital. It's very much market-oriented and 'tough love.'"

The banks' shareholders would probably scream bloody murder. And they did, especially after the results of the Fed's Supervisory Capital Assessment Program (SCAP) revealed that several large banks, including BoA, were woefully undercapitalized.

Meanwhile, the Fed continued to accept toxic assets from some of the same banks. By the end of February 2009, the Fed would hold $17.5 trillion in bank debt, mortgage-backed securities, and Treasury notes.

In a speech at the Kennedy School of Government in February, Fisher lamented "the very deep hole [our political leaders] have dug in incurring unfunded liabilities of retirement and health-care obligations" that "we at the Dallas Fed believe total over $99 trillion." The Fed's QE was digging the hole deeper.

The stock market continued its downward slide like a skier with a death wish on an icy slope. On March 6, 2009, the S&P 500 Index hit an intraday record low of 666.

It's rare to say a trading day can spook you. The sign of the devil—666—in the stock markets is not something you easily forget. Okay, call me superstitious. But the sentiment among those I knew on Wall Street could only be described as apocalyptic despair. By mid-2009, unemployment had reached a twenty-five-year high of 8 percent and was still climbing.

To send a message of confidence, Bernanke made a rare television appearance on CBS TV's *60 Minutes*—the first by a Fed chairman in more than twenty years. Correspondent Scott Pelley joked that when he initially approached the Fed a year earlier to interview Bernanke, his staff laughed him off.

But times had changed. Bernanke had finally gotten Fisher's message: Get your story out there. Repeat it. In February, Bernanke had spoken to the National Press Club. Earlier in March he spoke to the Council on Foreign Relations. Each time he made himself available for question-and-answer sessions.

"I'd just like to say to the American people that I have every confidence that this economy will recover, and recover in a strong and sustained way," Bernanke told Pelley. He was seated on a bench in his hometown of Dillon, South Carolina, where he had worked construction and waited tables while wearing a poncho, proof that Bernanke had experienced life on a bottom rung of the economic ladder.

Dillon had fallen on hard times. Plants had closed. Unemployment stood at 14 percent. The house where Bernanke grew up, sold a decade earlier by his parents, had been foreclosed on after the owners fell behind on their mortgage.

Bernanke realized that people were mad over the bailout of AIG. "I slammed the phone more than a few times on discussing AIG," Bernanke said. "It's absolutely unfair that taxpayer dollars are going to prop up a company that made these terrible bets."

But recovery couldn't happen until financial markets and banks were stabilized. Rest assured, Wall Street had gotten the message as well that "the era of this high living, this is over now." (I burst out laughing at Bernanke's naive idea that Wall Street was devastated.)

Bernanke admitted that the Fed had made mistakes amid the turmoil of September 2008. "I don't want to deny that we certainly could have done a better job, and others could have done a better job."

But the Fed had responded, and was effectively printing money to finance the rescue of the financial system rather than relying on taxpayer funds.

"When the economy begins to recover, that will be the time that we need to unwind those programs, raise interest rates, reduce the money supply, and make sure that we have a recovery that does not involve inflation," Bernanke said. He insisted that "green shoots" of positive growth were appearing in some areas.

If so, not everyone's garden had gotten the memo. During the March 2009 FOMC meeting, bank presidents described shriveled prospects for their local economies.

In Yellen's district, people were breaking into their piggy banks, literally. "The Cash Product Office reports huge increases in the amount of coins being brought into our inventory," Yellen said to laughter. "The December inventories of quarters and dollar coins were up more than 50 percent from 2007, and even pennies were up nearly 25 percent."

This tidbit of economic news was alarming. What would make people scour their homes for loose change except the inability to buy food and meet other immediate needs?

Yellen added that conditions were so bad "that I actually open the Greenbook economic projections with greater trepidation than my 401(k)."

Fisher reported that his business contacts were also pessimistic: "One [CEO] actually called me and said, 'Do you want some good news?' And I said, 'Please.' He said, 'Call somebody else.'"

Yellen pushed hard for additional monetary stimulus.

"Household wealth has plummeted," she said. "It fell more than $5 trillion in the fourth quarter alone. Unfortunately, households were not well positioned for such a shot to wealth. Instead, many had leveraged up to the hilt, and the combination of the dramatic loss in wealth and the massive household debt overhang portends years of subdued spending as households go through an extended period of deleveraging."

Skeptical aside: might this have had something to do with the housing bubble?

"Despite our best efforts at using both traditional and nontraditional monetary tools, the stance of credit market conditions has only improved modestly," Yellen said. "In past recessions, the Fed has been able to fuel a turnaround rapidly by stepping on the accelerator through sharp rate cuts. But in the current crisis, it feels more like we are desperately trying to power a bicycle uphill rather than pressing an accelerator on a high-powered sports car."

Yellen dismissed concerns expressed by Fisher and others who were trying to slam on the brakes, aware the Fed was being blasted as a political tool of the Obama administration.

"I don't think we've lost our independence," Yellen said. "I think people realize these are unusual and exigent circumstances, and taking a step like that now is a favorable thing for the economy."

By the end of the March 2009 FOMC meeting, the group approved a significant expansion of its bond-buying program. To the existing plan to buy $600 billion in mortgage bonds, the Fed tacked on an additional $1.05 trillion in mortgage bonds and Treasury securities.

Talk of stimulus growing from billions to trillions was music to investors' ears. They were finally convinced that the Greenspan Put would indeed be continued by Bernanke.

But that dramatic expansion of bond purchases wasn't enough for Yellen, who called for more stimulus at the April 2009 FOMC meeting.

"Now that we've tested the waters, it's time to wade in by substantially increasing our purchases of Treasury securities," Yellen said. "I prefer to take appropriate, bold action to stimulate the economy sooner rather than later." The FOMC held off in April, but she would come back with the same argument in May and June.

Yellen did nod to ultimate "exit strategies"—raising the interest rate and ending QE. But the Fed wouldn't need to worry about that until maybe 2012 or so, she said, when the economy had improved.

Neither Yellen nor Dudley had a strong argument for the likely benefit of QE. Though it seemed purchases of mortgage bonds was helping, the rationale for buying Treasury securities was sketchier.

"We don't know exactly how much a Treasury purchase program would do, but, if we start one, we'll be able to answer that question," Dudley had said in March 2009. So throw all the spaghetti on the wall and see what will stick.

At the April 28, 2009, FOMC meeting, it seemed Bernanke's "green shoots" had failed to propagate. The global recovery was "slow and tentative," said D. Nathan Sheets, director of the Fed's international finance division.

"In the realm of green shoots," Sheets said, "our forecast is much more like a small potted plant or a vulnerable asparagus garden than a large leafy tree."

The Fed's lack of clear direction distressed Lacker. "This last discussion has been fascinating against the backdrop of our not having a clear sense of exactly why and how expanding our balance sheet affects the world," Lacker said. "I think we're really groping in the dark here. I think we need to recognize that."

But doing nothing versus groping in the dark was untenable for this group of policymakers. The massive bond purchases continued.

The economy might have been nonresponsive, but the stock market was convinced. The Dow rallied in April and ended May up by 31 percent. Everyone breathed a sigh of relief. The Fed's ministrations had worked Wall Street magic.

I wasn't so sure. As Bernanke had told the FOMC in April at some unexpectedly good bit of economic news, "false dawns have occurred in previous recessions."

Fisher wanted the Fed out of the stimulus program, the sooner the better. He told the *Wall Street Journal* in May 2009 that "the perception of risk" created by the Fed's purchases of Treasury bonds, MBSs, and GSE paper was making investors nervous.

During a recent trip to China, Fisher had been grilled by senior officials of the Chinese government about "whether or not we are going to monetize the actions of our legislature." Made sense since the Chinese were among the biggest buyers of U.S. Treasuries.

"I think the trick here is to assist the functioning of the private markets without signaling in any way, shape or form that the Federal Reserve will be party to monetizing fiscal largesse, deficits or the stimulus program," Fisher said.

Fisher reiterated his belief that the Fed had played a large role in creating the financial crisis with ultralow interest rates.

"Throughout history, what the political class has done is they have turned to the central bank to print their way out of an unfunded liability," he said. "We can't let that happen. That's when you open the floodgates."

Fisher's constant refrain on debt was beginning to get on people's nerves. The *Wall Street Journal* reporter pointed out there had been "rumblings in Washington about revoking the automatic FOMC membership that comes with being a regional bank president."

"I am not losing a lot of sleep over it," Fisher said. "I don't think that it'd be the best signal to send to the market right now that you want to totally politicize the process."

In June, Fisher boarded a plane to Washington for the FOMC meeting. He didn't have a vote but he had a voice. Loaded for bear, Fisher blasted Bernanke with both barrels.

"I'm beyond particularly uncomfortable," Fisher told the FOMC at the June 2009 meeting. "I think we have to be very careful that we're not perceived as basically providing facilities to prop up institutions that are too big to fail at the expense of other institutions that desire to grow."

But Fisher had no vote; the FOMC continued on its path of QE and ZIRP.

As the fever of the crisis broke and some level of calm returned to the markets, Fisher no longer required my daily reports. In addition to the FOMC

Markets Brief, which were produced eight times a year, I began writing longer articles exploring the tight links of the credit and housing crisis to the financial markets. These became the basis for speeches I gave at conferences and for groups like Financial Executives International and the Lumbermen's Association of Texas.

I quickly discovered that these disparate audiences had an avid appetite for insight about the Fed. Initially nervous about public speaking, I embraced my new role as an educator. If this was my only contact with the public, I would have to get over my fears. And I always learned something from the audience Q&A.

In August 2009, it appeared as if the American economy was responding to ZIRP and QE. Home builders increased their building on both orders and speculation. Car dealers were running out of models eligible for finance under the government's "Cash for Clunkers" plan. Economists responded by tripling their second half GDP forecasts.

Markets are windows into the future; by definition current equity and bond prices already reflect forecasts for growth to come. (The National Bureau of Economic Research would determine that the recession triggered by the financial collapse had ended in June 2009. But the FOMC wouldn't know this for almost a year.)

A continued rise in the price of risky assets, however, stemmed from a steeper assumption: that new "mousetraps" were in the offing. Mousetraps refer to drivers of future growth, including job creation, external demand, and so-called animal spirits.

Animal spirits, a term famously coined by Keynes in 1936, are catnip to central bankers.

"Most, probably, of our decisions to do something positive, the full consequences of which will be drawn out over many days to come, can only be taken as the result of animal spirits—a spontaneous urge to action rather than inaction, and not as the outcome of a weighted average of quantitative benefits multiplied by quantitative probabilities," Keynes wrote.

In other words, the instinct to do something, *anything*, is powerful. You could see that being played out by the FOMC.

It was fitting that in 2009, Akerlof (Yellen's husband) and Shiller, both Nobel Laureates, published a book called *Animal Spirits: How Human Psychology Drives the Economy, and Why It Matters for Global Capitalism*.

"From blind faith in ever-rising house prices to plummeting confidence in capital markets, 'animal spirits' are driving financial events worldwide," read the publisher's catalog. The two warned that a steady hand of government was required to carefully manage animal spirits.

But it's really tricky to manage animal spirits once they're released.

Stocks kept rising despite bad news: the persisting oversupply in the home ownership and rental markets would keep a lid on GDP growth, and wage declines had settled in, inhibiting consumers' capacity to consume.

And yet stocks rose. "Money on the sidelines is still waiting to be put to work" summed up the conventional wisdom. That echoed the mind-set and steadfast resolve of investors during the Roaring Twenties, when the top 1 percent of U.S. families accounted for 24 percent of all personal income—as was the case in 2007.

On August 28, 1930, on the eve of the Great Depression, the *Wall Street Journal* put it thus: "There's a large amount of money on the sidelines waiting for investment opportunities; this should be felt in the market when 'cheerful sentiment is more firmly entrenched.' Economists point out that banks and insurance companies 'never before had so much money lying idle.'"

Almost seventy years later, on September 12, 2009, the *Journal* had this to say: "There is plenty of cash still to be put to work. In the U.S., money-market funds contained $3.54 trillion as of Wednesday [August 9], according to the Investment Company Institute, down from a March peak of $3.9 trillion but still a huge amount."

The problem was the bulk of these trillions was in the hands of few. Those who were most insulated from the need to earn a living were driving the rally. Any middle-class recovery was an illusion.

That's the problem with economic expansions driven by animal spirits. In the boom-boom days of the housing bubble, four of every ten jobs created were related to real estate. In the aftermath, economists began to realize how nonproductive it had been to build all those homes. Many of the jobs subsequently lost would never return.

And yet here was the Fed, with Yellen its biggest cheerleader, once again trying to build an economic recovery on the back of frenetic animal spirits.

Obama liked the Keynesian direction Bernanke, a Republican, was taking the Fed. In August, he announced his intention to reappoint Bernanke to a second four-year term, saying that his "background, temperament, his courage, and his creativity" had prevented another Great Depression.

The reaction from Bernanke's critics in Congress was mixed. A hearing in the Senate for his reconfirmation, said Minority Leader Mitch McConnell (R-Ky.), "will be an opportunity for the chairman to provide greater transparency on the actions the Fed has taken, and greater insight into the cumulative impact the administration's trillions in new spending, borrowing, and debt will have on the American taxpayer."

The mounting debt alarmed Fisher and Rosenblum, as did the growing concentration of deposits at just three banks. By August 2009, JPMC, Wells Fargo, and BoA held nearly one third of the country's deposits. Needless to say, they were glad to have fewer competitors.

At the briefing of the Dallas Board of Directors in September 2009, Rosenblum made a special presentation few will ever forget. Channeling country legend Merle Haggard, Rosenblum, wearing a cowboy hat, introduced himself as "Merle Hazard" and asked the tickled audience to guess if there would be inflation or deflation to come. (Actually, Merle Hazard is the nom de guerre of Nashville money manager Jon Shayne, who wrote the song and sings it on YouTube.)

Everyone join in at the chorus!

"Inflation or Deflation?"

As we go through this recession
As farther down we slip
Will our central bank get traction soon, or
Will it lose its grip?

It's a mini-Great Depression
Our markets went berserk
The Fed is printing trillions now, but
Will their efforts work?

Inflation or deflation?
Tell me, if you can

Will we become Zimbabwe
Or will we be Japan?

Credit markets came undone
And still are in distress
Will the dollars in my mattress
Buy much more next year or less?

It's a desperate situation
When you're at the zero bound
If a tree falls in a forest,
Is it making any sound?

New money makes inflation
If folks who have it spend
But if it only sits there,
Then the misery will not end.

Inflation or deflation?
The choice is looking grim
I wonder what John Maynard Keynes would say
If we asked him.

Inflation or deflation?
Tell me, if you can
Will we become Zimbabwe
Or will we be Japan?

Rosenblum joked that the Fed should sell T-shirts emblazoned with the motto: "We Manufacture Moral Hazard."

The September 2009 FOMC meeting would be a testing ground for yet another battle between what had evolved into the Yellen faction and the Fisher faction, with a few moments of thigh-slapping humor.

"I agree with Presidents Evans and Yeltsin—Yellen," said Boston Fed president Eric Rosengren at one point in the discussion. Getting the white-haired little lady with the Brooklyn accent mixed up with the vodka-swilling Russian president Boris Yeltsin provoked guffaws all around.

"I've gone drinking with Janet," Fisher interjected. "She's no Yeltsin."

More laughter. "Okay, the last two minutes will be struck," Bernanke said.

All still collegial. But the frequent clashes on the FOMC and the high-profile opposition Fisher was mounting against QE and ZIRP grated below the surface of the FOMC's cordial interactions.

At the beginning of every FOMC meeting, Fisher greeted Yellen with a kiss. She always responded with good humor and grace, maybe a giggle. But they represented the opposite ends of the spectrum. One camp within the Fed included those bank presidents from Boston, New York, Chicago, and San Francisco, which were home to big financial firms. The other camp included bank presidents from Dallas, Kansas City, St. Louis, and Philadelphia, which had more diverse economies. They wanted to look at costs versus benefits of each program.

After the September meeting, Fisher and Rosenblum published an op-ed in the *Wall Street Journal* called "The Blob That Ate Monetary Policy," contending that banks that the Fed deemed "too big to fail" had rendered the Fed's traditional monetary policy tools ineffective.

"While the list of competitive advantages TBTF institutions have over their smaller rivals is long, it is also well-known," they wrote. "We focus instead on an unrecognized macroeconomic threat: The very existence of these banks has blocked, or seriously undermined, the mechanisms through which monetary policy influences the economy."

The interest-rate channel was gummed up. Rates that mattered for the recovery of the economy—those paid by businesses and households through mortgages, auto loans, credit cards—had risen rather than fallen. The banks with the most toxic balance sheets restricted their lending activity to shore up their own margins.

"Japan paid dearly for propping up its troubled banks in the 1990s," wrote Fisher and Rosenblum. "We need to develop supervision and resolution mechanisms that make it possible for even the biggest boys to fail—in an orderly way, of course. We want creative destruction to work its wonders in the financial sector, just as it does elsewhere in the economy, so we never again have a system held hostage to poor risk management."

The conflict on the FOMC was being played out in public. In October

2009 alone, FOMC members fanned out and gave thirty speeches. Governor Warsh, who had experience on Wall Street, argued that the Fed shouldn't delay a rate hike.

"If policymakers insist on waiting until the level of real activity has plainly and substantially returned to normal," Warsh said, "they will almost certainly have waited too long."

Thomas Hoenig, president of the Kansas City Fed, didn't call for a rate hike but came close. "My experience tells me that we will need to remove our very accommodative policy sooner rather than later," he said in a speech to a business audience. "Even if we were to start immediately, much time would pass before incremental increases could be considered tight or even neutral policy."

At the November 3–4, 2009, FOMC meeting, Brian Sack, now head of the Markets Desk, said that investors had taken note of the "considerable volume" of recent commentary by Fed officials.

"I'm all for Central Bank transparency, but this may be going a bit far," Sack said. Everyone laughed, but who was he telling to shut up?

"Many of those speeches were seen by the markets as containing directional information about the likely course of monetary policy," Sack said, "and investors saw some of those messages as conflicting with one another."

Very perceptive on the part of investors.

The stock market had become "euphoric." Veteran market watchers followed Citigroup's proprietary Panic/Euphoria model to gain contrarian signals. Panic mode means expected returns are high, triggering savvy investors' salivary glands. A signal to buy. When investor sentiment is euphoric, expected returns are low. A signal to sell.

In early 2009, markets had been deep in panic territory, signaling a buying opportunity. But by November, I was warning Fisher that the model had pierced into euphoria—an extraordinary reversal in a short period of time. My concern was that rampant animal spirits had decoupled markets from the fundamentals of the underlying economy.

Not much had changed by December. If anything, markets were staging an early New Year's Eve celebration, behaving as if drunk on champagne. The economic data had continued to paint a mixed picture. But regardless of whether a given data release was good or bad news, as long as they understood rate hikes were not in the cards, investors would party, under the assumption that the Fed had their backs.

When Bernanke walked into the boardroom at the Eccles Building for the December 2009 FOMC meeting, everyone gathered around the massive table rose and gave him a standing ovation.

Time had just proclaimed Bernanke its "Person of the Year," singularly responsible for battling back recession, boosting employment, and restoring confidence to the financial markets.

That magazine cover left me unsettled, bringing back memories of the February 1999 issue with Greenspan, Rubin, and Summers, "The Committee to Save the World." More like destroy the world. Bernanke had spent the better part of two years cleaning up their mess—one that he was also complicit in creating.

Bernanke said he recognized that there were still "fairly substantial" calls for the Fed to be doing "a lot more" coming from many stakeholders: Congress, Wall Street, policy advocates. In other words, everyone wanted more stimulus spending. The wealth effect generated by spreading money around would promote consumer spending, which would increase employment, which would prompt more home sales.

To his credit, Bernanke voiced skepticism.

"Mortgage rates are already extraordinarily low," Bernanke said at the December 2009 meeting. "It's not clear that we can lower them much more."

Fisher pointed out that wage and salary increases had fallen sharply in the Eleventh District. The deteriorating performance of consumer and commercial real estate loans were exerting new pressures on the financial system. The overabundance of fresh regulatory initiatives had fomented uncertainty in corporate America. That uncertainty was holding back hiring and capital expenditures in the United States, threatening long-term economic growth.

In fact, many CEOs and CFOs had announced plans to deploy "CapEx" dollars outside the United States until there was greater clarity about future policy initiatives.

At the December meeting, the FOMC unanimously agreed it was time to stop buying bonds. "One-Note" Yellen acquiesced but told the committee that if the Fed's retreat from stimulus went badly, "I think we may need to resume purchases."

Yellen was fixated on spending as the solution to the country's continuing economic woes. Her staunch adherence to Keynesian theory blinded her to the reality that not every economic problem could be solved by throwing money at it.

I never did get that whole self-actualization concept in my required psychology courses in college. But that year, I flirted with the idea. I felt like my work had truly made a difference.

But I had a burr under my saddle—John V. Duca, my immediate supervisor in the bank's hierarchy. He began calling me into his office before each pre-brief and nit-picking my work to death, editing it to conform to "Fed" tone and style because it was being included in the Briefing Book. He derided various data sets because they were unconventional and not seasonally adjusted, thus unproven by the test of time. What if something I wrote embarrassed the Bank?

Never, ever embarrass the Bank.

I defended my work. Some data sets were new and provided insight into current market conditions. Others, for example a poll done by Gallup, were included to show investor sentiment. They let Fisher know what he needed to know right now, not next year.

Duca's scrutiny and mean-spirited attitude got so bad that at the end of 2009, I approached Rosenblum to ask him to intervene. My work was being molded to fit the Fed's paradigm, which effectively negated the unique perspective it provided to Fisher. My complaint fell on deaf ears.

"You're a professional," Rosenblum said. "I have the utmost confidence in you. Make it work."

Discouraged, I returned to my office determined to do just that. Against great odds, I had made it to the inner sanctum of Fed policymaking. I couldn't give up now.

CHAPTER 16

Dr. Ben Pulls a Bait and Switch

FED STATEMENT WORD COUNT: 697
EFFECTIVE FED FUNDS RATE: 0.09%
10-YR TREASURY RATE: 2.30%
FED BANKS TOTAL ASSETS: $3,478.67B
DATE: 6/1/2013

> For my own part, I did not see and did not appreciate what the risks were with securitization, the credit ratings agencies, the shadow banking system, the SIVs—I didn't see any of that coming until it happened.
>
> —JANET YELLEN, FINANCIAL CRISIS INQUIRY COMMISSION, NOVEMBER 15, 2010

Remember actor Bill Murray in the movie *Groundhog Day*? This cynical weatherman, sent to broadcast the emergence of Punxsutawney Phil from his burrow, was doomed to relive the same day over and over. In 2010, the markets began acting like it was precrisis 2007.

The stock market's manic behavior and perverse reactions to bad news suggested it was in an extremely fragile state. The worse the news was, the more markets seemed to rally.

As long as the Fed kept its QE machine up and running, the markets were pleased. So was the new Congress.

Even so, Bernanke faced surprising opposition in his bid to win reappointment as Fed chairman. In a contentious hearing before Congress in

December, he was even assailed by a staunch supporter, Sen. Chris Dodd (D-Conn). Though Dodd commended Bernanke's leadership, he said the Fed's poor supervision of the banking sector was at least partly to blame for the financial crisis.

"Why should I give an institution that failed in that responsibility the kind of exclusive authority we're talking about here?" Dodd asked, arguing for bank supervision to be given to a separate agency.

But Bernanke had gained the respect of District Bank boards of directors around the system. Even as political foes were saying they would never vote to reconfirm Bernanke, presidents like Fisher and board members like Herb Kelleher, who had great political contacts, went to bat for him.

"It wasn't just the Dallas directors," Rosenblum said. "It was the St. Louis directors, people around the system. Was he regarded as the perfect leader? No, but this was not time to change jockeys. The crisis was not fully behind us."

Bernanke may not have even known about these behind-the-scenes maneuvers. On January 28, 2010, the Senate voted 70 to 30 to confirm Bernanke for a second four-year term as Fed chairman. A few days before his official swearing-in, the Fed closed several of its emergency liquidity programs and its swap lines with foreign central banks, a signal that it believed the worst of the storm had passed.

In the spring of 2010 I got a real office inside the Dallas Fed instead of a cubicle. And I mean inside. No windows. Smaller than my walk-in closet. But at least I had four walls and a door that could be shut while I talked on the phone, deemed necessary because I was holding conversations with important contacts on Wall Street on matters of policy considered "restricted."

Overjoyed, I asked if I could get a TV monitor with CNBC.

Nope. Sorry, only Mr. Fisher and the break room can have a TV. The wiring in the bowels of the building was too complicated. Or so I was told.

By mid-2010, high-yield capital markets were sending asset prices soaring, leading some to question whether overly abundant liquidity had encouraged "bubblelike" behavior.

But these were "low conviction" rallies. Volumes dipped lower and lower, with fewer participants fueling the market. The lower the volume, the thinner the veneer of confidence.

Rosenblum started calling me the Fed's "worry beads." There was plenty to fret about. I was constantly revising my FOMC report for Fisher. On the morning of the formal briefing, I'd get up at the crack of dawn to update the document I'd finalized on Tuesday. Fisher especially valued direct feedback from traders on desks in New York. They were closer to the action than the New York Fed; in fact, they were the ones feeding the Markets Desk its intelligence.

The more proprietary it was to my ears—actual pricing on commercial mortgage-backed securities (CMBSs) or the vulnerability of certain securities to Fedspeak—the more it interested Fisher. He tracked information on credit spreads like a bloodhound. (A spread compares a riskier credit instrument, like a corporate bond, to a Treasury of similar maturity.)

A lot of the data came from big investment banks or ratings agencies like Moody's, but I also looked for unusual data sets that might shed light on a risk zone, like the Ceridian-UCLA Pulse of Commerce Index. Though it had only been around since 1999, in its young life the PCI tended to presage older, more historic sources.

Duca continued to complain about my use of unconventional data sets. He just didn't get it. I wasn't trying to compete with what Fisher was going to get from the Markets Desk, just augment it. The problem was that the financial crisis had changed so much that relying on historic data, released with long lag times, was a dangerous sport. The unconventional nature of QE distorted markets, lending further value to unconventional data.

In March 2010, the Federal Reserve found itself at its first major crossroads since the crisis erupted.

Not only was the Fed pulling back from being the largest buyer in two major credit markets, TALF was winding down and the FDIC had implemented stricter accounting rules that threatened consumers' access to financing even as the pace of the economic recovery remained fragile.

Fisher seemed to be the only member of the FOMC who was not frazzled at the prospect of the markets throwing a hissy fit. He knew there would be a rocky period but that markets adapt.

Looking past that, he ramped up his campaign for legislation to break up the "too-big-to-fail" banks.

"I think the disagreeable but sound thing to do regarding institutions that are [too big to fail] is to dismantle them over time into institutions that can be prudently managed and regulated across borders," Fisher said on March 3, 2010, in a speech before the Council on Foreign Relations.

Even Greenspan had come around to this position. "If they're too big to fail, they're too big," Greenspan had said in the autumn of 2009 in a speech before the same audience. "In 1911 we broke up Standard Oil—so what happened? The individual parts became more valuable than the whole. Maybe that's what we need to do."

Greenspan went on to what appeared to be an out-of-body experience, criticizing his successors at the Fed and Treasury—Bernanke and Paulson—for bailing out Bear Stearns and AIG.

"It's going to be very difficult to repair their credibility on that because when push came to shove, they didn't stand up," Greenspan said.

Let's get this straight. Bernanke and Paulson were the bad guys for bailing out Bear and AIG, even as Greenspan failed to supervise them from the get-go?

Little surprise that Dudley took umbrage at the notion that the big banks needed to be forced to downsize. While giving lip service to "too big to fail" creating moral hazard, Dudley's proposed solutions involved the creation of government authorities to wind down failing financial companies, raising bank capital requirements, improving regulatory abilities to assess risk, and insuring that firms were sufficiently liquid.

At no time did he mention the word "size." To my mind, the most elegant pathway out of TBTF was a modern-day version of the Glass-Steagall Act. Remove the taxpayer from the situation, leave the gambling to the investment banks, and call it a day.

An illusory calm hypnotized the markets in April 2010. In the three weeks after QE ended at the end of March, U.S. equity markets reached their highest level in two years.

Meanwhile the VIX, sometimes referred to as the stock market's "fear gauge," dropped to 15.23, its lowest point since July 2007—the eve of the credit crisis. All was well. But not for everybody.

Traders' lifeblood is volatility. If something is steady, you can't profit on its moves.

Therein lies the irony of Paul Volcker's 1979 decision to let interest rates float. Previously, they had always been held to a fixed rate, but Volcker—in a moment the markets will never forget—opted to cleave to his monetarist teachings with an attempt to control interest rates by using the money supply, not the fed funds rate.

Less than three years later, the Fed had to go back to setting interest rates. But in the interim Volcker had unleashed volatility in the bond market as never before. More trading meant money, money, money. As captured in *Liar's Poker*, Wall Street never looked back.

In time, securities brokers got so clever at this volatility game that they devised an index to trade: the VIX.

Now a household word, this ticker symbol for the Chicago Board Options Exchange Volatility Index was created to show the market's expectation of thirty-day volatility.

In practice, the VIX reflects the upper and lower bound of where investors perceive the S&P will trade over the next thirty days, gauging investors' attitude toward near-term risk in the stock market. The lower the VIX, the less concerned investors are. When it gets to be too low, however, it begins to flash a different kind of danger, that of complacency.

It stands to reason that as stocks rebounded by 80 percent, the VIX had declined by 70 percent. Maybe QE and other Fed actions had cured the market of any PTSD that lingered from the crisis.

But I couldn't shake my discomfort with the low-conviction nature of the rally. Trading volumes had declined by a third.

History wasn't repeating itself but it sure as heck was rhyming. Parallels emerged with events of 2007 and 2008. I had to wonder if they were scaring the tar out of Bernanke, given the worsening situation in Europe.

To its credit, America had taken the financial crisis as an opportunity to clean up its banking system. But the rot in European banks lingered. The bills were coming due.

On April 23, 2010, Greece's government asked the European monetary authorities for a bailout. In response, the European Central Bank handed down severe austerity measures: public sector salary cuts, higher taxes on alcohol and cigarettes (egad!), and stricter retirement policies.

In early May, German chancellor Angela Merkel told lawmakers in Berlin that a $140 billion plan proposed by the IMF to bail out Greece was "about nothing less than the future of Europe and the future of Germany in Europe."

In early May, enraged Greek workers went on strike, paralyzing transportation and shutting down schools and hospitals. Thousands of demonstrators took to the streets of Athens on May 5.

That morning, I awoke in a Windy City hotel room to troubling images on the television. Demonstrators stormed the Parliament building in Athens. Someone flung a gasoline bomb into the Marfin Egnatia Bank; three people were trapped by the fire and died from smoke inhalation. Tremors shook European financial markets, sending the euro to a fourteen-month low of $1.28.

I was attending the Chicago Fed's 46th Annual Conference on Bank Structure and Competition. I checked the headlines and trading levels between panel discussions and presentations. "Systemic risk" was a prominent topic. Athens, anyone?

At the evening Fed meet-and-greet reception, I shook hands with Bernanke, the next morning's keynote speaker. I was struck by how soft-spoken he was. No rock-star aura at all. Bernanke was a shy academic who had adjusted to fame, just barely, the antithesis of the socially savvy Greenspan.

The next morning, the ECB announced it would not offer Greece a bailout. More rioters took to the streets of Athens. As I walked into the conference's luncheon, the DJIA was down 300 points and dropping fast. After each course, I checked my phone under the table, trying to be discreet. Down 500 points. The buzz in the room started to rise. By 1:55 P.M., the market had collapsed, down 700 points and still dropping.

My heart racing, I looked around and was stunned to see the Fed economists chatting amiably in their seats. Enough was enough. I abandoned my dessert and made a mad dash for the exit with the handful of markets people in the room. We huddled around tall tabletops, staring at our phones in horror. By the end of lunch, the market had crashed 1,000 points.

Catastrophe. Billions of dollars lost! Frantic portfolio managers sweated bullets as they calculated their losses and wondered if they would still have jobs when they got back to their offices.

But then something even stranger happened. Within five minutes the market rebounded 600 points and stabilized, as if the seventeen-minute plunge never occurred. What the hell had just happened?

While stock markets do crash, immediate rebounds like that were unprecedented. I started calling all of my contacts on trading desks. They had no answers.

I spent time over the next few months consulting with my peers at the Markets Desk as they zeroed in on high-frequency trading (HFT) as the cause of the "flash crash," which wiped out $1 trillion of investors' equity.

I was surprised at how little proprietary data the Desk had on HFT and that there had not been more coordination between the Desk and the SEC. Lehman had failed eighteen months ago. What had happened to promises of regulatory coordination?

The crash's trigger was ultimately traced to a young British trader named Navinder Singh Sarao, who was accused of "spoofing" futures markets on the Chicago Mercantile Exchange (CME) by placing thousands of trades that were later canceled.

Arrested in April 2015, Sarao was dubbed "The Hound of Hounslow" by the British tabloids. At the time of the flash crash, Sarao was thirty-one years old and living with his parents at their home near Heathrow Airport.

That was hard to square with how one trader described him: "This guy, for want of a better word, had balls. He used to get into big positions, he saw the risk, then saw the reward, and he took the trades."

From his bedroom, Sarao launched what the Department of Justice alleged in 2015 to be "a massive effort to manipulate" the intraday price for "near month E-Mini S&P 500 futures contracts" on Globex, an electronic trading platform.

The DOJ maintained that Sarao turned a profit on March 6 of $900,000. In one day! Over the subsequent four years he had made $40 million using the same techniques. Sarao was charged with twenty-two counts of wire fraud and market manipulation.

His ability to manipulate the CME laid bare how vulnerable the markets had become to one rogue trader—and how important it was for the Fed to understand the new technologies that had overtaken the financial system.

On May 9, a few days after the flash crash, the FOMC held an unscheduled meeting and announced it would reopen swap lines with the ECB and other central banks to stem the chaos in the eurozone.

That summer, the Senate version of the proposed Dodd-Frank financial regulation overhaul bill finally lurched toward a vote.

In late 2009, the House had passed its version with zero Republican support. Two years of fierce lobbying by Wall Street had delayed Senate action. On July 15, 2010, the Senate approved the bill 60 to 39, with only three GOP votes in favor. The Dodd-Frank Wall Street Reform and Consumer Protection Act was signed into law by Obama on July 21.

At a staggering 2,300 pages, the running joke was the only two people who had read the legislation were Dodd and Frank. I doubted even they had the patience. Dodd-Frank opened up its own can of worms on Wall Street and pitted regulators against one another.

At thirty-five pages, a different sort of document was about to make history, at least in my world.

In July 2010, the Markets Desk released a shocking paper simply called "Shadow Banking," lead author Zoltan Pozsar, which diagrammed the Street's vast interconnections between financial subsidiaries like hedge funds, GSEs, securities lenders, and OBS entities like conduits and SIVs.

The paper went far beyond Pozsar's first effort in 2008, digging deeply into the role these entities had played in the financial crisis. JPMC and Bank of New York Mellon, the two banks that dominated the tri-party repo market, sat at the epicenter of an elaborate new map with hundreds of tiny boxes. It looked like the circuit board of a microprocessor.

Instead of just reading his papers, I had to meet the guy who'd designed the amazing map. The next time I was in New York, I made a beeline for the Fed fortress on Liberty Street.

I had imagined that Zoltan would be older, bigger, louder. He was a young, slender, and quiet man with an infectious energy, like a human exploding atom bomb, hungry to spread an understanding of the impossibly intricate map he had conceived.

If there's one thing I learned in all my years at the Fed it's that economists like to sound smart and confuse their audience. Zoltan was the opposite, keen to translate and ensure a deep understanding, mainly so I could be as alarmed as he was. He cared.

Shadow banking had not disappeared. It had gotten bigger.

The traditional banking system (estimated at $13 trillion in 2010) was dwarfed by a $16 trillion market that made up the "cash" and "synthetic" branches of the shadow banking system.

Two hours into a tutorial with Zoltan, I could hardly tear myself away, but I had another appointment and an FOMC briefing to write. I told him

I'd be back in New York next month and wanted another two hours of his time—the map was simply too much to take in.

We parted fast friends. Zoltan sent me a huge four-by-three-foot laminated color copy of his diagram in a tube. Even at that size, which took up half my office wall at the Fed, it was hard to read the tiny fonts on various pieces of the puzzle. The money flow was bizarrely complex. At the edge of the diagram were all the backstops created by the Fed and Congress that had kept the system afloat since 2008.

I wasn't the only one impressed.

"Looking at that map created a cognitive shift a little similar to the one that had occurred back in the sixteenth century, when the mathematician Nicholaus Copernicus showed in his diagrams that the earth revolved around the sun, not the other way around," wrote Gillian Tett of the *Financial Times*. She recommended that Pozsar's accompanying paper should be "mandatory reading for bankers, regulators, politicians and investors."

Tett pointed out that the "circuit board" had become so complex because "bankers were trying to arbitrage the last two sets of Basel rules." A third Basel Accord was in the works; the shadow system would arbitrage it as well. Would that lead to another crisis?

The August 10, 2010 FOMC meeting was tumultuous by the Fed's standards. Unemployment was stuck around 9 percent and inflation remained stubbornly low, less than 1 percent, at least by the Fed's preferred measure.

Bernanke wanted more QE, but more important, he wanted to ensure that the balance sheet would not be allowed to shrink. Enter MBS and Treasury securities reinvestment, which would become one of the most contentious issues at the central bank over the next few years.

As it stood, over time the Fed's balance sheet would naturally shrink as securities were prepaid or matured. For the hawks, this natural progression was a check and balance on the risk of the balance sheet getting too big. For the doves, reinvestment was a way to ensure that they never had to relinquish the power of a big balance sheet.

If there was little to no evidence that QE was effective, research on the benefits of reinvestment was nonexistent.

Yellen argued for yet more stimulus. "I consider it critical at this juncture that this [Fed] not be perceived as falling behind the curve, being unwilling to act or being out of touch with the mounting concerns we see in the markets and on Main Street," Yellen said. "The data show a considerable slowing of the economy during the summer and the near-term outlook has been marked down appreciably."

Bernanke argued that the sad-sack economy, particularly the stubbornly high levels of unemployment, demanded more QE.

"Even if you are a pure inflation targeter and don't give a damn about unemployment, we are too tight," Bernanke argued. "All of our nominal variables are coming in below target—we are forecasting inflation that is too low." Bernanke believed inflation needed to be around 2 percent to keep the economy growing.

But seven FOMC members expressed reservations.

"We cannot afford to fail," said Warsh, who had helped Bernanke maneuver through the crisis. He was concerned because the efficacy of the first round of QE was a complete unknown. "We are the grownups in town. We are the last folks, rightly or wrongly, fairly or unfairly, in a global economy that demands institutional credibility, and we should be thinking long about the decisions that we make."

Bernanke stood firm. "Some people argue that we shouldn't do the reinvestment because it won't be effective," Bernanke said, "and some seem to be arguing that we shouldn't do it because it will be too effective."

That statement alone proved the critics' point. The Fed wasn't confident that its easy money stimulus was having the desired effect.

Bernanke settled for half of his request. The FOMC announced that it would begin reinvesting proceeds of maturing MBS, halting the contraction taking place in the Fed's balance sheet. But Bernanke knew he had an ace up his sleeve.

Two weeks later, at the annual Jackson Hole conference on August 27, Bernanke gave a speech saying "policy options are available to provide additional stimulus."

Just the hint the heroin addict wanted to hear from his street vendor. On August 26, the S&P 500 Index had bottomed at 1047. The market listened to Bernanke's words and heard "more QE coming." The S&P 500 Index staged a full reversal and rose 20 percent by year's end.

His comments enraged the hawks. Fisher had implored Bernanke not to make this speech. Once the words left the chairman's mouth, they were as good as gospel.

Bernanke knew that the Fed would have to follow through on his hint or crash the markets. He'd effectively bypassed the FOMC, seeming more like the Maestro every day.

On cue, at the September 2010 FOMC meeting, David Stockton, the Board's director of Research, continued to sound the alarm about the underlying economy.

"Further downside surprises in a wide array of data could raise a concern that, rather than traversing a soft patch, we may have stumbled into something more like the La Brea tar pit," Stockton said. What an apt image. The Fed was starting to behave like a T. Rex trapped in California's infamous quagmire.

The doves' wings were on fire. They couldn't sit still and wait for the results. Maybe it would have been better for the FOMC to meet four times a year, the minimum required by law, instead of eight.

Stockton's assessment gave Yellen ammunition to ramp up her argument for more stimulus, insisting the Fed act even as she acknowledged the medicine was inexact in treating the underlying disease.

"It is not that monetary policy is the main problem facing businesses, as many of you have pointed out," Yellen said. "But I do think policy can contribute to the solution, even if it isn't a panacea for what ails businesses these days."

Yellen's drumbeat for more stimulus found favor with Obama's White House. In September, the Senate voted to confirm Yellen as the vice chair of the Board of Governors. The preening dove now had a permanent vote.

The Senate also confirmed Obama's nomination as a governor of Sarah Bloom Raskin, a lawyer and former Maryland Commissioner of Financial Regulation. But the president's nomination of MIT professor Peter Diamond for the remaining open governor seat was slapped down by Republicans.

In October 2010, Diamond became a corecipient of the Nobel Prize in Economics. The opposing Republicans considered Diamond too supportive of Bernanke's stimulus policies.

In an op-ed, Diamond said his detractors held "a fundamental misunderstanding: a failure to recognize that analysis of unemployment is crucial to conducting monetary policy."

They didn't misunderstand. They just didn't agree with Dr. Bernanke's prescription for the problem. Alabama Sen. Richard Shelby (R-Ala.) led the effort to keep Diamond off the board, calling him an "old-fashioned big government Keynesian." After two additional votes failed to win his confirmation, Diamond withdrew his name from consideration.

In October, the Fed sent a variety of messengers out to prepare the financial world for QE2. The economy's feeble state was "unacceptable," Dudley said in a speech, and "further Fed action was likely to be warranted."

But Fisher had a different message. "In my darkest moments I have begun to wonder if the monetary accommodation we have already engineered might even be working in the wrong places," he said in a speech on October 7, 2010. "Far too many of the large corporations I survey that are committing to fixed investments report that the most effective way to deploy cheap money raised in the current bond markets or in the form of loans from banks beyond buying stock or expanding dividends, is to invest it abroad where taxes are lower and governments are more eager to please."

The Fed was actually encouraging companies to move offshore!

A week before the November 2010 FOMC meeting, Hilsenrath wrote a story for the *Wall Street Journal*: "Fed Gears Up for Stimulus."

The Fed "is close to embarking" on another round of stimulus, the central bank "is likely to unveil" a program of Treasury bond purchases, the announcement "is expected to be made at the conclusion of a two-day meeting of its policy-making committee next Wednesday."

Unemployment stood at 9.6 percent, much higher than its goal of "maximum sustainable employment," and inflation was still too low, running a bit over 1 percent.

There was no formal inflation target in place at the time. But Bernanke had been relentlessly campaigning for the FOMC to adopt just such a target of 2 percent.

Inflation targeting had triggered a lively discussion in 1996 between Greenspan and Yellen, then a governor. She aggressively challenged the chairman, saying that a little inflation "greases the wheels" of the labor market and her preferred target was 2 percent. She asked Greenspan his preference. Could he put a number on it?

"I would say the number is zero, if inflation is properly measured," Greenspan said. The discussion spread around the table, most people agreeing with Yellen.

The next day, Greenspan summarized the discussion: "We have now all agreed on 2 percent." He reminded the FOMC of the "highly confidential nature" of their discussion. "I will tell you that if the 2 percent inflation figure gets out of this room, it's going to create more problems for us than I think any of you might anticipate."

In contrast, Bernanke wanted the world to know the Fed's inflation target was 2 percent. He all but willed the markets to box the Fed into a future corner.

David Stockman, former government economist and writer of the *Contra Corner* blog, later summarized the Fed's goals as a "voodoo style" formula of "2, 3, 4, 5"—meaning it wanted to hit 2 percent inflation, 3 percent real growth, a 4 percent "normalized" fed funds rate, and 5 percent unemployment, but unfortunately these benchmarks are virtually impossible to measure with any accuracy. He argued that there was no scientific proof that 2 percent inflation was better for growth than 1.20 or 0.02 percent.

"These are all self-serving fictions fabricated by a small community of monetary central planners and their Wall Street henchmen," Stockman wrote. "And they do one big but destructive thing: Namely, they are used to justify endless manipulation and falsification of the single most important set of prices in all of capitalism—the price of money and financial assets."

How billions of dollars of bond buying, which aimed to drive up the prices of long-term bonds and spur more investment and spending, would move unemployment up and inflation down remained unclear.

Don't get me wrong, I get the math. When bond prices go up, yields go down. The cheaper it is to finance X, Y, or Z, the more likely it is the borrower will bite.

But getting a borrower to bite was no longer as easy as it once was. Mortgage-lending standards had tightened in the aftermath of the housing crisis. Dodd-Frank made things worse because lenders could no longer estimate what their liability would be in case a mortgage went bad. My meetings with mortgage analysts increasingly focused on the subject of regulatory morass.

That's not to say that lower rates weren't beneficial to some parties. Pristine corporate borrowers in America barked with pleasure at every tick lower in yields. But extending credit to those who had ample access didn't do much to spur growth. It was a classic case of credit haves and have-nots.

The Fed had run out of ways to goose the economy. But it couldn't stand to do nothing, to let the economy find equilibrium. At the November FOMC meeting, Bernanke and his band of doves pushed for QE2.

The outspoken Hoenig infuriated Bernanke by calling the proposal "a bargain with the devil."

But the even-keeled Warsh, one of Bernanke's closest advisers, also opposed the move, going so far as to rally for mutiny among the District Bank presidents.

"If I were in your chair," Warsh told Bernanke, "I would not be leading the [Fed] in this direction, and frankly, if I were in the chair of most people around this room, I would dissent."

But Warsh understood that a dissenting vote by a governor would signal dissatisfaction with Bernanke's leadership; he voted in favor of QE2. "I wouldn't want to undermine at this important moment the chance that this program could be successful," Warsh said.

Hoenig cast the lone no vote, his seventh dissent of the year, and told the press it was "a dangerous gamble." He came in for scathing criticism.

"It seems odd to me that with 200 economists at the Federal Reserve in Washington, that Tom Hoenig has discovered some wisdom that escaped all those people," said Lou Barnes, a banker who tracked the Fed for Premier Mortgage Group in Colorado. "There's something undignified about all the dissenting and the questions it raises . . . makes you wonder whether he's grandstanding."

Bernanke would later describe Hoenig's rhetoric as "provocative," threatening the collegial tradition of the FOMC and undermining public confidence in the Fed. In fact, it's just the opposite. It's that same "group-think" that undermines the integrity of the Fed.

Hoenig and the nonvoting Fisher stood their ground to little effect. Against the permanent voters on the FOMC, dissenting District Bank presidents had little impact.

The big question: Would QE2 work?

Fisher argued in a speech after the vote that QE2 would not accomplish Bernanke's goal—and worse, it would reignite dangerous market speculation. Margin debt was "fast approaching levels that prevailed before the Nasdaq implosion in 2001."

Despite his yes vote, Warsh made his reservations known in a speech on November 8.

"Chronic short-termism in the conduct of economic policy has done much to bring us to this parlous point," Warsh said. "I am less optimistic than some that additional asset purchases will have significant, durable benefits for the real economy.... There are significant risks that bear careful monitoring...."

A group of prominent economists sent an open letter to Bernanke warning that yet another round of QE risked "currency debasement and inflation."

The Who's Who of Wall Street signers included John B. Taylor of Stanford University (eponymous with the so-called Taylor Rule), Niall Ferguson of Harvard, James Grant of *Grant's Interest Rate Observer,* and twenty other prominent economists.

"We disagree with the view that inflation needs to be pushed higher, and worry that another round of asset purchases, with interest rates still near zero over a year into the recovery, will distort financial markets and greatly complicate future Fed efforts to normalize monetary policy," the letter said.

"The Fed's purchase program has also met broad opposition from other central banks and we share their concerns that quantitative easing by the Fed is neither warranted nor helpful in addressing either U.S. or global economic problems."

Bernanke responded. "The Federal Reserve is committed to both parts of its dual mandate and will take all measures to keep inflation low and stable as well as promote growth in employment. *In particular, the Fed has made all necessary preparations and is confident that it has the tools to unwind these policies at the appropriate time*" (emphasis mine).

Cullen Roche's "Pragmatic Capitalist" column for *Business Insider* chided the economists as right for the wrong reasons. QE2 wouldn't cause inflation or currency debasement and did not involve "printing of new money."

Rather, Roche argued, the policy was counterproductive and should be ended "so as to maintain the credibility of the Federal Reserve and stop all market distortions that are occurring due to the sheer misconception surrounding the policy."

Financial journalist Alen Mattich warned that Bernanke (and his counterpart Mervyn King in the UK) were at risk of creating another asset bubble by launching yet more QE.

"Neither central banker seems to see the 70 percent-plus appreciation of their domestic equity markets over the past 20 months to significantly overvalued levels based on historic trends as a concern," Mattich wrote. "Indeed, Bernanke has openly admitted that the second round of quantitative easing he launched last week is designed to promote even further stock market appreciation. Not only has he never been able to identify a bubble in the past, he actively wants to create a new one now."

The response to QE2 from some sectors of Congress was equally ferocious. The political independence of the Fed was under fire. Rep. Paul Ryan (R-Wis.), incoming House Budget Committee chairman, launched an effort to organize opposition to more QE.

"Printing money is no substitute for pro-growth fiscal policy," said Rep. Mike Pence (R-Ind.). Those economists who signed the letter opposing the Fed plan "represent a growing chorus of Americans who know that we should be seeking to stimulate our economy with tax relief, spending restraint and regulatory reform rather than masking our fundamental problems and artificially creating inflation."

The White House and Democrats defended the Fed. Obama said the move "was designed to grow the economy," not cheapen the dollar. But even economists who usually agreed with the Keynesian view—Nobel Laureates Joseph Stiglitz and Paul Krugman—expressed skepticism that more QE was the answer to the country's economic problems.

Bernanke plowed ahead. *There, there, we know better than you.*

CHAPTER 17

A Turning Point

FED STATEMENT WORD COUNT: 790

EFFECTIVE FED FUNDS RATE: 0.07%

10-YR TREASURY RATE: 2.86%

FED BANKS TOTAL ASSETS: $4,102.14B

DATE: 1/1/2014

The plausible outcomes range from the gradual and benign to the more precipitous and damaging.

—TIMOTHY GEITHNER, JANUARY 23, 2006

By flooding the financial markets with easy money Bernanke had thrown a wrench into something investors call "price discovery." Wall Street legend Arthur Cashin, director of Floor Operations at UBS, gave me a priceless illustration of price discovery involving Charles Lewis Tiffany and J. P. Morgan, the banker who was instrumental in the creation of the Federal Reserve.

The legendary jeweler sends a diamond stickpin to Morgan in the classic Tiffany blue box, with a note that the price is $5,000. If he likes the pin, he may keep it and send a check back with the box.

Morgan sends the box back: "Dear Mr. Tiffany. The pin is truly magnificent. The price of $5,000 may be a bit rich. I have enclosed a check for $4,000. If you choose to accept, send my man back with the box. If not, send back the check and he will leave the box with you."

Tiffany tells Morgan's courier: "You may return the check to Mr. Morgan. My price was firm." The man takes the check and places the gift-wrapped box on Tiffany's desk. Tiffany unwraps the box to remove the stickpin and finds a check from Morgan for $5,000 and a note with a single sentence—"JUST CHECKING THE PRICE."

Instead of relying on the true pricing of assets as set by the markets, investors were "baking in" the Fed's largesse.

Even though I was writing policy recommendations for Fisher, which technically carried a higher security classification, in the middle of every FOMC briefing I'd have to get up and leave the room because I didn't have a high enough security clearance to participate in policy discussion.

Presence at this inner sanctum sanctorum was what every economist in the Research Department aspired to attain. I had no desire to have some label or title. I just wanted to be in on the discussion to defend my recommendations. Talk about being careful what you ask for.

Despite Rosenblum's dismissive attitude toward my increasingly inhospitable work environment, he went to bat for me. One day in the summer of 2010, I was summoned to his top floor office next door to Fisher's. With a big smile on his face, he gave me the news: My security clearance had been upgraded to Class I, which entailed filling out so much paperwork I felt closer to security than to my friendly neighborhood proctologist.

It was only a matter of days before there was a knock on my office door. Rosenblum's assistant delivered my first batch of classified documents from Washington in advance of the upcoming FOMC meeting. I stared with dismay at the foot-tall pile. Seeing the mountain of classified material was an eye-opener. I realized what an asset it was that Fisher needed so little sleep.

Because my Markets Brief was included in every Briefing Book, I attended every pre-FOMC meeting with Fisher. Most of the other economists attended only a couple a year, when they were called upon to do a brief.

Now, when the policy statements were discussed and others had to get up and leave the room, I remained, along with Fisher, Rosenblum, Duca, and a handful of others. I had gone from being the complete outsider to the ultimate insider. For the first time, I heard the discussion about the proposed FOMC statements that would be voted on at the meeting.

The moment of the statement release at 1 P.M. Texas time on "FOMC Wednesday" took on a different meaning for me. It felt like election night to see which statement would emerge victorious. When I ran up to the break room to watch CNBC's Steve Liesman read the FOMC statement, I was on tenterhooks, wondering which words had prevailed.

I fully grasped the ridiculous pageantry because I knew the markets would parse every single word. A Fed "computational linguistics" study of FOMC statements released in 2015 concluded: "natural language processing can strip away false impressions and uncover hidden truths about complex communications such as those of the Federal Reserve." The Street had it right all along.

Depressingly, the option Fisher preferred was rarely the one that came out of Liesman's mouth. The doves always seemed to have the upper hand.

Hawks and doves had become very political. It wasn't as much of an economic exercise as a political one, with a distinct irony. Hawk Fisher, who had served in two Democratic administrations and once ran for Senate as a Democrat, was effectively defending the Grand Old Party's fiscal prudence. (He'd sworn off partisan politics when he joined the Fed.) Dove Bernanke, who Bush had felt comfortable appointing because of his Republican roots, ended up supporting the Democrats' spendthrift agenda. (Fisher always liked to say he preferred to be labeled a "wise and thoughtful" owl, not a hawk.)

Aside from Rosenblum, the other economists in the inner sanctum were none too pleased at the news of my ascension, especially Duca, who ramped up his attacks on my work, demanding I remove every iota of personality from my Markets Brief and explain all market terms so that even the most junior research assistant could understand them. But I couldn't fit my brief into Duca's parameters and make it relevant to Fisher.

Duca started criticizing my work in public forums, and using stronger language. He went from dismissing my data for not being "seasonally adjusted" to outright proclaiming "This is stupid" in front of colleagues.

I bit my tongue and withstood the attacks. After every berating, I shut myself in my office, slowed down my breathing, and focused on what was important. Fisher and Rosenblum valued my work or I wouldn't be there. But the stress started to take a toll on my health. Hacking cough, exhaustion, insomnia.

Finally, I went to Rosenblum again in September 2010, just before my fortieth birthday. Torn between my desire to do a good job for Fisher and preserving my personal well-being, I pleaded with him to transfer me out of Duca's supervision.

"The situation has become untenable," I said. Rosenblum's face closed down. For the first time, I got no sympathy from my mentor.

"Make it work," he said. The Fed's bureaucracy made it virtually impossible to find another round hole for a square peg like me. My job was slotted at a certain pay level in a certain department under a certain supervisor.

Rosenblum had his own problems, as anyone managing a Research Department with three dozen economists would have. All those cats to herd.

Devastated, I felt my connection to Rosenblum had been severed. I contemplated leaving the bank. I could triple my salary the moment I walked out the door. Even the ignominious "equities in Dallas" jobs paid a lot more than the Fed.

But I couldn't in good conscience abandon my mission, the role I had earned with hard work and perseverance.

In November, Fisher invited me to lunch for a belated celebration of my birthday at the Mansion on Turtle Creek, the poshest restaurant in Dallas. I dressed up, prepared to talk about his concerns for one hour with no complaining. But I planned before the end of the meal to ask him for a teeny tiny favor.

Fisher beat me to the punch.

"So, how's it working out with Duca?" Fisher asked.

I was floored. He'd picked up on the antagonism though I hadn't said a word to him. I filled him in on the escalating acrimony of my work environment and pleaded for a transfer to another department.

"You know I'll be voting next year, and through December 2014," Fisher said. Two more voting rotations. As a District Bank president, he'd be forced to retire when he turned age sixty-five.

"Yes, sir," I said. "I know that."

"Well, if I do this for you, will you agree to stay through then?" he asked.

"Yes," I said without hesitation.

Immediately the weight of the world lifted from my shoulders. In exchange for four more years of loyalty, Fisher would give me the freedom to do my job. At that moment I committed to stay at the Fed.

As we finished our lunch, we talked about the direction of Fed policy, about income inequality and pension systems potentially going bust.

"Since we're talking about four years from now," I said, "what will you see in your lifetime that will be the most surprising?"

His answer stunned me.

"I think there's the potential for riots in our own streets, social unrest like we've never seen," Fisher said. I remembered what had happened in Greece. The Fed's policies have a real and potentially devastating impact on people's lives. At a time when I was thinking about my own problems, his answer made our mission all the more vital.

Fisher promised he would move me out of Research into a tiny autonomous division called Financial Industry Studies, within Sup & Reg. But the transfer might take some time, so he admonished me to stay mum. Even though he was bank president, Fisher had to delicately maneuver within the same Fed bureaucracy.

I attended the December formal briefing with a lighter heart, knowing that my time under Duca's thumb was near an end.

After Fisher left the room, Rosenblum asked everyone to stay for a few minutes. He had an announcement. In 2011 he would be starting a new initiative.

"I would like all of you to collaborate with Danielle on your given briefing documents," Rosenblum announced. "A closer collaboration with Danielle, weaving the financial markets into your economic analysis, will be key. She's proven herself. Her work's important. Accept it for what it is."

Duca looked like he had been given a cow-patty sandwich. The others stared, aghast. I wanted to crawl under the table. Fisher hadn't told Rosenblum that he'd decided to move me.

I sat there as everyone filed out, feeling like Judas, wondering why Rosenblum—if he had thought my work so valuable—hadn't responded to my pleas to be freed from Duca's interference in September. Rosenblum's stunning validation had an ironic twist. As horrified as the economists were, little did they know they would never have to work with me again.

Within a matter of days, the Research Department was a ghost town.

The seasoned veterans had long since earned European-length paid vacation time. The moment Fisher was safely off to Washington for the December FOMC, their holiday season began.

But there was none of that for me. I was engaged in an infuriating tussle with the editors in Research and Public Affairs, who were tasked with ensuring no document with the Dallas Fed's name on it incited even a scintilla of controversy.

Nine months earlier I had approached Rosenblum with the idea for my first primary-authored Economic Letter. I was convinced that the Fed's extraordinary efforts to mitigate the pain and suffering from the bursting of the housing bubble were doing more harm than good. Rosenblum disagreed, convinced that the Obama administration's policies to modify mortgages and prevent foreclosures were effective.

In the end Rosenblum relented, probably because he knew what the editors would do to my work before it was ever allowed out the door.

The thought police must have believed themselves quite clever, choosing to release my brainchild—"The Fallacy of a Pain-Free Path to a Healthy Housing Market"—between Christmas and New Year's Day, when nobody would be around to read it.

Clearly they didn't realize that *Zero Hedge* never sleeps. The heavily followed financial blog, written by the anonymous "Tyler Durden" in homage to the movie *Fight Club*, posted a link and described himself "stunned" that a Fed paper was honest about the continuing housing slump.

Another blogger wrote: "While we working stiffs were enjoying our families and taking a break from the world's cruel realities for the year end holidays, the Dallas Fed came out with a surprisingly refreshingly honest assessment of the housing market.... They even suggest that allowing it to crash and find its own level may ultimately be the least painful and correct thing to do."

That paper the Fed tried to bury is now suggested reading for economics courses at UCLA and NYU.

CHAPTER 18

Insider Trading?

FED STATEMENT WORD COUNT: 814
EFFECTIVE FED FUNDS RATE: 0.10%
10-YR TREASURY RATE: 2.60%
FED BANKS TOTAL ASSETS: $4,368.35B
DATE: 6/1/2014

One myth that's out there is that what we're doing is printing money.
We're not printing money.

— BEN BERNANKE, DECEMBER 3, 2010

End the Fed! End the Fed! End the Fed!"
 In early 2011, I looked out the window of my new office on the third floor of the Dallas Fed and saw angry elderly people on the street marching, carrying signs, and chanting "End the Fed!"

Retirees getting nothing for their jumbo CDs had started to realize the Fed had no intention of raising rates. Stuck at zero after a lifetime of saving.

"Damn Ron Paul," I thought every time I heard them outside. The congressman's 2009 book *End the Fed* called the bank corrupt and unconstitutional and urged its abolition. Though Paul made some good points, America is not a banana republic. It needs a strong and independent central bank. Though I didn't blame them for demonstrating, the chanting was distracting.

Moved to my new home in FIS, I was summarily stripped of my Class I clearance; no more access to economists' policy documents. That didn't bother me. I never learned anything from them that the markets hadn't already told me.

My sole regret: the sense that the bridge between me and my mentor Rosenblum had been burned.

Moving in, I asked my new boss, Jeffrey Gunther, with utter trepidation, "Could I, just possibly, understanding that this is an extraordinary and probably impossible request, get a TV with CNBC feed?"

He looked at me funny and said, "Sure, why not?"

I now had four screens: two for TV and live data streaming, two for writing and conducting research. Heaven. Plugged back into the real world, sunlight pouring through a window and a perfect view of downtown Dallas, I felt as if oxygen had been injected into the building.

It would take eighteen months for the bureaucracy to approve my new title: Senior Financial Analyst and Advisor. But I was happy to wait and my only run-ins with people in Research would be at FOMC briefs.

Fisher had the vote in 2011. I wanted to do whatever I could to make it count. In my four and a half years at the Fed, I had built a powerful network of players across the financial landscape, from the biggest investment banks to mutual fund families to the credit rating agencies.

To get a handle on a given corporate earnings season, I might pick up the phone and call renowned market watcher Jim Bianco. Then I'd travel to New York to visit Silverblatt at S&P. A few blocks west I'd meet with earnings guru Amanda Sneider at Goldman Sachs. I'd bring together what I learned in my meetings with what the data told me, and create one section of the Markets Brief.

Then it was up to midtown. Oleg Melentyev, then at Bank of America Merrill Lynch, would fill me in on the latest high-yield and emerging markets bond market developments.

Then a few blocks up to Morgan Stanley, where I'd settle in for a good visit with Ellen Zentner, a rising non-PhD economist and fellow Texan, for her views on where the economy was headed.

I'd cross the street to Barclays for my most grueling meeting with one of the best Treasury strategists on the street, Joseph Abate. More often than not, Abate's deep understanding of the efficacy of the Fed's so-called transmission mechanism would make its way into my policy recommendations.

Those restricted documents went straight to Rosenblum and Fisher.

Within a few weeks at FIS, Gunther, an inquisitive and refreshingly energetic PhD with an appreciation for the markets, suggested what I had always known. The FOMC cycle was much too drawn out for one markets briefing every six or so weeks.

Nodding to that reality, he suggested I start writing a mid-FOMC cycle briefing. My workload doubled overnight. But much to my delight, since it fell outside the deeply bureaucratic FOMC document preparation process, a different set of rules applied. This new brief would be seen by only six or seven individuals.

The midcycle briefings took on a life of their own, hidden from the view of the nit-picking cabal in Research. I was even able to throw in things I would have communicated verbally to Fisher.

Take the running joke on the trading desks back in 2011. "Do you know the name of the chairman of the People's Bank of China?"

The answer, of course, was "Ben Bernanke." *Rim shot.*

The joke highlighted the reality that QE was making its presence known all over the globe. Because the PBOC pegged the yuan to the dollar, China's central bank imported American monetary policy. It could not raise interest rates because doing so would induce more so-called hot money flows into the country.

In the final three months of 2010, regulators ascribed to speculators a record inflow of $199 billion into China. Given the ratio of about five to one, this translated into the need to print about one trillion yuan.

The more yuan the PBOC printed, the more speculative inflows fueled inflation. The growing concern was that the market would eventually strong-arm China into revaluing the yuan. How would that impact the growth of China's economy?

Freeing the yuan to appreciate would certainly cool inflation, but it would also make Chinese goods less attractive around the world. The consequences of QE would continue to pop up in unexpected places.

In theory, decision makers at the Fed were united in their quest to fulfill their formal mandates. In practice, the Fed was increasingly divided, with two armies marching in different directions.

The hundreds of PhDs under the doves' sway (DC, New York, Boston, Chicago, San Francisco) were desperately seeking the philosopher's stone, using their economic models and ZIRP and QE strategies to will America to respond: invest, buy, spend!

The hawks' army, though much smaller, was seeking exit strategies: get out of QE, break free of ZIRP, raise interest rates to a more realistic level, and in doing so, shrink the Fed's balance sheet.

That road less traveled would have sent a clear signal to the Fed's stakeholders that the worst of the crisis had indeed passed. Normalcy would return.

Fisher set the stage for his voting year with a speech at the Manhattan Institute in New York on January 12, 2011.

Though the recovery had been slow, particularly compared to those following other severe recessions of the past sixty years in 1973–75 and 1981–82, none of Fisher's business contacts were complaining about the cost of borrowing, the lack of liquidity, or the availability of capital.

"All express concern about taxes, regulatory burdens and the lack of understanding in Washington of what incentivizes private-sector job creation," Fisher said. "All are stymied by a Congress and an executive branch that have appeared to them to be unaware of, if not outright opposed to, what fires the entrepreneurial spirit."

The Fed had done all it could. Congress had to step up to the plate.

Fisher viewed the Fed's bond-buying program, which was purchasing nearly all new Treasury debt issuance, as running the risk that it would be viewed as "an accomplice" to Congress's fiscal misfeasance.

With a nod to Congressman Paul, Fisher said, "Those lawmakers who advocate 'Ending the Fed' might better turn their considerable talents toward ending the fiscal debacle that has for too long run amuck within their own house." The Fed "could not monetize the debt if the debt were not being created by Congress in the first place."

But as long as Bernanke's dream team of Yellen and Dudley had his back, the Fed would continue to have Congress's back. No one wanted to exit. That would turn off the money machine.

I preferred to think of QE2 as a "liquidity trap."

A liquidity trap, as defined years ago by Keynes, occurs when interest rates have been pushed so low that the expected rates of return on investments follow them down. When investment falls, the economy stagnates and cash holdings in banks rise. The cash is trapped, despite the central bank's exertions.

Chicago's Evans, a dove, acknowledged that monetary policy was hitting its outer bounds.

"Normally, monetary policy could reduce the incentives to save and stimulate spending by lowering short-term nominal interest rates," Evans said. "But with the federal funds rate already essentially at zero, we are in a liquidity trap."

Evans suggested the way out was to increase inflation expectations such that "the opportunity costs of holding cash goes up, tripping incentives toward higher spending and lending."

But how? Nothing the Fed did worked.

At the January 2011 FOMC meeting, everyone agreed that economic conditions remained tepid. Though unemployment had ended the year at 8.8 percent, evidence indicated it would be much higher if it included the Americans who had stopped looking for work or took part-time jobs.

The January statement explained that interest rates would remain at zero and the Fed expected to keep it there "for an extended period." Bernanke wanted to push investors out of Treasurys into other assets like corporate bonds and stocks.

January marked the first meeting of the FOMC without at least one dissent since December 2009. No longer voting, Hoenig had dissented at all eight FOMC meetings in 2010, receiving no small amount of criticism.

Hoenig hit back, saying that dissents at the Fed were as essential as they were at the Supreme Court. He added that the continued damage being done to more prudent players in the economy through ZIRP and QE would come back to haunt the Fed.

"Importantly," Hoenig said, "such actions as they continue are demanding the saving public and those on fixed incomes subsidize the borrowing public."

For now, Fisher remained quiet, choosing to hold his dissents for a time when change was afoot.

Signs had emerged that investors were becoming desperate in response to continued zero interest rates. The search for yield took on greater intensity. On February 18, 2011, junk bond yields hit a low of 6.80 percent, dipping below the prior December 2004 record of 6.86 percent.

Not only were corporations mired in a liquidity trap, so were households. Policymakers couldn't grasp that the longer interest rates stayed at the zero bound, the more savings consumers would have to siphon from their available funds for spending. You can't force all of Grandma's money into the casino. Hence, the "trap" in the "liquidity trap" for households.

Household formation, or the lack thereof, acted as a ball and chain on the economy. Census data showed that household formation had contracted in 2010 for the first time since World War II. This was backed by a Pew report that found a record one in six American households were multigenerational. Young adults who moved back home with parents instead of forming new households, combined with the persistent oversupply, would further delay the new home construction that typically led a recovery out of recession.

Home builders could see no end in sight as the traditional lever of low interest rates could no longer entice new buyers. The clearing of the housing market would not arrive until the foreclosures clogging the financial system and pent-up supply of vacant homes were finally listed and sold.

But the people at the top were doing great. The jumbo mortgage market remained open for business. Top-tier home prices had fallen by less and recovered to a greater degree, largely in line with the stock market to which they were tightly correlated.

In early February 2011, Warsh announced he was leaving the Fed, giving Obama the chance to put the Board of Governors almost entirely in the hands of his appointees.

Fisher was now one of the only members of the FOMC who had worked on Wall Street. Obama's first appointee, Daniel Tarullo, had been named to the board on January 28, 2009.

A law professor, Tarullo had emerged as a voice for stronger Fed oversight of Wall Street banks, in agreement with Fisher. Rosenblum called Tarullo a "bulldog on a meat truck." He meant it as a compliment, often characterizing his own tenacity in the same way. But other FOMC divisions ran deep.

On February 28, 2011, Dudley gave a speech at New York University to assure the country that the Fed would continue its bond-buying program.

"We are still very far away from achieving our dual mandate of maximum sustainable employment and price stability," Dudley said. "Faster progress toward these objectives would be very welcome and need not require an early change in the stance of monetary policy."

But on the same day, Bullard appeared on CNBC and contradicted Dudley.

Bullard maintained that the Fed was "determined" to return monetary policy "to a more normal stance" and might possibly finish the QE2 program "a little bit shy of where we intended initially, and then go on pause for a while."

Were these guys even in the same meetings?

Banks were struggling to comply with new rules and regulations. On April 1, the FDIC implemented a new fee system that charged banks between 10 and 45 basis points on their liabilities. The new system penalized big banks with wholesale lending operations and benefited smaller, deposit-only institutions.

Prior to the FDIC change, the fed funds effective rate had settled into a range that averaged 17 basis points; banks could earn between 10 and 12 basis points daily on the spread between the "interest on excess reserves" (IOER) and the fed funds rate on repo. The change prompted some banks to exit the fed funds repo market altogether, exacerbating the downward pressure on rates.

Though the FDIC "tax" might have been warranted, it revealed how delicate an operation it would be to lift the fed funds rate from the zero bound without disrupting the short-rate market.

"The fed funds rate is effectively broken," one Treasury analyst told me privately. "The Fed has lost control of it."

In these unusual times, anticipating the Fed's next moves had become even more highly valued in the financial world than ever. Some of those who left the central bank after serving either as a governor, Bank president, officer, or employee sold their advisory services to pension fund managers, hedge funds, and other investors trying to make sense of the Fed's unconventional policies.

Fisher had raised the issue at the November 2010 FOMC meeting,

"I think of it as akin to insider trading," Fisher said. "There are people who do profit. There is one former Governor who recently visited my bank while I was gone and who told the staff that the Reserve Bank Presidents are of no consequence at all to monetary policy, that their views are not considered, and that this individual—I'll let you guess who it is—was, in essence, the 18th or 19th member, depending on how many we have, of the FOMC, and the equivalent of a voting member."

Fisher suggested that the Fed "should seriously look at some kind of firm legal strictures that are equivalent to the prosecution of insider trading. If people make money off inside knowledge about our decisions, it's no different from people who make money off inside information trading securities. In fact, I think it's a more grievous abuse."

Hoenig weighed in with the same concern.

"President Fisher was referring to the idea that some people advertise themselves as in a consultancy role to the Fed, and that's an issue that's becoming more predominant," Hoenig said. "I had correspondence with, I think, the same individual that President Fisher did, and he also asserted that he was the 19th or 18th member of the FOMC, very important, and so on and so forth."

Even five years later, after the transcripts were released, Fisher would refuse to name names. But some sleuthing indicated he was talking about Laurence Meyer, who left the Board of Governors in 2002. Reuters reported in September 2010 that Meyer had provided information about Fed decisions not yet made public, to clients of Macroeconomic Advisers, which he cofounded. His fee: $75,000.

The cottage industry of Fed watching and consulting had exploded. Meyer's experience on the inside—and his continuing relationships with Bernanke and Yellen—were invaluable.

A year later, the FOMC adopted a policy, written by a committee headed by Yellen, saying that members "will strive to ensure" they do not provide financial firms or entities with "a prestige advantage over its competitors."

Ironically, Yellen would come under fire for leaking information to Medley Global Advisors, which advertised to clients that it provided information on central bank developments "by cultivating relationships with senior policymakers around the globe."

Yellen's refusal to cooperate with a congressional inquiry led the House Committee on Financial Services to issue a subpoena to the Fed requiring it to provide information about its internal investigation of the leak. The Fed has so far declined to comply.

On April 27, 2011, immediately after the close of that day's FOMC meeting—again, there were no dissents—Bernanke gave the first scheduled press conference in the Fed's ninety-eight-year history.

A quarterly presser was part of a new effort by the Fed to bring more transparency to the FOMC's decision making. The Fed invited about sixty print and broadcast journalists. In his professorial tone, Bernanke explained that the Fed was attempting to spur growth and increase employment, while keeping inflation low.

"While it is very, very important to help the economy create jobs and help to support the recovery," he said, "I think every central banker understands that keeping inflation low is absolutely essential to a successful economy, and we will do what we can to make sure that happens."

Bernanke said that though the Fed would let QE2 expire at the end of June, it would not start liquidating its $2.8 trillion portfolio of bonds and MBSs, and would continue to reinvest the proceeds in Treasurys.

In the twenty-one months since Bernanke had first sat down to talk to CBS correspondent Pelley, Bernanke's demeanor had noticeably changed. In March 2009, he'd seemed humble, an economist fully aware he'd been plucked from relative obscurity to act as savior of the free world. Now Bernanke seemed defensive, touchy about all the negative press he was getting.

The previous December Bernanke had told Pelley, "We're not printing money. The amount of currency in circulation is not changing. The money supply is not changing in any significant way. What we're doing is lowering interest rates by buying Treasury securities. And by lowering interest rates, we hope to stimulate the economy to grow faster."

Bloomberg writer Caroline Baum suggested in a column that Bernanke must have lost her list of questions. Her most pertinent regarded Bernanke's widely quoted 2002 speech on deflation.

"You explained that the Fed has 'a technology called a printing press that allows it to produce as many dollars as it wants at essentially no cost,'" Baum wrote. But Bernanke had told *60 Minutes* in December 2010 that the Fed was not printing money. "Please discuss."

Was the Fed printing money or not? Bernanke wouldn't answer that.

After Bernanke's press conference, Fisher went public with a call to cut QE2 short in a speech to the Society of American Business Editors and Writers.

"No amount of further accommodation would be wise—either by prolonging or 'tapering off' the volume of purchases of Treasurys past June, or adding another tranche of large-scale asset purchases," Fisher said, warning of the "intoxicating effects of the ambrosia of inexpensive and plentiful money."

Congress had to get the U.S. budget under control. "There cannot be robust direct investment in the United States without confidence in the nation's ability to reverse its budgetary death spiral," Fisher said, "especially the inexorable accumulation of national debt and unfunded liabilities of Medicare and Social Security."

Paradoxically, the economy of the Eleventh District was starting to perk up. By June 2011, 37 percent of all net new American jobs since the recovery began had been created in Texas.

Texas had added 265,300 jobs, out of 722,200 nationwide—far outpacing any other state since June 2009, when the recession ended. The next closest was New York, with 98,200 jobs. (Eighteen states had actually lost jobs.) Based on straight nonfarm payroll data, Texas accounted for 45 percent of all net U.S. jobs. Though energy was a plus, it provided for only 10.6 percent of the growth. Professional and business services (22.9 percent) and health care (30.5 percent) led the way.

As a result, the Texas economy had grown on average 3.3 percent per year for the last twenty years. The U.S. economy's average over the same period? Only 2.6 percent.

What was the Lone Star State's secret? Fisher argued that it had rejected the economic model prevailing in Washington by creating a business-friendly environment and low tax burden. Texas had a smaller government footprint, right-to-work labor laws, and was more open to global trade, particularly with Mexico. Texas had also seen a quicker rebound from the housing bust, because state law had limited mortgage borrowing to 80 percent of the appraised value of a home.

Nationwide, the news was not so positive, especially in the housing market.

Since 2007, the pool of renters had increased by more than 3.4 million. Baby boomers approaching their retirement years wanted to sell their large homes as they transitioned to a fixed-income lifestyle. If young buyers opted to rent instead of buying starter homes, how would they build equity and move up into the boomers' bigger residences?

Writing in *Barron's*, hedge fund manager Douglas Kass coined a perfect phrase: "screwflation."

Inflation—driven by food, fuel, and housing—was rising and the poor and middle class were getting screwed. "Unemployment has exacerbated screwflation's impact on all but the wealthiest Americans," he said.

Even as the housing bubble's aftermath continued to plague America, other asset bubbles were building.

By May 2011, an overabundance of QE was fueling a surge in commodity prices (especially oil), Asian corporate "perpetual bond" issuance, and tech IPOs. LinkedIn's valuation rose from $3 billion to $4.3 billion in two weeks. It opened on May 19 at nearly double its $45 offering price, this without discernible profits at the social networking site.

"Maybe it's time we revisit the idea of the market being in a bubble," said CNBC anchor Mark Haines, just days before the financial world was plunged into mourning by his unexpected death. I was devastated by the news. Haines's voice had been on every Wall Street trading floor the morning of September 11, 2001, a voice of calm. His quick wit and humor would never be replaced in the financial media.

Risk-takers seized upon the silver market. The precious metal surged 175 percent from August 2010 to a peak of almost fifty dollars a troy ounce in May 2011. The Chinese, in particular, were key players in the speculative rally (and subsequent crash), with silver turnover at China's main trading hub spiking 2,837 percent from the start of 2011.

More cautious investors had begun to position themselves in anticipation of the end of QE2; prime money market funds were drowning due to an overabundance of cash.

Money funds have a duty to put fresh funds to work but are forced to take a step down in terms of counterparty risk; they cast about for alternative investments against which to lend out their excess cash. They were finding it difficult to find safe havens.

Even as the end of QE2 neared, the financial press began to lust out loud for QE3.

Putting aside moral hazard, the mistaken belief that QE could generate jobs was entrenched and widespread, having been constantly repeated by the Fed. Even so, the weak jobs report in mid-2011 ramped up discussions of more QE among monetary policymakers.

The folly of using monetary policy to alleviate the stress across the spectrum of households had become plain.

The ability of the wealth effect to trickle down to the households most suffering from the vestiges of the credit crisis—the bottom half of earners—was virtually nil. This segment owns almost none of the country's financial assets.

If anything, the fruits of QE1 and QE2 had further skewed the distribution in favor of the top-earning cohorts. The spoils of the rebound in animal spirits had benefited the investment and shadow banks and those employed in the financial services industries to the greatest degree.

Of about six million firms in the United States (from GE to mom-and-pop shops), 90 percent have twenty or fewer employees. These sole proprietors drive the growth of the economy.

And they were still feeling the pain. A survey of 1,004 companies with annual revenues of $10 million or less found that 78 percent believed the economy was still in recession. A National Federation of Independent Businesses study revealed that 46 percent of small businesses reported their profits were still falling two years into the technical recovery.

QE2 officially ended on June 30, 2011, with the S&P 500 at 1320. It topped out a week later at 1353, then began sinking. (It would be trading as low as 1075 intraday by early October, a decline of 21 percent.)

The market had Bernanke's number.

The Fed had spawned a never-ending, self-reinforcing cycle of speculation and correction. Despite interest rates being held at the zero bound, despite higher asset prices, the economy remained comatose.

In late summer 2011, the stock market stuttered, prompting the financial media to sit up and beg for more.

From the *Wall Street Journal* this headline: "The Markets Are Betting on Fed Miracle."

From *Barron's*: "Will our central bank step up once again? After all, it was exactly a year ago when the Federal Reserve came to the market's rescue by spending $600 billion on a second round of quantitative easing. The traditional gift for a first anniversary happens to be paper, and Ben Bernanke sure knows how to print lots of it."

From *Bloomberg*: "The chairman knows the whole world is watching, so if he chooses not to say very much, the markets and the economy in some broader sense would be disappointed."

All this prompted Fisher to rebut: "Bernanke is not the tooth fairy."

The temptation to look at policymakers as sweet pixies that came in the night and left gifts under investors' pillows was irresistible. But Fisher knew any positive reaction in stock prices that flowed from QE3 would be muted and more short-lived than the previous iterations.

Each subsequent bullet shot from Bernanke's QE bazooka would be released with a lesser degree of velocity. A "blank" bullet carried the risk of inducing a sense of hopelessness, especially in light of the weak trajectory of economic data.

The price the Fed would pay in credibility for shooting such a blank would be immense. Fisher believed the Fed had to preserve its remaining easing mechanisms in the event bigger adversaries than spoiled investors arrived on the economic battlefield in the months to come.

Yet another fascinating paper by Pozsar, who had left the Fed and was now a visiting scholar at the IMF, shed some light on what was happening to the cash being held on the balance sheets of companies, custodial banks, securities lenders, and investment firms. These accounts had exploded in size over the previous twenty years, from under a half trillion dollars to $3.5 trillion.

Before the financial crisis, accounts were insured up to the first $100,000 by the FDIC. That limit kept enormous sums in the shadow banking system.

After the crisis, the FDIC raised the insured account limit to $250,000. But trillions of dollars still sat outside the traditional banking system. The "safe" money had no place to go except money market mutual funds and government securities, leading to a shortage of T-bills and a corresponding drop in yield. (The average yield of the ten-year Treasury bill since 1962 was 6.37 percent; it peaked in 1981 at 15.81 percent. By 2012, the yield would sink to 1.39 percent.)

Pozsar had started researching this paper while at the Fed, but had run into some of the same snobbery I had encountered.

Saying that Treasury needed to issue more T-bills? "That was like a cardinal going to the pope suggesting they needed to rethink celibacy," Pozsar said. "Then I'm told I'm not a PhD, so I should stop writing these papers."

When a PhD in Research demanded that Pozsar provide the data sets so he could write his own paper, Pozsar quit. Though he loved working at the Fed, he wanted to continue his research without interference.

Clearly the transmission mechanism was broken. And yet Bernanke insisted on whipping out another bottle of Liquid-Plumr at the August 2011 meeting. No surprise, he received stiff pushback. An unprecedented three of the ten voting members—Fisher, Plosser, and Narayana Kocherlakota of the Minneapolis Fed—cast dissenting votes.

They voted against the Fed's statement that committed the FOMC to maintaining ZIRP through the middle of 2013 at a minimum. Previously, the Fed had been saying it would keep rates down for an "extended period," meaning several months, not years. The more explicit the statement, the tighter the FOMC was boxed in.

It was the biggest mutiny since 1992. Though seen as dovish, Kocherlakota, a PhD economist who joined the Fed in 2009, had gone on the record as eager to begin raising rates. (There were only ten voting members because two vacancies on the Board of Governors remained unfilled.)

The dissatisfaction with forcing through unprecedented policy was clear. Two dissents could be viewed as a vote of no confidence in the Chairman; three meant "hell no."

Imagine how many dissents Bernanke would have faced had more hawks been eligible to vote, something the media was wise to. Despite his reputed desire to build consensus, Bernanke's actions spoke much louder than his hollow words.

Roberto Perli, a former Fed staffer now at an investment advisory firm, predicted that "the influence of the hawkish minority will diminish."

Perhaps, but few generals go on to win wars with deep dissension in their ranks. Volcker had faced similarly stiff opposition. Four members of the Board of Governors appointed by Reagan—Wayne Angell, Manuel Johnson, Martha Seger, and Preston Martin—outvoted Volcker during a heated meeting in February 1986, moving to lower the bank discount rate from 7.5 to 7 percent. A furious Volcker supposedly stormed out in a huff and threatened to resign.

On April 30, 1987, the Board of Governors again overruled Volcker, 3 to 2, to approve the applications of Citicorp, the Bankers Trust New York Corporation, and JPMorgan & Company to enter the brave new world of securities underwriting, allowing them to issue commercial paper, MBSs, and municipal revenue bonds. Other banks waited in the wings for similar approval.

A rare defeat for Volcker. Within weeks, faced with such a deeply divided board, Volcker resigned. Greenspan was appointed by President Reagan to lead the Fed.

Could Bernanke be on thin ice? Or were the District Bank presidents gambling with their power?

The three dissenters in August roused the ire of Rep. Barney Frank, who had introduced an unsuccessful bill earlier in the year to take away the District Bank presidents' right to vote. Bizarrely, Frank had proposed that only the governors, picked by the president, should get a policy vote because it would make the Fed "more democratic and accountable."

"The 7–3 vote of the FOMC in August in favor of keeping interest rates low is stark evidence of how much of a constraint" District presidents had become, Frank said in September. Why? Because their dissents were always in the direction of higher interest rates.

The Fed was quickly becoming more powerful than Congress. Why shouldn't it too be protected by the idea of checks and balances?

Fisher explained his dissent in a speech called "Connecting the Dots," that UBS's Cashin called, in his privately circulated column "Cashin's Comments," "required reading" for those on the Street and every member of Congress and the administration. (Given my constant contribution to Fisher's speeches, I delighted in Cashin's rave review. Vicarious beats invisible any day.)

"He describes in simple, fully understandable and non-partisan language how government efforts have been ineffective and even counterproductive in aiding business and the economy," Cashin wrote.

Fisher pointed out that it was a rare day when the discount windows— the lending facilities of the twelve District Banks—experienced significant activity. Domestic banks had on deposit at the Fed about $1.6 trillion in excess reserves, earning a mere one quarter of 1 percent per annum rather than earning more by making loans to operating businesses.

Nondepository firms likewise were sitting on an enormous pile of cash, with some estimates of excess working capital on the books of publicly traded companies exceeding $1 trillion.

"I do not believe it wise to commit to more than that, or to signal further accommodation, when the cheap and abundant liquidity we have made available is presently lying fallow," Fisher said, "and when the velocity of money remains so subdued as to be practically comatose."

Though repeatedly labeled a hawk, Fisher's major fear wasn't immediate inflationary pressure.

"My concern is with the transmission mechanism for activating the use of the liquidity we have created, which remains on the sidelines of the economy," Fisher said. "I posit that nonmonetary factors, not monetary policy, are retarding the willingness and ability of job creators to put to work the liquidity we have provided."

That was unlikely to change until the Federal Reserve—and other leaders—stopped sending the message that the sky was falling. Congress needed to create a tax, spending, and regulatory regime that "incentivizes businesses to invest in the United States and create jobs for American workers rather than gravitate to foreign shores."

Many of those I interacted with on Wall Street nodded their heads, even as they made money off the Fed's largesse.

As extensive as I thought my network was, it was about to expand beyond my wildest dreams.

In early 2011, I encountered David Kotok, chief executive of Cumberland Advisors, at a Richmond Fed conference. We'd first met in 2006 at my first BCA symposium.

Back then I was a complete unknown, but in 2011 Kotok knew exactly who I was.

"Interesting what you do for Fisher," Kotok said. "It's a unique role."

He mentioned that one of eight spots for women was still unfilled at Camp Kotok, his annual fishing trip. Kotok institutionalized it the year after 9/11, each August inviting about forty economists and money managers to a remote location in Maine to angle for smallmouth bass and talk about the markets and the Fed.

"Would you be interested in attending?" Kotok asked. He warned it wasn't easy to get there. From Dallas, I'd have to fly to New York or Boston, then to Bangor, Maine, and finally hop a floatplane to Grand Lake Stream. And everyone was required to fish.

Wow, I thought, *Harvey's fishing trip!*

Every year, when Harvey would leave for his annual trek to northeastern Maine, the Research Department would buzz with envy.

I was thrilled. To be invited to solve the world's problems with such a fascinating group for four days! Then he dropped the bomb.

"I'll put in a call to Harvey," Kotok said. "Just to get his blessing."

My heart sank. Rosenblum and I hadn't spoken much since my move into FIS. During Fisher's briefings, the tension between us was so uncomfortable it made my heart ache.

That night I couldn't sleep, sure Rosenblum would torpedo Kotok's invitation.

The next morning, Kotok greeted me with a smile. "Harvey sang your praises," he said. "Please come join us in Maine." That was one of the happiest moments of my career.

That August, I flew to Maine for the four-day Camp Kotok, the longest separation from my four children I'd had since their births. Mom and my stepfather arrived to fill the gap. The kids adored their Nana and Papa, a former railroad engineer who kept them laughing and was generous with the sugar.

I expected Camp Kotok to be a more glamorous affair. Leen's Lodge gave a whole new meaning to rustic and remote. No cell service? Inconceivable.

Rule number 1: Everybody fished. So attendees took their poles, their bait, and especially their cell phones out on the lake with their guides. You could see people standing up in canoes, holding their phones to the sky like ancient people seeking to connect with the gods.

In the mornings, I met market watchers like Barry Ritholtz, Josh Rosner, and other early risers who competed to tap what little Internet bandwidth was available in the camp's dining hall. I became fast friends with my roommate, Maryanne Waldman of Morgan Stanley. For four days, we all ate, drank, argued economics and financial markets, and, of course, fished with relish.

Camp Kotok introduced me to an unspoiled, beautiful part of Maine. I felt relaxed for the first time in months. The ice in my relationship with Rosenblum began to thaw. On the day we left, I hugged him. He smiled and hugged me back. I felt tremendous relief. I had my mentor back.

I would be reinvited to Camp Kotok the next year, and the next. It gave me more sources, more feedback, and friends for life.

In early September, as the presidential campaign got off the ground, Republican candidates began taking swings at Bernanke like he was a piñata.

Former Massachusetts governor Mitt Romney said he'd replace the Bush appointee. Thwack!

Former House Speaker Newt Gingrich said he'd fire Bernanke and audit the Fed. Double thwack!

Texas governor Rick Perry opined that Bernanke's easy money policy was "almost treasonous." On the stump in Iowa, Perry ventured that "if this guy prints more money between now and the election, I don't know what you would do to him in Iowa but we would treat him pretty ugly now in Texas." Triple thwack!

With such animosity coming from fellow Republicans, Bernanke was feeling the heat.

On September 7, 2011, Hilsenrath laid out Bernanke's perspective going into the next FOMC meeting with this lead: "The recent slew of bad economic news has raised expectations in financial markets that the Federal Reserve will take new actions to spur growth and hiring." (What could be wrong with that?)

"One option that has gained favor in some corners of the Fed: Lower long-term interest rates by shifting the composition of the Fed's holdings of government securities so the average maturity is longer." Or sell some shorter-term securities and reinvest in those with longer-term rates. Or stop paying banks the 0.25 percent interest they received for cash held on reserve at the Fed. Or, of course, more QE. Pathetic.

The September 21, 2011, FOMC meeting marked the tenth anniversary of the close of the most memorable week in U.S. stock market history.

After the terrorist attacks on 9/11, the NYSE shut down for four trading days. It was a hiatus not seen since President Franklin Roosevelt declared the 1933 Bank Holiday.

During the week of September 17, 2001, the S&P 500 Index fell 12 percent. That Friday's close for traders was somber yet resolved. The economic catastrophe the terrorists hoped to trigger had not occurred. Still, the investment community struggled to find its compass, plagued by uncertainty, the most potent bacteria to infect risky assets.

The Fed injected huge amounts of liquidity into markets to allow the economy to function. Ten years later, the S&P 500 Index was trading 20 percent higher than it had a decade earlier, a sign of the resiliency of our financial markets. But uncertainty lingered, as illustrated by the confusion that reigned at the Fed.

In a speech given before the meeting, Kocherlakota brushed off the suggestion of more QE, saying "it is unlikely the data in September will warrant adding still more accommodation."

But Bernanke could not stop. On September 21, 2011, in the face of the declining stock market, the FOMC announced what the financial press would dub "Operation Twist," a hybrid version of QE in which the Fed would buy long-term bonds, while selling short-term bonds, giving a blast of oxygen to market players.

Fisher again dissented, explaining why in a speech on September 27, though he had to be circumspect because the FOMC minutes had not yet been released.

He showed a photograph of the sign outside the Jan Mayen Arctic weather station, a desolate volcanic island about six hundred miles west of Norway's North Cape. Subject to brutal winters, the station was described by writer Tom Clancy in *The Hunt for Red October* as "Loran-C," a NATO tracking and transmission station.

The sign greets visitors in the Norsk language, which translated to English reads: "Theory is when you understand everything, but nothing works. Practice is when everything works, but nobody understands why. At this station, theory and practice are united, so nothing works, and nobody understands why."

CHAPTER 19

Spinning Fedwire

FED STATEMENT WORD COUNT: 569

EFFECTIVE FED FUNDS RATE: 0.11%

10-YR TREASURY RATE: 1.88%

FED BANKS TOTAL ASSETS: $4,500.06B

DATE: 1/1/2015

While admirers of capitalism, we also to a certain extent believe it has limitations that require government intervention in markets to make them work.

—JANET YELLEN, 2012

At the January 25, 2012, FOMC meeting, Bernanke was determined to push the FOMC to officially adopt the goal of a formal inflation target of 2 percent.

That was like saying, okay guys, in addition to this straitjacket we're already wearing—getting unemployment to a magic number—let's strap on another one, even if we all agree that our inflation metrics are imprecise. Fisher argued against it. Bernanke got his way. In a historic vote, the FOMC set an official inflation target rate of 2 percent.

A few months later, market watchers were puzzled by weird movements in some credit markets; gossip began circulating about a rogue trader everyone dubbed the London Whale for the large positions he was taking in credit default swaps.

The mystery was solved in April, when JPMC, now the biggest bank in the United States, revealed that a trader in its little-known Chief Investment Office in London had made enormous bets on derivatives that triggered $2 billion in losses for the bank. (The price tag would ultimately total $6 billion.)

The French-born employee, Bruno Iksil, became the perfect illustration of Fisher's argument that nothing had changed. Dimon at first called the debacle "a tempest in a teapot."

But an investigation revealed serious management failings that allowed trades that, as Dimon later admitted, were "flawed, complex, poorly reviewed, poorly executed, and poorly monitored."

A report by the Fed's inspector general showed that the losses stemmed from JPMC's "failures in prioritization, loss of institutional knowledge through turnover, and poor coordination among agencies."

The Whale's losses revealed that even under the SEC's new "Volcker Rule," designed to put a governor on proprietary trading, a bank could still place a massive bet as a hedge against a decline in its entire portfolio. One author of the bill, Sen. Carl Levin (D-Mich.), called the gap "a big enough loophole that a Mack truck could drive right through."

The other author of the bill, Sen. Jeff Merkley (D-Ore.), had a message for Dimon: "If you want to be a head of a hedge fund, be a hedge fund. Terminate your access to the Fed's discount window, terminate your access to deposits, and then we have no quarrel."

The Whale provided more proof that big banks were too complex to manage, "not just for top bank executives, but too complex as well for creditors and shareholders to exert market discipline," wrote Fisher and Rosenblum in a *Wall Street Journal* op-ed in April. "And too big and complex for bank supervisors to exert regulatory discipline."

In June 2012, Fisher spoke in Scotland at the University of St. Andrews as part of the commemoration of that institution's 600th birthday, which also happened to be the 129th birthday of John Maynard Keynes.

The FOMC sets monetary policy for all fifty states, Fisher pointed out, thus its influence was uniform across the country. The same rate of interest is charged on bank loans whether you live in Texas or New York.

Why, then, had the Texas economy surpassed other states since the financial crisis? Though Texans were equally impacted by Washington's regulatory policies and the Fed's interest rates, employment in the Lone Star State had outperformed job creation in almost every other major industrialized economy worldwide.

Oil accounted for some of the effect; but only 2 percent of employment in Texas was directly generated by energy. Fisher credited state and local governments whose tax, spending, and regulatory policies were oriented toward job creation.

But the Fed continued to look at the nation's unemployment metrics as a whole without examining what was working at the state level.

In addition to businesses not knowing what the Fed was going to do, Obamacare, signed into law by the president on March 23, 2010, added another level of uncertainty, encouraging businesses to wait until the dust settled.

Even before the August 2012 FOMC meeting, Bernanke began making dozens of phone calls to FOMC members to gather support for a proposal he planned to present at the September meeting.

To continue downward pressure on long-term rates, Bernanke wanted to extend Operation Twist. Bernanke was determined to push inflation up to scare money out of the hidey-holes where it had been stashed. The theory: that people would lend and spend rather than see their money depreciate.

Bernanke was chasing his tail. You cannot force inflation higher if incomes aren't rising.

But like a dog with a bone Bernanke worked the committee, identified allies and dissenters, and then focused on the fence-sitters.

And meanwhile his allies went to work spinning the press.

"They have gone about their usual pre-FOMC leak frenzy where they talk to this reporter and that reporter," Steve Roach told Bloomberg TV on July 25, 2012. Former chairman of Morgan Stanley Asia, he had worked on the Fed's research staff in Washington during the 1970s.

"Jon Hilsenrath is actually the chairman of the Fed," Roach said. "When he writes something in the *Wall Street Journal*, Bernanke has no choice but to deliver on what he wrote." Roach predicted that QE3—more "crack" for investors—was in the offing, and "it's not going to work."

My buddy Jim Bianco wrote an e-mail to several senior Fed officials, including Chicago's Evans, who also served as the head of the FOMC's communications committee.

"These leaks are co-opting Fed policy," Bianco wrote. "They only seem to come out when the stock market is suffering and the market believes that they are timed for a short-term reaction."

Bianco created a timeline that showed vividly how Hilsenrath's stories tracked with three-day declines of the market, goosing it every time.

"It is almost like clockwork that every time the stock market has a bad day or two, we get a Hilsenrath story that more money printing is on the way," Bianco wrote. "Whether fair or not, given Hilsenrath's position as the 'Fedwire,' the market takes this as evidence the Federal Reserve will act to prevent a decline in equity prices."

The Fed maintained that Hilsenrath's stories were coincidental, triggered by worsening economic conditions. But the market had concluded it was no happenstance. A Bloomberg FOIA request had resulted in the release of Dudley's calendar, showing that he both placed and received dozens of calls to and from Hilsenrath every year. A cottage industry had sprung up among market watchers to track Hilsenrath's stories, the DJIA, and Fed announcements.

"To put it bluntly, the Fed is creating a monster," Bianco wrote, "and if they do not act to rein in these repeated Hilsenrath stories that suggest more QE is coming after three bad days in the stock market, the FOMC's reputation is going to devolve into it being a bunch of short-term market manipulators and not a body to determine traditional monetary policy."

In addition to the cottage industry tracking Fedwire, the Street had started counting the number of words in the FOMC statement. Usually under two hundred words, the statement had ballooned to eight hundred by the end of 2013. People even tracked the use of certain words, like "inflation" and "geopolitical." All in the service of understanding what the heck the Fed was thinking.

At the August 2012 meeting Bernanke set the stage to rev up more bond buying.

Plosser wanted Bernanke to wait until the end of the year, to see if the economy leveled out. Fisher compared Bernanke's insistence on more QE to a doctor overprescribing Ritalin to traders with attention deficit disorder. The only hawk with a vote, Lacker dissented for the fifth time that year.

Bernanke got his way in September, when the FOMC announced it would purchase an additional $40 billion in agency MBSs each month.

Bernanke had wooed Kocherlakota—a scholarly PhD—into the dove camp. "I've learned a lot by talking to him," Kocherlakota said, adding that Bernanke's "thinking is framed by data and models. It beats coming in there with just your gut."

Another one bites the dust.

Only Lacker voted against the chairman. "The larger we make our balance sheet, the riskier we make the exit," Lacker warned, saying he dissented because "the additional monetary stimulus was unlikely to result in a discernible improvement in economic growth."

Bernanke talked a good game, making it appear he cared about Main Street. "My colleagues and I are very much aware that holders of interest-bearing assets, such as certificates of deposit, are receiving very low returns," Bernanke said at a press conference in September 2012. "But low interest rates also support the value of many other assets that Americans hold, such as homes and businesses large and small."

It's true, the prices of some homes had been propped up. Private equity investors had snapped up foreclosures, boosting home prices at the lower end, while wealthy individuals were bidding up prices of luxury homes.

The second stated goal of ultralow interest rates was job creation.

"Healthy investment returns cannot be sustained in a weak economy and of course it is difficult to save for retirement or other goals without the income from a job," Bernanke said at the same press conference. "Thus, while low interest rates do impose some costs, Americans will ultimately benefit most from the healthy and growing economy that low interest rates help promote."

But that healthy and growing economy didn't happen. So savers were getting hammered for no good reason for the benefit of rich people.

By December 2012, the Fed was pumping $85 billion a month into the economy: $40 billion in mortgage-backed securities and $45 billion in Treasuries.

The public had been outraged by that same one-time ticket price for the bailout of AIG just four years earlier. What was once extraordinary financial intervention to save the global economy had become the equivalent of an AIG bailout a month. The markets had built up such a resistance to the drug of QE that it took larger doses to get the same result.

A few days later, Fisher gave a speech at the New York Harvard Club.

"We are blessed at the Fed with sophisticated econometric models and superb analysts," Fisher said. "The truth, however, is that nobody on the committee, nor on our staffs at the Board of Governors and the 12 Banks, really knows what is holding back the economy.... And nobody—in fact, no central bank anywhere on the planet—has the experience of successfully navigating a return home from the place in which we now find ourselves."

On June 3, 2009, Bernanke had been asked during a congressional hearing if the Federal Reserve would monetize U.S. government debt. In other words, print money. No way, no how, Bernanke had promised. "The Federal Reserve will not monetize the debt."

But that was effectively what he had done by becoming underwriter extraordinaire to Congress's bidding.

Hoenig left the Fed in 2012 to become vice chairman of the FDIC. Plosser and Fisher soldiered on, joined by fellow hawks Bullard and Esther George of Kansas City.

"With Mr. Fisher as a thought leader, some of the best new ideas are being developed within the Federal Reserve System," MIT professor Simon Johnson wrote in the *New York Times*. I bet Bernanke loved that.

However, the actions of the doves would always supersede the words of the hawks. Wall Street's quip "QEternity" no longer seemed far-fetched.

The December 2012 FOMC statement featured Fedspeak in its full glory: "This exceptionally low range for the federal funds rate will be appropriate at least as long as the unemployment rate remains above 6½ percent, inflation between one and two years ahead is projected to be no more than a half percentage point above the Committee's 2 percent longer-run goal, and longer-term inflation expectations continue to be well anchored."

But it couldn't hide the fact that the Fed had painted itself into a corner.

CHAPTER 20

The Taper Tantrum

FED STATEMENT WORD COUNT: 545

EFFECTIVE FED FUNDS RATE: 0.13%

10-YR TREASURY RATE: 2.36%

FED BANKS TOTAL ASSETS: $4,495.06B

DATE: 6/1/2015

I don't think [Fed policies are] causing a danger. . . . Is our policy a magic wand? No, it's not. But is it working? Yes, I think it is working.

—JANET YELLEN, NOVEMBER 2012

Wall Street was in full-blown rotation mode by 2013. The best and the brightest, knowing their incomes would be restrained under the new regulatory regime, could be seen jumping ship, their Hermès ties billowing in the wind. Their destination? Private equity firms.

I began to cover the subject of collapsing bond inventories at the biggest banks. The twenty-one primary dealers that traded with the Federal Reserve had trimmed their debt holdings to $56 billion by March 27, 2013, down from $235 billion in 2007. The combination of Dodd-Frank, with its aim of limiting risk-taking, and Basel III, with its increased capital requirements, had proved to be a toxic combination.

Was it any wonder that commercial bank officers were stumped? The stated aim of QE was to encourage banks to loan money. But other rules required they hold more capital against fresh loans if they did—to say nothing of the risk they assumed if yield curve normality ever made a comeback.

Private equity kingpins had become the new overlords of the corporate bond market. They had also discovered the profitability of being landlords.

Money was cheap for those who could access it. And investors were eager to buy into the next private equity fund in the hopes they could eke out positive returns. So private equity set its sights on the "sand states," ground zero of the housing crisis.

Home prices took off, especially in places like Phoenix and Las Vegas, where investors purchased distressed properties to hold, flip, or put on the rental market. Goldman Sachs and its clients contributed 10 percent to a $1 billion fund called Fundamental REO to purchase single-family properties.

Private equity firms lured investors into their funds to buy rental homes with promises of outsized returns. One company acquired a house in Riverside, California, for $131,000 and flipped it later the same month for $171,000. Do that enough and it adds up to real money.

But investors were crowding out buyers who intended to live in the homes. In 2012, they accounted for nearly a third of all sales in Miami, and about one in five sales in Phoenix and Las Vegas.

Absentee purchasers making all-cash offers for houses sight unseen indicated another kind of housing bubble in the works. Low-hanging fruit was being plucked by investors with a first-mover advantage. The real estate markets in Southern California and the Bay Area were some of the hottest markets, buoyed by the ability to monetize equity in technology companies.

After depleting the inventories of distressed homes on the East and West coasts, private equity looked inland. Texas markets held special appeal, given the hearty job growth and sheer number of companies relocating to the area.

Investors swarmed in, triggering a disturbing moment at the supermarket newsstand. Out of the corner of my eye, I saw the front cover story on real estate in *D Magazine*: "The Hottest Dallas Housing Market Ever."

Not all were sold.

"Betting on home price appreciation is not a sure thing," economist Shiller reminded investors. "Right now we have the Fed with a massive subsidy to the housing market, but you can't have a housing recovery without a jobs recovery."

Underneath the optimism lay a dormant employment sector and lackluster consumer spending. With no raises in sight, soaring rents, high prices for gasoline, and an increase in payroll taxes, "paycheck" consumers' wallets had been sucked dry.

The mere mention in May 2013 by Bernanke that the Fed might begin to wind down its bond-buying program triggered alarm as investors fled the bond market in terror. One strategist called it the three phases of tapering: denial, acknowledgment, and panic.

The "taper tantrum" showed just how difficult it would be for the Fed to retreat from its positions, for manipulated markets to regain a footing based on fundamentals.

On June 19, Jon Hilsenrath appeared on CNBC and was blindsided by an antagonistic Rick Santelli, who explained there are market "players" and "tailors." He accused Hilsenrath of being a "tailor," spinning in advance for Bernanke, lobbing softballs and not holding the Fed accountable for the extraordinary ballooning of the balance sheet. The startled Hilsenrath defended his work. Just doing his job, he said, working his sources.

But Santelli wasn't mollified. He demanded to know why Hilsenrath refused to challenge Bernanke about the obviously ineffective and risky QE programs. Hilsenrath complained that at Bernanke press conferences he rarely got a chance to ask follow-up questions, not a good answer to give the in-your-face Santelli.

At the Dallas Fed's briefing for the September 16–17, 2013, FOMC meeting, I advised Fisher that data indicated bond investors had moved to the final stage of grief, that of acceptance of the inevitability of higher interest rates. The ten-year Treasury note yield had moved from 1.63 percent in May 2013 all the way to 3 percent by September.

Besides, the Fed had become the elephant in the room, by far the largest player in the Treasury and mortgage markets. "Market functionality" was at risk. The Fed had crowded out natural buyers like mutual funds and other central banks and its credibility would be further eroded if they blinked once again.

The day before the FOMC meeting, I called Fisher, who was on his way to Washington. Fisher's executive assistant and I shared the same birthday, so Fisher never forgot mine.

"I'd like a fifteen-billion-dollar birthday gift," I said. "Go get me that taper."

"You know I'll always try my best," he said.

But Fisher and the hawks failed. The FOMC voted no, both on raising interest rates and ending QE. The excuse du jour? Policymakers feared economic turmoil because the government would be shutting down on September 30.

Bernanke's disastrous decision not to lean against the wind devastated the Fed's credibility with financial market veterans. Later in the year, the FOMC would agree to a modest taper, but the moment to show independence had been lost.

The world did not end with the government shutdown. In fact, financial markets perked up, concluding that the Fed would not start tapering until the March 2014 FOMC meeting.

"This episode should engender humility on all sides," Warsh wrote in the *Wall Street Journal*. "It should also correct the misimpression that QE is anything other than an untested, incomplete experiment."

Fisher had harsher words.

"If the members of the FOMC could manage to get themselves to once again be thought of as humble, competent people on the level of dentists, that would be splendid," Fisher said. "I would argue that the time to reassume a more humble central banker persona is upon us."

Bernanke's Herculean efforts to fix the economy with Keynesian remedies stumbled even as he pulled up to the finish line. As if in hiding, he skipped that year's Jackson Hole conference, marking the first time in twenty-five years the chairman of the Fed had not attended.

In early fall, the Fed-watch industry ramped up its speculation about who Obama would appoint as Bernanke's successor when his second term expired in January.

Among those mentioned—Geithner, former governors Kohn and Ferguson, and Stanley Fischer, former chairman of the Bank of Israel and the reigning "godfather" of central banking—was the ubiquitous Summers, the odds-on favorite. But Obama had inadequate political capital to make it happen.

During his short stint as president of Harvard, Summers had ignited controversy through numerous conflicts with faculty, and his opinion, offered at a small seminar, that women's lack of representation in the top tiers of math and science was probably due to "intrinsic aptitude," not discrimination.

Fisher, who served on Harvard's Board of Overseers, described Summers to me as "a bull who carried around his own china shop." The economist's comments infuriated women and triggered an acrimonious international debate. In February 2006, Summers stepped down from the presidency of Harvard in disgrace.

Since then, Summers had refused to take an aggressive stance on the need for greater financial reform of Wall Street. Democrats deluged Obama with letters of protest. After it became clear that he could not win confirmation in the Senate, Summers withdrew his name from consideration as Fed chairman.

Simon Johnson, ever a fan, tried to throw Fisher's name in the ring in one of his columns. "He would be the ideal candidate to become the next Fed chair," he said. "Unfortunately, the political power of megabanks means Mr. Fisher is unlikely to be called upon." Besides, he wasn't a PhD, for heaven's sake.

Yellen emerged as the top choice to succeed Bernanke, swept along by an avalanche of prominent female leaders lobbying the White House to appoint the first female Fed chair. Ironic since, once appointed, Yellen refused to be referred to as chairwoman, preferring the title "chair." (I favor "Fair Chair.")

Since 2008, Yellen, Bernanke, and Dudley had formed the Fed's inner circle. She had managed to build a reputation as an excellent forecaster and Cassandra about the housing bubble.

But FOMC transcripts from 2007 and 2008 show it wasn't until the spring of 2008 that it dawned on Yellen a financial crisis was hurtling toward the economy. Before then, Yellen even managed to downplay the concerns of others.

Reflecting back in 2010 during testimony to the Financial Crisis Inquiry Commission (FCIC), Yellen astonished her interviewers by saying, "I did not see and did not appreciate what the risks were with securitization, the credit rating agencies, the shadow banking system, the SIVs—I didn't see any of that coming until it happened."

As for the mortgage lenders in her own backyard, like the obviously out-of-control Countrywide: "I am not going to say that we saw in that institution all the dangers that were lurking there," Yellen told the FCIC. "Did we have a thorough appreciation of the flaws in the securitization process, and so forth, and the way they could affect the financial system as a whole?

No. But we certainly saw we had the largest mortgage lender in the United States."

Duh. No wonder her regulators were asleep at the switch.

In a subsequent speech in the fall of 2010, Yellen further conceded that "despite volumes of research on financial market metrics and weighty position papers on financial stability, the fact is that we simply didn't understand some of the most dangerous systemic threats. Meanwhile, things went along so well for so long that the common belief came to be that nothing *could* go disastrously wrong."

She mentioned the financial system stresses of LTCM, the Asian crisis, and the stock market crashes of the late 1980s and early 2000s.

"With each crisis, policymakers rolled up their sleeves and beat back the systemic threat," she said. "The levees held. . . . We appeared to have entered a new era of stability. We even gave it a name: the Great Moderation. We were left with the mirage of a system that we thought was invulnerable to shock, a financial Maginot Line that we believed couldn't be breached. We now know that this sense of invincibility was mere hubris."

Hubris and myopia. Yellen's admission had been stunning.

Would this prompt a harsh look in the mirror, a revisiting of her intellectual orthodoxy? No. Her faith in her models of monetary stimulus had grown stronger in the years that followed. Yellen was Bernanke in lipstick and a skirt.

But the reality was that hubris and myopia permeated the Fed system, as it can in any large, entrenched enterprise—government or private—that has few checks and balances. How to effect change? First it takes recognition that there's a problem. Though there were those inside the Fed who saw the need for change, like Rosenblum, they were not the ones at the top.

Critics maintained that Yellen's radical interventionist approach to the labor market would make even Keynes blush. Even so, her (undeserved) reputation as an economic forecaster, gender, and staunch belief in the value of continued and extraordinary monetary stimulus pushed Yellen to the front of the field.

Not everyone saw her as the strong leader the Fed needed to get out of its morass.

"Yellen's abrasive, intimidating style is probably more suited for a 'Mad Men' era as opposed to a modern office environment," Dick Anderson, who served for two years as the chief operating officer of the Fed Board, told the *Wall Street Journal*.

Hilsenrath wrote that Yellen would bring a "demanding and harder-driving leadership style" to the Fed, in contrast to the low-key, consensus-building Bernanke. She was regarded by some current and former Fed staffers as a "polarizing figure."

She had a tense relationship with Governor Tarullo, the Fed's point person on bank regulation. And there was the fact that she reminded everyone of their ninth-grade math teacher, not a plus in front of Congress.

At any rate, Yellen was the right PhD in the right place at the right time. On October 9, 2013, Yellen was nominated by President Obama to become chair of the Fed. The most liberal Fed leader since Marriner Eccles, going back to the Roosevelt and Truman administrations, she assumed the post in February 2014.

There was nothing unclear in Obama's message: maintain the status quo. The doves rejoiced. The hawks' tail feathers drooped, but Fisher vowed to keep fighting. As for me, I was determined to go down with the ship. There was no way I would quit given where the Fed was taking the country. My resolve had been strengthened.

Fisher had one last voting year to make a difference. So did I.

CHAPTER 21

The New Sheriff in Town

FED STATEMENT WORD COUNT: 558
EFFECTIVE FED FUNDS RATE: 0.034%
10-YR TREASURY RATE: 2.09%
FED BANKS TOTAL ASSETS: $4,482.35B
DATE: 1/1/2016

The truly unique power of a central bank, after all, is the power to create money, and ultimately the power to create is the power to destroy.
—PAUL VOLCKER, 1994

Soon after ringing in the New Year, a hilarious column by one of my closest friends, market analyst Peter Boockvar of the Lindsey Group, made me laugh out loud.

I forwarded "Beer Goggles" to Fisher, who loved it when I shot great metaphors his way.

On January 14, 2014, Fisher quoted Boockvar, giving what would become his most famous speech: "QE puts beer goggles on investors by creating a line of sight where everything looks good."

For his "wine and martini" audience, the National Association of Corporate Directors, Fisher defined the term "beer goggles," described in the Urban Dictionary as the effect that alcohol has in rendering a person alluring who one would ordinarily regard as unattractive.

"Things often look better when one is under the influence of free-flowing liquidity," Fisher said. "This is one reason why William McChesney Martin, the longest-serving Fed chairman in our institution's 100-year history, famously said that the Fed's job is to take away the punch bowl just as the party gets going."

Punch bowl, beer goggles. Different eras but the same thing.

The Fed's bull market had numerous unintended consequences, Fisher said. It fueled share buybacks, financed by debt issuance, which flattered earnings per share, but over the long haul chipped away at top-line growth: dividend payments financed by cheap debt bolstered share prices, and margin debt pushed up against all-time records.

But what goes up must come down, sometimes abruptly. And recessions can severely harm—even kill—profitable businesses.

Fisher said he would be heartened if his colleagues adopted the First Law of Holes: If you find yourself in a hole, stop digging. "We should stop digging. I plan to cast my votes at FOMC meetings accordingly."

The Fed had decided in December to reduce its monthly bond purchases by $10 million, though that left accommodation essentially unchanged. Markets didn't even flinch. Fisher believed the cut should have been twice as large. But it was a move in the right direction.

The *New York Times* profiled both Fisher and Kocherlakota, who would be voting members in 2014. One hawk, one dove.

"The gas tank is full," Fisher said. "Having gone down this path, which I believe was not necessary, of adding these last few gallons in the tank, and if you're going to withdraw that stimulus, how do you do so without creating market havoc?"

As Fisher and former Dallas Fed board chairman Kelleher, "an iconic consumer of Wild Turkey bourbon," agreed: "You can't go from Wild Turkey to cold turkey overnight."

Fisher's CEOs were sounding more positive, but still wanted more clarity about taxes, federal spending, and regulation. "I hear an enormous disdain for the current administration and for the Congress," Fisher said. "I haven't heard in over a year that they need cheaper money or more access to money."

Bernanke had left the Fed. Yellen was the new sheriff in town. She and Fisher still exchanged a hug and a kiss before FOMC meetings. All was cordial. But both must have been a little wary as her regime began.

Yellen had promised during her nomination hearings to put a human face on the high cost of unemployment. Even during her swearing-in, Yellen pledged to "never forget the individual lives, experiences and challenges that lie behind the statistics we use to gauge the health of the economy."

Clearly, she had forgotten her fellow seniors. They counted for nothing in Yellen's worldview.

During her first public speech as Fair Chair, Yellen managed to botch both the substance and the "theater," as Fisher would say. In very personal and impassioned remarks, Yellen mentioned three residents of Chicago struggling to find full-time jobs.

"They are a reminder that there are real people behind the statistics," Yellen told the National Interagency Community Reinvestment Conference on March 31, 2014. Their experiences "tell us important things that the unemployment rate alone cannot." She implied the Fed would continue its path until they and people like them had good jobs.

Yellen neglected to mention that two of the three people she held up as examples had criminal records—one for felony theft and the other for heroin possession—deterrents in gainful employment with companies that did routine background checks. What was shocking: they had told Yellen about their pasts. She chose to leave out those salient facts in her speech.

Predictable result: The resulting news stories were not about the Fed's efforts to bolster the labor market but Yellen's lie by omission.

What can ultraeasy monetary policy do to help those with criminal records find long-term meaningful work? Nothing. Of course people with criminal records need jobs too, but that's a different speech. Why gamble with the Fed's credibility? To me, it was just another example of an economist's selective use of data to prove a point.

By the time Yellen took over, only two District Bank presidents, including Fisher, had previous banking experience. He had branded himself as the proud man on the street, unashamed that he was not a PhD. And though he chose to be judicious with his dissents, Fisher continued to make it clear what he thought about Yellen's continued insistence on maintaining ZIRP and QE, which was having little impact on the labor market.

"I don't think there is any doubt that quantitative easing enabled the rich and the quick," Fisher said in a speech at the London School of Economics in March. "It was a massive gift."

I had found my own public voice, making twenty speeches in 2014 (always pointing out at the beginning, as did Fisher, that my views were my own, not that of the Federal Reserve). My audiences were hungry for the truth about what was going on inside the Fed.

I dropped the word "well-intentioned" from my talks; by now, I considered the Fed completely politicized, reckless, and harmful.

At each FOMC meeting, Yellen refused to raise interest rates. To justify her inaction, she kept moving the "target" unemployment rate down to 6.5 percent, when she finally said "never mind"—the Fed would no longer employ a target level. Evidence mounted that monetary policy was the wrong tool to bring people into the labor force.

Businesses shed good full-time jobs with benefits, not knowing what the economy would be a year down the road. People dropped out of the workforce and didn't return, content to go on unemployment or get Social Security disability if they could qualify. Thanks to the Fed, the expanding welfare state had become so cheap to finance that it actually created the illusion the deficit was falling.

In March, I reported to Fisher that indicators like corporate forward price-to-earnings, Shiller CAPE P/E 10 ratios, and market capitalization as a percentage of GDP had reached levels not seen since the dot-com boom of the late 1990s. Margin debt was pushing up against an all-time record.

The statement after the March 2014 FOMC meeting said explicitly for the first time that it would keep short-term rates lower than normal *even after inflation and employment returned to their longer-run trends* (my emphasis). Kocherlakota dissented; Fisher kept his powder dry.

In April, Toyota shocked officials in Torrance, California, by announcing it would move its North American sales headquarters—with about three thousand employees—to Plano, a booming suburb north of Dallas. With cheaper housing, better public schools, and lower taxes, Plano and other Dallas suburbs were a magnetic draw for corporations that wanted a business-friendly environment and lower cost of living.

What if other states followed the Texas model? Would the American economy improve?

In early April, I boarded a plane to fly to Georgia for the Atlanta Fed's annual Financial Markets Conference at Stone Mountain.

I was upbeat for two reasons. I intended to meet one of my heroes,

Jeremy C. Stein, a member of the Board of Governors who would be giving a speech. And I was awaiting good news about my stepfather's treatment at MD Anderson Cancer Center in Houston.

Papa had been diagnosed a few months earlier with small cell lung cancer but was admitted into a clinical drug trial that showed great promise. His visit with the oncologist to determine whether or not the new medicine worked would take place while I was in the air, but all signs looked good.

After takeoff, I pulled my Fed laptop from my computer bag, slid my security "token" into the USB port, and tried to work.

The token was a device that locked unauthorized users out of the computer; if not in use, Fed security rules dictated it had to be held in a different bag from the laptop.

The aircraft flew into bad weather, bucking like a bronco at a Texas rodeo. Always an anxious flyer, I gritted my teeth and dug my fingernails into the arms of the window seat. That flight was the most turbulent I'd ever endured.

As the plane prepared for landing, a flight attendant barked at me to put my computer away. I slammed it shut and tucked it between the wall of the fuselage and the metal bar of the seat in front of me, since I couldn't stand up to reach my laptop bag.

When the plane touched down at the Atlanta airport, the passengers cheered. I turned on my phone and saw a message from my mother. Only two words: "Please call."

As the plane taxied to the gate, I phoned her.

"Danielle, the news is bad," mom said. "The trial didn't work. They gave Papa three months to live."

Shocked, I burst into tears. My children would be devastated to lose their grandfather. I grabbed my things and rushed out of the aircraft to find a place to weep in private.

After pulling myself together, I took a taxi to the conference center. In my room I reached into my carry-on for my computer.

No laptop. I dug around in my purse. No security token.

Panic rising, I closed my eyes and retraced my steps. Taxi, bathroom, crying, window seat. Federal Reserve computer on the floor. With the security token plugged in.

My job was at stake—but so was much more. I had numerous policy documents on my computer that were considered "restricted controlled," circulated only to a handful of people inside the Fed. A leak of discussions at the September 2012 FOMC meeting about possible actions in December had prompted a "mole hunt" at the highest levels inside the bank, illustrating the lengths people would go to get information about the Fed's future actions. (The alleged mole was never identified.)

I got on the phone. No one had turned in the computer at the Atlanta airport. The plane had not been cleaned, but had flown immediately back to Dallas. But the aircraft wasn't there either.

Early the next morning, I raced to the airport to get answers. They found the plane in Albuquerque. Finally, I learned my laptop had been found by the cleaning crew, security token still in place.

But I was still in trouble. Had someone downloaded everything? I had the laptop shipped overnight to Dallas and with trepidation returned to the conference.

I got back in time to hear Jeremy Stein's speech. Widely regarded then as the brightest mind on the Board of Governors, he delivered an alarming prediction based on the behavior of high-yield bond spreads.

Bond spreads behave like an accordion. As the price to finance riskier credit increases, spreads widen, meaning investors demand more compensation to take on the risk of default.

As economic cycles peak and inevitably turn, the accordion contracts and the compensation investors demand decreases. Stein's concern was that spreads were so narrow investors were not demanding nearly enough in payment for the risk they were taking on. His research showed that every time the inevitable widening occurred, the economy landed in recession.

My brain raced. If what Stein said was accurate, the Fed had missed a whole rate-hiking cycle.

After weaving through rows of chairs, I planted myself in front of Stein and stuck out my hand.

"Hi, I'm Danielle," I said. "I advise Richard Fisher on the financial markets." We shook hands.

"I know exactly who you are," Stein said.

Stein had joined the Board in May 2012 with an impressive background: former president of the American Finance Association, educated at Princeton and MIT, professor at Harvard.

As an academic known for papers exploring imperfections in financial markets, Stein studied how investors actually behaved instead of the way Fed economists thought they would behave.

I knew Fisher had shared some of my briefings with Stein. He and Stein had even signed and forwarded one of my memos to Bernanke, underscoring their own concerns about the ABS market in October 2012, when alarm bells about auto-backed subprime loans started ringing.

"I paid avid attention to your presentation," I said. "If what you're saying is correct, then the discussion around the FOMC table this month should not even be about the taper. We're already too late. The train has left the station."

Stein looked glum, but nodded.

"You are exactly right," Stein said.

We chatted briefly, but I didn't ask him the question everyone wanted to know: Why had Stein just announced he would resign from the Board after serving only two years? Appointed to fill an unexpired term, he had been expected to serve six years.

Stein had told the media he wanted to preserve his tenured professorship at Harvard. But a seat on the Board with a vote at every FOMC meeting is one of the most powerful jobs in the world, pure gold on any economist's résumé.

"He's exhausted from the fight," Fisher told me. Since Yellen had been appointed Fed chair "he knows he'll never win. He can do more on the outside than on the inside."

In the midst of my own drama, the meeting with Stein slapped me back into reality. Not even a Harvard professor on the Board of Governors could fight the Fed's DNA, the Jell-O pyramid.

As soon as I returned to the Dallas Fed, I was summoned to a security tribunal that included two of my bosses and the head of technology services in Sup & Reg.

They grilled me. I had no good answers. Humiliated, I imagined my career at the Fed ending in disgrace.

They revealed my computer showed no signs of being turned on after my last shutdown. Even so, they hammered home the magnitude of my security breach. I left the room aware my job hung in the balance.

Rosenblum had recently retired. In a standing-room-only auditorium at the Dallas Fed, he'd given me a shout-out at his retirement ceremony, one of the proudest moments of my life.

But he couldn't save me now. Other allies had moved on to jobs outside the bank. I refused to send an SOS up to Fisher.

I had been praying to find grace for my children and myself in the weeks to come with Papa. The next day I arrived early, went to the fourteenth floor, and knocked on the door of Ann Worthy's office. She was head of Sup & Reg, and my only remaining potential advocate.

Worthy had a Bible open on her desk. She looked up, invited me in. I spilled out my woes, my fear of losing my job, of leaving Fisher in the lurch over my stupidity. Over my fears for Papa.

Patiently, Worthy reassured me that Fisher valued my work too highly for me to lose my job, and that I would find spiritual strength for the days ahead. A much appreciated moment of redemption.

I wasn't fired but informed that I could no longer label my policy recommendations to Fisher with the word "policy," which equaled classified. From now on, they would be titled "Markets Brief, Part 2." As punishment, they killed my midcycle FOMC brief, effectively cutting my workload in half. Classic.

My stepfather declined rapidly. So Papa could spend his last days surrounded by his family, we moved him into our home in Dallas. He died on July 9, 2014. I felt deep sorrow but also relief he didn't suffer long.

Worthy retired, triggering an epiphany. I had no allies left inside the bank besides Fisher. If the Fed couldn't figure out how to exit QE, my work there was done when Fisher's voting year ended.

In June, Dudley and/or Yellen had shocked markets by venturing—through Hilsenrath—that maybe markets were too complacent. "The worry at the Fed is that when investors become unafraid of risk," Hilsenrath wrote, "they start taking more of it, which could lead to trouble down the road."

But the Fed had encouraged that sense of calm by saying rates would stay low for the foreseeable future.

"It is a problem of their own making," said Martin Barnes, chief economist at BCA Research. "If they want to sustain zero interest rates and push up asset prices, how can they expect to have that with no excesses and no risk taking?"

In July 2014, Yellen presented the Federal Reserve's Semiannual Monetary

Policy Report to the Congressional Committee on Banking, Housing, and Urban Affairs.

Sen. Elizabeth Warren (D-Mass.), then the most junior member of the Senate Banking Committee, took the Fair Chair to task over JPMC's "living will," an exercise required by Dodd-Frank to determine if it could be liquidated without taxpayer funds.

Warren pointed out that in 2008, Lehman had $639 billion in assets; by 2014, JPMC had nearly $2.5 trillion in assets. In 2008, Lehman had 209 subsidiaries. Warren expressed "shock" that JPMC now had 3,391 subsidiaries. Shadow banking was alive and well.

JPMC had filed three living wills; the Fed had not rejected any of them. "Can you honestly say that JPMorgan can be resolved in a rapid and orderly fashion as described in its plans with no threat to the economy and no need for a taxpayer bailout?" Senator Warren asked.

Yellen said that the Fed was continuing to work with firms like JPMC to give them feedback on their living wills. Warren looked with disdain over her glasses at Yellen. Has JPMC "ever gotten to a plan, which you can say with a straight face, is credible?"

"I've understood this to be a process," Yellen said. "These are extremely complex documents to produce. In our second round of submission, we're looking at plans that run into tens of thousands of pages."

What had been released to the public was thirty-five pages long. Essentially nothing had changed except that the banks had gotten bigger, more complex to manage, more impossible to understand.

"I remind you, there are very effective tools that you can use if those plans are not credible," Warren lectured Yellen, "including forcing those financial institutions to simplify their structure or forcing them to liquidate some of their assets. In other words, break them up."

That would never happen on Yellen's watch. And another Fischer knew it.

At Camp Kotok that August, Jim Bianco and I sat in a canoe and debated for nearly three hours, trying to understand why Stanley Fischer would come out of retirement to work under Yellen, or for that matter, any other central banker in the world.

The accepted giant among his peers, Fischer had received universal plaudits for his steering of the Bank of Israel through the aftermath of the global financial crisis. Insiders joked that if Mario Draghi, head of the European Central Bank, was suffering an existential policy crisis in the night, he would reach for the phone and ask Stan for advice. He had been Bernanke's thesis adviser at MIT.

Fischer had retired less than a year earlier. But he'd agreed to come out of retirement and in June had been confirmed as vice chairman of the Board of Governors.

We concluded that Fischer had answered a higher calling. It was no secret that Yellen was a pure-play academic, a sharp contrast to Fischer's reputation as a commonsense central banker.

Anything but bashful at his first FOMC meeting, Governor Fischer asked why the Fed relied on the core personal consumption expenditure (PCE) measure of inflation.

Fischer said he lived his life by the Consumer Price Index (CPI), as did his children. In his opinion, the only realistic measures of inflation were the CPI and the Dallas Fed Trimmed Mean PCE. (I bet Fisher got a kick out of that, since this relatively young metric had been nurtured under his leadership.)

One brave Fed staffer explained that the models the Fed used to set interest rates wouldn't function if they didn't use PCE. The no-nonsense Bullard jumped in.

"Let me get this straight," Bullard said, according to a Fed official who was present. "Crap in, crap out? That's how we make policy?"

Speaking of inflation, Yellen's duplicity had become so obvious that her use of one word—"transitory"—had become the brunt of jokes on Wall Street.

She used it to explain her reason for shifting her favored inflation metric from "core" to "headline" PCE.

As previously mentioned, headline inflation is what we see on the front page of the newspaper. It's got everything in it: food, energy, the whole basket. Core inflation measures, however, strip out food and energy prices, which reduces the volatility of reported inflation.

Want to get under any retiree's skin? Try explaining how they are supposed to live on a fixed income based on core anything. But something unusual happened in the summer of 2014.

After peaking at $110 per barrel early that summer, crude oil plunged to a low of $28.

The dramatic move prompted Janet Yellen to introduce the word "transitory" to the phenomenon of exceedingly low energy prices. This allowed her to shift the focus to using the headline inflation metric, as she contended that low oil prices wouldn't hang around for very long. Hence their transitory nature. Over two years later, headline inflation was still below core inflation.

Had she stuck with core inflation, Yellen would have been compelled to raise interest rates—something she didn't want to do. So she brandished a word to give herself cover—transitory—and simply changed the measure. Bad economic data? Transitory. Weakness in job growth? Transitory.

With Yellen changing the rules to fulfill her academic agenda, Bianco and I concluded that Stan Fischer would offer another check and balance to steer others on the FOMC back down to planet Earth.

It was pie-in-the-sky monetary policymaking, after all, that had landed the Fed at the epicenter of the financial crisis. If there was one thing Fischer understood, it was financial stability, making him the antithesis of the woman at the helm, who appreciated little about the complexity of the financial system and its capacity for financial contagion.

At least the other Fisher, my boss, would soon be extricating himself from what can only be described as a broken decision-making framework.

In November 2014, Fisher and I were gearing up for his last vote in December. He happened to be in New York at the same time I was there, a rare occasion when our paths crossed.

I invited Fisher to meet some of my closest Wall Street contacts: Arthur Cashin, director of Floor Operations for UBS Financial Services at the NYSE; Peter "Beer Goggles" Boockvar, chief market analyst for the Lindsey Group; and Howard Silverblatt, high priest of stats at S&P Dow Jones Indices.

With a chill in the night air, we gathered at the historic King Cole Bar at the St. Regis Hotel to "marinate ice cubes," as Cashin was fond of saying.

We ordered drinks beneath the gaze of *Old King Cole*, the massive, ribald mural painted by Maxfield Parrish.

It was a bittersweet few hours, almost like a wake. Intelligence from my closest confidantes had armed me with the ammunition to send Fisher off to battle. The recognition that we'd been on the losing end of a long-waged war was the silent sixth guest. We had fought the good fight, but we agreed that Yellen was an intractable foe, more married to her models than Greenspan and Bernanke combined.

The December 2014 FOMC ended with another rare "hat trick" of dissent, with Fisher and two others voting no to the proposed panel recommendation for widely different reasons, a reflection of how contentious and divided the committee had become.

This was Fisher's last vote at the Fed. His swan song was included in the statement released by the FOMC:

"Voting against the action were Richard W. Fisher, who believed that, while the Committee should be patient in beginning to normalize monetary policy, improvement in the U.S. economic performance since October has moved forward, further than the majority of the Committee envisions, the date when it will likely be appropriate to increase the federal funds rate; Narayana Kocherlakota, who believed that the Committee's decision, in the context of ongoing low inflation and falling market-based measures of longer-term inflation expectations, created undue downside risk to the credibility of the 2 percent inflation target; and Charles I. Plosser, who believed that the statement should not stress the importance of the passage of time as a key element of its forward guidance and, given the improvement in economic conditions, should not emphasize the consistency of the current forward guidance with previous statements."

Yet another convoluted FOMC statement that made little sense.

All three dissenters—Plosser, Kocherlakota, and Fisher—would soon be gone from the Fed.

CHAPTER 22

Culture Shock

If it were possible to take interest rates into negative territory, I would be voting for that.

—Janet Yellen, February 2010

After flinging my baited hook into Grand Lake Stream, I plopped down in the canoe and tried not to tip over my fishing buddy, Charles Plosser.

On a sunny, blazing hot afternoon in August 2015 at Camp Kotok, I angled for smallmouth bass with the former hawk who in March had retired as president of the Philadelphia Fed. We had a lively conversation.

I'd come full circle. In June, a few months after Fisher left the Dallas Fed, I also resigned. I relished the prospect of spending time with friends as I envisioned the next chapter of my life. And caught some fish.

By Camp Kotok's rules, what's said on the lake stays on the lake. But Plosser gave an interview that week to The Street. Though everyone anticipated that the Fed would raise interest rates in September, Plosser doubted the FOMC's ability to normalize rates after seven years stuck at zero.

"We're in uncharted territory," Plosser said. "This is something we've never done before, and central banks have rarely done. . . . I think financial markets should get away from this notion that everything the Fed does is so important. Lots of things go on to determine the path of the economy that have nothing to do with the Fed."

In September 2015, the FOMC would again fail to raise rates. The excuse this time: an unexpected move by China to devalue its currencies had sent shock waves through the global financial markets. And yet, as with the "taper tantrum," the markets were ready for the Fed to move and actually surprised that it didn't. Another wasted opportunity.

Staring up at the stars in Maine gave me time to look back on the near decade I had spent at the Federal Reserve. Two words came to mind: abdication and complicity. Congress and the White House are guilty of abdicating their leadership to the Fed. The Fed facilitates their misfeasance, hence its complicity.

I began to recognize my mission: to educate the public about what goes on inside the Fed. It's no black box and it's certainly not worthy of the mystique that surrounds it.

Back to my boogeyman: debt. Driving me is the awareness of the high price of debt, psychologically and in real terms. Rather than take on hard decisions, the leadership in Washington has used debt. The Fed is their banker.

The unintended consequences of unconventional monetary policy run amok: pension systems at risk, unaffordable housing, malinvestment, rampant financial engineering by America's top companies, stagnant wages, millions who have dropped out of the labor force, the stealth growth of the safety net financed by record low interest rates. And of course, more asset price bubbles than ever before.

"Such environments raise the not-so-fine art of financial engineering to a 'botox state,'" Art Cashin said. "It's no secret that companies have been gorging themselves on share buybacks and mergers and acquisitions, nonproductive but highly lucrative endeavors. When combined, the results are magnificent—costs are cut, profits juiced and bonus season becomes the most wonderful time of the year."

It could all be laid at the feet of the Fed, which has essentially become the fourth branch of the U.S. government.

The Fed's balance sheet stood at $4.5 trillion. I wondered what Yellen's husband, George Akerlof, who had railed against the deficit racked up by the Bush administration, thought about the outrageous balance sheet and Yellen's obvious role in exacerbating income inequality.

Bizarrely, Bernanke's renunciation of his GOP affiliation was lauded as brave when his self-congratulatory memoir, *The Courage to Act*, was released in 2015. But how exactly is income inequality the fault of any political party when the Fed is in charge?

At a press conference in June 2016, Yellen reiterated that the Fed would continue to reinvest proceeds from maturing securities and that she anticipated continuing this policy "until normalization of the level of the fed funds rate is well underway."

She may as well have said never and been done with it.

In fact, signs indicate that Yellen intends to continue the expansion of the balance sheet. Other central banks are buying corporate bonds and stocks. As of mid-2016, the Bank of Japan owned over half of the nation's exchange-traded fund (ETF) market. If central banks keep chasing the White Rabbit, they risk running out of things to buy.

Through surrogates and back channels, Yellen is preparing the nation for the possibility of instituting negative interest rates, a nightmare that's landed on Japan's shore. A top-selling item in Japan these days: safes, where Japanese can stash their currency rather than pay a bank for the privilege of keeping their money. The Tokyo manufacturer Eiko reported in April 2016 that shipments of home safes had doubled since the previous fall.

Maybe she should pick up a European newspaper. A few headlines from the eurozone, where negative rates are a reality, might show Yellen how bad things could get in the United States.

An early 2016 report from a German regulator warned that the country's life insurance companies, which hold over 80 percent of their investments in fixed bond instruments, will start to fold in 2018. If Draghi keeps rates in negative territory, he will succeed in driving them out of business.

So bye-bye money market funds, see you later pensions, and adios insurance companies. Does this seem strange to anyone?

Fisher and others on the FOMC tried to fight ZIRP and QE because they were not married to their models. What they received in return for their rational resolve was the "boy who cried wolf" treatment from their ivory tower counterparts and much of the financial press.

But remember, at the end of the fairy tale, the wolf shows up. The Federal Reserve's radical monetary policy—imposed by academics with no experience in the business world—has proved a disaster on an unprecedented scale. Global systemic risk has been exponentially amplified by the Fed's actions.

Who will pay when this credit bubble bursts? The poor and middle class, not the elites. If those injured most by Fed policy could understand, they would be marching at Yellen's door with protest signs, screaming "Show us the wealth effect!"

The fundamental changes wrought by Fed policies over the last eight years will prove difficult if not impossible to unravel, especially with unexpected events like Brexit that promise to keep the global economy in turmoil. As long as Europe remains mired in slow economic growth and negative interest rates, any efforts to hike rates in America will be fraught with hazard.

As the balance sheet of the United States ballooned, the Fed and Treasury missed a singular opportunity created by the crisis. The Irish government sold a 100-year bond for 2.35 percent. Spain issued 50-year debt. Mexico sold a first-of-its-kind century bond priced in euros. Pension funds and insurance companies snatched them up. What about the U.S. of A.? Crickets chirping.

I'll give them this much. It is a statement of fact that the United States is paying less in interest than the average of the past half century. In 1995, the government shelled out $232 billion in net interest payments. In 2015, it had dropped to $223 billion.

Is this a reflection of good behavior? Not hardly. According to the CBO's math, if the yield on the ten-year Treasury note rises to 4.1 percent over the next ten years, interest payments will swell to $839 billion. A nightmare.

In early 2015, a revived effort in Congress to "audit the Fed" gathered steam with the introduction of a bill by Sen. Rand Paul (R-Ky.).

Critics demanded the central bank return to its roots, when it was a "bankers' bank," an entity that provided liquidity for banks in trouble. No monetary central planning. No pointless attempts to manipulate the GDP, inflation, or the job market. No issuance of cheap debt to encourage Wall Street to invest and float all boats.

The call to audit the Fed—which has been around in various forms for decades—was in some ways misleading. The Fed's internal financial processes are audited every year by the GAO and are made public. But the "secret" loans made to Wall Street's big banks in the aftermath of the financial crisis engendered deep suspicion. Paul's bill would allow the GAO to question the Fed's decision-making process.

"I want to be completely clear. I strongly oppose 'Audit the Fed,'" Yellen told Congress. "Central bank independence in conducting monetary policy is considered a best practice for central banks around the world. Academic studies, I think, establish beyond the shadow of a doubt that independent central banks perform better."

Can't argue with those "academic studies." (Except that devilish detail that most can't be replicated.)

Fisher also opposed Paul's bill. "It is always politically convenient to make something sound mysterious, if not malevolent, by claiming it is opaque," Fisher said in a speech to the Economic Club of New York. "My suspicion is that many of those in Congress calling for 'auditing' the Fed are really sheep in wolves' clothing. Having proven themselves unable to cobble together with colleagues a working fiscal policy or to construct a regulatory regime that incentivizes rather than discourages investment and job creation—in other words, failed at their own job—they simply find it convenient to create a bogeyman out of an entity that does its job efficiently."

I doubt he believed that part about "efficiently." But he did believe in the independence of the Fed and the representation of Main Street the District Bank presidents brought to the discussion.

Meanwhile, the Fed advertised that it was trying to clean up one of its most problematic operations: Sup & Reg at the New York Fed.

If all was working the way the Fed intended, the bank examiners who supervised Lehman Brothers, Bear Stearns, Merrill Lynch, and others should have seen and sounded the alarm about the extraordinary risk that had built up in the system long before 2008.

After the collapse, the New York Fed had under its supervision six of the top seven bank holding companies; its examiners were the front line of defense.

To address lingering cynicism, Dudley had established a "Listening to Our Critics" series in 2011, bringing in detractors for discussions over lunch.

Rosenblum was skeptical of these efforts. The Fed has a long history of politely "listening" to its antagonists in seminars and luncheons, then showing them the door and disregarding their views. The culture wouldn't change, but the Fed could boast, "Hey, we're listening to our critics!"

Dudley had even sat in the front row of a screening of the documentary *Inside Job,* which blamed the Fed—and Wall Street, Treasury, and others—for the financial crisis. The scathing critique prompted some squirming and peevish comments.

"Why do we get blamed for everything?" one New York Fed employee whined to Sheila Bair, former head of the FDIC, at one such event. Bair had often clashed with Geithner about the New York Fed's cozy relationship with banks.

"I do think they are trying to effectuate culture change," Bair told the *Wall Street Journal.*

Few knew how bad it really was. A secret report outlined the widespread cultural dysfunction inside the New York Fed.

In 2009, Dudley deputized an outsider, Columbia University finance professor David Beim, to find out why his Sup & Reg department had so spectacularly failed. Dudley gave Beim unlimited access to investigate internal problems and produce a report that would remain confidential.

Beim's team asked members of the New York Fed's Financial Risk Committee (FRC) why it had not seen rising risk from 2004 to 2007.

He learned the FRC had focused appropriately on a number of systemic issues, including subprime lending and related securities, "but its conclusions were quite moderate and no action was ever recommended," Beim reported. "Team members noted that the FRC meetings tended to be quite presentational, like lectures, where most participants listened rather than debated. Skeptical voices or disagreements were rarely heard in these large and formal sessions."

During 2007 and 2008, the FRC recognized problems such as the freezing up of short-term lending markets and the sizable credit losses in MBSs. But it sounded no warning. "Contrarian and skeptical views (if there were any) were not heard in the large and largely formal meetings in the Board Room with the Bank's most senior management."

Beim's group interviewed about two dozen senior supervisors. They found a "culture that is too risk averse to respond quickly and flexibly to new challenges. Officers are intensely deferential to their superiors, similar to an army. Knowledge is too often hoarded in silos."

The parallels with the Dallas Fed were uncanny.

Many assumptions made by the Fed, from Greenspan and Bernanke on down, turned out to be utterly wrong, Beim said, starting with the belief that due to self-interest, "banks can be relied upon to provide rigorous risk control."

In fact, risk management was often marginalized within Wall Street banks. Internal governance broke down under the temptations to skew bonus pool calculations. "One of our [Fed] interviewees said that principled risk managers in banks were fired. Conversation with some bank risk managers themselves confirms that they felt powerless to stand up to the business side."

What about another of Greenspan's oft-quoted phrases, that "markets will always self-correct"? That Fed attitude at the top trickled down to disastrous result. From the Beim report: "A deference to the self-correcting property of markets inhibited supervisors from imposing prescriptive views on banks. . . . Many felt the deference to be excessive."

Some telling quotes from New York Fed employees:

"Grow up in this culture and you learn that small mistakes are not tolerated."

"Don't want to be too far outside from where the management is thinking."

"No opportunity to earn enough merit from ten right policy decisions to compensate for one wrong decision."

"After you get shot down a couple of times you tend not to 'go there' any more."

"Until I know what my boss thinks I don't want to tell you."

Above all, New York Fed employees strove for consensus. "Internal consensus is needed to move issues forward, but it can also become a source of delay, imprecision, and avoidance of responsibility," the Beim report said. Back to that crazy Jell-O pyramid!

Beim recommended that Dudley "launch a sustained effort to overcome excessive risk-aversion and get people to speak up when they have concerns, disagreements or useful ideas. Encourage a culture of critical dialogue and continuous questioning. . . . [Senior managers] need to encourage dissent rather than stifle it."

I thought of the sneers about the District Bank presidents, the dissenters who stood up to Bernanke and Yellen. The Beim report could apply to the Federal Reserve System across the board. Indeed "having made these points, interviewees believe that the silos in the New York Fed are nowhere near as rigid as within the [Washington] Board staff or other agencies."

Beim advised that the "mission of financial stability should be made more public, more explicit and put on a par with monetary stability. Future bank supervision will require a degree of sophistication, contrarian thinking and imagination beyond anything thought needed in the past."

Changing the Fed's internal culture had always been Rosenblum's most important goal. But as Beim pointed out, "cultures resist change" and only happen when there is a determined "push from the top."

Beim's report even addressed internal processes at the FOMC. "Discussion of systemic issues should either become a regular part of FOMC meetings, or a parallel process for this issue should be created. . . . Unless this support is strong and visible, actions at FRBNY to uncover systemic risk are unlikely to have real effect."

The Beim report was finished by September 2009. Dudley quietly began to make changes. His Sup & Reg recruited specialized and presumably hard-nosed examiners to station within each systemically important financial institution (SIFI) it supervised.

Carmen Segarra, a lawyer with thirteen years of experience in compliance, was hired as a senior bank examiner on October 31, 2011, and embedded with a New York Fed team at Goldman Sachs. Educated in the Ivy League and at the Sorbonne, Segarra, a passionate and strong-minded individual, believed she was following the new attitudes sought by Dudley.

Several large Goldman transactions had come under scrutiny for possible violations. When Segarra concluded that Goldman did not have an adequate firmwide conflict-of-interest policy in place she clashed with other Fed employees and her boss. She claimed she was told to change her findings. After she refused, Segarra was fired on May 23, 2012, having lasted only seven months.

Then Segarra shocked the Fed by going public with forty-six hours of secret audiotapes she'd made of internal discussions that allegedly showed the New York Fed going easy on Goldman Sachs.

Segarra's wrongful dismissal lawsuit was thrown out of court, as was her appeal, for technical reasons. Hearings on the merits were never held. Her boss said she was fired because the New York Fed had "lost confidence" in Segarra's ability "to not substitute [her] own judgment for everyone else's."

The tapes Segarra made of her conversations among colleagues revealed the same attitudes still prevailed between Goldman and its regulators. On one tape, her boss can be heard pleading with her, "But can't we say they have a policy?" Go along and get along. So-called regulatory capture—where the regulator acts in ways that benefit the entity it is regulating instead of the public—is a powerful force.

"The simple answer is that it's become standard practice for Fed employees to go to work for Wall Street firms," writer Michael Lewis said in the aftermath of the Segarra episode. "So the last thing they want to do is to alienate those firms and come across as people who don't 'get it.'" Not to mention the problem of having an examiner making $150,000 a year standing up to a banker who makes ten times that salary.

Segarra's revelations provoked outrage. Goldman immediately released a new and improved conflict-of-interest policy. During a congressional hearing in November 2014, Senator Warren declared that there was "a cultural problem" at the New York Fed. She told Dudley to fix it "or we need to get someone who will."

Behind the scenes, by the time the Segarra bombshell erupted, an obscure committee headed by Governor Tarullo had been at work for two years putting into place new regulations that would rein in the power of the New York Fed, which the *Wall Street Journal* called "once the most-feared banking regulator on Wall Street." (Obviously Hilsenrath's inside joke.)

Created in 2010, the powers of Tarullo's Large Institution Supervision Coordinating Committee (LISCC) were outlined in a paper called the "Triangle Document," which shifted the Washington Fed to the center of bank supervision.

Dodd-Frank had required the White House to appoint a Fed vice chairman for bank supervision. The Obama administration had failed to do so but never explained why—probably because Yellen knew removing the power of bank supervision would dilute the Fair Chair's power. LISCC was the compromise.

Tarullo had lowered the hammer on New York Fed supervisors in 2009 for not pushing hard enough to compel Citigroup to repay $45 billion it borrowed during the financial crisis. Then, during the London Whale debacle, Tarullo had demanded to know how New York Fed supervisors had let such massive bets occur without their knowledge and oversight.

So Tarullo was a logical choice to lead LISCC. At Bernanke's direction Tarullo and a sixteen-person committee began looking at the Fed's internal regulatory structure and practices.

Tarullo's team pulled most examiners out of banks and relocated them in a separate building near 33 Liberty Street. In early 2015, the Fed released results of annual bank stress tests run by Tarullo's committee, drawing attention to the power shift.

LISCC now oversees banks that pose the most risk to the financial system if they fail. The goal is to give Washington—and the FOMC—a better understanding of risks across the banking system and a more balanced method of oversight. Most supervisors of bank examiners now report to Washington, not the New York Fed.

The change undisputedly compromised Dudley's clout. Fisher had long argued that the New York Fed president should be treated the same as the other eleven District Bank presidents.

"I understand the suspicions that surround the New York Fed," Fisher said in early 2015. He called for power to be moved away from New York— and from the Board of Governors—and shifted toward the other eleven District Banks to give the rest of the country a greater voice in the Fed's decisions.

After all, why should the president of the "Wall Street" Fed have a stranglehold on the post of vice chairman of the FOMC and get a permanent vote? Why should political appointees of the party in power have so much dominance over a system that affects the economic well-being—and future—of the entire nation?

The New York Fed remains first among equals and probably always will, unless Congress acts, because Wall Street banks have subtle but overwhelming control of the system. In particular, "Government Sachs" has continued to dominate the Fed.

In July 2015, Patrick Harker, who had been chairman of the Philadelphia Fed's board of directors, switched seats when he was named the bank's new president. He had served as trustee of a handful of Goldman Sachs Trusts and as "independent manager" of the Goldman Sachs Hedge Fund Partners Registered Fund. (These are not included in his bio on the Philadelphia Fed's Web site.)

The next month, Harvard professor Robert S. Kaplan was named president of the Dallas Fed. During his twenty-three years at Goldman Sachs, Kaplan rose to vice chairman of Goldman Sachs Group and cohead of the firm's Investment Banking Division. When he left Goldman in 2006, he was bestowed the honorary title of Senior Director.

The longest-serving president in the Dallas Fed's history, Fisher had announced he would retire on November 13, 2014. The bank's seven-month search for a president had been handled by executive recruitment firm Heidrick & Struggles. On the firm's board of directors: Robert Kaplan.

If celebrity deaths come in threes, apparently so do new Fed appointees.

In November 2015, the Minneapolis Fed tapped Neel Kashkari to be its new president. He started working at Goldman during an internship while getting his MBA at Wharton and joined the firm upon graduating. During the heat of the financial crisis, Paulson plucked him from Goldman's ranks to manage TARP. (Actually, Kashkari cold-called Paulson and volunteered to come to DC to help.) In 2009, Kashkari left his post to join Pimco, then ran unsuccessfully for governor of California. Of course the Fed was the next stop.

Kashkari's appointment meant one third of the Fed District Banks—four out of twelve, including Dudley—were now controlled by Goldman alums. The result was predictable. In March 2016, Hilsenrath wrote a story in the *Wall Street Journal* with a picture of Kaplan and the headline: "The Decline of Dissent at the Fed."

Like Garry Kasparov, Goldman has positioned players on the Fed's chessboard, including paying $675,000 to Democrat presidential candidate Hillary Clinton for three speeches, probably to get her insight on the permutations of bank regulations under Dodd-Frank.

In 2017, four out of the five District Bank presidents eligible to vote on the FOMC will be Goldman alums. And let's not forget Bank of England governor Mark Carney and Mario Draghi, head of the ECB, just two of the many former Goldman Sachsonites now in overseas central banking posts.

Economist Joseph Stiglitz, who taught Yellen at Yale, told the *New Yorker* that he campaigned for her over Summers for Fed chairman because, as he put it: "Where was the soul of the Democratic Party? Was it about making the world safe for Goldman Sachs?" Apparently!

Central banking around the world has become a growth industry, populated with PhD economists and a few former investment bankers. These unelected men—and a few women, most notably Yellen—control the world's economic system. They are arguably more powerful than the world's political leaders chosen by voters. Under the banner of "central bank independence," they manipulate the monetary system based on their models and their connections.

And they are increasingly scary. In May 2016, Vitas Vasiliauskas, a Governing Council member of the ECB, told Bloomberg that central bankers still had tools to handle economic shocks despite negative interest rates.

"Markets say the ECB is done, their box is empty," said Vasiliauskas, head of Lithuania's central bank. "But we are magic people. Each time we take something and give to the markets—a rabbit out of the hat."

Because what she does impacts her counterparts around the world, Yellen has found herself in a quandary: what if following the Fed's dual mandate adversely affects the economies of other countries?

Events of the summer of 2015 vividly demonstrated how difficult it will be to raise interest rates back to what economists consider a normalized level of 3 to 4 percent in a global economy.

After keeping interest rates at zero for seven years, Yellen began signaling the Fed would initiate a rate-hiking cycle. But, as mentioned earlier, in August 2015, China had cleverly fought back with a minuscule devaluation, staying the Fed's hand at its September FOMC meeting.

By the time December 2015 rolled around, the nation was technically in an industrial recession. Never in the history of the Fed had a rate-hiking cycle been initiated with manufacturing in contraction. Yet Yellen, as if hypnotized by some outside influence, finally hiked rates 0.25 percent, sending financial markets into a tailspin.

Why was Yellen so insistent? Concurrent with the rate hike, the Fed quietly lifted the cap on a recently created lending facility to $2 trillion, insuring that in case of future disruption, the Fed's balance sheet would act as a backstop to the financial system.

Yellen had to hike the rate into positive territory to engage that lending option, which requires money market fund participation. With interest rates at the zero bound, money market funds have been operating in the red for years.

As her fame has grown, Janet Yellen is recognized in restaurants and airports around the world. But her world has narrowed. Because the Fed chairman can so easily move markets with a few casual words, Yellen can't get together regularly and shoot the breeze with businesspeople or analysts who follow the Fed for a living. She must rely on her instincts, her Keynesian training, and the MIT Mafia.

"You can't think about what is happening in the economy constructively, from a policy standpoint, unless you have some theoretical paradigm in mind," Yellen had told Lemann of the *New Yorker* in 2014.

One of Lemann's final observations: "The Fed, not the Treasury or the White House or Congress, is now the primary economic policymaker in the United States, and therefore the world."

But what if Yellen's theoretical paradigm is dead wrong?

The woman who "did not see and did not appreciate what the risks were with securitization, the credit rating agencies, the shadow banking system, the SIVs . . . until it happened" has led us straight into an abyss.

It's time to climb out. The Federal Reserve's leadership must come to grips with its role in creating the extraordinary circumstances in which it now finds itself. It must embrace reforms to regain its credibility.

Even Fedwire finally admitted in August 2016 that the Federal Reserve had lost its mojo, with a story headlined "Years of Fed Missteps Fueled Disillusion with the Economy and Washington." In an effort to explain rising extremism in American politics in a series called "The Great Unraveling," Jon Hilsenrath described a Fed confronting "hardened public skepticism and growing self-doubt."

Mistakes by the Fed included missing the housing bubble and financial crisis, being "blinded" to the slowdown in the growth of worker productivity, and failing to anticipate how inflation behaved in regard to the job market. The Fed's economic projections of GDP and how fast the economy would grow were wrong time and again.

People are starting to wake up. A Gallup poll showed that Americans' confidence that the Fed was doing a "good" or "excellent" job had fallen from 53 percent in September 2003 to 38 percent in November 2014. Another poll in April 2016 showed that only 38 percent of Americans had a great deal or fair amount of confidence in Yellen, while 35 percent had little or none—a huge shift from the early 2000s when 70 percent and higher expressed confidence (however misguided) in Greenspan.

In early 2016, Yellen told an audience in New York that it was too bad the government had leaned so heavily on the Fed while "tax and spending policies were stymied by disagreements between Congress and the White House." Maybe if she hadn't been throwing money at them, lawmakers might have gotten their house in order.

"The Federal Reserve is a giant weapon that has no ammunition left," Fisher told CNBC on January 6, 2016.

The Fed must retool and rearm.

First things first. Congress should release the Fed from the bondage of its dual mandate.

A singular focus on maintaining price stability will place the duty of maximizing employment back into the hands of politicians, making them responsible for shaping fiscal policy that ensures American businesses enjoy a traditionally competitive landscape in which to build and grow business.

The added bonus: shedding the dual mandate will discourage future forays into unconventional monetary policy.

Next, the Fed needs to get out of the business of trying to compel people to spend by manipulating inflation expectations. Not only has it introduced a dangerous addiction to debt among all players in the economy, it has succeeded in virtually outlawing saving.

Most seniors pine for a return to the beginning of this century when they could get a five-year jumbo CD with a 5 percent APR, offset by inflation somewhere in the neighborhood of 2 percent. Traditionally, 2 to 3 percentage points above inflation is where that old relic, the fed funds rate, traded. The math worked.

Under ZIRP, only fools save for a rainy day. The floor on overnight rates must be permanently raised to at least 2 percent and Fed officials should pledge to never again breach that floor. Not only will it preserve the functionality of the banking system, it will remind people that saving is good, indeed a virtue. And that debt always has a price.

Limit the number of academic PhDs at the Fed, not just among the leadership but on the staffs of the Board and District Banks. Bring in more actual practitioners—businesspeople who have been on the receiving end of Fed policy, CEOs and CFOs, people who have been on the hot seat, who have witnessed the financialization of the country and believe that American companies should make things and provide services, not just move money around.

Governors should be given terms of five years, like District Bank presidents, with term limits to bring in new blood and fresh ideas.

Grant all the District Bank presidents, not just New York's, a permanent vote on the FOMC. Why should Wall Street, not Main Street, dominate the Fed's decision making?

While we're at it, let's redraw the Fed's geographical map to better reflect America's economic powerhouses.

California's economy alone is the sixth biggest in the world. Add another Fed Bank to the Twelfth District to better represent how the Western states have flourished over the last hundred years.

Why does Missouri have two Fed banks? Minneapolis and Cleveland can be absorbed into the Chicago Fed. Do Richmond, Philadelphia, and Boston all need Fed District Banks? Consolidate in recognition of the fact that it isn't 1915 anymore.

Slash the Fed's bloated Research Department. It's hard to argue that a thousand Fed economists are productive and providing value-added insight when their forecasting skills are no better than the flip of a coin and half of their studies cannot be replicated.

Send most of the PhD economists back to academia where they belong. Require the rest to focus on research that benefits the Fed, studying how its policies impact American taxpayers and citizens. (Did the Fed do any studies about how ZIRP and QE would impact banking and consumers before it imposed them? No.)

Now take all the money you've saved and aim it squarely at Wall Street investment banks intent on always staying one step ahead of the Fed's regulatory reach. Hire brilliant people for the Fed's Sup & Reg departments and pay them market rates. Rest assured this will be ground zero of the next crisis.

And mix it up. One of Rosenblum's students applied for a job at the New York Fed. He came from a blue-collar background, spent seven years in the military, and earned his MBA from SMU on the GI Bill. Smart guy. But he couldn't get to first base at the New York Fed. They hire people from Yale and Harvard and NYU—people just like themselves. Others need not apply.

Then the top Ivy Leaguers stay for two years and move on to bigger money at Citibank or Goldman Sachs. It's a tribe that's been bred over ninety years and slow to change.

But if the culture of extreme deference at the New York Fed (which also exists in District Banks to a lesser degree) is not quashed, regulatory capture will continue with disastrous results. The Fed must give bank examiners the resources they need to understand the ever-evolving financial innovations created by Wall Street and back them up when they challenge high-paid bankers who live to skirt the rules.

Regulators must focus on the big picture as well as nodes of risk. Interconnectedness took down the economy in 2008, not just the shenanigans of a few rogue banks.

Focus on systemic risk and regulation around the FOMC table. Create a post with equal power and authority to that of the chair to focus on supervision and regulation. Yellen talks about monetary policy ad nauseam, but when challenged by the press or Congress on regulatory policy she stumbles and mumbles and does her best doe-in-the-headlights impersonation. Markets need predictability and transparency when it comes to Fed policy, not guesswork, parsing of the chair's words, and manipulation of FOMC minutes.

Finally, let nature take its course. Reengage creative destruction. Markets by their nature are supposed to be volatile. Zero interest rates prevent the natural failures of weak companies, weighing down the economy with overcapacity for generations.

Recessions might have been more frequent, the financial losses greater for some, but if the Fed had let the economy heal on its own, America would have been stronger in the end and the bedrock of our nation, capitalism, would not have been corrupted.

I could never have imagined how my near decadelong journey at the Federal Reserve would play out.

In the beginning, I had been a "risk radar" to benefit myself and those closest to me. I wanted to stay out of debt and make certain that my children had great educations and a foundation of financial savvy so that they could pursue their versions of the American dream.

But I realize now the stakes are much higher.

We've become a nation of haves and have-nots thanks to Fed policies that benefit the wealthiest investors, punish the savers and the retired, and put the nation's balance sheet at risk.

As consumers on the receiving end of Fed policies, we must reform our education system so that the American dream can be accessible to everyone. We must campaign for Congress to stop hiding behind the Fed's skirts.

And we must demand that the Fed stop offering excuse after excuse for its failures. Short-term interest rates must return to some semblance of normality and the Fed's outrageously swollen balance sheet must shrink in size. And most of all, the Fed must never follow Europe by taking interest rates into negative territory.

No more excuses. The Fed's mandate isn't to have a perfect world. That only exists in fairy tales, dreams, and the Fed's econometric models.

ACKNOWLEDGMENTS

The idea for this book was conceived over ten years ago in the heat of the great financial crisis. I joined the Federal Reserve in 2006, hoping to serve my country through what I saw coming: the greatest economic calamity to test our leadership since the 1930s. Way back as a rookie saleswoman on Wall Street, I had felt the invisible hand of Alan Greenspan, and sensed a force in the markets working against mom-and-pop investors. It was my hope that perhaps on the inside of the Fed, I could work to make a difference. What better opportunity than a crisis to revolutionize the approach to the monetary policymaking framework, and to stunt the drivers of the boom-and-bust cycles facilitated by intrusive intervention?

Several years later, the prospect did present itself to revisit the inflation metrics that missed the runaway prices in homes and financial assets that culminated in the crisis. The moment, though, passed and squandered. From that sad vista, the vision of this book was born.

During the buildup to the crisis, before I joined the Fed, I had become friends with David Rosenberg who was then at Merrill Lynch. "Rosie," as his friends call him, inspired me with his courage from the day we met, a gift that has yet to stop giving. He redefined true grit on the "sell-side" of Wall Street, calling the housing frenzy what it was, a bubble, long before most of his peers would have dared.

As far as my colleagues inside the Fed: to Harvey Rosenblum, I owe a tremendous debt of gratitude. Looking back, I realize I would have never connected the dots between monetary policy and the markets were it not for Harvey who imparted his four decades of wisdom to me. The early work that he and I collaborated on at the Fed opened my eyes to the dangers of moral hazard and its intentional consequences. To Michael Cox and Rick Alan, two fellow former insiders, thank you for setting the example of how to think critically and question the internal orthodoxy. David Luttrell and Joshua Zorsky were also the best wingmen I could have ever hoped to work with. The reams of briefs produced over the years would have never happened without you both.

Those briefs would also have never been possible without my tremendous network of colleagues who are now friends in New York. Without your collective market intelligence, I would have never been able to see clearly through your many prisms. At the risk of omitting someone, for which I hope you do forgive me if that's the case, many thanks to Joseph Abate, Joseph Astorina, Jonathan Basile, Hayley Boesky, Chris Flanagan, George Goncalves, Michael Hartnett, Richard Hill, Tobias Levkovich, Michelle Meyer, Oleg Melentyev, Leland Miller, Priya Misra, Tiina Siilaberg, Amanda Sneider, Vishwanath Tirupattur, Oliver Wiener, Ted Wieseman, and Ellen Zentner.

And then there is Zoltan Pozsar. Your patient approach to educating me on the plumbing of the financial system was and remains one of the greatest gifts bestowed upon me. Thank you.

To David Kotok, I give you many thanks for bringing me into the fold. My brothers and sisters at Camp Kotok in Maine have been a constant source of support and encouragement throughout the process of writing this book. There are too many of you to name, but to my big brothers including Jim Bianco, Barry Ritholtz, Josh Rosner, and Chris Whalen, thanks for never sugarcoating what was to come. To my sisters Natalie Cohen, Philippa Dunne, and Maryanne Waldman, thanks for sharing your wisdom and grace with me. And to J. R. Mabee, thanks for being a guide to so much more than fishing.

Looking back a bit further, thank you Dr. Keith Brown for introducing me to the wonders and discipline of finance during in my business school days at the University of Texas. I officially forgive you for dragging me through the longhand derivation of the Black–Scholes model. You were right. It helped build my character. As for my days at Donaldson, Lufkin & Jenrette, you know I'm eternally grateful to you, Raymur Plant Walton Rachels, my sweet friend from the South and fellow MBA trainee of the class of 1996; thank you for your unwavering support of my vision and friendship for all these years.

There are four other very special women in my life who have shown me, not told me, how to succeed in making this book a reality, helping me every step along the way. Christine Breck, Virginia Hassell, Glenna Rimmer, and Tracy Wallingford, you are my rocks and rock stars as such.

As for good fortunes, my friendship with Gillian Tett over the years led me to my agent, Amanda "Binky" Urban, who fought tirelessly to convince the world this book was anything but your typical tome on the Fed.

Had it not been for Binky, there would never have been a Niki, or for that matter my Penguin family. I am deeply fortunate to have landed in the capable hands of my editor, Niki Papadopoulos, who knew me before she met me and still put up with me.

I would also like to thank Adrian Zackheim for taking a flyer on an unknown and unproven first-time author. It goes without saying that it takes a village, even at a firm as well-oiled as Penguin. With that in mind, thank you to Leah Trouwborst, Kelsey Odorczyk, Tara Gilbride, Ali Rickards, and Will Weisser for your patience more than anything else.

The research, the poring over of transcripts, the editing, the second set of eyes and ears—for this the prize of my undying gratitude goes to Glenna Whitley whose attention to detail and historical references were invaluable. This book would never have made it to the finish line if it were not for your efforts.

Richard Fisher, it is safe to say, served as my surrogate in fighting the good fight, in not playing along for the sake of getting along, for never forgetting about the little guy suffering at the hand of misguided policy. I'd like to extend a very direct personal debt of gratitude for never wavering in your convictions. Our country could use a few more strong voices like yours to break through the cacophonic consensus that's bringing it down.

And then there are the three advisers who helped make me adviser to Richard Fisher.

To Howard Silverblatt, it seems like we've been lifelong friends. Thank you for the years of data, data, data, and then wise guidance. You are the very essence of the stock market to me. You personify how things in the world of price discovery should work and remind me constantly of how they need to be once again.

And to you Peter Boockvar, my dear friend, "thank" and "you" are two words that fail—the weekends you gave to read the manuscripts in their many iterations and your bottomless font of fact checks here and suggestions there. You have always been there for me as this book marched from conception to reality and I cannot thank you enough.

I have finally had the honor of getting to know Arthur Cashin as a result of life placing me on the path to working with Richard Fisher at the Fed. Richard and I came to call Arthur "King Arthur" and with good reason. Wall Street will forever be indebted to its King for passing down the stories that remind us all that markets are designed to act as natural price discovery mechanisms. Thank you, Arthur, for anchoring me in my determination to write this book and write it right. Know your friendship and support over the years have been a priceless gift to which I can assign no value.

And then there is my family. Aunt Janice and Uncle Phil, thank you two for being there in every way from the day I was born. Your love, guidance, and pride in my achievements make me smile deep down. I love you right back.

Aunt Gail, what can I say? You are my researcher, my editor, my compass, my greatest critic, and my new best friend. For all, I am in awe.

To my husband, John, all I can say is I will never be able to express in words how much it means that you sacrificed so much for this book. Raising our four children, our sweet William, Henry, Carolyn, and John, Jr., throughout the researching, writing, and editing of this book, simply would have been impossible were it not for what you gave of yourself to offset what I gave to the book. Thank you for surrendering yourself to help make this book a reality. 3.*

And finally, to you, Mom. I am me because of you. I would not be anything were it not for you. You gave so very much and lost so much more to ensure that what you could not have, I would, in every way. If this book was not dedicated to those you have inspired me to in turn inspire, it would be dedicated to you.

---

* My husband will know what this means.

NOTES

CHAPTER 1: "GROUPSTINK"

1 **"Never in the field of monetary policy":** Michael Hartnett, "The Thundering Word: When Janet Met Mario," Bank of America Merrill Lynch Global Investment Strategy newsletter, November 1, 2015.

2 **Created in 1913:** Mark Koba, "The Federal Reserve: CNBC Explains," CNBC.com, March 18, 2015, www.cnbc.com/id/43752521. There are innumerable books and magazine articles that describe the origin and structure of the Federal Reserve. Koba's piece provides a short, succinct summary.

4 **By mid-2016:** Timothy W. Martin, "Pension Returns Slump, Squeezing States and Cities," *Wall Street Journal*, July 25, 2016.

4 **And then there are the millennials:** "Why Millennials Are Delaying Home Buying More Than Ever," Knowledge@Wharton, Wharton School of Business, University of Pennsylvania, November 18, 2015, knowledge.wharton.upenn.edu/article/why-millennials-are-delaying-home-buying-more-than-ever/.

5 **With interest rates on CDs:** Scott Burns, "How to Scrape By in a Yield Famine," *Dallas Morning News*, March 6, 2016.

7 **Companies in the S&P 500 Index:** Will Deener, "Many Shun the Bull," *Dallas Morning News*, September 2, 2016.

7 **This strategy has been employed:** Joe Carroll and Asjylyn Loder, "Exxon Mobil Loses Top Credit Rating It Held Since Depression," Bloomberg.com, April 26, 2016, www.bloomberg.com/news/articles/2016-04-26/exxon-mobil-loses-top-credit-rating-it-held-since-depression.

7 **Since 2005, U.S. corporations:** William Watts, "For Every Job Created, Companies Spent $296K on Buybacks," MarketWatch.com, November 2, 2015, www.market

watch.com/story/for-every-job-created-companies-spent-296k-on-buybacks
-2015-11-02?dist=beforebell.

7 **"No wonder share buybacks":** Rana Foroohar, "Too Many Businesses Want a
Piece of the Financial Action," *Financial Times*, May 15, 2016, www.ft.com/cms/s
/0/ed421ea4-1925-11e6-b197-a4af20d5575e.html#axzz4EPfdS5Ru.

7 **Compared to the immediate:** Ibid.

7 **By mid-2015, only by 62.6 percent:** Andrew Soergel, "Where Are All the Workers?,"
U.S. News & World Report, July 16, 2015, www.usnews.com/news/the-report/articles
/2015/07/16/unemployment-is-low-but-more-workers-are-leaving-the-workforce.

7 **The so-called shadow unemployment rate:** "John Williams' Shadow Government Statistics: Analysis Behind and Beyond Government Economic Reporting,"
shadowstats.com, last updated September 2, 2016, www.shadowstats.com/alter
nate_data/unemployment-charts.

8 **Proof: a third of all cars:** Wolf Richter, "What Will Sink the US Auto Boom?,"
wolfstreet.com, May 24, 2016, wolfstreet.com/2016/05/24/this-sinks-auto-boom
-negative-equity-loan-to-value-ratio-used/.

8 **In five thousand years:** Matt O'Brien, "It's the Best Time in 5,000 Years to Get
Loan," *Dallas Morning News*, September 28, 2015.

8 **The percentage of U.S. adults:** Justin McCarthy, "Just Over Half of Americans
Own Stocks, Matching Record Low," Gallup, April 20, 2016 www.gallup.com/poll
/190883/half-americans-own-stocks-matching-record-low.aspx.

8 **Inflows into U.S. stock mutual funds:** Deener, "Many Shun the Bull."

9 **Since 2007, world debt has grown by about $60 trillion:** Matthew Philips, "The
World's Debt Is Alarmingly High. But Is It Contagious?," Bloomberg.com, February 22, 2016, www.bloomberg.com/news/articles/2016-02-22/the-world-s-debt-is
-alarmingly-high-but-is-it-contagious.

9 **The acclaimed Noam Chomsky:** *Requiem for the American Dream*, directed by
Peter D. Hutchison, Kelly Nyks, and Jared P. Scott (2015; n.p.: Naked City Films).

9 **The ostentatiousness with which:** Shawn Donnan, "Trump, Jobs Data and Economic Anger in the US," *Financial Times*, March 3, 2016.

9 **Central bankers have invited politicians:** Douglas Kass, "Sorry Janet, the Fed Has No
Cred," RealMoney.TheStreet.com, August 26, 2016, realmoney.thestreet.com/articles
/08/26/2016/sorry-janet-fed-has-no-cred. Founder and president of Seabreeze Partners
Management, Kass has a gift for coining words like "screwflation" and "groupstink."

9 **Annual borrowing costs:** Jim Grant, "Make America Solvent Again," *Time*, April
25, 2016, 28–33.

10 **If this lunacy doesn't end:** Ibid.

10 **But it's done nothing to staunch:** Ibid.

Chapter 2: Who Would Buy That Crap?

11 **How do we know when irrational exuberance:** FRB: Alan Greenspan, "Central Banking in a Democratic Society" (speech, American Enterprise Institute for Public Policy Research, Washington, DC, December 5, 1996), www.federalreserve.gov /boarddocs/speeches/1996/19961205.htm.

13 **He had adopted the maxim:** FRBD: Mark Wynne, "How the FOMC Talks" (speech, Sul Ross University, Alpine, Texas, October 29, 2014), www.dallasfed.org /assets/documents/educate/events/2014/14summit_wynne.pdf.

14 **The brainchild of John Meriwether:** Stephanie Yang, "The Epic Story of How a 'Genius' Hedge Fund Almost Caused a Global Financial Meltdown," BusinessInsider Singapore, July 11, 2014.

14 **As markets sank, the hedge fund lost $2 billion:** Ibid.

14 **At least $1 trillion was at risk:** Ibid.

14 **The heads of more than a dozen:** Michael Fleming and Weiling Lui, "Near Failure of Long-Term Capital Management," Federal Reserve Bank of New York, Federal Reserve History, September 1998, www.federalreservehistory.org/Events/DetailView/52.

15 **"Had the failure of LTCM":** FRB: Testimony of Chairman Alan Greenspan, "Private-Sector Refinancing of the Large Hedge Fund, Long-Term Capital Management," Committee on Banking and Financial Services, U.S. House of Representatives, October 1, 1998, www.federalreserve.gov/boarddocs/testimony/1998 /19981001.htm.

15 **On February 15, 1999:** Joshua Cooper Ramo, "The Three Marketeers," *Time*, February 15, 1999, content.time.com/time/world/article/0,8599,2054093,00.html.

15 **In August 2000:** Randall Smith and Charles Gasparino, "Credit Suisse Confirms Agreement to Acquire DLJ in a $11.5 Billion Deal," *Wall Street Journal*, August 30, 2000.

16 **They and Wall Street's dog pack:** "The Warning," *Frontline*, transcript, PBS, www .pbs.org/wgbh/pages/frontline/warning/etc/script.html.

17 **Realizing she could not effect change:** "Interview: Brooksley Born," *Frontline*, PBS, www.pbs.org/wgbh/pages/frontline/warning/interviews/born.html.

17 **I never sold any Credit Suisse CDOs:** Richard Tomlinson and David Evans, "CDO Boom Masks Subprime Losses, Abetted by S&P, Moody's, Fitch," Bloomberg Markets, May 30, 2007.

17 **Greenspan had slashed interest rates:** "Fed Makes Surprise Rate Cut," CNN Money.com, January 3, 2001, money.cnn.com/2001/01/03/economy/fed/.

17 **By 2008, the derivatives market had quintupled:** Peter S. Goodman, "Taking a Hard Look at a Greenspan Legacy," *New York Times*, October 8, 2008.

18 **In the DLJ training program:** Michael Lewis, *Liar's Poker* (New York: W. W. Norton, 2014), 44.

Chapter 3: Saint Greenspan

19 **The notion of a bubble bursting:** Tom Dooley, "Industry Watch: No Bubble, Says Fed Governor," RealtorMag.com, March 2003.

19 **Harvard-Stanford-Oxford smart:** Press release, Federal Reserve Bank of Dallas, December 21, 2004.

19 **In June 2005:** Sue Kirchhoff, "Rate Increases May Be Near End, Official Says," *USA Today*, June 1, 2005.

20 **"It may have to go into extra innings":** Eduardo Porter, "The Economy: On One Hand, but Then . . . ," *New York Times*, June 2, 2005.

20 **Fisher's comments that the Fed:** Jonathan Fuerbringer, "Red Ink? Yes. But Not as Much," *New York Times*, June 5, 2005.

20 **Blamed for a 95-point drop:** Scott Patterson, "Fed Comments Roil the Market," *Wall Street Journal*, October 6, 2005, www.wsj.com/articles/SB112859671097461506.

20 **Unlike many other Fed District Bank presidents:** Mark Gongloff, Scott Patterson, and David Gaffen, "Who Will Wield Influence After Greenspan Departs?," *Wall Street Journal*, November 18, 2005, www.wsj.com/articles/SB113225663185000372.

21 **The classic definition of an asset bubble:** Robert J. Shiller, "Speculative Asset Prices," Nobel Prize Lecture, nobelprize.org, December 8, 2013, 460–61. His more detailed version of a bubble: "A situation in which news of price increases spurs investor enthusiasm which spreads by psychological contagion from person to person, in the process amplifying stories that might justify the price increase and bringing in a larger and larger class of investors, who, despite doubts about the real value of the investment are drawn to it partly through envy of others' successes and partly through a gambler's excitement."

21 **I preferred Warren Buffett's definition:** Jason Zweig, "Buffett: Real Estate Slowdown Ahead," CNNMoney.com, May 8, 2006.

21 **"There's definitely a housing bubble":** Danielle DiMartino, "A Tough Hike Ahead," *Dallas Morning News*, January 2, 2003.

21 **The greatest real estate market in history:** Danielle DiMartino, "Housing Market's Glory Days Are Fading," *Dallas Morning News*, August 31, 2003.

21 **In 1993, in response to initiatives:** FRBB: "Closing the Gap: A Guide to Equal Opportunity Lending," Federal Reserve Bank of Boston, April 1993, www.thebrokenwindow.net/papers/c/closingt.pdf.

22 **Jeff Jacoby of the *Boston Globe*:** Jeff Jacoby, "Frank's Fingerprints Are All Over the Financial Fiasco," *Boston Globe*, September 28, 2008, archive.boston.com/boston globe/editorial_opinion/oped/articles/2008/09/28/franks_fingerprints_are _all_over_the_financial_fiasco/.

23 **The enigmatic Greenspan did admit:** Edmund L. Andrews, "Greenspan Concerned About 'Froth' in Housing," *New York Times*, May 21, 2005.

23 **In mid-2004, Greenspan:** FRBSL: "Chart: Effective Federal Funds Rate," Economic Research, Federal Reserve Economic Data (FRED), Federal Reserve Bank of St. Louis, fred.stlouisfed.org/series/FEDFUNDS.

23 **"So, what I think is more likely":** Jonathan McCarthy and Richard Peach, "Is There a Bubble in the Housing Market Now?," Federal Reserve Bank of New York, NFI Policy Brief No. 2005-PB-01, papers.ssrn.com/sol3/papers.cfm?abstract_id=923867.

23 **Greenspan told Congress:** Danielle DiMartino, "Reality, Fed Are at Odds," *Dallas Morning News*, July 26, 2005.

23 **Two of the top economists:** Ibid.

25 **Those lasted until the NASDAQ peaked:** Associated Press, "Turbulent Market Forces Shifts in Strategy," *Deseret News*, May 29, 2000.

25 **My master's thesis:** Danielle DiMartino, "The Daily Crystal Ball" (master's thesis, Columbia University, August 2001).

26 **Like watching a "subtitled, multilanguage":** Ibid.

26 **"Though I have immense respect":** Danielle DiMartino, "Fed Chief's Mercy May Have Costs," *Dallas Morning News*, January 30, 2006.

26 **The mortgage market in the United States:** Danielle DiMartino, "Systemic Risk Is on the Bubble," *Dallas Morning News*, March 27, 2006.

27 **Is it any wonder that years later:** Julia La Roche, "Warren Buffett's Right Hand Man Gave a Dark Warning about Finance," BusinessInsider.com, April 11, 2016, www.business insider.com/charlie-munger-warns-about-american-finance-2016-4.

27 **Known as the "econotrarian":** Danielle DiMartino, "Banks Have Put Huge Bets on Housing," *Dallas Morning News*, March 28, 2006.

27 **But then MBSs and CDOs were adopted:** Ibid.

27 **By 2006, sales of these derivatives:** "CDO Issuance Up Two Thirds To $503 Billion In 2006, Says FT." Global Custodian, www.globalcustodian.com/Securities-Finance/CDO-Issuance-Up-Two-Thirds-To-$503-Billion-In-2006,-Says-FT/.

28 **The value of the $340 million Credit Suisse CDO:** Richard Tomlinson and David Evans, "CDO Boom Masks Subprime Losses, Abetted by S&P, Moody's, Fitch," Bloomberg.com, May 30, 2007.

28 **If the housing bubble bursts:** DiMartino, "Banks Have Put Huge Bets on Housing."

28 **With great timing, William "Bill" Dudley:** Danielle DiMartino, "Fed Has a Different Take on Bubbles," *Dallas Morning News*, March 31, 2006.

28 **But Dudley helpfully pointed out:** Ibid.

29 **After working at Goldman Sachs:** Jon Hilsenrath, "For New York Fed Chief, a New Fix-It Job," *Wall Street Journal*, May 15, 2010, www.wsj.com/articles/SB10001424052748704414504575244733500441298.

29 **Despite evidence that the housing market:** FR: FOMC Statement, March 28, 2006, www.federal reserve.gov/newsevents/press/monetary/20060328a.htm.

29 **"It just doesn't make any sense":** Danielle DiMartino, "Fed Hike Seen As Certainty," *Dallas Morning News*, October 31, 2005.

Chapter 4: Inside the Black Box

30 **Lunch is for wimps:** *Wall Street*, directed by Oliver Stone (1987; Los Angeles: Twentieth Century Fox).

33 **"The ramifications extend far beyond":** Danielle DiMartino, "For Many, Homes Becoming a Liability," *Dallas Morning News*, September 14, 2006.

34 **The entire first floor of the bank:** FRBD: "About the Dallas Fed," www.dallasfed .org/fed/dallas.cfm.

35 **The dwindling need for check processing:** Chris Edwards, "Federal Reserve Pay Soars," Cato Institute, October 9, 2010. Cato.org/blog/federal-reserve-pay-soars.

36 **In 2015, it posted record earnings:** Jim Puzzanghera, "Federal Reserve Sends Record $97.7-billion Profit to Treasury," *Los Angeles Times*, January 11, 2016.

36 **But its expenses are borne by the taxpayer:** United States General Accounting Office, Testimony Before the Committee on Banking, Housing, and Urban Affairs, U.S. Senate, "Federal Reserve System: Current and Future Challenges Require Systemwide Attention, Statement of Charles A. Bowsher, Comptroller General," July 26, 1996.

36 **The Central Bank, he reminded:** Henry B. González, History, Art & Archives, United States House of Representatives, www.history.house.gov/People/Detail /13906?ret=True.

36 **At any given time, the vault:** FRBD: "The Economy in Action," www.dallasfed.org /assets/documents/fed/eia/eia_brochure.pdf.

37 **The Dallas Fed's vault:** Erica Greider, "Money Makes the World Go Round." *Texas Monthly*, October 2013. www.texasmonthly.com/politics/money-makes-the-world -go-round/.

37 **As the Dallas Fed tells visitors:** Stephen Clayton, ed., *Money.* Everyday Economics Series, Federal Reserve Bank of Dallas, 5, www.dallasfed.org/educate.

38 **The face of each Federal Reserve Note:** Ibid.

38 **Paper money is composed:** Jill Cowan and Michael Houge, "Made in Fort Worth," *Dallas Morning News*, May 9, 2016,

38 **Hundred-dollar bills:** FRB: "How Long Is the Life Span of US Paper Money?," Current FAQS, www.federalreserve.gov/faqs/how-long-is-the-life-span-of-us-paper-money.htm.

38 **The Bureau of Engraving and Printing uses:** Clayton, ed., *Money*, 14.

38 **In the basement of the Dallas Fed:** On the first floor of the Federal Reserve District Bank of Dallas is a multimedia exhibit that provides a plethora of information about currency operations at the bank. After going through security, visitors hear a short talk by a guide, then can tour the exhibit at their own pace. Be sure to get your little bag of shredded cash before you leave.

41 Their papers appeared in prestigious academic journals: N. Kundan Kishor and Evan F. Koenig, "VAR Estimation and Forecasting When Data Are Subject to Revision," *Journal of Business and Economic Statistics* (2010): 1–10, doi:10.1198/jbes.2010.08169AUTHOR.

41 And "Lifestyle-Consistent Female Labor Supply": Anil Kumar, "Lifecycle-Consistent Female Labor Supply with Nonlinear Taxes: Evidence from Unobserved Effects Panel Data Models with Censoring, Selection and Endogeneity," *Review of Economics of the Household* 14.1 (2013): 207–29.

41 Each morning I greated Carlos: Carlos Zarazaga, "Inflation Processes in Latin America" (Diss., University of Minnesota, 1992), abstract.

41 In a corner office reigned: John V. Duca, "Mutual Funds and the Evolving Long-Run Effects of Stock Wealth on U.S. Consumption," *Journal of Economics and Business* (May/June 2006).

42 The Fed mother ship: Neil Irwin, "Nine Questions About the Federal Reserve You Were Too Embarrassed to Ask," *Washington Post*, September 18, 2013.

42 Though the Fed's "factory" functions: Jim Kudlinski, *The Tarnished Fed: Behind Closed Doors: Forty Years of Successes, Failures, Mystique, and Humor* (New York: Vantage, 2010).

42 By law, the FOMC: Jon Hilsenrath, "Go Behind the Fed's Closed Doors," *Wall Street Journal*, December 13, 2011.

42 Save for the New York Fed: FRBNY: "About the Fed: Federal Open Market Committee," www.newyorkfed.org/aboutthefed/fedpoint/fed48.html.

43 Their pay is somewhat parsimonious: FRB: "About the Federal Reserve Board: Who Are the Members of the Federal Reserve Board, and How Are They Selected?, www.federalreserve.gov/faqs/about_12591.htm.

43 The head of the European Central Bank: Jana Randow, "ECB Report Shows Draghi Pay More than Twice as High as Fed Chief," Bloomberg.com, February 20, 2014, www.bloomberg.com/news/articles/2014-02-20/ecb-report-shows-draghi-pay-more-than-twice-as-high-as-fed-chief.

43 One member of the Board: Harriet Torry, "Fed Governor Brainard Donated to Clinton Campaign," *Wall Street Journal*, March 8, 2016.

44 The president's pay outstrips: Edwards, "Federal Reserve Pay Soars."

44 One former insider has described: Kudlinksi, *The Tarnished Fed.*

46 Economist John Kenneth Galbraith: Scott Rasmussen, "2016 Forecast: The Experts Will Be Wrong," Realclearpolitics.com, December 28, 2015, www.realclearpolitics.com/articles/2015/12/28/2016_forecast_the_experts_will_be_wrong_129141.html.

46 Their absurd collective blunder prompted: FRBD: Richard Fisher, "A Perspective on the U.S. Economy and Monetary Policy" (speech, Market News International Seminar, New York, New York, June 6, 2011), www.dallasfed.org/news/speeches/fisher/2011/fs110606.cfm.

46 **It concluded that the programs:** Oleg Komlik, "Economic Sociology and Political Economy," EconomicSociology.org, September 28, 2014, economicsociology.org/2014 /09/28/economics-graduate-programs-may-be-turning-out-a-generation-with-too -many-idiot-savants-skilled-in-technique-but-innocent-of-real-economic-issues/.

46 **At one top university:** Thomas T. Vogel Jr., "Berkeley's Economists Attack Policy Issues," *Wall Street Journal,* December 1, 1995, people.umass.edu/~maash/berkecon.wsj.

47 **"Central banking thrives on":** FRBD: Mark Wynne, "How the FOMC Talks" (speech, Sul Ross University, Alpine, Texas, October 29, 2014), www.dallasfed.org /assets/documents/educate/events/2014/14summit_wynne.pdf.

47 **Even Greenspan dinged his chosen profession:** Edmund L. Andrews, "The Doctrine Was Not to Have One," *New York Times,* August 26, 2005.

47 **Because high-paid economists' predictions:** Peter Passell, "This Model Was Too Rough; Why Economic Forecasting Became a Sideshow," *New York Times,* February 1, 1996.

47 **"Research economists have shown little interest":** Ibid.

47 **According to the San Francisco Fed:** FRBSF: "What Kinds of Research and Analysis Do Economists at the Federal Reserve System Do, What Types of Information Do They Use, and What Kinds of Presentations Do They Make?," January 2006, www.frbsf.org/education/publications/doctor-econ/2006/january/economist -research-fed.

47 **For decades, the Fed:** Robert Auerbach, "When 500 Economists Is Not Enough," HuffingtonPost.com, October 23, 2009, updated May 24, 2011, www.huffington post.com/robert-auerbach/when-five-hundred-economi_b_278418.html.

48 **By 2006, when Bernanke:** Justin Fox, "How Economics PhDs Took Over the Federal Reserve," *Harvard Business Review,* February 3, 2014, hbr.org/2014/02/how -economics-phds-took-over-the-federal-reserve/.

48 **Under his tenure:** Ibid.

48 **The first Fed chairman to have a PhD:** Ibid.

48 **He's widely regarded as one of the best:** Ibid.

49 **But his paper went missing:** Jim McTague, "Dr. Greenspan's Amazing Invisible Thesis," *Barron's,* March 31, 2008. Also see Jim McTague, "Looking at Greenspan's Long-Lost Thesis," *Barron's,* April 28, 2008.

49 **A study at the Cleveland Fed:** Matthew Bryan and Linsey Molloy, "Mirror, Mirror, Who's the Best Forecaster of Them All?," Federal Reserve Bank of Cleveland, March 15, 2007, www.clevelandfed.org/en/newsroom-and-events/publications/economic -commentary/economic-commentary-archives/2007-economic-commentaries /ec-20070315-mirror-mirror-whos-the-best-forecaster-of-them-all.aspx.

49 **When researchers at the Federal Reserve:** David Matthews, "Papers in Economics 'Not Reproducible,'" Reuters.com, October 21, 2015. See also Andrew C. Chang

and Phillip Li (2015), "Is Economics Research Replicable? Sixty Published Papers from Thirteen Journals Say 'Usually Not,'" Finance and Economics Discussion Series 2015-083. Washington, DC: Board of Governors of the Federal Reserve System, dx.doi.org/10.17016/FEDS.2015.083.

49 **One researches involved:** Sarah Necker, "Scientific Misbehavior in Economics," *Research Policy* 43, no. 10 (2014): 1747–59, doi:10.1016/j.respol.2014.05.002.

50 **"Janet Yellen followed quickly":** Fox, "How Economics PhDs Took Over the Federal Reserve."

50 **The Yale economist expressed:** Paul Solman, "Nobel Laureate Bob Shiller on Why the Fed Can't Say There's a Housing Bubble," *PBS Newshour*, December 11, 2013, Pbs.org/newshour/making-sense/nobel-laureate-bob-shiller-on/.

CHAPTER 5: THE FIRST TREMORS

51 **With respect to their safety:** Kristin Jones, "Top Regulators Once Opposed Regulation of Derivatives," ProPublica.org, October 6, 2008, www.propublica.org/article/top-regulators-once-opposed-regulation-of-derivatives.

52 **Fed economists had "growing confidence":** Timothy Geithner, *Stress Test: Reflection on Financial Crises* (New York: Broadway Books, 2015), 80.

52 **Geithner—though an intelligent man:** "Opening at the Fed: How to Think About the World's Most Important Job Vacancy," *Review & Outlook, Wall Street Journal*, December 5, 2008.

52 **Born in 1961:** Greg Ip, "Fed's Fireman on Wall Street Feels Some Heat," *Wall Street Journal*, May 30, 2008.

52 **The the elder Geithner's moves:** Robert Wenzel, "A Note on Tim Geithner's Father as CIA Agent," EconomicPolicyJournal.com, May 20, 2014, www.economicpolicyjournal.com/2014/05/a-note-on-tim-geithners-father-as-cia.html.

53 **Geithner's took only one economics class:** James Freeman, "Book Review: 'Stress Test' by Timothy Geithner," *Wall Street Journal*, May 11, 2014.

53 **Geithner's new job:** FRBNY: "About the New York Fed: Historical Speeches," www.newyorkfed.org/aboutthefed/historical_speeches.html. In addition to historical information are short bios of New York Fed presidents.

53 **Rubin described Geithner as "elbow-less":** Jeff Gerth, "How Citigroup Unraveled Under Geithner's Watch," ProPublica.org, January 14, 2009, www.propublica.org/article/how-citigroup-unraveled-under-geithners-watch.

53 **Geithner later admitted that his previous:** Andrew Ross Sorkin, "What Timothy Geithner Really Thinks," *New York Times*, May 8, 2014.

54 **He sensed Geithner was:** Andrew Huszar, "Tim Geithner's Lack of Nerve Drove Me from the New York Fed," BusinessInsider.com, May 14, 2014.

54 **"The only thing it seemed to excel at":** Ibid.

54 **In the senior regulatory strategy sessions:** Ibid.

54 **"I tried to push back against complacency":** Geithner, *Stress Test*, 80, 81.

55 **In fact, beyond reiterating:** FRBNY: Timothy Geithner, "Change and Challenges Facing the U.S. Financial System" (speech, New York Bankers Association Annual Financial Services Forum, March 25, 2004), www.newyorkfed.org/newsevents /speeches/2004/gei040325.

57 **The Fed could endear itself:** Danielle DiMartino Booth, internal Dallas Fed memorandum, October 27, 2006.

Chapter 6: Front-running the Fed

59 **My answers to these questions:** FRBSF: Janet Yellen, "The U.S. Economy and Monetary Policy" (speech, Conference on US Monetary Policy convened by the European Economics and Financial Centre, London, England, September 27, 2005), www.frbsf.org/our-district/press/presidents-speeches/yellen-speeches/2005 /september/the-us-economy-and-monetary-policy-london/.

59 **The film would celebrate:** "Free to Choose: The Complete Television Series," PBS, 1980, www.amazon.com/Free-Choose-Television-Milton-Friedman/dp/B001DHTHZ8.

59 **a companion book:** Milton and Rose Friedman, *Free to Choose: A Personal Statement* (New York: Harcourt Brace and Company, 1979).

60 **Rosenblum had joined:** Roger Lowenstein, "The Education of Ben Bernanke," *New York Times Magazine*, January 29, 2008.

60 **Speak out of school:** Cheryl Hall, "Harvey Rosenblum Ready to Go with the Flow After Leaving Dallas Fed," *Dallas Morning News*, August 31, 2013.

60 **That happened a few times:** Ibid.

61 **One of Fisher's early mentors, Robert Roosa:** FRBD: Press release, December 21, 2004.

62 **When Rosenblum arrived:** Interview with Michael Cox. February 19, 2016.

63 **But the field of economics:** Peter T. Kilborn, "'Fresh Water' Economists Gain," *New York Times*, July 23, 1988.

64 **While he was in the air:** Donald Bernhardt and Marshall Eckblad, "Black Monday: The Stock Market Crash of 1987," Federal Reserve Bank of Chicago, Federal Reserve History, www.federalreservehistory.org/Events/DetailView/48.

64 **"Black Monday," when the market fell:** Ibid.

64 **Investors lost about $1 trillion:** Christopher Matthews, "25 Years Later: In the Crash of 1987, the Seeds of the Great Recession," Bloomberg.com, October 22, 2012.

64 **Then the mother of all storks:** Bernhardt and Eckblad, "Black Monday: The Stock Market Crash of 1987."

65 **Sometimes, as an added bonus:** Ibid.

CHAPTER 7: THE MAVERICK

66 **It is not the responsibility:** Ben Bernanke, *The Courage to Act* (New York: W. W. Norton & Company, 2015), 156.

67 **The Dallas Fed is a $100 billion bankers' bank:** FRBD: Richard Fisher, "A Need for Innovative Fiscal Policy (With a Nod to John Stemmons, Ronald Reagan and Paddy McCoy" (speech, Stemmons Corridor Business Association, Dallas, Texas, February 8, 2011), www.dallasfed.org/news/speeches/fisher/2011/fs110208.cfm.

67 **He was also one of the wealthiest:** Binyamin Appelbaum, "How the Fed Presidents' Assets Stack up," *New York Times,* January 31, 2012.

67 **Despite his patrician appearance:** Erica Grieder, "Money Makes the World Go Round," *Texas Monthly,* October 2013, www.texasmonthly.com/politics/money-makes-the-world-go-round/.

67 **On the wall of his office:** Will Deener, "Dallas Fed President Richard Fisher Known to Speak Out on Inflation, Deficit Issues," Stanford Business Magazine Online, n.d., public-prod-acquia.gsb.stanford.edu/news/bmag/sbsm1008/feature-fisher.html.

68 **They barely escaped the mainland:** Alan Peppard, "Dossier Dallas: Richard Fisher, President and CEO of the Federal Reserve Bank of Dallas," *Dallas Morning News,* September 29, 2012.

68 **"But I was manufactured in China":** Ibid.

69 **"I'll never make it here":** Greider, "Money Makes the World Go Round."

69 **In Fisher's words:** Ibid.

70 **In one speech:** FRBD: Richard Fisher, "Confessions of a Data Dependent" (speech, New York Association for Business Economics, November 2, 2006), www.dallasfed.org/news/speeches/fisher/2006/fs061102.cfm.

70 **He wasn't afraid to take on sacred cows:** Ibid.

70 **"Poor data led to a policy action":** Greg Ip, "Fed Official Says Bad Data Helped Fuel Rate Cuts, Housing Speculation," *Wall Street Journal,* November 3, 2006.

70 **Describing his failed effort:** FRBD: Richard Fisher, "A New Perspective on Policy" (speech, Midwestern State University, Wichita Falls, Texas, April 4, 2006), www.dallasfed.org/news/speeches/fisher/2006/fs060404.cfm.

71 **Kelleher's philosophy of life:** Katrina Brooker, "Can Anyone Replace Herb?," *Fortune,* April 17, 2000.

71 **Joe Kim King:** FRBD: "King Elected to Dallas Fed," press release, December 13, 2007.

71 **"Credit is exactly like morphine":** FRBD: "About the Dallas Fed, History and Timeline," www.dallasfed.org/fed/dalhistory.cfm.

72 **The journalist was wowed:** Interview with Harvey Rosenblum, February 4, 2016.

72 **But the tide had turned:** FR: FOMC Meeting, transcript, December 13, 2005, www.federalreserve.gov/monetarypolicy/files/FOMC20051213meeting.pdf.

72 **In fact, to listen to boastful staffers:** Sudeep Reddy, "Does Fed Policy Marginal-
ize Regional Bank Presidents?" *Wall Street Journal*, December 20, 2008.

73 **The transformation of my role:** "Table: Subprime-Related Losses At Major Banks,"
Financial Times, February 7, 2008, www.ft.com/cms/s/0/9622326c-d5b8-11dc
-8b56-0000779fd2ac.html#axzz4EPfdS5Ru.

74 **"The impact on the broader economy":** Testimony of Chairman Ben Bernanke,
"The Economic Outlook," Before the Joint Economic Committee of Congress, March
28, 2007, www.federalreserve.gov/newsevents/testimony/Bernanke20070328a.htm.

74 **Defaults had escalated:** Seth Lubove and Daniel Taub, "Subprime Fiasco Exposes
Manipulation by Mortgage Brokers," BloombergMarkets.com, May 29, 2007.

74 **On April 2, 2007:** FRBSL: "The Financial Crisis: Full Timeline," www.stlouisfed
.org/financial-crisis/full-timeline. This is one of the most thorough and useful time-
lines of the financial crisis, integrating events and actions by the Federal Reserve.

74 **With Rosenblum's encouragement:** FRBD: Danielle DiMartino and John V. Duca,
"The Rise and Fall of Subprime Mortgages," Economic Letter, November 2007,
www.dallasfed.org/assets/documents/research/eclett/2007/el0711.pdf.

74 **The next month, Duca:** FRBD: Danielle DiMartino, John V. Duca, and Harvey
Rosenblum, "From Complacency to Crisis: Financial Risk Taking in the 21st Century," Economic Letter, Vol. 2, No. 12, December 2007, www.dallasfed.org/assets
/documents/research/eclett/2007/el0712.pdf.

CHAPTER 8: THE INNER SANCTUM

76 **While the decline:** FRBSF: Janet Yellen, "The U.S. Economy in 2007: Prospects and Puzzles" (speech, Joint Rotary Clubs of Reno and the East Bay, SF Bay Area, Reno, Nevada,
January 22, 2007), www.frbsf.org/our-district/press/presidents-speeches/yellen
-speeches/2007/january/the-u-s-economy-in-2007-prospects-and-puzzles-reno/.

76 **Just minutes into the morning session:** FR: FOMC Meeting, transcript, June
29–30, 2005, 74, www.federalreserve.gov/monetarypolicy/files/FOMC20050630meet
ing.pdf.

77 **"Market participants briefly flirted":** Ibid.

77 **"Just speak the truth, Richard":** Binyamin Appelbaum, "Q&A: An Advocate for a
Quicker Taper," *New York Times*, January 27, 2014, economix.blogs.nytimes.com
/2014/01/27/qa-an-advocate-for-a-quicker-taper/?_r=0.

77 **Fisher mentioned his background:** FR: FOMC Meeting, transcript, May 3, 2005,
40, www.federalreserve.gov/monetarypolicy/files/FOMC20050503meeting.pdf.

77 **Fisher described "a noticeable dissonance":** Ibid., 38.

78 **Core inflation measures:** Ibid., 42.

78 **No nationwide housing bubble:** FR: FOMC Meeting, transcript, June 29–30, 2005,
www.federalreserve.gov/monetarypolicy/files/FOMC20050630meeting.pdf.

78 **The Fed even van simulations:** FRB: "FRB/US Model," Federal Reserve Board, www.federalreserve.gov/econresdata/frbus/us-models-about.htm.

79 **"Assuming that the FRB/US model":** Jon Hilsenrath, "Years of Fed Missteps Fueled Disillusion with the Economy and Washington," *Wall Street Journal*, August 25, 2016.

79 **There were no dissents:** FR: FOMC Statement, June 30, 2005, www.federalreserve .gov/boarddocs/press/monetary/2005/20050630/default.htm.

79 **"Ben Bernanke told me":** Edmund L. Andrews, "Fed Chief Swears Off Improvising," *New York Times*, May 24, 2005.

79 **"Senator, that episode":** Ibid.

80 **"Fisher's comment was at odds":** Ibid.

80 **Gossips often fingered:** Steven Perlberg, "Meet the 6 Reporters Who Can Make Markets Go Crazy," BusinessInsider.com, June 18, 2013, www.business insider. com/the-6-fed-reporters-who-can-move-markets-2013-6.

81 **The statement was spare:** FRBD: Mark Wynne, "How the FOMC Talks" (speech, Sul Ross University, Alpine, Texas, October 29, 2014), www.dallasfed.org/assets /documents/educate/events/2014/14summit_wynne.pdf.

81 **In May 1999:** FRBSF: "What Steps Has the Federal Reserve Taken to Improve Transparency?," Mr. Econ, September 2006, www.frbsf.org/education/publica tions/doctor-econ/2006/september/transparency.

83 **Dallas Fed senior economist:** FRBD: Jim Dolmas, "Trimmed Mean PCE Inflation," Research Department Working Paper 0506, July 25, 2005, www.dallasfed .org/assets/documents/research/papers/2005/wp0506.pdf.

83 **"Why would you want to do":** Interview with Harvey Rosenblum, May 23, 2016.

84 **Bernanke would later tell:** Jeffry Bartash, "Bernanke Reveals What Really Happens at Fed Meetings," MarketWatch.com, December 30, 2014.

84 **"I was a bit loquacious":** FR: FOMC Meeting, transcript, January 30–31, 2007, 104, www.federalreserve.gov/monetarypolicy/files/FOMC20070131meeting.pdf.

84 **She did offer that:** Kristina Peterson, Michael S. Derby, Eric Morath, and Jon Hilsenrath, "Three Stages of Fed Grief: Key Quotes from 2007," *Wall Street Journal*, January 18, 2013.

85 **Her parents were born:** Nicholas Lemann, "The Hand on the Lever," *New Yorker*, July 21, 2014, www.newyorker.com/magazine/2014/07/21/the-hand-on-the-lever.

85 **"What I really liked about economics":** Ibid.

85 **"Tobin was a person ":** Ibid.

86 **She and her husband frequently coauthored:** Dylan Matthews, "Seventeen Academic Papers of Janet Yellen's That You Need to Read," *Washington Post*, October 9, 2013.

86 **She described herself:** James Risen, "Clinton Names 2 Economists to Fed Board," *Los Angeles Times,* April 23, 1994.

86 **She described herself as:** Clay Chandler, "Blinder, Yellen Named to Fed Board," *Washington Post,* April 23, 1994, www.washingtonpost.com/pb/archive/business/1994/04 /23/blinder-yellen-named-by-clinton-to-fed-board/86e0e452-6f71-45b5-a02b-b44ea9c 9016a/?outputType=accessibility&nid=menu_nav_accessibility forscreenreader.

86 **"Who would be prepared to believe":** Binyamin Appelbaum, "The Gorilla and the Maginot Line," *New York Times,* April 25, 2013.

87 **Her husband is George A. Akerlof:** Josh Boak, "A Marriage of Equals: Janet Yellen's Husband Also a Renowned Economist," Associated Press, *San Jose Mercury News,* March 18, 2014.

87 **"Not only did our personalities mesh":** Marilyn W. Thompson and Jonathan Spicer, "A Fed Love Story: Janet Yellen Meets Her Match," Reuters.com, September 29, 2013, www.reuters.com/article/us-usa-fed-yellen-idUSBRE98S07N20130929.

87 **A public disclosure statement:** Victoria McGrane and Eric Morath, "Fed's Yellen, Husband Worth up to $13.2 Million in 2012," *Wall Street Journal,* August 27, 2013.

87 **He went for the jugular:** Louis Uchitelle, "Encouraging More Reality in Economics," *New York Times,* January 6, 2007.

87 **He posited that there was a "natural rate":** Ibid.

88 **Friedman's "misleading" theories:** Ibid.

88 **"It has engaged in":** Matthias Streitz, "The Worst Government the US Has Ever Had," *Der Spiegel* Online, July 29, 2003, www.spiegel.de/wirtschaft/akerlof -interview-im-englischen-original-the-worst-government-the-us-has-ever -had-a-258983.html.

88 **"I'm sorry that light bulbs didn't go off":** Lemann, "The Hand on the Lever."

89 **In May 2006, Ameriquest:** Kathy M. Kristof and David Streitfeld, "Ameriquest Plans to Cut 3,800 Jobs," *Los Angeles Times,* May 3, 2006.

89 **That same month, Merit Financial:** Dan Richman, "'Bottom Fell Out' at Merit Financial," *Seattle Post-Intelligencer,* May 4, 2006.

89 **In early January 2007, Ownit Mortgage Solutions:** Kristina Doss, "Ownit Mortgage Files for Bankruptcy Protection," *Wall Street Journal,* January 2, 2007.

89 **"While the decline":** FRBSF: Yellen, "The U.S. Economy in 2007: Prospects and Puzzles."

89 **"Outside of housing":** FRBSF: Janet Yellen, "The U.S. Economy in 2007" (speech, Silicon Valley Leadership Group, Santa Clara, California, February 21, 2007), www.frbsf.org/our-district/press/presidents-speeches/yellen-speeches/2007 /february/the-u-s-economy-in-2007-silicon-valley/.

89 **Though Yellen perceived:** William Derby, "Fed Official Expects Economy to Weather Subprime Fallout," *Wall Street Journal,* April 4, 2007.

89 **"On the housing front":** Peterson et al., "Three Stages of Fed Grief: Key Quotes from 2007."

89 **At the June 2007 FOMC meeting:** Jon Hilsenrath and Kristina Peterson, "Records Show Fed Wavering in 2007," *Wall Street Journal*, January 18, 2013.

90 **"I do think there is enormous risk":** Peterson et al., "Three Stages of Fed Grief: Key Quotes from 2007."

90 **The Bear Stearns High-Grade:** Reuters, "2 Bear Stearns Funds Are Almost Worthless," *New York Times*, July 17, 2007.

90 **Bear injected money:** FRBSL: "The Financial Crisis: Full Timeline," www.stlouis fed.org/financial-crisis/full-timeline.

90 **She called the housing sector:** Hilsenrath and Peterson, "Records Show Fed Wavering in 2007."

90 **"I think the odds are":** Peterson et al., "Three Stages of Fed Grief: Key Quotes from 2007."

90 **"Now could that change quickly?":** Ibid.

90 **Standing in my aunt's kitchen:** Jeffrey Frankel, "Getting Carried Away: How Carry Trade and Its Potential Unwinding Can Explain Movements on International Financial Markets," *Milken Institute Review*, November 19, 2007, www.hks.harvard .edu/fs/jfrankel/CarryTradeNov19-2007.pdf.

91 **At the 2007 FOMC meeting:** FR: FOMC Statement, September 18, 2007, www .federalreserve.gov/newsevents/press/monetary/20070918a.htm.

91 **The Fed, Fisher argued:** Ben Bernanke, *The Courage to Act* (New York: W. W. Norton & Company, 2015), 162.

91 **But the chairman:** Ibid.

91 **Throughout the FOMC transcripts:** Annie Lowry, "Inside the Fed's 2007 Deliberations," *New York Times*, January 18, 2013.

CHAPTER 9: "LUDDITE!"

92 **Not only have individual:** FRB: Alan Greenspan, "Remarks by Chairman Alan Greenspan" (speech, American Bankers Association Annual Convention, New York, New York, October 5, 2004), www.federalreserve.gov/BOARDDOCS/Speeches/2004 /20041005/default.htm.

92 **They knew Chairman Volcker:** Associated Press, "Central Bankers Can Thank Paul Volcker's Love for Fly Fishing for the Jackson Hole Symposium," BusinessIn sider.com, August 31, 2012. See also FRBKC: Public Affairs Department of the Federal Reserve Bank of Kansas City, *In Late August: The Federal Reserve Bank of Kansas City's Jackson Hole Economic Policy Symposium*, 2001, www.kansascityfed .org/publicat/InLateAugust/InLateAugust.pdf.

93 **Donald Kohn usually led:** Ben Bernanke, *The Courage to Act* (New York: W. W. Norton & Company, 2015), 154.

93 **Rajan was invited:** Justin Lahart, "Mr. Rajan Was Prescient (But Unpopular) at Greenspan's Party," *Wall Street Journal*, January 2, 2009.

93 **On August 26, one:** FRBKC: George A. Kahn, "The Greenspan Era: Lessons for the Future—A Summary of the Bank's 2005 Economic Symposium," August 25–27, 2005, *Economic Review, Fourth Quarter 2005*, www.kansascityfed.org.

94 **"Has Financial Development":** FRBKC: Raghuram G. Rajan, "Has Financial Development Made the World Riskier?" (paper, Jackson Hole Economic Symposium, sponsored by the Federal Reserve Bank of Kansas City, Jackson Hole, Wyoming, August 27, 2005), www.kansascityfed.org/publicat/sympos/2005/pdf/Rajan2005.pdf.

94 **According to a study:** Paul Hodgson, Greg Ruel, and Michelle Lamb, "Wall Street Pay: Size, Structure and Significance for Shareholders," November 2010, White Paper prepared for the Council of Institutional Investors. online.wsj.com/public /resources/documents/CIIWhitePaperWallStreetPayFINAL11302010.pdf.

95 **"The interbank market":** Justin Lahart, "Mr. Rajan Was Prescient (But Unpopular) at Greenspan's Party."

95 **"I felt like an early Christian":** Mark Bergen, "Line of Credit," *Caravan*, October 1, 2013, www.caravanmagazine/in/reportage/line-credit.

95 **Summers, then president:** Dylan Matthews, "Raghuram Rajan Is India's New Central Banker. God Help Him," *Washington Post*, August 7, 2013.

95 **Summers had championed:** Charles Ferguson, "Larry Summers and the Subversion of Economics," *The Chronicle of Higher Education*, October 3, 2010, chronicle .com/article/Larry-Summersthe/124790/.

95 **Public disclosure forms showed:** Ibid.

95 **"As a consequence":** FRB: Governor Donald L. Kohn, "Panel Discussion: Financial Markets, Financial Fragility, and Central Banking" (remarks, Jackson Hole Economic Symposium, sponsored by the Federal Reserve Bank of Kansas City, Jackson Hole, Wyoming, August 27, 2005), www.kansascityfed.org/Publicat/sympos /2005/PDF/Kohn2005.pdf.

CHAPTER 10: HELPLESS

100 **My first action:** The Mortgage Lender Implode-O-Meter is still online at ml -implode.com.

100 **The troubled Countrywide:** David Ellis, "Countrywide Rescue: $4 Billion," CNNMoney.com, January 11, 2008, money.cnn.com/2008/01/11/news/companies /boa_countrywide/.

101 **Born in 1953, Bernanke:** Roger Lowenstein, "The Education of Ben Bernanke," *New York Times Magazine*, January 20, 2008.

101 **When vetted for the job:** James B. Stewart, "Eight Days," *New Yorker*, September 21, 2009, www.newyorker.com/magazine/2009/09/21/eight-days.

101 **"We did it"**: Sebastian Mallaby, "How the Fed Flubbed It," *Atlantic*, January /February 2015.

102 **The markets were in turmoil, and:** Google Finance, S&P 500 Index, www.google .com/finance/historical?cid=626307&startdate=jan+1%2C+2008&enddate=feb +1%2C+2008&num=30&ei=TZDJV9msLeW1iQLxvLq4Cg.

102 **On Monday, January 21:** Binyamin Appelbaum, "Fed Misread Crisis in 2008, Records Show," *New York Times*, February 21, 2014.

102 **"Obviously it's not our job":** FR: FOMC Teleconference, transcript, January 21, 2009, 6, www.federalreserve.gov/monetarypolicy/files/FOMC20080121confcall.pdf.

102 **Bernanke admitted in his memoir:** Ben Bernanke, *The Courage to Act* (New York: W. W. Norton & Company, 2015), 188.

102 **"What do we get":** FR: FOMC Teleconference, transcript, January 21, 2009, 17.

102 **"This action will not be viewed":** Ibid., 13.

103 **The next morning, the Fed:** FR: FOMC Statement, January 22, 2008, www.federal reserve.gov/newsevents/press/monetary/20080122b.htm.

103 **The unexpected rate cut:** David Gauthier-Villars, Carrick Mollenkamp, and Alistair MacDonald, "French Bank Rocked by Rogue Trader," *Wall Street Journal*, January 25, 2008.

104 **On March 13, Treasury:** Glenn Setzer, "Paulson Releases Presidential Working Group Recommendations," MortgageNewsDaily.com, March 13, 2008, www .mortgagenewsdaily.com/3132008_Presidents_Working_Group.asp.

104 **In 1997, a *Washington Post* reporter:** Brett Fromson, "Plunge Protection Team," *Washington Post*, February 23, 1997.

105 **Since 1993, Bear had been headed:** Daily Intelligencer, "Jimmy Cayne Almost Died Trying to Save Bear Stearns," *New York Magazine*, August 4, 2008, nymag.com/dailyin telligencer/2008/08/jimmy_cayne_speaks.html.

105 **He'd been hired by Alan "Ace" Greenberg:** William Cohan, "The Rise and Fall of Jimmy Cayne," *Fortune*, August 25, 2008, archive.fortune.com/2008/07/31/maga zines/fortune/rise_and_fall_Cayne_cohan.fortune/index.htm.

105 **He once told a mother:** Kate Kelly, "Bear CEO's Handling of Crisis Raises Issues," *Wall Street Journal,* November 1, 2007, www.wsj.com/articles/SB119387369474078336.

106 **Cayne earned $34 million:** Ibid.

106 **Cayne exhibited a bizarre indifference:** Ibid.

106 **But the investing community:** Kelly, "Bear CEO's Handling of Crisis Raises Issues."

107 **Beginning on March 10:** Matthew Goldstein, "Bear Stearns' Big Bailout," Bloomberg.com, March 14, 2008.

107 **Early on March 12:** Ibid.

107 **Schwartz denied it:** John Carney, "Goldman Sachs and Bear Stearns: A Financial-Crisis Mystery Is Solved," *Wall Street Journal*, March 28, 2016.

108   **On March 14, Schwartz:** Goldstein, "Bear Stearns' Big Bailout."

108   **The *Financial Times* reported:** Gillian Tett and Krishna Guha, "The Cost of a Lifeline: Humbled Financial Groups Brace for More Regulation," *Financial Times*, April 23, 2008.

109   **Geithner, the elbow-less civil servant:** Greg Robb, "Bernanke's Quiet Skipper Makes Waves," MarketWatch.com, March 21, 2008.

109   **In the *New Yorker*:** Stewart, "Eight Days."

109   **He had seized control of the firm:** Jessica Holzer, "A Loophole for Poor Mr. Paulson," *Forbes*, June 2, 2006.

109   **His estimated equity stake:** Ibid.

109   **But the move to government service:** Ibid.

110   **The rule is intended:** Ibid.

110   **Paulson went so far:** Gretchen Morgenson and Don Van Natta Jr., "Paulson's Calls to Goldman Tested Ethics," *New York Times*, August 8, 2009.

110   **I had been on Wall Street:** Eric Owles, "Timeline: Jamie Dimon, the Chief of Too Big to Fail," *New York Times*, updated January 25, 2014, www.nytimes.com/interactive /2013/05/20/business/DealBook/20130520-jamie-dimon-timeline.html.

110   **Despite their long relationship:** Ibid.

110   **To top if off, in January, 2007:** FRBNY: "Dimon, Bollinger to Join New York Fed Board of Directors, Nooyi Reelected to Second Term," press release, November 20, 2006, www.newyorkfed.org/newsevents/news/aboutthefed/2006/oa061120.

111   **"We have a real issue":** Michael J. De La Merced, "Happy Birthday, Jamie Dimon," *New York Times*, March 13, 2013.

111   **At Bernanker's budding:** Edmund L. Andrews, "Fed Acts to Rescue Financial Markets," *New York Times*, March 17, 2009.

111   **The New York Fed loaned Maiden Lane:** Office of the Special Inspector General for the Troubled Asset Relief Program (SIGTARP), Quarterly Report to Congress, July 21, 2009, oversight.house.gov/wp-content/uploads/2012/01/7-21-09-SIGTARP-Report.pdf.

112   **The fire sale included:** Maria Godoy, "Bear Stearns Bought Out by JP Morgan Chase," NPR.com, March 17, 2008, www.npr.org/templates/story/story.php?storyId=88405777.

112   **A decade after:** William D. Cohan, "The Rise and Fall of Jimmy Cayne," *Fortune*, August 25, 2008, archive.fortune.com/2008/07/31/magazines/fortune/rise_and _fall_Cayne_cohan.fortune/index.htm.

112   **Bear's fourteen thousand employees:** Kristina Cooke, "Tough Job Market Awaits Bear Stearns Staff Who Leave," *New York Times*, March 18, 2008.

113   **"Gambling has been fed":** "The Financial System: What Went Wrong," *Economist*, May 19, 2008.

113   **The youngest governor:** "A Golden Boy on the Federal Reserve Board," PrudentIn vestor.com, March 20, 2006, www.prudentinvestor.com/2006/03/golden-boy -on-federal-reserve-board.html.

113 **At the March 18, 2008, FOMC meeting:** FR: FOMC Meeting, transcript, March 18, 2008, 62, www.federalreserve.gov/monetarypolicy/files/FOMC20080318meeting.pdf.

113 **"It is very hard to make":** Ibid., 75.

114 **Geithner insisted that:** Stephen Labaton, "Testimony Offers Details of Bear Stearns Deal," *New York Times*, April 4, 2008.

114 **Bear's CEO Schwartz:** Henry Blodget, "Government Screwed Bear Stearns: NY Fed Welched On Loan, Forcing Sale," BusinessInsider.com, April 14, 2008, www.businessinsider.com/2008/4/u-s-government-screwed-bear-stearns-ny-fed-welched-on-loan-forcing-sale.

114 **"Buying a house":** Labaton, "Testimony Offers Details of Bear Stearns Deal."

114 **Economist Nouriel Roubini:** Stewart, "Eight Days."

114 **"Our system has many strengths":** Labaton, "Testimony Offers Details of Bear Stearns Deal."

114 **The mystery was finally solved:** Carney, "Goldman Sachs and Bear Stearns: A Financial-Crisis Mystery Is Solved."

115 **Bass had asked other:** Ibid.

115 **Late on Tuesday:** Ibid.

115 **"Our trading desk would prefer":** Ibid.

115 **"The news hit the Street":** Ibid.

115 **In retrospect, in hindsight:** David Lawder and Rachelle Younglai, "Bear Stearns' Cayne Concedes Leverage Was Too High," Reuters.com, May 5, 2010.

116 **The Fed was "fighting against the wind":** "Excerpts from Bernanke's Testimony," *Los Angeles Times*, April 3, 2008.

116 **"With financial conditions fragile":** FRB: Testimony of Ben S. Bernanke, "The Economic Outlook," Before the Joint Economic Committee, U.S. Congress, April 2, 2008.

116 **Bernanke predicted that:** Ibid.

116 **"It has never happened before":** Associated Press, "Reluctantly, Bernanke Admits Recession Is Possible," *New York Daily News*, April 2, 2008.

CHAPTER 11: SLAPPED IN THE FACE BY THE INVISIBLE HAND

117 **You want to put out the fire first:** John Cassidy, "Anatomy of a Meltdown: Ben Bernanke and the Financial Crisis," *New Yorker*, December 1, 2008, www.newyorker.com/magazine/2008/12/01/anatomy-of-a-meltdown.

117 **He and I began collaborating:** Harvey Rosenblum, Danielle DiMartino, Jessica J. Renier, and Richard Alm, "Fed Intervention: Managing Moral Hazard in Financial Crises," Economic Letter, Vol. 3, No. 10, Federal Reserve Bank of Dallas, October 2008, www.dallasfed.org/assets/documents/research/eclett/2008/el0810.pdf.

117 **The *Economist* wrote:** "The $2 Bail-out," *Economist*, March 19, 2008.

118 **The *Economist* expressed skepticism:** Ibid.

118 **Fisher told the FOMC that:** Ben Bernanke, *The Courage to Act* (New York: W. W. Norton & Company, 2015), 150.

118 **To encourage lending:** FR: FOMC Statement, March 18, 2008, www.federalre serve .gov/newsevents/press/monetary/20080318a.htm.

118 **"I find myself conciliating":** Bernanke, *The Courage to Act*, 238. Kohn responded to Bernanke's e-mail by pointing out that "after a honeymoon period of three meetings without dissent in 1987, the Maestro had faced dissents in nineteen of his next twenty-one meetings."

118 **The Fed's traditional of:** Ibid.

119 **"You mean you cannot push on a string?":** John H. Wood, *A History of Central Banking in Great Britain and the United States* (Cambridge: Cambridge University Press, 2005), 231.

119 **"It's really a question":** Sudeep Reddy, "Fisher: Fix the Credit System First," *Wall Street Journal*, April 22, 2008.

120 **In mid-April 2008:** Maurna Desmond, "IMF: Subprime Losses Could Hit $1 Trillion," Forbes.com, April 8, 2008, www.forbes.com/2008/03/31/subprime-costs -writedowns-markets-equity-cx_md-0331markets21.html.

120 **As if on one:** "UBS Reports 1Q Net Loss of $11 billion," *USA Today*, May 6, 2008.

120 **On May 13:** Gretchen Morgenson and Vikas Bajaj, "MBIA Debt Is Setting Up a Quandary," *New York Times*, June 18, 2008.

120 **The $5.4 billion loss announced:** "S&P Sees No Affect on AIG's Ratings from Q2 Loss," insurancejournal.com, August 8, 2008, www.insurancejournal.com/news/national /2008/08/08/92615.htm.

120 **On July 11:** Kathy Kristof and Andrea Chang, "Federal Regulators Seize Crippled IndyMac Bank," *Los Angeles Times*, July 12, 2008.

120 **That week, Congressman Barney Frank:** Gretchen Morgenson and Joshua Rosner, *Reckless Endangerment: How Outsized Ambition, Greed and Corruption Led to Financial Armageddon* (New York: Times Books, 2011), 71.

120 **I think we see entities:** Gretchen Morgenson, "Suggested Safeguards Irk Fund Industry," *New York Times*, June 24, 2012, www.nytimes.com/2012/06/24/busi ness/mutual-fund-industry-resists-sec-proposals.html.

121 **Merrill Lynch reported write-downs:** Elinor Comlay, "Merrill Post $4.9 Billion Loss, Sells Bloomberg Stake," Reuters.com, July 18, 2008.

121 **followed by Citigroup:** Donald R. Van Deventer, "A Credit Crisis Chronology, Part 2 from March 2008 through March 2009: This Time Isn't Different," May 14, 2011, Kamakuraco.com, Kamakura Corporation. Don R. Van Deventer's blog summarizes events that Kamakura's risk professionals judged to be important milestones in the credit crisis. It's a treasure trove of material. www.kamakuraco .com/Blog/tabid/231/EntryId/305/A-Credit-Crisis-Chronology-Part-2-from -March-2008-Through-March-2009-This-Time-Isnt-Different.aspx.

121 **Wachovia with a loss:** Ibid.

121 **On July 31, 2008:** Ibid.

121 **Though many banks were swept:** Louise Story, "A Deal at Merrill Puts Spotlight on Others," *New York Times*, July 30, 2008.

121 **He attached a paper:** Zoltan Pozsar, "The Rise and Fall of the Shadow Banking System," *Regional Financial Review*, July 2008, Moody's Analytics, Inc., www.econ omy.com/sbs.

122 **The term "shadow banking":** Paul McCulley, "Teton Reflections," PIMCO Global Central Bank Focus, September 2007, www.pimco.com/insights/economic-and -market-commentary/global-central-bank-focus/teton-reflections.

122 **Though he got a better job offer:** Personal interview with Zoltan Pozsar, April 25, 2016.

122 **Pozsar's initial paper:** Pozsar, "The Rise and Fall of the Shadow Banking System," 16.

124 **At their peak in 2008:** Ibid.

125 **Called "The Panic of 2007":** FRBKC: Gary Gorton, "The Panic of 2007" (speech, Jackson Hole Economic Symposium, sponsored by the Federal Reserve Bank of Kansas City, Jackson Hole, Wyoming, August 2008), aida.econ.yale.edu/~nordhaus/homep age/documents/gorton.08.04.08.pdf.

125 **After hearing Gorton's ideas:** FRBM: Douglas Clement, ed., "Interview with Gary Gorton," The Region, December 1, 2010, www.minneapolisfed.org/publications/the -region/interview-with-gary-gorton.

125 **"Economists view the world as being the outcome":** FRBA: Gary Gorton, "Slapped in the Face by the Invisible Hand: Banking and the Panic of 2007" (paper, Federal Reserve Bank of Atlanta 2009 Financial Markets Conference: Financial Innovation and Crisis, May 11–13, 2009), 2, frbatlanta.org/-/media/Documents /news/conferences/2009/financial-markets-conference/gorton.pdf.

125 **He'd described the first thing:** Adam Smith, *An Inquiry into the Nature and Causes of the Wealth of Nations*, first published in 1776. The book by the Scottish economist and moral philosopher was widely influential. I was surprised to learn that he never uses the term "laissez-faire" in the book.

126 **"The credit crisis raises":** Gorton, "Slapped in the Face by the Invisible Hand," 2.

126 **"Instead," Gorton said:** Ibid., 10.

127 **"A dealer or other holder":** "Money Market: Repos," Investopedia.com, www.investo pedia.com/terms/r/repurchaseagreement.asp?ad=dirN&qo=investopedia SiteSearch&qsrc=0&o=40186.

128 **A year later, the price shot up:** Gorton, "Slapped in the Face by the Invisible Hand," 33.

128 **And the Fed didn't have:** FRBNY: "About the New York Fed, Purchase and Reverse Purchase Transactions," 2007, www.newyorkfed.org/aboutthefed/fedpoint/fed04 .html.

CHAPTER 12: HEADS MUST ROLL

130 **Some critics have argued:** FRBKC: Alan S. Blinder and Ricardo Reis, "Understanding the Greenspan Standard" (speech, Jackson Hole Economic Symposium, sponsored by the Federal Reserve Bank of Kansas City, Jackson Hole, Wyoming, August 25–27, 2005), www.kansascityfed.org/publicat/sympos/2005/pdf/Blinder-Reis2005.pdf.

130 **"Is Lehman next?":** "Lehman CFO Erin Callan: Back From Bloody Monday," bloomberg.com, March 19, 2008, www.bloomberg.com/news/articles/2008-03-19/lehman-cfo-erin-callan-back-from-ugly-monday.

131 **A few days after her:** Steve Fishman, "Burning Down His House," *New York Magazine*, November 30, 2008, nymag.com/nymag/rss/business/52603/.

131 **Lehman's stock price jumped 46 percent:** Ibid.

131 **"The worst of the impact":** Ibid.

131 **On June 9:** Ibid.

131 **"The board has to deliver a head":** Ibid.

131 **Wall Street's lean, mean:** Ibid.

132 **"Every day is a battle":** Ibid.

132 **Fuld would later describe:** Evelyn Chang, "Lehman's Fuld: No One Thing Caused the Crisis," CNBC.com, May 28, 2015, www.cnbc.com/2015/05/28/lehmans-fuld-no-one-thing-caused-the-crisis.html. The Web site provides a link to Fuld's speech at the Marcum MicroCap Conference in New York City the same day, in which he describes his arrival at Lehman Brothers.

132 **Professor Mark Stein:** Mark Stein, "When Does Narcissistic Leadership Become Problematic? Dick Fuld at Lehman Brothers," *Journal of Management Inquiry* 22, no. 3 (2013): 282–93, doi:10.1177/1056492613478664.

133 **By 2008, Lehman had borrowed:** Fishman, "Burning Down His House."

133 **From 2003 through 2007:** Allan Sloan and Roddy Boyd, "How Lehman Brothers Veered Off Course," *Washington Post*, July 3, 2008.

133 **By one friend's assessment:** Joshua Green, "Where Is Dick Fuld Now? Finding Lehman Brothers' Last CEO," Bloomberg.com, September 13, 2013, www.bloomberg.com/news/articles/2013-09-12/where-is-dick-fuld-now-finding-lehman-brothers-last-ceo.

133 **On May 29, 2007:** Sloan and Boyd, "How Lehman Brothers Veered Off Course."

133 **McAllistair Ranch was:** Ibid.

133 **He slashed Lehman's:** Joe Bel Bruno, Associated Press, "Lehman Shares Slip on Plans to Auction Off Unit, Consider Sale of Company," *Seattle Times,* September 10, 2008, old.seattletimes.com/html/businesstechnology/2008171076_weblehman10.html.

134 **Years later Fuld:** Jonathan Marino, Linette Lopez, and Julia La Roche, "Ex-Lehman CEO: 'Why Don't You Bite Me?,'" BusinessInsider.com, May 28, 2015, www.business insider.com/rich-fuld-speech-2015-5.

134 **Private equity firms:** Richard Fuld (speech, Marcum MicroCap Conference, New York, New York, May 28, 2015), www.cnbc.com/2015/05/28/lehmans-fuld-no-one -thing-caused-the-crisis.html.

134 **In 2000, about four thousand:** Ibid.

134 **The crisis became:** David Gelles, "Breaking Silence, Richard Fuld Speaks on Love, Putin and 'Rocky,'" *New York Times*, May 28, 2015. The *Times* also posted the full video.

134 **But Lehman had to come up with:** Carrick Mollenkamp, Susanne Craig, Jeffrey McCracken, and Jon Hilsenrath, "The Two Faces of Lehman's Fall," *Wall Street Journal,* October 6, 2008, www.wsj.com/articles/SB12232493764800 6103.

134 **"As long as I am alive":** Susanne Craig, Jeffrey McCracken, Aaron Lucchetti, and Kate Kelly, "The Weekend that Wall Street Died," *Wall Street Journal*, December 29, 2008.

134 **Though the firm wasn't saddled:** Joshua Green, "Where Is Dick Fuld Now?"

135 **"I began to worry":** Timothy Geithner, *Stress Test: Reflection on Financial Crises* (New York: Broadway Books, 2015), 179.

135 **"If you don't believe":** Ibid., 177.

136 **According to Paulson:** Fishman, "Burning Down His House."

136 **As Paulson put it:** DealBook, "The Financial Crisis Through Paulson's Eyes," *New York Times*, February 1, 2010.

136 **"Everybody, in some part":** James B. Stewart, "Eight Days," *New Yorker*, September 21, 2009, www.newyorker.com/magazine/2009/09/21/eight-days.

136 **Lehman filed for bankruptcy:** DealBook, "Lehman's Big Bankruptcy Filing," *New York Times*, September 15, 2008.

136 **He later insisted:** Gelles, "Breaking Silence, Richard Fuld Speaks on Love, Putin and 'Rocky.'"

137 **The largest insurance company:** Gretchen Morgenson, "Behind Insurer's Crisis, Blind Eye to a Web of Risk," *New York Times*, September 27, 2008.

137 **AIGFP had written about $500 billion:** Ibid.

137 **The unit's revenues in 1999:** Ibid.

137 **At a conference in 2007:** Ibid.

138 **"It is hard for us":** Ibid.

138 **On the evening of September 13:** Stewart, "Eight Days."

138 **"There will be no public support" for AIG:** Ibid.

138 **On September 15, all:** Matthew Karnitschnig, Deborah Solomon, Liam Pleven,

and Jon E. Hilsenrath, "U.S. to Take Over AIG in $85 Billion Bailout; Central Banks Inject Cash as Credit Dries Up," *Wall Street Journal*, September 16, 2008.

138 **The next day, the Fed injected $70 billion:** Stewart, "Eight Days."

139 **"I have eight hundred billion":** Ibid.

139 **On September 17, the Fed:** Karnitschnig, et al., "U.S. to Take Over AIG in $85 Billion Bailout: Central Banks Inject Cash as Credit Dries Up."

139 **Eventually the bailout:** Leslie Scism, "Hank Greenberg Challenges AIG Bailout," *Wall Street Journal*, September 28, 2014. See also Damian Paletta and Leslie Scism, "Geithner Testifies in AIG Bailout Suit," *Wall Street Journal*, October 7, 2014.

139 **Paulson informed Willumstad:** Paletta and Scism, "Geithner Testifies in AIG Bailout Suit."

CHAPTER 13: BREAKING THE BUCK

140 **Will capitalist economies:** Rich Miller, "Yalies Yellen-Hamada Put Tobin Twist Theory to Work in QE," Bloomberg.com, October 21, 2013, www.bloomberg.com /news/articles/2013-10-31/yalies-yellen-hamada-putting-tobin-s-twist -theory-to-work-in-qe.

140 **The chairman of the Reserve Management Company:** James B. Stewart, "Eight Days," *New Yorker*, September 21, 2009, www.newyorker.com/magazine/2009/09 /21/eight-days.

140 **By the time the senior Bent:** Ibid.

141 **No other MMF had:** Diya Gullapalli, Shefali Anand, and Daisy Maxey, "Money Fund, Hurt by Debt Tied to Lehman, Breaks the Buck," *Wall Street Journal*, September 17, 2008.

141 **The news was "really, really bad":** Ibid.

141 **"Paulson and Bernanke totally":** Stewart, "Eight Days."

141 **"Lehman Brothers begat":** Ibid.

142 **"We cannot do this alone":** Ibid.

142 **Finally, someone in New York:** Timothy F. Geithner, "The Paradox of Financial Crises," *Wall Street Journal*, May 13, 2014.

142 **"Hank! Listen to me":** Stewart, "Eight Days."

142 **Bernanke went on:** Ibid.

142 **Treasury announced it would provide:** U.S. Department of the Treasury, "Treasury Announces Temporary Guarantee Program for Money Market Funds," press release, September 29, 2009, www.treasury.gov/press-center/press-releases/Pages/hp1161.aspx.

142 **"We are in danger":** Stewart, "Eight Days."

142 **"The kind of financial collapse":** Ibid.

142 **He predicted that:** Ibid.

142 **With the blessing of President Bush:** "Statement by Secretary Henry M. Paulson

Jr. on Comprehensive Approach to Market Developments," press release, September 19, 2008, U.S. Department of the Treasury, www.treasury.gov/press-center /press-releases/Pages/hp1149.aspx.

143 **At the urging of:** Stewart, "Eight Days."

143 **WAMU was sold:** John Letzing, "WaMu Seized, Sold to JP Morgan Chase," Market Watch.com, September 26, 2009.

143 **The bloody, bloody Monday:** Chris Isidore, "Bailout Plan Rejected—Supporters Scramble," CNNMoney.com, September 29, 2008.

143 **But the biggest bloodletting:** Alexandra Twin, "Stocks Crushed," CNNMoney .com, September 29, 2008.

144 **A story in the *New York Times*:** Timothy Geithner, *Stress Test: Reflection on Financial Crises* (New York: Broadway Books, 2015), 171.

144 **So Paulson requested:** Gretchen Morgenson and Don Van Natta Jr., "Paulson's Calls to Goldman Tested Ethics," *New York Times*, August 8, 2009.

144 **But phone records:** Ibid.

144 **"We don't know what":** Ibid.

144 **But two "senior government officials":** Ibid.

145 **"It's clear he":** Ibid.

145 **Bernanke had insisted:** John Cassidy, "Bernanke Changes Story on Lehman Collapse," *New Yorker*, September 2, 2010.

145 **"The Federal Reserve and the Treasury":** Editorial, "Questions for Mr. Geithner," *Wall Street Journal*, December 14, 2008.

145 **"The only why we could have":** Cassidy, "Bernanke Changes Story on Lehman Collapse."

146 **"The view was that failure":** Ibid.

146 **In December 2008:** Opinion Page, "Questions for Mr. Geithner," *New York Times*, December 14, 2008.

146 **A person involved:** Steve Fishman, "Burning Down His House," *New York Magazine*, November 30, 2008, nymag.com/nymag/rss/business/52603/.

146 **At a hearing before Congress:** Brian Ross and Alice Gomstyn, "Lehman Brothers Boss Defends $484 Million in Salary, Bonus," ABC News, October 6, 2008, abcnews .go.com/Blotter/story?id=5965360.

146 **But the collapse of Lehman cost:** Fishman, "Burning Down His House."

146 **After all, soon after:** "Merrill Lynch CEO Thain Spent $1.22 Million on Office," CNBC.com, January 22, 2009, www.cnbc.com/id/28793892.

146 **"Some have faulted Dick":** Joshua Green, "Where Is Dick Fuld Now? Finding Lehman Brothers Last CEO," Bloomberg.com, September 13, 2013, www.bloomberg .com/news/articles/2013-09-12/where-is-dick-fuld-now-finding-lehman -brothers-last-ceo.

146 **"You can't look at Lehman":** Ibid.

147 **"I think I missed the violence":** David Gelles, "Breaking Silence, Richard Fuld Speaks on Love, Putin and 'Rocky,'" *New York Times*, May 28, 2015. The *Times* posted the full video.

147 **"I just wanted to point out":** Ben Bernanke, *The Courage to Act* (New York: W. W. Norton & Company, 2015), 347.

147 **And Dudley, the former Goldman Sachs chief economist:** "Opening at the Fed: How to Think About the World's Most Important Job Vacancy," *Review & Outlook, Wall Street Journal*, December 5, 2008.

147 **The revolving door:** Julie Creswell and Ben White, "The Guys from 'Government Sachs,'" *New York Times*, October 17, 2008.

148 **But Paulson's actions:** Ibid.

148 **But in October 6:** Kate Kelly and Jon Hilsenrath, "New York Fed Chairman's Ties to Goldman Raise Questions," *Wall Street Journal*, May 4, 2009.

148 **The Fed waiver was approved:** Ibid.

148 **Goldman's stock rallied:** Ibid.

148 **"You can't get permission":** Ibid.

148 **By the end of 2008:** Geithner, "The Paradox of Financial Crises."

CHAPTER 14: BREACHING THE ZERO BOUND

150 **The U.S. government has:** FRB: Ben Bernanke, "Deflation: Making Sure 'It' Doesn't Happen Here" (speech, National Economists Club, Washington, DC, November 21, 2002), www.federalreserve.gov/boarddocs/speeches/2002/20021121/default .htm.

150 **Bernanke gave a speech:** FRB: Ben Bernanke, "Federal Reserve Policies in Financial Crisis" (speech, Greater Austin Chamber of Commerce, Austin, Texas, December 1, 2008), www.federalreserve.gov/newsevents/speech/bernanke20081201a.htm.

150 **The nickname referred:** Bernanke, "Deflation: Making Sure 'It' Doesn't Happen Here."

151 **In the "fog of war,":** Ylan Q. Mui, "Ben Bernanke on Why He Was Right About the Economy," *Washington Post*, October 14, 2015.

151 **Geithner would later call:** David M. Jones, *Understanding Central Banking: The New Era of Activism* (London: M. E. Sharpe, Inc., 2014), 105.

152 **From 1936 to 1995:** FRBSL: Daniel L. Thornton and David C. Wheelock, "Making Sense of Dissents: A History of FOMC Dissents," Federal Reserve Bank of St. Louis *Review*, Third Quarter 2014, 96(3): 213–27, research.stlouisfed.org/publications /review/2014/q3/thornton.pdf.

153 **Greenspan ignored the blackout:** Laurence H. Meyer, *A Term at the Fed: An Insider's View* (New York: HarperBusiness, 2004), 99.

153 **Once he arrived, Meyer:** Ibid., 6.

153 Meyer was once stunned: Ibid., 99.

153 At the FOMC meeting on: FR: FOMC Meeting, transcript, January 29–30, 2008, 7, www.federalreserve.gov/monetarypolicy/files/FOMC20080130meeting.pdf.

153 But there was no call to arms: FRBSL: Bryan J. Noeth and Rajdeep Sengupta, "Is Shadow Banking Really Banking?" *Regional Economist,* October 2011, www.stlou isfed.org/Publications/Regional-Economist/October-2011/Is-Shadow-Banking -Really-Banking.

154 "We have had extensive conversations": FR: FOMC Meeting, transcript, January 29–30, 2008, 17, www.federalreserve.gov/monetarypolicy/files/FOMC20080130 meeting.pdf.

154 The January 2008 meeting: Ben Bernanke, *The Courage to Act* (New York: W. W. Norton & Company, 2015), 197.

154 "When the market is": FR: FOMC Meeting, transcript, January 29–30, 2008, 139, www.federalreserve.gov/monetarypolicy/files/FOMC20080130meeting.pdf.

154 Fed governor Frederic Mishkin: Ibid., 93.

154 "This proposal crosses a bright line": FR: FOMC Conference Call, transcript, March 10, 2008, 21, www.federalreserve.gov/monetarypolicy/files/FOMC20080310 confcall.pdf.

154 "The root problem is a problem of liquidity": FR: FOMC Meeting, transcript, March 18, 2008, 55, www.federalreserve.gov/monetarypolicy/files/FOMC20080318meeting.pdf.

155 "I am not going to vote": Ibid., 56.

155 Plosser and Fisher dissented: Associated Press, "Recession Worries Drove Rate Cut, Minutes Show," *New York Times,* April 8, 2008.

155 Unintentionally, the March 2008 meeting: FR: FOMC Meeting, transcript, March 18, 2008, 109–11.

157 "Let me first say": FR: FOMC Meeting, transcript, April 29–30, 2008, 136, www .federalreserve.gov/monetarypolicy/files/FOMC20080430meeting.pdf.

157 She expected GDP growth: Ibid., 47.

157 Yellen added that the: Ibid., 48.

157 Fisher and Plosser again dissented: FR: FOMC Statement, April 30, 2008, www .federalreserve.gov/newsevents/press/monetary/20080430a.htm.

157 "Although downside risks": FR: FOMC Statement, June 25, 2008, www.federalre serve.gov/newsevents/press/monetary/20080625a.htm.

157 Fisher dissented, again insisting: Sudeep Reddy and Phil Izzo, "The Dissent: Fisher Stands Alone," *Wall Street Journal,* June 25, 2008.

157 "I think it would be wise": FR: FOMC Meeting, transcript, August 5, 2008, 117, www .federalreserve.gov/monetarypolicy/files/FOMC20080805meeting.pdf.

158 "Frankly, I am decidedly confused": FR: FOMC Meeting, transcript, September 16, 2008, 74, www.federalreserve.gov/monetarypolicy/files/FOMC20080916meeting.pdf.

158 One Fed chief economist: Ibid., 20.

158 "For example, East Bay plastic surgeons": Ibid., 33.

158 "The interaction of": Ibid., 33.

158 "Money doesn't talk": Ibid., 54.

159 "I also agree with those": Ibid., 76.

159 In the end, Fisher voted: Phil Izzo, "The End of Dissent: Fisher Joins the Majority," *Wall Street Journal*, September 16, 2008.

159 The economic news and forecasts: FR: FOMC Statement, October 29, 2008, www.federalreserve.gov/newsevents/press/monetary/20081029a.htm.

159 "We are fighting an uphill battle": FR: FOMC Meeting, transcript, October 28–29, 2008, 71, www.federalreserve.gov/monetarypolicy/files/FOMC20081029meeting.pdf.

159 "Given the seriousness": Ibid., 28–29.

160 "The recent sharp deterioration": FR: FOMC Meeting, transcript, December 15–16, 2008, 5, www.federalreserve.gov/monetarypolicy/files/FOMC20081216meeting.pdf.

160 Bernanke had outlined: FRB: Ben S. Bernanke, Vincent R. Reinhart, and Brian P. Sack, "Monetary Policy Alternatives at the Zero Bound: An Empirical Assessment," Finance and Economics Discussion Series. www.federalreserve.gov/pubs/feds/2004/200448/200448abs.html.

160 "I am the least well-educated": FR: FOMC Meeting, transcript, December 15–16, 2008, 36, www.federalreserve.gov/monetarypolicy/files/FOMC20081216meeting.pdf.

160 "We don't have any models": Ibid., 36.

161 "That will be a tricky task": Ibid., 37.

161 "We could also consider using the FOMC minutes": Ibid., 43.

161 "Mr. Chairman," Fisher said: Ibid., 83.

161 Friedman suggested to a colleague: Jim Kudlinski, "Memo to the Fed: First, Do No Harm," *Wall Street Journal*, June 15, 2015, A17.

161 Fisher maintained that cutting: FR: FOMC Meeting, transcript, December 15–16, 2008, 84.

161 "Adding to our difficulties": Ibid.

161 "I have worked and lived in Japan": Ibid., 84–85.

163 Fisher insisted that establishing: Ibid., 210.

163 Fisher mentioned one CEO: Ibid., 146.

163 "We have hit zero": Ibid., 213–14.

163 "With some reluctance": Ibid., 215.

163 Fisher entered the only: Ibid.

163 "On consideration, in order": FR: FOMC Meeting, transcript, December 15–16, 2008, 216.

CHAPTER 15: THE WALKING DEAD

164 **I will be the first:** FRBSF: Janet Yellen, "A View of the Economic Crisis and the Fed's Response" (speech, Commonwealth Club of California, June 30, 2009), www .frbsf.org/our-district/press/presidents-speeches/yellen-speeches/2009/june /yellen-economic-crisis-federal-reserve-response/.

166 **In January, the S&P 500 Index:** Google Finance Historical Chart, S&P 500 Index, January 2009, www.google.com/finance/historical.

166 **DJIA was down more than 50 percent:** Big Charts, Dow Jones Industrial Average, marketwatch.com, bigcharts.marketwatch.com/advchart.

166 **Blackstone Group CEO Steve Schwarzman:** Megan Davies and Walden Slew, "45 Percent of World's Wealth Destroyed: Blackstone CEO," Reuters.com, March 10, 2009.

167 **The *Wall Street Journal* revisited:** Justin Lahart, "Mr. Rajan Was Prescient (But Unpopular) at Greenspan's Party," *Wall Street Journal*, January 2, 2009.

167 **As the *New York Times* put it, Lehman:** Landon Thomas, "Funds Try to Lose Ties to Lehman," *New York Times*, October 1, 2008.

168 **Released in late November 2011:** Luca Di Leo and Maya Jackson Randall, "Fed Data Shows Firms on the Brink," *Wall Street Journal*, December 1, 2010.

169 **The single neediest day?:** Bob Ivry, Bradley Keoun, and Phil Kuntz, "Secret Fed Loans Gave Banks $13 Billion Undisclosed to Congress," Bloomberg.com, November 27, 2011.

169 **"We took an enormous amount of risk":** Di Leo and Randall, "Fed Data Shows Firms on the Brink."

169 **"It strikes me that":** FR: FOMC Meeting, transcript, January 27–28, 2009, 47, www .federalreserve.gov/monetarypolicy/files/FOMC20090128meeting.pdf.

170 **"The buggy whip industry":** Ibid., 59.

170 **Geithner was sworn in:** Kenneth R. Bazinet, "Senate Votes 60–34 to Confirm Timothy Geithner as Treasury Secretary," *New York Daily News*, January 26, 2009.

170 **"It's like selling a car":** FR: FOMC Conference Call, transcript, February 7, 2009, 4, www.federalreserve.gov/monetarypolicy/files/FOMC20090207conf call.pdf.

170 **Calling BoA and Citigroup:** Ibid., 4.

171 **And they did, especially:** David Enrich, Dan Fitzpatrick, and Marshall Eckblad, "Banks Won Concessions on Tests," *Wall Street Journal*, May 9, 2009.

171 **By the end of February 2009:** FRBSL: "Mortgage-backed Securities Held by the Federal Reserve: All Maturities," Economic Data, Federal Reserve Economic Data (FRED), Federal Reserve Bank of St. Louis, fred.stlouisfed.org/series /MBST.

171 **In a speech at the Kennedy School:** FRBD: Richard Fisher, "Comments on the Current Financial Crisis" (speech, John F. Kennedy School of Government, Harvard University, February 23, 2009), www.dallasfed.org/news/speeches/fisher /2009/fs090223.cfm.

171 **On March 6, 2009:** John Authers, "Numbers Games: Was 666 Low Enough in 2009?," *Financial Times*, March 7, 2014.

171 **By mid-2009, unemployment:** U.S. Department of Labor, Bureau of Labor Statistics, Labor Force Statistics from the Current Population Survey (unemployment rate), data.bls.gov/timeseries/LNS14000000.

172 **"I'd just like to say":** DealBook, "Bernanke Sees Recovery Beginning in 2010," *New York Times*, March 15, 2009.

172 **Dillon had fallen on hard times:** Bryan Blackstone, "Bernanke Defends Recovery Efforts in Rare TV Interview," *Wall Street Journal*, March 15, 2009.

172 **In Yellen's district, people:** FR: FOMC Meeting, transcript, March 17–18, 2009, 134, www.federalreserve.gov/monetarypolicy/files/FOMC20090318meeting.pdf.

173 **"He said, 'Call somebody else'":** Ibid., 123.

173 **"Household wealth has plummeted":** Ibid., 136.

173 **But in the current crisis:** Ibid., 135.

173 **By the end of the March 2009:** FR: FOMC Statement, March 18, 2009, www.feder alreserve.gov/newsevents/press/monetary/20090318a.htm.

174 **"I prefer to take appropriate, bold action":** FR: FOMC Meeting, transcript, April 28–29, 2009, 121, www.federalreserve.gov/monetarypolicy/files/FOMC2009 318 meeting.pdf.

174 **"We don't know exactly":** FR: FOMC Meeting, transcript, March 18, 2009, 73.

174 **The global recovery was "slow and tentative":** FR: FOMC Meeting, transcript, April 28–29, 2009, 33.

174 **"I think we're really groping in the dark":** Ibid., 129.

174 **The Dow rallied:** Big Charts, Dow Jones Industrial Average, Marketwatch.com . bigcharts.marketwatch.com/advchart/.

174 **As Bernanke had told:** FR: FOMC Meeting, transcript, April 28–29, 2009, 98.

175 **He told the *Wall Street Journal*:** Mary Anastasia O'Grady, "Don't Monetize the Debt," *Wall Street Journal*, May 23, 2009.

175 **"That's when you open the floodgates":** Ibid.

175 **The *Wall Street Journal* reporter:** Ibid.

175 **"I think we have to":** FR: FOMC Meeting, transcript, June 23–24, 2009, 78, www.fed eralreserve.gov/monetarypolicy/files/FOMC20090624meeting.pdf.

176 **The National Bureau of Economic Research:** Chris Isidore, "Recession Officially Ended in June 2004," cnnmoney.com, September 20, 2010.

176 "Most, probably, of our decisions": "Animal Spirits—J. M. Keynes," economicshelp
     .org, November 28, 2012. Keynes describes animal spirits in his 1936 book *General
     Theory of Employment, Interest and Money* (London: Macmillan, 1936), 161–62.

176 It was fitting that in 2009: George Akerlof and Robert Shiller, *Animal Spirits: How
     Human Psychology Drives the Economy, and Why It Matters for Global Capitalism*
     (Princeton, N.J.: Princeton University Press, 2009).

177 "There's a large amount of money": Cullen Roche, "1930's Déjà Vu," Business
     Insider.com, September 4, 2009.

177 "There is plenty of cash": Richard Barley, "Fretful Investors Sidelined by Rally,"
     Wall Street Journal, September 12, 2009.

177 In August, he announced: Jennifer Liberto, "Obama Taps Bernanke for Second
     Term," CNNMoney.com, August 25, 2009.

178 A hearing in the Senate: Ibid.

178 Channeling country legend: Jon Shayne, "Inflation or Deflation?," lyrics, YouTube,
     www.youtube.com/watch?feature=player_embedded&v=2fq2ga4HkGY, www.merle
     hazard.com.

180 "She's no Yeltsin": FR: FOMC Meeting, transcript, September 22–23, 2009, 144,
     www.federalreserve.gov/monetarypolicy/files/FOMC20090923meeting.pdf.

180 One camp within the Fed: Gretchen Morgenson, "At the Fed in 2009, Rolling the
     Dice in a Crisis," *New York Times*, March 7, 2015.

180 After the September meeting: Richard W. Fisher and Harvey Rosenblum, "The
     Blob That Ate Monetary Policy," *Wall Street Journal*, September 27, 2009, www.wsj
     .com/articles/SB10001424052748704471504574438650557408142.

180 "If policymakers insist on waiting": FRB: Kevin Warsh, "Longer Days, Fewer
     Weekends" (speech, 12th Annual International Banking Conference, Chicago, Il-
     linois, September 25, 2009), www.federalreserve.gov/newsevents/speech/warsh
     20090925a.htm.

180 "My experience tells me": Edmund L. Andrews, "Fed Is Split Over Timing of Rate
     Rise," *New York Times*, October 9, 2009, www.nytimes.com/learning/students
     /pop/articles/09bernanke.html.

181 At the November 3–9, 2009: FR: FOMC Meeting, transcript, November 3–4, 2009,
     4, www.federalreserve.gov/monetarypolicy/files/FOMC20091104meeting.pdf.

181 *Time* had just proclaimed: Michael Grunwald, "Person of the Year 2009: Ben Ber-
     nanke," *Time*, December 16, 2009.

182 "Mortgage rates are already extraordinarily low": Binyamin Appelbaum, "In
     Eye of Economic Storm, the Fed Blinked," *New York Times*, March 4, 2015.

182 "One-Note" Yellen: FR: FOMC Meeting, transcript, December 16, 2009, 105, www
     .federalreserve.gov/monetarypolicy/files/FOMC20091216meeting.pdf.

Chapter 16: Dr. Ben Pulls a Bait and Switch

184 **For my own part, I did not see:** FRB: Interview with Janet Yellen, FCIC staff audiotape, Financial Crisis Inquiry Commission, November 15, 2010, fcic-static .law.stanford.edu/cdn_media/fcic-audio/2010-11-15%20FCIC%20staff%20audio tape%20of%20interview%20with%20Janet%20Yellen,%20Federal%20Reserve %20Board.mp3.

185 **Though Dodd commended:** Chris Isidore, "Bernanke Faces Fire at Confirmation Hearing," MoneyCNN.com, December 3, 2009, money.cnn.com/2009/12/03/news /economy/bernanke_hearing/.

185 **On January 28, 2010:** Ben Leubsdorf, "A Timeline of the Federal Reserve in 2010," *Wall Street Journal*, January 15, 2016.

186 **A lot of the data:** The Ceridian-UCLA Pulse of Commerce Index has been discontinued. For historical reference see: ycharts.com/indicators/ceridian_ucla_pulse _of_commerce_index.

186 **"I think the disagreeable but sound thing":** FRBD: Richard Fisher, "Lessons Learned, Convictions Affirmed" (speech, Council on Foreign Relations, New York City, New York, March 3, 2010), www.dallasfed.org/news/speeches/fisher/ 2010/fs100303.cfm.

187 **"If they're too big to fail":** DealBook, "Greenspan Calls to Break Up Banks 'Too Big to Fail,'" *New York Times*, October 15, 2009, DealBook.nytimes.com/2009/10/15 /greenspan-break-up-banks-too-big-to-fail/?_r=0.

188 **But in the interim Volcker:** Michael Lewis, *Liar's Poker* (New York: W. W. Norton, 2014), 44.

188 **Now a household word:** The CBOE VIX measures stock market volatility, www .cboe.com/micro/VIX/vixintro.aspx.

189 **Demonstrators stormed the Parliament:** Dan Bilefsky, "Three Reported Killed in Greek Protests," *New York Times*, May 5, 2010.

190 **The crash's trigger:** Bernard Goyder, "Navinder Sarao Faces U.S. Extradition," *Wall Street Journal*, March 23, 2016.

190 **"This guy, for want":** Suzi Ring, John Detrixhe, and Liam Vaughan, "The Alleged Flash-Trading Mastermind Lived with His Parents and Couldn't Drive," Bloomberg .com, June 9, 2015, www.bloomberg.com/news/articles/2015-06-09/the-alleged -flash-trading-mastermind-lived-with-his-parents-and-couldn-t-drive.

190 **The DOJ maintained:** Jane Croft and Philip Stafford, "Sarao Loses First Round of US Extradition Fight," *Financial Times*, March 23, 2016, www.ft.com/fastft/2016 /03/23/flash-crash-trader-sarao-to-be-extradited-to-us/.

191 **That summer, the Senate version:** Signed by President Barack Obama, July 21, 2010, www.whitehouse.gov/blog/2010/07/21/president-obama-signs-wall-street -reform-no-easy-task.

191 **In July 2010:** FRBNY: Zoltan Pozsar, Adrian Tobias, Adam Ashcraft, and Hayley Boesky, "Shadow Banking," Federal Reserve Bank of New York Staff Reports No. 458, July 2010; revised February 2012.

191 **The traditional banking system (estimated):** Ibid.

192 **"Looking at that map created a cognitive shift":** Gillian Tett, "Road Map That Opens Up Shadow Banking," *Financial Times*, November 18, 2010.

192 **Yellen argued for yet more stimulus:** FR: FOMC Meeting, transcript, August 10, 2010, 100, www.federalreserve.gov/monetarypolicy/files/FOMC20100810meeting.pdf.

193 **"Even if you are a pure inflation targeter":** Ibid., 135.

193 **"We cannot afford to fail":** Ibid., 126.

193 **"Some people argue":** Ibid., 135.

193 **The FOMC announced that it:** FR: FOMC Statement, August 10, 2010, www.fed eral reserve.gov/newsevents/press/monetary/20100810a.htm.

193 **Two weeks later, at the:** FRB: Ben Bernanke, "The Economic Outlook and Monetary Policy" (speech, Jackson Hole Economic Symposium, sponsored by the Federal Reserve Bank of Kansas City, Jackson Hole, Wyoming, August 27, 2010), www .federalreserve.gov/newsevents/speech/bernanke20100827a.htm.

193 **On August 26, the S&P 500:** Google Finance Historical Prices, S&P 500 Index, www.google.com/finance/historical?cid=626307&startdate=Aug+1%2C+2010 &enddate=Dec+1%2C+2010&num=30&ei=rBTHV4mvJ8imebfCioAL.

193 **The S&P 500 Index staged a full reversal:** Ibid.

194 **"Further downside surprises":** FR: FOMC Meeting, transcript, September 2010, 20, www.federalreserve.gov/monetarypolicy/files/FOMC20100921meeting.pdf.

194 **"But I do think policy":** Ibid., 87.

194 **In September, the Senate:** Corey Boles, "Senate Confirms Yellen, Bloom Raskin as Fed Board Members," *Wall Street Journal*, September 30, 2010.

194 **But the president's nomination:** Ibid.

194 **In an op-ed, Diamond:** Joshua Zumbrun, "Nobel Laureate Diamond Withdraws Nomination to Fed Board," Bloomberg.com, June 6, 2011.

195 **Alabama Sen. Richard Shelby:** Ibid.

195 **After two additional votes:** Ibid.

195 **The economy's feeble state:** Jon Hilsenrath, "Fed Gears Up for Stimulus," *Wall Street Journal*, October 26, 2010.

195 **"In my darkest moments":** FRBD: Richard Fisher, "To Ease, Or Not To Ease?" (speech, Economic Club of Minnesota, Minneapolis, Minnesota, October 7, 2010), www.dallasfed.org/news/speeches/fisher/2010/fs101007.cfm.

195 **The Fed "is close to embarking":** Hilsenrath, "Fed Gears Up for Stimulus."

195 **She aggressively challenged the chairman:** Laurence H. Meyer, *A Term at the Fed: An Insider's View* (New York: HarperBusiness, 2004), 42.

196 **"I will tell you that if the 2 percent"**: Ibid., 43.

196 **David Stockman, former government economist:** David Stockman, "Sell the Bonds, Sell the Stocks, Sell the House—Dread the Fed!," DavidStockmanContra Corner.com, December 18, 2015.

197 **The outspoken Hoenig:** Ben Bernanke, *The Courage to Act* (New York: W. W. Norton & Company, 2015), 488.

197 **"If I were in your chair":** FR: FOMC Meeting, transcript, November 3, 2010, 182, www.federalreserve.gov/monetarypolicy/files/FOMC20101103meeting.pdf.

197 **"I wouldn't want to undermine":** Neil Irwin, "Federal Reserve Started 2010 with Hope, Then Fear and Fitful Activism," *New York Times*, January 15, 2016.

197 **Hoenig cast the lone no vote:** Sewell Chan, "Fed's Contrarian Has a Wary Eye on the Past," *New York Times*, December 13, 2010, www.nytimes.com/2010/12/14/busi ness/14fed.html.

197 **"It seems odd to me":** Paul M. Barrett and Scott Lanman, "Fed Dissenter Hoenig Wages Lonely Campaign Against Easy Credit," Bloomberg.com, September 24, 2010, www.bloomberg.com/news/articles/2010-09-24/fed-dissenter-hoenig-s -campaign-against-easy-credit-has-roots-in-prairie.

197 **Bernanke would later describe:** Bernanke, *The Courage to Act*, 488.

197 **Fisher argued in a speech:** FRBD: Richard Fisher, "Recent Decisions of the Federal Open Market Committee: A Bridge to Fiscal Sanity?" (speech, Association for Financial Professional, San Antonio, Texas, November 8, 2010), www.dallasfed.org/news /speeches/fisher/2010/fs101108.cfm.

198 **"Chronic short-termism":** FRB: Kevin Warsh, "Rejecting the Requiem" (speech, Securities Industry and Financial Markets Association, New York, New York, November 8, 2010), www.federalreserve.gov/newsevents/speech/warsh20101108a.htm.

198 **A group of prominent economists:** Cullen Roche, "Huge List of Investors and Economists Pen Open Letter to Ben Bernanke Slamming QE," BusinessInsider .com, November 15, 2010.

198 **"We disagree with the view":** Ibid.

198 **"*In particular, the Fed*":** Ben Bernanke, "What the Fed Did and Why: Supporting the Recovery and Sustaining Price Stability," *Washington Post*, November 4, 2010, www .washingtonpost.com/wp-dyn/content/article/2010/11/03/AR2010110307372.html.

198 **Financial journalist Alen Mattich:** Alen Mattich, "Macro-Prudential Nonsense from Bernanke and King," *Wall Street Journal*, November 10, 2010.

199 **Rep. Paul Ryan:** Peter Wallsten and Sudeep Reddy, "Fresh Attack on Fed Move," *Wall Street Journal*, November 15, 2010.

199 **"Printing money is no substitute":** Ibid.

199 **Obama said the move:** Ibid.

199 **But even economists:** Ibid.

Chapter 17: A Turning Point

200 **The plausible outcomes:** Christopher Swann, "US Current Account Deficit 'Unsustainable'—NY Fed Chief," *Financial Times,* January 23, 2006.

200 **Wall Street legend Arthur Cashin:** Linette Lopez, "Art Cashin Just Gave a Hilarious Wall Street History Lesson Going Back to the 1950s," BusinessInsider.com, October 8, 2013.

202 **A Fed "computational linguistics":** FRB: Miguel Acosta and Ellen Meade, "Hanging on Every Word: Semantic Analysis of the FOMC's Postmeeting Statement," FEDS Notes, September 30, 2015, www.federalreserve.gov/econresdata/notes /feds-notes/2015/semantic-analysis-of-the-FOMCs-postmeeting-statement -20150930.html.

205 **The thought police:** FRBD: Danielle DiMartino Booth and David Luttrell, "The Fallacy of a Pain-Free Path to a Healthy Housing Market," Economic Letter, Vol. 5, No. 14, December 2010, www.dallasfed.org/assets/documents/research/eclett/2010 /el1014.pdf.

205 **Clearly they didn't realize:** Tyler Durden, "Refuting the Housing Recovery Fallacy Courtesy of . . . The Fed?" zerohedge.com, December 22, 2010, www.zerohedge.com /article/refuting-housing-recovery-falacy-courtesy.

205 **"While we working stiffs":** "The Fed Finally Tells the Truth," city-data.com, January 4, 2011, www.city-data.com/forum/economics/1166860-fed-finally-tells-truth.html.

Chapter 18: Insider Trading?

206 **We're not printing money:** Scott Pelley, "Fed Chairman Ben Bernanke's Take on the Economy," *60 Minutes,* CBS News, December 3, 2010, www.cbsnews.com /news/fed-chairman-ben-bernankes-take-on-the-economy/2/.

206 **The congressman's 2009 book:** Ron Paul, *End the Fed* (New York: Grand Central Publishing, 2009).

208 **In the final three months:** "China Currency Reserves Rise to Record $2.85 Trillion," Bloomberg.com, January 11, 2011, www.bloomberg.com/news/articles/2011-01-11 /china-s-currency-reserves-rise-to-record-domestic-lending-exceeds-target.

209 **"All express concern":** FRBD: Richard Fisher, "The Limits of Monetary Policy: Monetary Policy Cannot Substitute for Government Irresponsibility" (speech, Manhattan Institute, New York, New York, January 12, 2011), www.dallasfed.org /news/speeches/fisher/2011/fs110112.cfm.

210 **"But with the federal funds rate":** FRBC: Charles Evans, "Thoughts on the Future Course of Monetary Policy" (speech, ASSA-AEA Conference, Denver, Colorado, January 7, 2011), www.Chicagofed.gov.

210 **The January statement:** FR: FOMC Statement, January 26, 2011, www.federal reserve.gov/newsevents/press/monetary/20110126a.htm.

210 **No longer voting:** Sudeep Reddy, "The Lone Dissenter: Kansas City's Hoenig Goes Out with a Record," *Wall Street Journal*, December 14, 2010.

210 **Hoenig hit back:** Gregg Robb, "Hoenig Defends String of Dissents in 2016," Marketwatch.com, January 5, 2011.

210 **On February 18, 2011:** Aline van Duyn and Nichole Bullock, "'Junk' Bonds Hit Record Low," *Financial Times*, February 18, 2011.

211 **This was backed by:** Richard Fry and Jeffrey S. Passel, "In Post-Recession Era, Young Adults Drive Continuing Rise in Multi-Generational Living," Pew Research Center: Social and Demographic Trends, July 17, 2014.

211 **In early February 2011:** Neil Irwin, "Kevin Warsh to leave Federal Reserve Board," *Washington Post*, February 10, 2011.

211 **A law professor:** Jon Hilsenrath and Damian Paletta, "Fed's Tarullo Shakes Up Bank Rules," *Wall Street Journal*, October 27, 2009.

211 **"We are still very far away":** Michael S. Derby, "Dudley and Bullard Complicate QE2 Outlook," *Wall Street Journal*, February 28, 2011.

212 **Bullard maintained that:** Ibid.

212 **On April 1, the:** "Current Rates Effective April 1, 2011—Present," Assessment Rates, FDIC.com, www.fdic.gov/deposit/insurance/assessments/proposed.html.

212 **"I think of it as akin to insider trading":** FR: FOMC Meeting, transcript, November 2–3, 2010, 8, www.federalreserve.gov/monetarypolicy/files/FOMC20101103 meeting.pdf.

213 **"President Fisher was referring":** Ibid., 10.

213 **But some sleuthing:** Josh Zumbrun, "Fed Officials Concerned about Use of Insider Information as Early as 2010," *Wall Street Journal*, January 15, 2016.

213 **A year later, the FOMC:** Pedro Nicolaci Da Costa and David Harrison, "Yellen Meetings of Medley Global Come Under Scrutiny," *Wall Street Journal*, May 5, 2015.

213 **Ironically, Yellen would come under fire:** Ibid.

213 **Yellen's refusal to cooperate:** U.S. House of Representatives, "Federal Reserve Subpoenaed Over Leak," press release, House Committee on Financial Services, May 15, 2015, financialservices.house.gov/news/email/show.aspx/.

213 **On April 27, 2011:** Binyamin Appelbaum, "Bernanke Defends Fed's Role in Running Economy," *New York Times*, April 27, 2011.

214 **In his professorial tone:** Ibid.

214 **The previous December:** Scott Pelley, "Fed Chairman Ben Bernanke's Take on the Economy," *60 Minutes*, CBS News, December 3, 2010, www.cbsnews.com/news /fed-chairman-ben-bernankes-take-on-the-economy/.

214 **"You explained that the Fed":** Carolyn Baum, "Bernanke Must Have Lost My List of Questions," Bloomberg.com, April 27, 2011.

214 **"No amount of further accommodation":** Michael S. Derby, "Fed's Fisher: May Need to Consider Curtailing QE2," *Wall Street Journal*, April 8, 2011.

215 **By June 2011:** "The Lone Star Jobs Surge," *Review & Outlook, Wall Street Journal*, June 10, 2011.

215 **Texas had added 265,300 jobs:** Ibid.

215 **As a result, the Texas economy had grown:** Ibid.

215 **Since 2007, the pool of renters:** "America's Rental Housing: Evolving Markets and Needs," Joint Center for Housing Studies of Harvard University, 2013, www.jchs.harvard.edu/sites/jchs.harvard.edu/files/jchs_americas_rental_housing_2013_1_0.pdf.

215 **Writing in *Barron's*:** Douglas Kass, "The Threat of Screwflation," *Barron's*, June 11, 2011.

216 **LinkedIn's valuation rose:** Renee C. Quinn, "LinkedIn IPO Huge Success, Valuation of $8.79 Billion," IPWatchdog.com, May 22, 2011.

216 **"Maybe it's time we revisit":** Jeff Cox, "CNBC Anchor Mark Haines Dies Unexpectedly at Age 65," CNBC.com, May 25, 2011.

216 **The precious metal surged:** "Silver Prices," 100-Year Historical Chart, macrotrends.net, www.macrotrends.net/1470/historical-silver-prices-100-year-chart.

216 **The Chinese, in particular:** Rockefeller Strategic Currency Briefing, May 13, 2011, www.rtsforex.com/wp-content/uploads/051311_Morning_Forex_Briefing.pdf.

217 **Of about six million firms:** "Small Business Facts & Data," Small Business & Entrepreneurship Council, sbecouncil.org/about-us/facts-and-data/.

217 **A survey of 1,004 companies:** "U.S. Bank Small Business Annual Survey," stories.usbank.com/dam/Documents/SlideDeck.pdf.

217 **A National Federation of Independent Businesses study:** William C. Dunkelberg and Holly Wade, "NFIB Small Business Economic Trends," National Federation of Independent Businesses, December 2011, www.nfib.com/Portals/0/PDF/sbet/sbet201112.pdf.

217 **QE2 officially ended:** Steven C. Johnson, "Market Debates Fed's Next Move as QE2 Ends," Reuters.com, June 30, 2011.

217 **It would be trading as low as 1075:** Google Finance Historical Prices, S&P 500 Index, www.google.com/finance/historical?cid=626307&startdate=Jan+20%2C+2011&enddate=Dec+31%2C+2011&num=30&ei=6SfHV8CCFIKnmAGsk4uQBg.

217 **From the *Wall Street Journal*:** Stephen Grocer, *Marketbeat* blog "The Markets Are Betting on Fed Miracle," *Wall Street Journal*, August 24, 2011.

217 **From *Bloomberg*: "The chairman":** Caroline Salas Gage and Jeannine Aversa, "Jackson Hole Bankers Reflect on QE2 Amid Pressure for Stimulus," Bloomberg.com, August 12, 2011.

217 **All this prompted Fisher:** "Bernanke's No 'Tooth Fairy,' Fisher Says—FBN," Market News, Reuters.com, August 22, 2011.

218 **Yet another fascinating paper:** Zoltan Pozsar, "Institutional Cash Pools and the Triffin Dilemma of the US Banking System," IMF Working Paper No. 11/190, 2010. See also Gillian Tett, "Cash-Rich Investors Choose Crazy Treasury Returns," *Financial Times*, August 11, 2011.

219 **An unprecedented three of the ten:** FR: FOMC Statement, August 9, 2011, www .federal reserve.gov/newsevents/press/monetary/20110809a.htm.

219 **It was the biggest mutiny since 1992:** FRBSL: Daniel L. Thornton and David C. Wheelock, "Making Sense of Dissents: A History of FOMC Dissents," Federal Reserve Bank of St. Louis *Review*, Third Quarter 2014, 96(3): 213–27, research .stlouisfed.org/publications/review/2014/q3/thornton.pdf.

219 **Roberto Perli, a former Fed staffer:** Luca Di Leo and Carol Lee, "Bernanke Overrides Opposition to Low Rate Policy, Suggesting Weaker Voice for Fed's Inflation Hawks," *Wall Street Journal*, August 10, 2011.

219 **A furious Volcker:** Tom Redburn, "Reagan Appointees Override Volcker on Cut in Discount Rate," *Los Angeles Times*, March 19, 2986, articles.latimes.com/1986 -03-19/business/fi-22778_1_discount-rate.

219 **On April 30, 1987:** Nathaniel C. Nash, "Bank Curb Eased in Volcker Defeat," *New York Times*, May 1, 1987.

220 **Bizarrely, Frank had proposed:** Luca Di Leo, "Barney Frank Takes on Fed District Presidents," *Wall Street Journal*, September 12, 2011.

220 **"The 7–3 vote":** Ibid.

220 **Fisher explained his dissent:** Art Cashin, "Cashin's Comments," UBS Financial Services, September 28, 2011. "Cashin's Comments" is privately circulated.

220 **"I do not believe it wise":** FRBD: Richard Fisher, "Connecting the Dots: Texas Employment Growth; A Dissenting Vote; and the Ugly Truth (With Reference to P. G. Wodehouse)" (speech, Midland Community Forum, Midland, Texas, August 17, 2011), www.dallasfed.org/news/speeches/fisher/2011/fs110817.cfm.

221 **He mentioned that:** Kathleen Madigan, "At Camp Kotok, the Chatter Is About Fed Rate Rise, China and How the Fish Are Biting," *Wall Street Journal*, August 10, 2015.

223 **Former Massachusetts governor Mitt Romney said:** Colleen McCain Nelson, "Romney Reiterates He Would Replace Bernanke," *Wall Street Journal*, August 23, 2011.

223 **Former House Speaker Newt Gingrich said:** "While Romney Ignores the Fed, Gingrich Offers Bold Reforms," press release, The American Presidency Project, November 2, 2011, presidency.ucsb.edu.

223 **Texas governor Rick Perry opined:** Phil Izzo, "Fed Policies Gave Big Boost to Texas," *Wall Street Journal*, September 23, 2011.

223 **"The recent slew of bad economic news":** Jon Hilsenrath, "Bernanke Takes on Balancing Act," *Wall Street Journal*, September 7, 2011.

223 **After the terrorist attacks:** Suzanne Kapner, "Wall Street Unrecognizable Now, but Not Just Because of 9/11," *Wall Street Journal*, September 6, 2011.

223 **During the week:** Marc Davis, "How September 11 Affected the U.S. Stock Market," *Investophedia.com*, September 9, 2011.

224 **Ten years later, the:** Ibid.

224 **In a speech given:** FRBM: Narayana Kocherlakota, "Communication, Credibility, and Implementation: Some Thoughts on Current, Past and Future Monetary Policy" (speech, University of Minnesota, September 6, 2011).

224 **On September 21, 2011:** FR: FOMC Statement, September 21, 2011, www.federal reserve.gov/newsevents/press/monetary/20110921a.htm.

224 **He showed a photograph:** FRBD: Richard Fisher, "Explaining Dissent on the FOMC Vote for Operation Twist (With Reference to Jan Mayen Island, Paul Volcker and Thor's Hammer)" (speech, Dallas Assembly, September 27, 2011), www .dallasfed.org/news/speeches/fisher/2011/fs110927.cfm.

Chapter 19: Spinning Fedwire

225 **While admirers of capitalism:** Binyamin Appelbaum, "Yellen's Path from Liberal Theorist to Fed Voice for Jobs," *New York Times*, October 10, 2013, www.nytimes .com/2013/10/10/business/economy/for-yellen-a-focus-on-reducing -unemployment.html.

225 **At the January 25, 2012:** FR: FOMC Statement, January 25, 2012, www.federal reserve.gov/newsevents/press/monetary/20120125a.htm.

225 **In a historic vote:** Ibid.

225 **A few months later, market:** Jessica Silver-Greenberg and Nelson D. Schwartz, "'London Whale' Said to Be Leaving JP Morgan," *New York Times*, May 16, 2012.

226 **Dimon at first:** Stephen Gandel, "The 10 Stages of Jamie Dimon's Blubbering London Whale Grief," Fortune.com, April 11, 2013.

226 **But an investigation:** Robert Lenger, "JPM Trade 'Flawed, Complex, Poorly Reviewed, Executed, Monitored,'" Forbes.com, May 12, 2012.

226 **A report by the Fed's:** FR: Office of the Inspector General, "Evaluation Report: The Board Should Enhance Its Supervisory Processes as a Result of Lessons Learned from the Federal Reserve's Supervision of JPMorgan Chase & Company's Chief Investment Office," October 17, 2014, oig.federalreserve.gov/reports/2015-0030 _-_Document_To_Release.pdf.

226 **The Whale's losses revealed:** FRB: Volcker Rule, www.federalreserve.gov/bankin foreg/volcker-rule/.

226 **One author of the bill:** John H. Cushman Jr. and Edward Wyatt, "Bank Regulations Gain Fresh Support," *New York Times*, May 11, 2012.

226 **The other author:** Ibid.

226 **The Whale provided:** Richard Fisher and Harvey Rosenblum, "How Huge Banks Threaten the Economy," *Wall Street Journal*, April 4, 2012.

226 **Why, then, had the Texas economy surpassed:** FRBD: Richard Fisher, "The Limits of the Powers of Central Banks (With Metaphoric References to Edvard Munch's *Scream* and Sir Henry Raeburn's *The Reverend Robert Walker Skating on Duddingston Loch* (speech, St. Andrews University, June 5, 2012), www.dallasfed .org/news/speeches/fisher/2012/fs120605.cfm.

227 **In addition to businesses:** Obamacare bill: The Patient Protection and Affordable Care Act, obamacarefacts.com/obamacarebill/.

227 **Even before the August 2012:** Jon Hilsenrath, "How Bernanke Pulled the Fed His Way," *Wall Street Journal*, September 28, 2012.

227 **"They have gone about their usual":** Mamta Badkar, "Stephen Roach: WSJ Report Jon Hilsenrath Is the Chairman of the Fed," BusinessInsider.com, July 25, 2012.

228 **"These leaks are co-opting Fed policy":** Jim Bianco, e-mail to Danielle DiMartino Booth, July 26, 2012, used by permission.

228 **The only hawk:** FR: FOMC Statement, August 1, 2012, www.federalreserve.gov /newsevents/press/monetary/20120801a.htm.

228 **Bernanke got his way:** FR: FOMC Statement, September 13, 2012, www.federal reserve.gov/newsevents/press/monetary/20120913a.htm.

229 **Bernanke had wooed Kocherlakota:** Hilsenrath, "How Bernanke Pulled Fed His Way."

229 **Only Lacker voted against:** FR: FOMC Statement, December 12, 2012, www .federalreserve.gov/newsevents/press/monetary/20121212a.htm.

229 **"The larger we make":** Michael S. Derby and Kristina Peterson, "Fed's Lacker Is Skeptical of More Explicit Policy," *Wall Street Journal*, November 20, 2012.

229 **Bernanke talked a good game:** Joe Weisenthal, "If You're a Saver, Ben Bernanke Has a Special Message for You," BusinessInsider.com, September 14, 2012, www .businessinsider.com/ben-bernankes-message-to-savers-2012-9.

229 **By December 2012:** FR: FOMC Statement, December 12, 2012.

230 **"The truth, however":** FRBD: Richard Fisher, "Comments to the Harvard Club of New York City on Monetary Policy (With References to Tommy Tune, Nicole Parent, the FOMC, Velcro, Drunken Sailors and Congress)" (speech, Harvard Club of New York, New York, September 19, 2012), www.dallasfed.org/news/speeches /fisher/2012/fs120919.cfm.

230 **On June 3, 2009:** FRBM: David Fettig, "Who Do You Trust With Your Money: Two Books Take a Hard Look at Federal Reserve Independence," The Region,

September 2009, www.minneapolisfed.org/publications/the-region/who-do-you
-trust-with-your-money.

230 **Hoenig left the Fed: FDIC Board of Directors:** Thomas M. Hoenig, fdic.gov, www
.FDIC.gov/learn/board/hoenig/bio/html.

230 **"With Mr. Fisher as a thought leader":** Simon Johnson, "The London Whale, Richard Fisher and Cyprus," *New York Times*, March 21, 2013.

230 **The December 2012 FOMC statement:** FR: FOMC Statement, December 12, 2012.

CHAPTER 20: THE TAPER TANTRUM

231 **Yes, I think it is working:** Jim Tankersley, "Janet Yellen in Her Own Words: An Exclusive Interview," *Washington Post*, October 9, 2013, www.washingtonpost
.com/news/wonk/wp/2013/10/09/janet-yellen-in-her-own-words-an-exclusive
-interview/.

231 **I began to cover:** Lisa Abramowicz, "Bond Dealer Retreat Seen in Trades Shrinking 39%: Credit Markets," Bloomberg.com, November 19, 2013.

232 **Goldman Sachs and its clients:** Heather Perlberg and John Gittelsohn, "Goldman Backs Mullen in Rentals After Subprime Short," Bloomberg.com, April 22, 2013, www.bloomberg.com/news/articles/2013-04-22/goldman-backs
-mullen-in-rentals-after-subprime-short.

232 **One company acquired:** Ibid.

232 **But investors were crowding out buyers:** "The State of the Nation's Housing 2013," Joint Center for Housing Studies of Harvard University, 25, www.jchs.harvard.edu
/sites/jchs.harvard.edu/files/son2013.pdf.

232 **Out of the corner of my eye:** Joseph Guinto, "The Hottest Dallas Housing Market Ever," *D Magazine*, July 2013.

232 **"Betting on home price appreciation":** Matthew Goldstein, "Special Report: Cheap Money Bankrolls Wall Street's Bet on Housing," Reuters.com, May 2, 1013.

233 **The "taper tantrum":** Antaole Kaletsky, "The Markets and Bernanke's 'Taper Tantrums,'" Reuters.com, September 19, 2013, blogs.reuters.com/anatole-kaletsky
/2013/09/19/the-markets-and-bernankes-taper-tantrums/.

233 **On June 19, Jon Hilsenrath appeared:** "Santelli to Hilsenrath: Why Do We Still Need QE?," CNBC.com, June 19, 2013. video.cnbc.com/gallery/?video=3000176036.

233 **The ten-year Treasury note yield:** Ben Rooney, "Treasury Yields Hit 3%," CNNMoney.com, December 26, 2013.

234 **The FOMC voted no:** FR: FOMC Statement, September 18, 2013, www.federal
reserve.gov/newsevents/press/monetary/20130918a.htm.

234 **"It should also correct":** Kevin Warsh, "QE Untested, Incomplete Experiment," *Wall Street Journal*, November 12, 2013.

234 **"I would argue":** FRBD: Richard Fisher, "Comments on Monetary Policy (With Praise for Urban Lehner, Norman Borlaug and Dentists)" (speech, DTN/Progressive Farmer AG Summit, Chicago, Illinois, December 9, 2013), www.dallasfed.org /assets/documents/news/speeches/fisher/2013/fs131209.pdf.

234 **During his short stint:** Damian Paletta, "Larry Summers Circles as Fed Opening Looms," *Wall Street Journal*, July 7, 2013, www.wsj.com/articles/SB1000142412788 732426020457858823002479170.

235 **In February 2006:** Ibid.

235 **Since then, Summers had refused:** Simon Johnson, "Yellen's Credentials to Lead the Fed," *New York Times*, September 19, 2013.

235 **After it became clear:** David Wessel, "Summers Withdraws His Name for Fed Chairmanship," *Wall Street Journal*, September 16, 2013, www.wsj.com/articles /SB10001424127887323981304579077442028100408.

235 **"He would be the ideal candidate":** Simon Johnson, "Sadly, Too Big to Fail Is Not Over," *New York Times*, August 1, 2013.

235 **Reflecting back in 2010:** FRB: Interview with Janet Yellen, FCIC staff audiotape, Financial Crisis Inquiry Commission, November 15, 2010, fcic-static.law .stanford.edu/cdn_media/fcic-audio/2010-11-15%2FCIC%20staff%20audio tape%20of%20interview%20with%20Janet%20Yellen,%20Federal%20Reserve% 20Board.mp3.

236 **In a subsequent speech:** FRBSF: Janet Yellen, "Macroprudential Supervision and Monetary Policy in the Post-Crisis World" (speech, Annual Meeting of the National Association for Business Economists, Denver, Colorado, October 11, 2010), www.federalreserve.gov/newsevents/speech/yellen20101011a.htm.

236 **"Yellen's abrasive, intimidating style":** Jon Hilsenrath, "Yellen Would Bring Tougher Tone to Fed," *Wall Street Journal*, September 22, 2013, www.wsj.com/arti cles/SB10001424052702303983904579091521754109480.

237 **Hilsenrath wrote that:** Ibid.

CHAPTER 21: THE NEW SHERIFF IN TOWN

238 **The truly unique power:** Ralph Benko, "The Global Importance of Paul Volcker's Call For a 'New Bretton Woods,'" *Forbes*, June 16, 2014.

238 **I forwarded "Beer Goggles":** Peter Boockvar, "I'm Not a Soothsayer, but I'll Do as Wall Street Does," Lindsey Group, January 2, 2014.

238 **"QE puts beer goggles":** FRBD: Richard Fisher, "Beer Goggles, Monetary Camels, the Eye of the Needle, and the First Law of Holes" (speech, National Association of Corporate Directors, Dallas, Texas, January 14, 2014), www.dallasfed.org/news /speeches/fisher/2014/fs140114.cfm.

239 **"The gas tank is full"**: Binyamin Appelbaum, "Q&A: An Advocate for a Quicker Taper," *New York Times*, January 27, 2014, economix.blogs.nytimes.com/2014/01 /27/qa-an-advocate-for-a-quicker-taper/.

239 **"You can't go from Wild Turkey to cold turkey"**: FRBD: Richard Fisher, "Comments on Tailored Regulation and Forward Guidance (With Reference to Dr. Seuss, Strother Martin in *Cool Hand Luke* and Other Serious Economists)" (speech, Louisiana Bankers Association, New Orleans, Louisiana, May 9, 2014), www.dal lasfed.org/assets/documents/news/speeches/fisher/2014/fs140509.pdf.

240 **Even during her swearing-in**: FRB: Janet Yellen, "Remarks at the Ceremonial Swearing-In," March 5, 2014, www.federalreserve.gov/newsevents/speech/yel len20140305a.htm.

240 **Yellen neglected to mention**: Jon Hilsenrath, "Janet Yellen's Human Message Gets Clouded," *Wall Street Journal*, April 1, 2014.

240 **"I don't think there is any doubt"**: Phalguni Soni, "Why Richard Fisher Says Quantitative Easing Has Enabled the Rich," MarketRealist.com, April 7, 2014, marketre alist.com/2014/04/richard-fisher-says-quantitative-easing-enabled-rich/.

241 **To justify her inaction**: Adriene Hill, "Fed Stops Targeting 6.5% Unemployment," MarketPlace.org, March 18, 2014, www.marketplace.org/2014/03/18/economy/fed -stops-targeting-65-unemployment.

241 **In March, I reported**: From Investopedia: "The P/E 10 ratio uses smoothed real earnings to eliminate the fluctuations in net income caused by variations in profit margins over a typical business cycle. The ratio was popularized by Yale University Professor Robert Shiller, who won the Nobel Prize in Economic Sciences in 2013. It attracted a great deal of attention after Shiller warned that the frenetic U.S. stock market rally of the late 1990s would turn out to be a bubble," www.in vestopedia.com/terms/p/pe10ratio.asp.

241 **The statement after**: FR: FOMC Statement, March 19, 2014, www.federalreserve .gov/newsevents/press/monetary/20140319a.htm.

241 **In April, Toyota shocked officials**: Virginia Postrel, "Why Toyota Moved to Texas," Bloomberg.com, April 29, 2014.

243 **A leak of discussions**: Craig Torres, "Fed Leak Handed Traders Profitable Tip, Prompted Secret Inquiry," Bloomberg.com, December 1, 2014.

243 **Widely regarded then**: FRB: Jeremy Stein, "Incorporating Financial Stability Considerations into a Monetary Policy Framework" (speech, International Research Forum on Monetary Policy, Washington, DC, April 16, 2014), www.federalreserve .gov/newsevents/speech/stein20140321a.htm. Governor Stein presented identical remarks at the International Monetary Fund 2014 Spring Meetings on April 13, 2014, and at the 2014 Financial Markets Conference on April 16, 2014,

243 **Stein had joined:** FRB: "Jeremy C. Stein, Governor (Board)," Federal Reserve History: www.federalreserve.org/People/.

245 **In June, Dudley:** Jon Hilsenrath, "Fed Officials Growing Wary of Market Complacency," *Wall Street Journal*, June 3, 2014.

245 **"It is a problem of their own making":** Ibid.

246 **Warren expressed "shock":** Myles Udland, "Elizabeth Warren Destroys Janet Yellen over JP Morgan's 'Living Will,'" BusinessInsider.com, July 15, 2014.

246 **"Can you honestly say":** "Warren Presses Yellen to Get Tougher on Big Banks and Their Living Wills," MarketWatch.com, July 15, 2014.

246 **Has JPMC "ever gotten":** Udland, "Elizabeth Warren Destroys Janet Yellen over JP Morgan's 'Living Will.'"

246 **"These are extremely complex documents":** Ibid.

246 **"In other words, break them up":** Ibid.

247 **He had been Bernanke's thesis adviser:** Roger Lowenstein, "The Education of Ben Bernanke," *New York Times Magazine*, January 20, 2008.

247 **But he'd agreed:** Don Lee, "Stanley Fischer Confirmed by Senate for Federal Reserve Board Seat," *Los Angeles Times*, May 21, 2014.

247 **After peaking at $110:** Russell Gold, "Back to the Future? Oil Replays 1980s Bust," *Wall Street Journal*, January 13, 2015.

249 **The December 2014 FOMC:** Luca Di Leo and Carol Lee, "Bernanke Overrides Opposition to Low-Rate Policy, Suggesting Weaker Voice for Fed's Inflation Hawks," *Wall Street Journal*, August 10, 2011.

Chapter 22: Culture Shock

250 **If it were possible:** Ann Saphir, "Update 2—Fed's Yellen: U.S. Economy Still Needs Ultra-Low Rates," Reuters.com, February 22, 2010, www.reuters.com/article/usa-fed -yellen-idUSN2222725320100222.

250 **"We're in uncharted territory":** Rhonda Schaffler, "Former Philly Fed President Plosser: 'Not a Bad Idea' to Raise Rates," TheStreet.com, August 10, 2015, www .thestreet.com/story/13250133/1/former-philly-fed-president-plosser-not-a-bad -idea-to-raise-rates.html.

251 **"Such environments raise":** Steve Blumenthal, "On My Radar: An Optimist Sees Opportunity in Every Difficulty," CMGWealth.com, August 15, 2015, www.cmg wealth.com/ri/7388-2/.

251 **Bizarrely, Bernanke's renunciation of his GOP affiliation:** Chad Stone, "Ben Bernanke Has Had It with Stupid GOP Economics," *U.S. News & World Report*, October 9, 2015, www.usnews.com/opinion/economic-intelligence/2015/10/09/ben-bernanke -has-had-it-with-stupid-gop-economics.

252 **At a press conference in June 2006:** FR: FOMC Statement, December 16, 2015, www.federal reserve.gov/newsevents/press/monetary/20151216a.htm.

252 **As of mid-2016:** Yuji Nakamura, Anna Kitanaka, and Nao Sano, "Bank of Japan Owns More Than Half of Nation's ETFs: Chart," Bloomberg.com, www.bloomberg.com/news /articles/2016-04-25/bank-of-japan-owns-more-than-half-of-nation-s-etfs-chart.

252 **Through surrogates and back channels:** Larry Kudlow, "Message Matters: Trump Succeeded, Yellen Failed," Townhall.com, February 13, 2016, townhall.com/colum nists/larrykudlow/2016/02/13/message-matters-trump-succeeded-yellen-failed -n2118954.

252 **The Tokyo manufacturer:** Simon Kennedy, "The Sub-Zero Club: Getting Used to the Upside-Down World Economy," Bloomberg.com, April 18, 2016, www.bloomberg .com/news/articles/2016-04-19/the-sub-zero-club-getting-used-to-the-upside -down-world-economy.

252 **An early 2016 report:** Madeleine Nissen and Paul J. Davies, "Germany: Where Negative Rates Are Lethal," *Wall Street Journal*, April 14, 2016.

253 **The Irish government sold a 100-year bond:** Dara Doyle, "Ireland Sells First 100-Year Bond, Saying on Comeback Trail," Bloomberg.com, March 30, 2016, www.bloomberg .com/news/articles/2016-03-30/ireland-sells-first-100-year-bond-to-complete -comeback-trail.

253 **Spain issued 50-year debt:** Anooja Debnath, "Europe's Ultra-Long Debt Trend Builds with 50-Year Spanish Bond," Bloomberg.com, May 11, 2016, www .bloomberg.com/news/articles/2016-05-10/spain-joins-euro-area-s-ultra-long -trend-with-new-50-year-bond.

254 **"I strongly oppose 'Audit the Fed'":** Shane Ferro, "Janet Yellen Testified to Congress, Opposed Audit the Fed, and Gave No New Clues on Monetary Policy Going Forward," BusinessInsider.com, February 24, 2015.

254 **Fisher also opposed Paul's bill:** Jim Puzzanghera, "Fed's Fisher Calls 'Audit the Fed' Backers 'Sheep in Wolves' Clothing,'" *Los Angeles Times*, February 11, 2014. See also FRBD: Richard Fisher, "Suggestions After a Decade at the Fed (With Reference to Paul Volcker, Roosa Boys, Hogwarts, the Death Star, Ebenezer Scrooge, Mae West, Herb Kelleher, Worms and Camels, Peter Weir, Charles Kindleberger, Pope Francis and Secretariat) (speech, Economic Club of New York, New York, February 11, 2015), www.dallasfed.org/news/speeches/fisher/2015/fs150210.cfm.

254 **To address lingering cynicism:** Jon Hilsenrath, "Washington Strips New York Fed's Power," *Wall Street Journal*, March 4, 2015.

255 **The scathing critique:** Ibid.

255 **He learned the FRC:** David Beim and Christopher McCurdy, "Federal Reserve Bank of New York: Report on Systemic Risk and Bank Supervision," Discussion Draft,

August 18, 2009, 12, www.propublica.org/documents/item/1303305-2009-08-18-frbny
-report-on-systemic-risk-and.html.

256 "One of our [Fed] interviewees": Ibid., 6.

256 "Many felt the deference to be excessive": Ibid., 2.

256 Beim recommended that Dudley: Ibid., 10.

257 "Future bank supervision": Ibid., 14.

257 "Unless this support is strong": Ibid., 15.

257 Carmen Segarra, a lawyer: Jake Bernstein, "Inside the New York Fed: Secret Record-
ings and a Culture Clash," ProPublica.org, September 26, 2014, www.propublica.org
/article/carmen-segarras-secret-recordings-from-inside-new-york-fed.

257 After she refused, Segarra was fired: Ibid.

257 Then Segarra shocked: Ibid.

257 Her boss said: Ibid.

258 "On one tape": Ibid.

258 "The simple answer": C. Thompson, "Here's Theory Why Segarra Drove New York
Fed Crazy: Opening Line," Bloomberg.com, September 30, 2014.

258 "During a congressional hearing in": Antoine Gara, "Elizabeth Warren Grills
William Dudley Over 'Cultural Problem' at New York Fed," Forbes.com, November
21, 2014.

258 Behind the scenes, by: Jon Hilsenrath, "Washington Strips New York Fed's Power,"
Wall Street Journal, March 4, 2015.

259 "I understand the suspicions": Michael S. Derby, "Fisher Says Fed Should Move
Power Away from New York Fed," *Wall Street Journal*, February 11, 2015.

259 In July 2015, Patrick Harker: Binyamin Appelbaum, "Philadelphia Fed Picks Harker, University of Delaware President, to Lead It," *New York Times*, March 2, 2015.

259 The next month, Harvard: FRBD: Press release, August 17, 2015, www.dallasfed
.org/news/releases/2015/nr150817.cfm.

260 In November 2015: Kate Davidson and Anupreeta Das, "Fed's New Bank Critic,
Neel Kashkari, Keeps Heat On," *Wall Street Journal*, April 4, 2016, www.wjs.com
/articles/feds-new-bank-critic-keeps-heat-on-1459720148.

260 In March 2016, Hilsenrath: Jon Hilsenrath, "The Decline of Dissent at the Fed,"
Wall Street Journal, March 24, 2016.

260 Like Garry Kasparov: Marisa Schultz, "Inside Hillary's $675K Worth of Speaking
Fees," *New York Post*, February 5, 2016, nypost.com/2016/02/05/inside-hillarys
-675k-worth-of-goldman-speaking-fees/.

260 "Was it about making the world safe for Goldman Sachs?": Nicholas Lemann,
"The Hand on the Lever," *New Yorker*, July 21, 2014, 51, www.newyorker.com/mag
azine/2014/07/21/the-hand-on-the-lever.

261 **"But we are magic people":** Alessandro Speciale and Milda Seputyte, "ECB Can Still Pull Rabbits Out of the Hat, Council Member Says," Bloomberg.com, May 11, 2016.

261 **But, as mentioned earlier:** Charles Riley, "China Devalues Yuan in Shocking Move," CNNMoney.com, August 11, 2015, money.cnn.com/2015/08/11/investing /china-pboc-yuan-devalue-currency/index.html.

261 **Yet Yellen, as if:** FR: FOMC Statement, December 16, 2015, www.federalreserve .gov/newsevents/press/monetary/20151216a.htm.

262 **"You can't think about":** Lemann, "The Hand on the Lever," 53.

262 **Even Fedwire finally admitted:** Jon Hilsenrath, "Years of Fed Missteps Fueled Disillusion with the Economy and Washington," *Wall Street Journal*, August 25, 2016.

262 **Mistakes by the Fed:** Ibid.

262 **A Gallup poll showed:** Ibid.

263 **In early 2016:** Ibid.

263 **"The Federal Reserve is a giant":** Myles Udland, "Former Fed President: 'The Federal Reserve Is a Giant Weapon That Has No Ammunition Left," BusinessInsider.com, January 6, 2016, www.businessinsider.in/FORMER-FED-PRESIDENT-The-Federal -Reserve-is-a-giant-weapon-that-has-no-ammunition-left/articleshow/50470721.cms.

INDEX